"[A] COMPREHENSIVE, CONS(AND TRUSTWORTHY COOKBOOK ...
Brody, with Flaste, delivers the goods, as always."
—Publishers Weekly

"Written in her usual instructive style, the book is packed with soothing advice for seafood novices and more challenging recipes for intermediate cooks."
—USA Weekend

"Tempt your palate . . . It's time to get in the swim of things—with fashionable, flavorful, positively good-for-you fish."
—The Baltimore Sun

"*Jane Brody's Good Seafood Book* tackles the important questions of nutrition, safety, selection and storage while providing a huge variety of innovative and immensely palatable low-fat recipes."
—Detroit Free Press

"A good all-around reference for seafood tips and techniques [that] encourages cooks to get creative with fish."
—Atlanta Journal & Constitution

"[These] creamy pages are bound to grow soft and stained from constant use."
—Elle

"Brody introduce[s] readers to the health benefits and delicious possibilities of all manner of seafood. . . . She provides easy-to-follow charts illustrating the fats and cholesterol in various seafood, also comparing them to other high-protein foods and the many other important vitamins and minerals that bless this wonderful food."
—World News Features

Also by Jane E. Brody

SECRETS OF GOOD HEALTH *(with Richard Engquist)*
YOU CAN FIGHT CANCER AND WIN *(with Dr. Arthur I. Holleb)*
JANE BRODY'S NUTRITION BOOK
JANE BRODY'S THE NEW YORK TIMES GUIDE TO PERSONAL HEALTH
JANE BRODY'S GOOD FOOD BOOK
JANE BRODY'S GOOD FOOD GOURMET

JANE BRODY'S GOOD SEAFOOD BOOK

By Jane E. Brody

with Richard Flaste

Illustrations by Pat Stewart

Fawcett Columbine • New York

A Fawcett Columbine Book
Published by Ballantine Books

This edition published by arrangement with W.W. Norton & Company, Inc.

The recipe for Steamed Shrimp (p. 129) is reprinted with the permission of Nina Simonds and *Gourmet Magazine*. The recipe for Octopus Appetizer (p. 146) is adapted from *Tapas: The Little Dishes of Spain*, by Penelope Casas, with the permission of Alfred A. Knopf, Inc., copyright © 1985 by Penelope Casas. The recipe for Fish Tacos with Cilantro Pesto (p. 490) is reprinted with the permission of Norman Fieros and *Simply Seafood Magazine*.

Library of Congress Catalog Card Number: 95-90149

ISBN: 0-449-91021-0

Cover photo by Michael McLaughlin

Manufactured in the United States of America
First Ballantine Books Edition: October 1995
10 9 8 7 6 5 4 3

Contents

At Home on the Range   *339*

Great on the Grill 437

Magic in the Microwave 469

A Saucier's Apprentice: Salsas, Sauces, and Marinades 497

Fish in Their Finite Variety: A Seafood Glossary 511

Acknowledgments

In more ways than one, this book was a great adventure. It represents my first professional collaboration and my first in-depth exploration of a singular foodstuff. And what a grand time I had! No small thanks to my inspired and inspiring collaborator, Rick Flaste, and to the forbearance of my family and friends, especially my husband, Richard Engquist; my son, Erik Engquist; Rick's wife, Dale Flaste; and our special friend, Kris Kim, who night after night dined willingly on all manner of seafood as Rick and I tested hundreds of recipes to cull the best for the volume you now hold in your hands.

Thanks, too, to Ana Deboo for her meticulous and industrious assistance both in gathering facts and figures and in retesting recipes; to Richard Lord, who probably knows more about fish and shellfish than any living creature with or without fins, for checking the manuscript for technical accuracy; to Fran Korein for her generous supply of source material; to my editor, Mary E. Cunnane, for her continuing encouragement and support of the Jane Brody schema; to Carol Flechner, a manuscript editor who goes far beyond the call of duty to polish a work to perfection; to Andy Marasia, a production manager whose can-do attitude and humor take all the pain out of producing a book; to designer Margaret Wagner for turning rough pages into artistry that serves both cook and author; to artist Patricia Stewart for drawings that seem to leap from the page; to my agent, Wendy Weil, who continues to champion my causes; and, last but by no means least, to the myriad friends (especially Betty Marks), relatives, and acquaintances who served as tasters of our many preparations.

Jane E. Brody
April 1994

JANE BRODY'S
GOOD SEAFOOD BOOK

1
Beyond Fish Sticks— From the Familiar to the Fantastic

Most of us, as we were growing up, knew fish in one of two forms: as frozen, batter-covered, deep-fried fish sticks or fillets that left us wondering "Where's the fish?" and as oil-packed, canned tuna or, perhaps, sardines, mixed with lots of mayonnaise, chopped celery, and onion and further hidden between two slices of pasty white bread.

Maybe, like me, you had a mother who was somewhat adventurous in the kitchen and occasionally prepared salmon croquettes (fried, of course) or simply seasoned broiled fillets of flounder. My mother had one other fish dish in her repertoire: she was masterful (and patient) at breading and frying those dozens of tiny but succulent sunfish and perch that I and my kid brother managed to extract from lakes in the Catskills each summer, baiting them with dough balls (the perfect fate for that pasty white bread) and night crawlers that we gathered from the lawn before our extended summer bedtime.

Considering how quick and easy to prepare and, in those days, inexpensive most fish were, it is surprising that fish was never popular when I was growing up. My Catholic friends endured it on Fridays, when meat was forbidden, and many other people I knew never ate it at all, except, perhaps, when they indulged in an occasional shrimp or lobster dish at a Chinese restaurant.

Well, folks, times have changed. While still a poor runner-up to meat and chicken, seafood is finding its way onto American tables, both in restaurants and at home. Despite some recent setbacks, seafood consumption has increased by about 22 percent in the last decade and has now reached an average of well over 15 pounds per person a year, a level that some experts expect will rise as nutritional and culinary savvy reach ever-higher levels and as more and better varieties of finfish and shellfish reach the American marketplace.

Still, considering the many benefits that seafood has to offer the American consumer, 15 or even 30 pounds a year is a paltry sum. Meat, which lately has suffered the slings and arrows of nutritional condemnation (as well as several contamination scares), still lords it over fish at a per capita consumption level of about 100 pounds a year. This inequity has ruffled the scales of the seafood industry, which has begun to survey consumer views and develop strategies that promise to give this fine food a big boost.

The industry found, for example, that while many consumers happily order fish in restaurants, the primary reason most people do not prepare more seafood dishes at home is "pescaphobia"—fear of fish, a fear arising from unfamiliarity. While most people know how to buy and broil a steak or burger, few consumers grew up knowing how to select and prepare the various kinds of fish and shellfish. When staring at a salmon steak priced at $6.99 a pound or at swordfish at $10.99, a rational cook is not going to risk any culinary errors.

I know because I, too, was once one of those timid seafood consumers. Oh, I long ago learned how to throw a lobster into a kettle of boiling water, stir-fry shrimp, broil a piece of flounder, and even grill a salmon steak. And because my sons, like me, were avid fishermen in their youth, I was also good at filleting, breading, and frying the dozens of sunfish and occasional bullheads (a kind of catfish) they would catch on a good morning. I even once successfully stuffed and baked a 5-pound carp the boys had pulled from the Minnesota side of the St. Croix River. It was either that or risk insulting their fishing skills and try to find a way to dispose of a large dead fish.

But for much of my cooking life, I had no idea of what to do with clams or crabs, haddock or halibut, marlin or monkfish, shark or swordfish, not to mention squid or skate or most of the more than 2,000 varieties of finfish and shellfish commercially available in American markets. And while I added significantly to my fish preparation skills in developing and testing recipes for *Jane Brody's Good Food Book* and *Jane Brody's Good Food Gourmet,* it was not until *Jane Brody's Good Seafood Book* that I began to feel comfortable both in the fish market and, once back home, in the kitchen with my "catch."

I'm not sure I would have been willing to tackle such a project on my own had not my good friend and former boss at *The New York Times,* Richard

(Rick) Flaste, suggested a joint venture in producing a collection of recipes that show off the finest qualities in seafood, fit into the demanding lives of modern cooks, and foster the principles of healthful, low-fat eating. Rick was an old hand in the kitchen, having worked on three cookbooks with noted chef Pierre Franey, including *Pierre Franey's Low-Calorie Gourmet.* He had watched Pierre prepare all manner of seafood—from the mundane to the exotic—and he was sold on the importance of seafood to a well-rounded and healthful diet.

It took only one sentence to get my pectoral fins flapping with excitement over the idea. After all, I was a health and nutrition writer, fully aware of the remarkable findings about fish that were emerging from universities and medical centers here and abroad. Red meat, cheese, and eggs, riddled as they are with cholesterol-raising saturated fat, had become occasional items on our household menu. And there are just so many ways to prepare skinless chicken breasts before the cook starts clucking. My sons have never become enamored of dried beans and peas, and no one in the family likes tofu outside of hot and sour soup. So what better choice of a high-protein food could there be besides fish? Seafood gave me—and can give you—a way to save hearts and waistlines without having to sacrifice taste and variety. There is no other high-protein, nutritious food that is as versatile.

In the title and throughout the text of this book, I use the word "seafood" generically to represent all fish and shellfish, be they from salt or fresh water. Nearly all the fish and shellfish that people consume these days is either captured in the wild in bays and oceans or raised in ponds on fish farms, both freshwater (for fish like tilapia and catfish) and saltwater (for salmon and shellfish like shrimp and mussels). Except for some locally caught species, about the only freshwater wild fish eaten these days are those caught by sports fishermen, many of whom now catch and release rather than consume their prey.

GETTING COZY WITH SEAFOOD

In working with Rick to devise and prepare hundreds of recipes for this book and in perusing probably a thousand others in scores of cookbooks and in the wonderful new magazine *Simply Seafood* (see page 114), I have also discovered that cooking with seafood is simple. Anyone who can tie a shoelace can learn to purchase and prepare it well. To become comfortable with seafood, you simply have to start "doing" it: buying it, cooking it, and savoring each delicious, nutritious mouthful.

If you are a novice in this area, this book can quickly bring you to the level of a seafood gourmet. If you are an experienced seafood cook, you're likely to find dozens of recipes that will expand your repertoire. If you are only familiar with high-fat cooking techniques, you'll learn new, delectable ways to prepare seafood with little or no added fat. And you won't feel afraid or ashamed to serve such dishes to company since these recipes include some of the most beautiful and delicious meals I have ever prepared. And so many of them are simple and quick to cook. In fact, few fish dishes take longer than 20 minutes of cooking time, and whole fish meals can be put together in an hour.

Seafood can be prepared using the techniques and seasonings from virtually every cuisine in the world. It can be boiled, broiled, steamed, stir-fried, braised, baked, grilled, sautéed, smoked, poached, cured, microwaved. And, if properly handled, some seafood can be savored raw. In this book, you'll find a potpourri of international as well as regional dishes—from Mexico to Morocco, Italy to India, California to China. And you'll discover that many of the dishes you now make with meat or chicken can be prepared with seafood instead. Note, for example, my use of seafood in a Moroccan salad (page 242), a taco and a burrito (pages 490 and 316), a chili (page 434), a lasagna (page 322), a pasta primavera (page 391), and a hot and sour soup (page 210).

And, if my ideas aren't enough for you, chances are you'll find recipe cards for many kinds of seafood stacked on your market's fish counter. Be careful, though—the recipes distributed by stores may not be low in fat or calories. But the techniques I use in this book can help you adapt some of them to a low-fat diet.

GETTING VALUE FOR YOUR MONEY

Lack of experience in buying and cooking seafood is the leading, but not the only, factor that the seafood industry has identified as discouraging to consumers. Another is the cost. Most—though not all—seafood is priced significantly higher per pound than meat or poultry. It is a matter of supply and demand. The majority of seafood on the American market comes from the sea, and harvesting these ocean animals is far more difficult (and, thus, more expensive) than rounding up cattle from a feedlot. Also, the United States is the leading exporter of seafood, so we compete worldwide for the available supplies. As more and more species are raised on fish farms (see page 25), the cost of seafood may come down, but it will be quite a few years before the supply of farmed fish is large enough to meet the growing demand.

As prices stand now, consumers watching their budget, and even those who don't have to, may hesitate to spend $6 to $12 on just the protein portion of a meal for a family of four, and I don't blame them. But look at it this way: eating fish may significantly reduce your family's health-care costs; it's a kind of insurance policy—you pay a little more now to be protected in a big way later.

Still, there are ways around the cost issue. One is to serve reasonable portions. You'll note that my recipes rarely call for individual serving sizes of more than 4 to 6 ounces of uncooked fish, which means that four people can dine on 1 to 1½ pounds of seafood (see the buying guide on page 42). That's more than enough protein for any adult at a single meal. Healthful dining calls for only 3 ounces of a cooked high-protein food, with bellies filled by ample servings of a starchy food like pasta, rice, couscous, bulgur, beans, or potatoes as well as by one or more nonstarchy vegetables and/or salad and—don't forget—bread. Keep in mind, too, that there is little waste when preparing seafood. When you cook fillets and boneless fish steaks, you eat everything you pay for. Even bone-in steaks and shrimp in their shells have little waste.

Then there's the matter of selection. Not every form of seafood is expensive. Mussels and squid (calamari) are downright bargains. So is the processed fish called surimi, which is made mostly from Alaskan pollock. In general, the less well-known varieties of seafood are the least expensive—fish like skate, dogfish, and jack, for example. Get to know these, for they'll give you more than your money's worth.

Like fruits and vegetables, fish caught in the wild have seasons, and they are least costly when the supply is greatest. However, what's in season varies from area to area, year to year, so you'd be wise to stay alert to local good buys on seasonal seafood. Most markets that have fish counters also run weeklong specials on one or more varieties of fish. If the fish is fresh (see page 41), this is your chance to stock up and save; buy extra, repackage it, label it, and freeze it for future use (see page 64 for tips on freezing seafood). Incidentally, seafood that is sold frozen (see pages 62–63) is often considerably cheaper than the same variety sold "fresh."

"FRESH" VERSUS FROZEN

I put the word fresh in quotation marks because, when it comes to fish, "fresh" to the consumer means that the fish has never been frozen. What "fresh" really should mean is "not old." Since weeks can elapse between the time fish are taken from the water and the time they reach the cook's kitchen at home or in a restaurant, the freshest fish are usually those that were flash-frozen at sea and delivered, still frozen, to the retail market or restaurant and not thawed until they were ready to be put on sale or, in the case of a restaurant, cooked and served.

As Roger Fitzgerald, a former fisherman and now an editor and writer on seafood, put it in his column in *Simply Seafood,* "The highest standard of freshness might well be the fish captured on the high seas—far away from any polluted waters—by our American factory trawler fleet: fish that are cleaned and frozen within two hours and delivered months later to the market. Superb!" I couldn't agree more. It is time we stopped making a fetish of "fresh" as in "not frozen" and started buying "fresh" as in "not old."

"WE DON'T ALL LIKE FISH"

Worried about guests? A wise host will check beforehand to be sure invited guests have no aversion or allergy to any seafood that he or she plans to serve. Unless you are setting out a buffet with a wide range of dishes, food-preference checks should be routine now that so many Americans spurn meat and poultry or all animal foods. Happily, though, fish-eating "vegetarians" are much in vogue these days.

Home cooks who have no trouble getting everyone in the family to eat burgers and fried chicken may hesitate to invest time and money in fish if their children or their spouses say they don't like it. Children, of course, have a million dislikes, most of which they eventually outgrow. Meanwhile, parents can increase the chances that fish will remain popular with their offspring by preparing it in simple ways, making sure it has no bones, and perhaps serving it with a favorite condiment—for example, ketchup, barbecue sauce, or tartar sauce.

Chances are, when an adult spurns fish, the reasons stem from negative fish experiences that date way back. Perhaps this person was "forced" to eat fish as a child, or the fish served was not fresh or was too bony, or the method of preparation used (usually deep-frying) smelled up the house for a day or more. Reintroducing seafood to such a person may require a little ingenuity. This book is replete with recipes that "disguise" fish in dishes normally made with other ingredients. Try serving the reluctant fish consumer a seafood chili (page 434), a seafood pizza (pages 324, 326, 328, and 330), fish kebabs (pages 438, 440, and 442), or pasta and seafood (for example, those recipes on pages 242, 322, and 390). Again, start with boneless fillets or, even better, fish steaks that have a meatlike consistency—tuna, shark, or swordfish.

If you still have trouble selling adults on seafood, you might point out that the Chinese character for fish—*yu*—means "abundance" and "prosperity." The Chinese eat just about everything that comes out of the water, from carp to sea cucumbers, and have been farming fish for more than 2,000 years. In all likelihood, they know something about this wonderful food that we could stand to learn.

Now read, shop, cook, and enjoy!

2
Good Seafood, and Low-Fat, Too!

This is no ordinary seafood cookbook. Those of you familiar with Jane Brody's nutritional credo and recipes no doubt assumed that this book would be more of the same—low in fat, high in flavor. You will not be disappointed. Many cookbooks that purport to be low in fat aren't. Sure, they use less oil, butter, cheese, and other high-fat ingredients found in what I call fat-careless cooking. But they are not *low in fat*. These recipes are. And many cookbooks with recipes that really are low in fat seem to have forgotten that people rarely eat foods that are not tasty. I haven't forgotten. My recipes must pass muster not only with me and my family and Rick Flaste and his family, but also with discerning guests who are invited to taste-test them.

But back to the fat issue. Fat, as you probably know, is the most unhealthy ingredient in the American diet, and far too much of our dietary fat is the hazardous, cholesterol-raising saturated kind. Seafood is naturally low in saturated fats (see the table on page 19), and my seafood recipes rarely contain more than 1 tablespoon of added fat—usually heart-sparing monounsaturated olive oil or canola oil—for 4 servings. In fact, many of my recipes are made with no or only a trace or 1 teaspoon of added fat. That leaves only the fat naturally present in the seafood, which—I repeat—is usually very little, to boost the calorie count of your meal.

As if that were not enough of a selling point, what fat there is in seafood, including the fattier varieties like salmon, herring, and mackerel, is rich in health-promoting omega-3 fatty acids. See pages 15 to 17 for the many established and suggested nutritional virtues of omega-3s.

Even though I had had considerable experience with low-fat cooking, this book is replete with remarkable new ideas and techniques, many of which you should be able to use to lower the fat content of some of your own favorite recipes. In devising these new methods, Rick Flaste and I proved to be an inspired team. At times through pure invention and at other times by modifying approaches that we had learned elsewhere, we came up with creative solutions to such problems as how to keep nonfat and low-fat dairy products from separating when they are heated, how to prepare good-tasting reduced-fat versions of standard sauces like beurre blanc and red pepper sauce, and how to make delicious "creamed" soups without cream. We tested these unique recipes several times—and even had an ordinary home cook (that is, nonprofessional cook), Ana Deboo, try many of them, too—to be sure they would work in anybody's hands.

Too many low-fat foods on the market today are unpalatable and have given low-fat food a bad name. According to an article in the May 1993 issue of *Consumer Reports,* many fat-free products that promise pleasure without guilt unfortunately miss out on the pleasure. Despite an initial flurry of consumer enthusiasm (most people will try—once, at least—foods that purport to offer something for nothing), sales of these products have fallen off considerably. *Consumer Reports* put it this way: "As food companies have pushed to take fat reduction to the limit, they have often made foods unfit for the normal palate." Let's face it, most people don't sit down to dinner for punishment, and they are not inclined to eat food that doesn't taste good.

With the recipes in this book, you need not worry about flavor and texture. There's plenty of both. I am generous with healthful seasonings, especially fresh herbs and peppers of all kinds. Nor should you worry about counting calories, fat grams, or any other such statistic. I do not believe, as I have said in my previous cookbooks, that people should eat by number (see page 125). People should eat by *concept.* If you fail to learn the concepts of nutritious, low-fat eating, all the numbers in the world will do you no good. These concepts are simple: load up on low-fat grain-based and other starchy foods (the base of the new U.S. Department of Agriculture "eating pyramid"), vegetables, and fruits; then "flesh out" your meal with a moderate portion of a high-protein food like finfish or shellfish. My recipes are designed to help you do just that. In addition to being low in fat, the seafood portions are moderate. When seafood is mixed with other ingredients such as pasta and vegetables, it is these other ingredients that are plentiful. In other cases, the serving suggestions with the recipe are likely to recommend a filling starchy food as an accompaniment. The lesson here is that even if a high-protein food is highly nutritious—as seafood is—your body needs just enough; it cannot use too much of it. And the wise consumer will not overdo even a good thing.

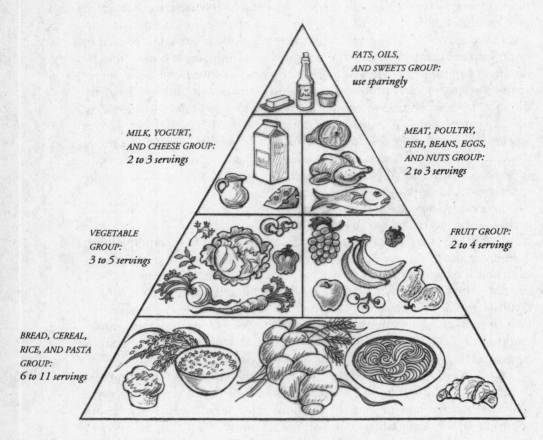

UNITED STATES DEPARTMENT OF AGRICULTURE EATING PYRAMID: DAILY DIETARY GUIDELINES

What is a serving?
- *1 cup milk or yogurt; 1½ ounces natural cheese*
- *2 to 3 ounces cooked lean meat, poultry, or fish; ½ cup cooked dry beans; 1 egg; 2 tablespoons peanut butter*
- *1 cup raw leafy vegetables; ½ cup other vegetables; ¾ cup vegetable juice*
- *1 medium apple, banana, or orange; ½ cup chopped, cooked, or canned fruit; ¾ cup fruit juice*
- *1 slice of bread; 1 ounce of cereal; ½ cup rice or pasta*

Here, then, is how I went about devising recipes as rich in variety and fun as they are low in fat. While I don't believe in rigidity, I did establish a few guidelines to keep my recipes lean and luscious. Some of my approaches are based on the more inspired low-fat cooking techniques that have emerged in recent years from spas, cooking schools, and restaurants. Others Rick and I devised on our own. Feel free to use them to modify some of your own favorite recipes.

- In general, I limit recipes designed for 4 servings to 1 tablespoon or less of added fat—usually as vegetable oil, occasionally as butter or margarine. The exceptions include a few sauces and dressings in which I sometimes allowed the quantity to rise to 2 tablespoons, usually of heart-safe vegetable oil; marinades in which much of the oil is not consumed; and recipes in which an additional touch of vegetable-oil spray is used to prevent sticking or to aid in browning.

- Wherever possible, I use only vegetable-oil spray as my "added" fat, which greatly decreases the amount of oil in my recipes.

- There is no deep-frying in this book. But I have found that every other method of cooking fish—from sautéing to microwaving—lends itself well to a low-fat approach.

- In place of whole milk, cream, and other fat-laden dairy products, I use nonfat and low-fat versions such as evaporated skimmed milk, nonfat and low-fat milk, nonfat yogurt and sour cream, and low-fat buttermilk and ricotta cheese.

- When thickening is required, as in a "creamed" soup, I often turn to pureed vegetables such as potato and occasionally to cornstarch or browned flour to do the job, rather than using cream or butter mixed with flour.

- Instead of relying on fats for flavor, I lean heavily on fresh herbs, garlic and various members of the onion family, peppers of all kinds, citrus juices, and the nearly endless variety of spices and dried seasonings.

- Proper cookware is almost as important as the ingredients. Nonstick surfaces are the name of the game if you are watching your fat intake, and I urge you to use nonstick pots and pans.

- I follow modern nutritional guidelines with regard to amounts of protein and suggest servings of cooked seafood of 3 to 4 ounces per person. As spectacular as seafood is, excessive amounts of protein should not supplant the vegetables, grains, and fruit that are now known to be so important in healthful eating.

3
Fish Is a Health Food (Mom Was Right!)

I almost hesitated to write this chapter because so many people seem to equate "health foods" with foods that lack flavor and interest. But those of you already familiar with the hundreds of tasty dishes in *Jane Brody's Good Food Book* and *Jane Brody's Good Food Gourmet* know better. And those who don't yet appreciate the fact that fabulous food can be as good to your body as it is to your taste buds are about to find out otherwise. But first a word about why it is worth your while to become more familiar with seafood and to make it a regular part of your weekly diet.

When it comes to nutrition, seafood is a natural. Nearly all edible finfish and shellfish emerge from the water offering many of the nutrients you most need to achieve and maintain health—lean protein, B vitamins, phosphorus, iron, and zinc—and some varieties are especially rich in such essential nutrients as calcium, iodine, and potassium. And you get all this at a caloric price that makes seafood a dieter's delight, especially if the dish is prepared—as it is in this book—without the addition of many high-calorie ingredients.

But the nutrient density of seafood turns out to be almost an incidental health reason for recommending that it become a more prominent feature in the American diet. Most important is the fact that nearly all seafood is relatively low in fat, especially in the so-called saturated fat that is now regarded as the primary culprit in heart and blood-vessel diseases. Even the fish with the highest fat content, such as farm-raised salmon, falls well within current guidelines. As if that were not enough, medical researchers recently discovered that a significant amount of the fat in seafood is a type that is actually health-promoting. These fats, known as omega-3 fatty acids, are primarily EPA (for eicosapentaenoic acid) and DHA (for docosahexaenoic acid). But don't worry, you need not remember the chemical names, just that these fats (really oils) seem to play a vital—though as yet incompletely understood—role in preventing heart attacks and strokes caused by blood clots.

How is the fat in fish able to perform these miracles? At least two probable mechanisms have been identified. One is the ability of omega-3 fatty acids to lower blood levels of triglycerides, fats that, when elevated in the blood, are associated with an increased risk of heart attack. The second, and perhaps most important, mechanism is the ability of omega-3 fatty acids to act as natural anticoagulants. They reduce the tendency of the blood to form clots, and it is clots trying to squeeze through narrow coronary arteries that are the primary cause of heart attacks. A third possibility, for which current evidence is contradictory, is the ability of fish oils to raise blood levels of HDL, the cholesterol-carrying blood protein that is believed to act as a kind of Drāno for coronary arteries, cleansing them of fatty deposits. Many studies have shown that the higher a person's blood level of HDL, the lower the coronary risk.

Some studies indicate that omega-3 fatty acids may also play a role in lowering blood pressure, preventing or treating autoimmune diseases like lupus and rheumatoid arthritis, and blocking the spread of cancer. But even if they do none of these, their widely acknowledged ability to lower the risk of blood clots that cause heart attacks and most strokes should award them a prominent place in the diet of all health-conscious people who also like to enjoy good food.

As with most new discoveries on the nutrition front, this one prompted several companies to try to package the "wonder nutrient" in a bottle. Fish-oil supplements (mainly sold as capsules) soon became the rage among those who worry about their long-term health. To many, taking a fistful of capsules a day seemed infinitely easier than buying and preparing fish to eat, even if the capsules did not cost any less—and often cost more—than their equivalent "dose" in fish.

But those who opt for the easy way out may be fooling themselves while lining the pockets of fish-oil entrepreneurs. First, most of the evidence for the health benefits of fish oils comes from studies not of people taking supplements, but of people who have eaten fish regularly for most of their lives. One large, well-designed study in the Netherlands showed that eating fish only

OMEGA-3 FATTY ACIDS IN SEAFOOD

This table gives the average amount of omega-3 fatty acids found in 3½ ounces (the raw edible portion) of finfish and shellfish. Keep in mind that even seafood with the smallest quantity of omega-3 fatty acids still contains beneficial amounts. See also the table on page 20 for the differences in total fat content between seafood raised on farms and seafood harvested from the wild.

MOST (MORE THAN 1 GRAM)	MODERATE (0.5 TO 1 GRAM)	LEAST (LESS THAN 0.5 GRAM)
Anchovy	Chum salmon	Carp
Atlantic halibut	Pompano	Channel catfish
Bluefish	Rainbow trout	Cod ("scrod")
Herring	Shark	Flounder
Mackerel	Smelt	Grouper
Pilchards	Striped bass	Haddock
Sablefish	Swordfish	Mahi-mahi
Salmon, Atlantic	Pacific oysters	Ocean perch
Salmon, coho	Squid	Orange roughy
Salmon, pink		Pacific halibut
Salmon, sockeye		Pacific rockfish
Sardines		Pike
Spiny dogfish		Pollock
Whitefish		Snapper
		Whiting
		Clams
		Crab
		Crayfish
		Eastern oysters
		Lobster
		Mussels
		Scallops
		Shrimp

SOURCE: United States Department of Agriculture.

twice a week can reduce the risk of having a heart attack by 50 percent, a benefit far greater than would result simply from eliminating two meat meals. Given that most people eat 21 meals a week (or should), making two of them fish meals should not be that difficult. Fish or shellfish can be eaten for dinner, lunch, or breakfast. If you think seafood is not a breakfast food, think again of the traditional fish-and-soup breakfast in Japan, the kippers eaten in England, and the lox (smoked salmon) that is a popular breakfast treat in many American cities. Seafood is an excellent, low-fat, low-calorie, stick-to-the-ribs breakfast food. On chilly mornings, I have breakfasted on the seafood soups and chowders in this book.

A second reason for eating fish rather than taking fish-oil supplements is that no one knows what quantity of supplements is needed to provide the most benefit at the least risk. Greenland Eskimos, who offered the first clues to the health-saving value of fish oils, suffer high rates of hemorrhagic strokes probably because their large intake of omega-3 fatty acids (in fish and blubber) interferes with the ability of their blood to clot. In addition to raising the risk of hemorrhagic stroke, those of us who take too much fish oil may end up with internal bleeding in the digestive tract or a tendency to bruise easily. Furthermore, there is a risk associated with contaminants in commercial fish-oil supplements, a danger of consuming too much vitamins A and D, a risk of depleting the body's supply of protective vitamin E, and a possibility of damaging cells of the immune system that help defend the body against harmful invaders.

A third reason for eating seafood in lieu of supplements is that the fish-oil supplements are high in calories, just as high as any other oil—about 120 calories per tablespoon. Taking fish oils in addition to eating regular meals could add a significant number of pounds to your frame in a year's time. Furthermore, to get the maximum benefit from seafood, fish should replace some of the animal protein foods now prominent in your diet that are considerably higher in total fats, especially in artery-damaging saturated fats: red meats, cheese, eggs, and most forms of poultry (see the table on page 19). Fish oils will not help much, if at all, if you continue to dine regularly on hamburgers, steak, fried chicken, and cheese-and-sausage pizza. Far better to tickle your taste buds and fill your stomach regularly with seafood dishes, saving those high-fat, high-calorie foods for occasional meals.

Finally, nutritionally speaking, seafood gives you far more than any supplement. It is an excellent source of protein, completely balanced and much leaner than any common animal protein food except, perhaps, chicken breast cooked without skin or added fat. Lean means you get more protein and less fat for your calories. A typical portion of fish (3 ounces, cooked) contains only about 100 calories and provides one-third to one-half of a day's protein needs for most adults. Even the richest fish, such as king salmon, have only about 230 calories in a 4-ounce portion (before cooking), as against 400 calories in a comparable piece of steak. Most fish are less than 5 percent fat (by weight), and all shellfish are less than 3 percent fat, whereas most cuts of beef are 20 to 30 percent fat by weight (75 to 85 percent fat by calories). Interestingly, even the low-fat fish and shellfish are reasonably good sources of omega-3 fatty acids, which are not found in any other animal protein food. Fish is also easy to chew and digest, making it an ideal protein food for small children and the elderly as well as everyone in between.

Like red meat, seafood is a good source of all the B vitamins, especially

B_{12}, which is virtually absent from strict vegetarian diets. Many types of shellfish—particularly oysters, mussels, and clams—and finfish—sardines, mackerel, bluefish, and bonito—are rich in iron. Fish that are eaten with their small bones, such as smelts and canned salmon and sardines, are excellent sources of calcium. All kinds of seafood are good sources of phosphorus; many—like catfish and canned tuna—are rich in magnesium; oysters, mussels, and clams are excellent sources of zinc; and mussels, scallops, and many finfish have lots of potassium. Many mollusks—clams, mussels, and oysters—are rich in the trace minerals selenium (a cancer protector), iodine (needed to prevent thyroid disease), and fluorine (essential for strong bones and teeth). And for those concerned about salt and its effects on blood pressure and water retention, nearly all fish are naturally low in sodium, even those that live in the sea.

When seafood is cooked, virtually all the essential nutrients it starts out with are preserved. Part of the reason is that seafood cooks so quickly and most often in a small amount of liquid or none at all.

THE FATS IN FISH

The fish that are richest in omega-3 fatty acids are the fattier fish: mackerel, king salmon, sablefish, shad; then herring, pompano, lake trout, whitefish, sockeye and coho salmon, and albacore tuna (see the table on page 16). Such fish can be found in both marine and freshwater environments and in both cold and warmer waters. However, even many low-fat varieties of seafood—especially shellfish like shrimp—are good sources of omega-3 fatty acids. Fish and shellfish acquire these protective fats from the foods they eat. The original source is phytoplankton, the microscopic plants consumed by fish and shellfish that are filter feeders. Bigger fish that eat these plankton feeders also acquire the omega-3 fatty acids. But these fats are found in almost no land animal that people consume.

Fish raised on farms (see page 20) will have omega-3 fatty acids only if they are given these fats in their feed. Farmed trout routinely have them because trout farmers have long known that these fish need such fats to develop properly. But the amount of omega-3 fatty acids in farmed catfish, salmon, tilapia, and other fish and shellfish can be highly variable. Hopefully, fish farmers, who by now must be aware of the sales value of omega-3 fatty acids, will soon all be providing their charges with feeds rich in these health-preserving oils.

Also variable is the amount of total fat—and, therefore, the amount of omega-3 fatty acids—found in fish and shellfish that live in natural environ-

THE FAT IN FISH: HOW DOES IT MEASURE UP?

The following chart compares the fat content of the 10 most popular seafoods in America with that of competing sources of animal protein. Overall, it shows that seafood generally has less total fat, less artery-clogging saturated fat, and usually less cholesterol than most meats, poultry, eggs, and cheese. Also, unlike other animal foods, seafood contains health-promoting omega-3 fatty acids. The amount of fat in Atlantic salmon, for example, rivals that of other animal protein foods; but very little of the salmon's fat is saturated, and wild-caught and some farm-raised salmon are among the richest sources of omega-3 fatty acids. Except where indicated, in each case the portion size is 3½ ounces (100 grams) of uncooked fish.

	SATURATED FAT (g)	OMEGA-3 (g)	CHOLESTEROL (mg)	TOTAL FAT (g)
Fish				
Catfish, farmed	1.77	0.27	47	7.59
Clams	0.09	0.14	34	0.97
Cod	0.13	0.18	43	0.67
Crabs	0.22	0.32	78	1.08
Flounder/sole	0.28	0.20	48	1.19
Salmon, Atlantic	2.18	1.9	59	10.85
Scallops	0.08	0.20	33	0.76
Shrimp	0.33	0.48	152	1.73
Surimi (from pollock)	n/a	n/a	30	0.90
Tuna, canned in water	0.23	0.27	30	0.82
Other animal proteins				
Beef (round)	7.44	—	66	17.54
Cheese, Cheddar (1 oz.)	5.98	—	30	9.40
Chicken (no skin)	0.79	—	70	3.08
Eggs (2 large)	3.10	—	426	10.02
Pork loin (lean only)	2.85	—	64	8.25

n/a = data not available.

SOURCE: USDA Handbooks 8-15, 8-1, 8-5, 8-10, 8-13.

ments. The fat content of seafood varies according to season, stage of development, food supply, and environmental conditions. The amounts listed in tables (such as the table above) represent an average found in seafood samples taken under varying conditions. Thus, the seafood you find on your plate on any particular day could have a different fat content than the one listed. But over the course of a year, if you eat that same kind of seafood repeatedly, you will consume approximately the amount per serving listed.

THE FAT CONTENT OF FARMED VERSUS WILD SEAFOODS

As aquaculture grows rapidly in the United States and around the world, it is useful to keep in mind that more than availability, safety, and flavor are affected by efficient farm breeding and feeding. Nutritional characteristics are also altered—for better or worse. Farmed fish may have more of the essential nutrient beta-carotene, which may reduce the risks of heart disease and cancer, but many are also higher in fat than their wild cousins. Here are a few fat-content examples, according to data from the United States Department of Agriculture.

	SATURATED FAT (g)	OMEGA-3 (g)	CHOLESTEROL (mg)	TOTAL FAT (g)
Atlantic salmon, farmed	2.18	1.90	59	10.85
Atlantic salmon, wild	0.98	1.44	55	6.34
Catfish, farmed	1.77	0.27	47	7.59
Catfish, wild	0.72	0.36	58	2.82
Coho salmon, farmed	1.82	1.21	51	7.67
Coho salmon, wild	1.26	1.08	45	5.93
Eastern oysters, farmed	0.44	0.39	25	1.55
Eastern oysters, wild	0.77	0.56	53	2.46
Rainbow trout, farmed	1.55	0.93	59	5.40
Rainbow trout, wild	0.72	0.59	59	3.46

THE CHOLESTEROL IN FISH

I stated earlier that saturated fats, the kind that are hard at room temperature and found in only very small amounts in seafood, are the primary dietary culprit in artery-clogging disease. Many studies of animals and people have shown that saturated fats in the diet are far more important than dietary cholesterol in raising the cholesterol levels in the blood of people. This does not mean, however, that the cholesterol you eat is unimportant to health; it just means that it is less important than the kind and amount of fats consumed.

In general, finfish and many kinds of shellfish have less cholesterol per serving than most high-protein foods from land animals. Whereas a single large egg is loaded with about 213 milligrams of cholesterol, a 3½-ounce hamburger may have 100 milligrams, and a 3½-ounce chicken breast typically has 85 milligrams, the same size portion of monkfish, Pacific cod, or sea scallops has only 35 milligrams. And this is not unusual: 3½ ounces (before cooking) of swordfish, red snapper, ocean perch, and northern pike have only 40 milligrams; flounder, 50 milligrams; channel catfish, 60 milligrams; haddock, 65 milligrams; brook trout, 70 milligrams; chum salmon, 75 milligrams; and mackerel, 80 milligrams.

Contrary to long-standing (and now known to be mistaken) beliefs, most shellfish are not high in cholesterol. Even shrimp, with 125 to 160 milligrams of cholesterol in 3½ ounces (depending on the variety), are not astronomically high and are now considered an acceptable alternative to red meat by the American Heart Association. The only really high-cholesterol shellfish commonly consumed are squid, with 200 to 300 milligrams per 3½ ounces, depending on the type. Clams have only 25 to 40 milligrams, oysters only 45 to 55 milligrams, and mussels only 45 to 60 milligrams per 3½ ounces of meat. Even lobster, which many cholesterol watchers mistakenly think is a forbidden food, has only 70 to 95 milligrams of cholesterol per 3½ ounces.

Still not convinced? Perhaps this 1990 study by Marian T. Childs and colleagues at the University of Washington will ease your qualms about enjoying shellfish. The study examined the effects on men's cholesterol and triglyceride levels of a diet featuring various kinds of shellfish. Men who ate lots of oysters, clams, and crab had lower levels of cholesterol and triglycerides at the end of the study than before they switched to a shellfish diet. Those who indulged on mussels were only slightly behind the first group but also ended up with improved cholesterol profiles. And those who dined on a diet rich in shrimp and squid, which have the highest cholesterol content, experienced no change in their cholesterol levels despite their consumption of high-cholesterol (but very low-fat) shellfish.

4

Fish out of Water: Our Seafood Supply

There are, as the saying suggests, plenty of fish in the sea—and in the rivers, lakes, ponds, and streams. The unsettling fact, however, is that the supply seems to change continuously. Too often, one species or another is overfished or falls into catastrophic decline as the result of some environmental assault. Haddock comes quickly to mind because I'd been searching for it recently without much luck and wondered where it had gone. Then I learned that the annual American catch, which was 14 million pounds not so long ago, had plummeted to nearly 4 million pounds. No wonder it was a rare offering at fish counters. It's an old, familiar story: too many haddock had been taken from the North Atlantic, forcing the government to restrict the catch until the species recovers, as it is believed it will. Grouper has been overfished, too. A few years back, redfish went into a free fall in availability not long after the dish called blackened redfish emerged from Louisiana to became the rage. Even shark is facing declines, not only because we have discovered its culinary virtues, but because it is being killed in vast numbers solely for its fins to satisfy the Chinese demand for shark-fin soup.

MORE AND BETTER FISH

At the same time, all this bad news has been countered by some terrific turn-arounds. Striped bass is returning as an edible fish harvested from some of its old estuaries; one of its breeding grounds, the Hudson River, is regaining its health so emphatically these days that the pollution-sensitive barnacles that had disappeared from piers are back in force to plague boat hulls again. The "trash" fish of yesterday that most fishermen discarded because few people would eat them—monkfish, catfish, and skate, among others—are now widely appreciated and have greatly added to the panoply of seafood available to us. And while some fish purists may bemoan this fact, the techniques of big (and not so big) business have significantly increased the supply of some seafood; efficient breeding, freezing, and transportation methods now get the fish from here to there in greater quantity and variety—and in better shape—than ever before.

It is now commonplace, for instance, for huge fishing boats to travel 700 miles or more out to sea to find tuna, stay out a week or two, and still manage to keep the fish in excellent condition. They preserve the fish aboard ship by bleeding them first and then either freezing them at once or submerging them in a slurry of salt water and ice. This way, the tuna does not freeze, but bacterial growth—and, thus, spoilage—is effectively squelched until the giant fish makes it to the dock.

And Latin America, in particular, has proved a boon to fish lovers north of the border, with enormous catches of mahi-mahi (it used to be called dolphin fish, but people were confusing it with the lovable mammal) and the widespread development of fish and shellfish farming. The significant jump in shrimp consumption in the United States since the 1970s—from about 1.5 pounds per person annually to 2.5 pounds—has been made possible largely by the staggering production of shrimp in places as far-flung as Ecuador and Thailand, both sending us frozen shrimp by the ton (almost all the shrimp you eat has been frozen at one time or another).

How the range of choices in seafood has grown! In the *Official Fulton Fish Market Cookbook,* which includes a history of New York City's Fulton Fish Market, the largest wholesale fish market in the Western Hemisphere, Bruce Beck says that in the early days its produce was limited to an area reaching only from Cape Hatteras to the banks off the coast of New England. Now, refrigerated trucks and airplanes speed across the country and around the world every day to markets everywhere. They bear fresh Dover sole from Holland to restaurants in Seattle and Boston and even to neighborhood markets in Middle America, where fish shops were once unknown. And in the sky, perhaps right now, orange roughy is on its way to somewhere in the States from New Zealand, and salmon is speeding from the Pacific to the Atlantic. These days, just about every fish is a flying fish.

On the coasts, a great variety of fish is already in residence. A surprising aspect of our fish supply is that many of the same fish—with slight variations—exist in widely separated areas. The story goes that the French, arriving in America by the boatload in the 1930s and 1940s and poised to promulgate their haute cuisine, were desperate to find their lovely, treasured fish known as bar. There was none to be found until one day they discovered that the relatively unappreciated American striped bass was virtually a bar. Soon, as you might imagine, it soared in popularity here. Also close cousins, despite the geographic distance that separates them, are the Atlantic and Pacific salmon. Their breeding habits differ and the flavor of Atlantic salmon is said to have less character, but they are all salmon nevertheless.

Although the recent news about salmon has been dominated by its struggle for survival in many parts of the world, particularly in the Pacific Northwest, salmon are, undeniably, something of an American success story. In Alaska—where the frigid, clear waters produce great quantities of halibut, pollock, cod, shrimp, and crab—the pristine sea yields much of the world's salmon as well. So successful, in fact, is the salmon haul that fishermen complain they are catching too many pinks to bring a decent price for them. Pinks are the little fellows, on average only about 3 pounds (as compared to the more desirable and monstrous king salmon, which can weigh in at about 120 pounds). The pinks are used primarily for canning, and the surplus probably accounts for all the bargains we've seen recently in canned-salmon prices.

A visit to southeastern Alaska on just about any summer day to talk to the fishermen or the state officials explains why productivity has remained high. Not only is the state so sparsely populated that water cleanliness can be maintained, but management of the fish has been stringent. To flourish, the salmon must forge their way from the deep ocean into the Alaskan streams to breed. But the fishermen can prevent that by dropping long seines (nets) into the ocean near the mouth of the streams, thereby hauling in whole schools of fish as the salmon attempt to follow nature's calling. To make sure breeding salmon are not overfished, the government has strictly regulated the times that the fishermen can deploy their barricades—some days on, some days off—and the type of salmon that can be caught, depending on the season. Beyond that, government hatcheries spawn salmon that they release in the wild to give the species another boost.

FARM-RAISED FISH AND SHELLFISH

Wild salmon have been assisted in their survival, too, by one of the most significant developments in the production of food in years: aquaculture, or fish farming, which has augmented the supply from oceans and streams. All over the world, from Ireland to Chile to Washington State, salmon are farmed specifically for human consumption. Because the feed, conditions, and other variables affecting farmed salmon are different in many ways from those in the wild, all of it affecting taste, a debate has flared among some chefs and other salmon lovers over the relative merits of each. While one chef would never dream of buying farmed salmon (too mild in flavor, he says, and the texture isn't quite right), another actually prefers the farmed variety because he can rely on consistent quality and a constant year-round supply. Still others detect little difference between farmed and fresh salmon and are just grateful for the ready availability. The same debate goes on with equal vigor over some of the other farmed fish—striped bass, for example. However, the argument is moot in this instance because restrictions on the commercial catch have meant that farmed hybrid striped bass is nearly the only game in town.

With regard to many of the new seafood products to emerge from farms, there is little or no argument. Catfish, for instance, was eaten by relatively few people until only recently. Some caught the fish in the wild, where it often acquired a muddy, oily flavor because of the fish's proclivity for dining on algae. That flavor problem was eliminated when fish farmers learned to control the water quality in their ponds better. The result was, in most instances, a sweet, buttery-flavored catfish with pleasant white flesh. The price was kept relatively low, thanks to the ease of farming, and catfish production and eating in the United States took an astonishing leap so that now 300 million pounds of the farmed fish are shipped every year.

Another success involves mussels and for much the same reason. Wild mussels are wonderful to eat, though they are sometimes a bit of a nuisance because they can be gritty and encrusted with barnacles, a logical result of a lifetime spent clinging to pilings and rocks. But in 1971, a Maine man named Edward Myers traveled to Spain to learn mussel farming from the industry that was established there. He started the first mussel aquaculture business in America using a technique called raft culture, and soon other farmers in America tried this and similar approaches to mussel aquaculture. Myers hung ropes from floating rafts, and the mussels flocked to the dangling tendrils. When mussels cling to such ropes in the protected waters of some beautiful cove off Maine or Washington State, they grow in great numbers, are easy to harvest, and are generally much cleaner than their wild brethren. Once the mussels are harvested, the processor frequently will clean them still further.

They can be shipped in bags, and, properly refrigerated (38°F), they will live for about a week. Now, steamed mussels (see the recipe on page 436) are no longer the sort of delicacy you find mainly in restaurants or abroad; they have become a wonderful food that practically any home cook in America can prepare in no time—a great pile of them all at once—to wow family and friends.

Aquaculture has resulted in some strange products on the market. Tilapia, for example, a fine, sweet fish that comes from Africa, reproduces beautifully on a farm and is now showing up everywhere in the country to the mystification of many shoppers. Aquaculture also must be thanked for the current bounty of trout, available to grace any table at almost any time. (Oh, I know that the wild ones, just out of the stream, are more flavorful, but not many of us get the opportunity to go trout fishing.) Most of America's farmed trout comes from a 15-mile stretch of the Snake River in Idaho, where a canyon has sliced through an aquifer. The fresh, clear water, exactly 58°F year round, cascades out of the canyon wall to feed the river. And it is there that some of the water is diverted—just for a little while—so that it can run through the trout ponds constructed all along the river. The trout are bred, raised to varying sizes, filleted or butterflied or left whole, and then hurried off to fish shops and restaurants around America.

There are more than 3,400 aquaculture farms in the United States alone, some now raising even abalone, crayfish, redfish, and sturgeon. Their numbers are expected to keep growing as the demand for fish does. With that expansion, however, has come some lamentable problems: uneven quality and some contamination in poorly kept ponds, making it all the more important that you find a reliable supplier and complain when the fish has an off flavor. But on the whole, aquaculture is a marvelous development for those of us looking for healthful, flavorful fish.

5

Aliases and Substitutions: The "Hake," You Say?

Although this nation is beginning to embrace the glories of fish, seafood is still confusing and mysterious to many of us. Even the best efforts at self-education run smack into the chaotic realities of seafood nomenclature. Take weakfish, for instance—not so named because it is actually weak, but because its mouth is easily torn by a hook. That makes enough sense, I suppose. But this same fish is also known as sea trout although it is not really a trout. Now, salmon trout is, in fact, a trout—it is not a salmon. (Although salmon and trout are in the same fish family, trout are generally freshwater fish whereas salmon spend most of their lives in salt water.) A fish called Saint Peter's is an illegal name for tilapia, the widely farmed fellow originally from Africa that biblical scholars believe to be the fish with which Jesus fed the multitudes. Perenially popular scrod isn't a recognized fish at all, but the name for a small cod—or, rather, that is what it's supposed to be. These days, the name is sometimes used loosely to describe other fish in the cod family, too, such as hake or pollock. Surimi, which some will tell you is fake fish, isn't so much fake as reconstituted and flavored fish: pollock that has been processed and seasoned, frequently to resemble crab. Whew!

The possibility for confusion—and, with it, the loss of confidence you may feel (as if unfamiliarity with a particular name reaffirms your inability to get a handle on this seafood stuff)—is endless. It is caused by everyone from the fishermen who love to invent colorful names for their catch (often more than one colorful name) to the few fish shops that try to make an inexpensive-sounding fish more exotic. The government, too, is indirectly at fault for being unable to cut through the dizzying name game.

I came to my own intense exploration of seafood a bit late, driven in part by a desire to lessen my dependence on meats and to leave saturated fats behind. And I suspect that, as in learning a foreign language, a lot of this would have been easier if I had started earlier. I remember the time I came home with a fine, big fish that the lovely woman at the fish store said was a blue snapper. Now, maybe there is something called that, but I never did find it in any of my reference books. Baby bluefish are called snappers, but this was too big; there is something called a blue-striped snapper, but this fish had no stripes. Anyway, it was great eating, whatever it was.

Despite the rampant confusion out there, I hope you won't despair any more than I have. It is certainly possible to diminish, if not eliminate, a lot of the mix-ups and flimflam. The rest of this chapter, the tables, and the glossary at the back of the book should help. So should your own sense of adventure because as you try different fish, you quickly start to see their similarities and differences. With familiarity comes a comfortable intimacy. It's like visiting a foreign country where everyone looks the same—that is, until you get to know people as individuals. And it's like learning to appreciate wine. At first, all you know is red and white, and then, slowly and with great personal satisfaction, you begin to taste and smell and actually feel the important differences. But wine is a subtle thing; seafood, by comparison, is a cinch and far less encumbered with pretension.

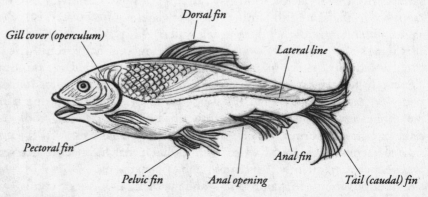

ANATOMY OF A FISH

FLATFISH

I don't know of anything simpler and, at the same time, more baffling than the fish known as *flatfish*, so named because they resemble elongated pancakes rather than cylinders. This is a collection of similar, fascinating fish, mostly called flounders but also widely known as sole (even though the only "true" sole is the Dover sole caught in Europe and generally not available in the United States). If you see something called sole in the market, just remember it's a flounder. These fish spend much of their life hiding on the bottom of the ocean on their sides, with the white side of their bodies resting on the sand and the darker top side acting as camouflage to fool predators. This would be a very awkward position for them to maintain if it were not for the fact that although they start out life like normal two-eyed fish, as they grow up and flop over onto their sides to spend their adult life on the ocean sand, one of their eyes migrates to the top side to get out of the sand so that both of their eyes are now on the same side of their face. (Well, it seems to work for them.)

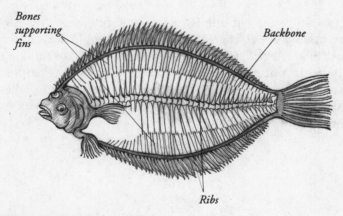

BONE STRUCTURE OF A FLATFISH

All of these fish can be neatly filleted, which is why they are so often sold that way. Since flounders are among the most delicate and mildest of the fish we have available, people who say they don't like fish often find them palatable. Logically, these fragile fish are usually cooked in ways that involve gentle and minimal handling, such as sautéing and baking rather than grilling, and they are typically flavored gently so as not to overwhelm them with intense seasonings. Only the big members of this group, like the halibut (a flounder that can grow to hundreds of pounds), has flesh that is firm enough for rougher handling.

ROUNDFISH

The designation *roundfish* has to do with the fact that if the fish were to be sliced crosswise, the resulting steak would form an oval or circle. Among the most common roundfish we see in the markets are members of the cod family: Atlantic and Pacific cod, pollock, and haddock. They are all large, cold-water, mildly flavored fish. Most often you see them as steaks, although fillets are not uncommon (particularly the smaller cod, often sold as scrod fillets). Haddock will generally cost more, when you can find it, because it seems to have a little more character and is rarer. A fish called hake should probably also be included here. I say probably because for the longest time it was considered a cod, although a bit less bland. Then, as I worked my way through various articles by fish experts, I saw emerging another train of thought indicating that maybe hake was only a cousin of the cod, maybe, in fact, it was a whiting (which is in a different family), or perhaps only some hakes were cods and some were whitings. Relax. They all taste pretty much alike. And if you buy hake thinking it's cod or thinking it's whiting, you'll do just fine either way. All of these fish are excellent in chowders and salads or simply broiled or baked. But none of them has the cachet of some of the other wonderful roundfish available to us, each with its own distinctive flavor and appearance.

Hake

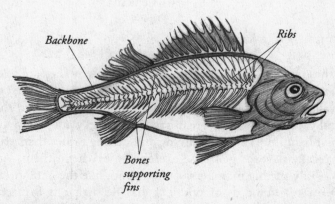

Backbone   *Ribs*

Bones supporting fins

BONE STRUCTURE OF A ROUNDFISH

Tuna, in particular, has gone from that too familiar precooked commodity in a can to being one of the most desirable of all the fresh fish. This is partly due to the passion of the Japanese for raw tuna and to successful marketing in the United States, where fresh tuna is sold as if it were red meat: "Just like beef, but better for you." That marketing ploy has backfired somewhat: the reddest fresh tuna doesn't necessarily taste the best. Since the Japanese treasure tuna for their sushi bars (see, for example, the recipe on page 162 for tuna maki), they will pay the highest price and purchase the best specimens, often at some huge auction. As it is being judged for quality, a beheaded tuna, which can weigh several hundred pounds and look like a tapered barrel, is stroked and examined by merchants as if it were a racehorse. One thing the experts look for is a kind of marbling that indicates how much desirable fat is in the flesh. The tuna's flesh (which, like beef, is muscle tissue) is so firm because its strength is needed to help propel these powerful fish through the seas during migration like so many trailer trucks barreling across the highways. Fresh tuna is nothing like the canned version and does, in fact, stand up beautifully to the rough handling of grilling, pan-searing, or anything else your imagination leads you to. (*A hot tip:* the lowly, relatively inexpensive mackerel is in the tuna family. Eat it now, before anybody else finds out.)

Among other commonly sold species of roundfish are those in the grouper, snapper, and salmon families. As different as they may be in flavor and looks, they have important similarities. For one thing, you can't go wrong with any of them. Buy them filleted, buy them whole, cook them as you like: poached, baked, steamed, sautéed, whatever. It will all work just fine. Each is a moderately firm fish with sublime flavor. The true striped bass, which many consider the best eating fish of all, is now in limited supply because of the environmental assaults it has suffered. But a hybrid striped bass is farmed widely and is a fine substitute. The black sea bass is also widely sold, and although its flavor is perhaps less spectacular, it is a marvelous fish.

As for snappers, there is only one true, official red snapper, caught primarily in the warm Atlantic waters off the coast of the United States. But part of the desirability in this case is in the name; lots of other reddish snappers, wherever they come from, are excellent fish, most of them tasting pretty much alike. So the high price of the true red snapper is often an artificial gauge of its relative value.

Salmon, unlike the snappers, show vast differences according to type (see the glossary on pages 540 to 542), but what most of us see year round in the stores, especially on the East Coast, are the Atlantic salmon. They are almost never caught in the waters off the United States anymore, but are farmed with great success around the world. Just to confuse matters, they are sometimes called Norwegian salmon (to give it more class) regardless of where they come from. On the West Coast, you're likely to find Pacific salmon, mostly wild-caught but some that have been raised on farms.

TRASH FISH

I don't know if there are any so-called trash fish that are treated with disdain anymore. Once, these were the fish that fishermen tossed away as nuisances. They were too ugly, too fearsome, too strange. Now, to take one example, we eat monkfish all the time even though the industry has wisely chosen to show us only the tail and never the head. The head is gigantic and frightening. There are stories about this fish reaching up out of the sea to eat a duck. But the tail of the powerful monkfish (also called anglerfish and a bunch of other things), when properly cleaned, yields firm, sweet meat that clever marketers have dubbed "poor man's lobster." Although the story may be apocryphal, monkfish is said to have acquired its popular name because monks of yore happily dined on it even when most fishermen discarded it. Others say the name comes from the hooded appearance of its huge head.

Monkfish

And who would have thought we would be eating sharks? Not only do we consume them, but some types are now threatened by overfishing. Another great surprise is the skate, a relative of the ray, whose wings provide us with a fine, flavorful flesh, white and delicate, with an interesting corduroy-like ribbed texture.

SHELLFISH

There are few generalizations to make about these animals with their skeletons on the outside (how convenient for cooks and diners since the flesh just has to be plucked free one way or another) except that each in its way is wonderful, both as a creature and as a food. The lobster, I suppose, is my favorite, a complicated animal whose whole exterior is covered with receptors that allow it to track down morsels of food at great distances by detecting the molecular trails its prey leave in the sea. That superb homing-in capacity often brings these lobsters right into the local lobsterman's trap, to the lobster's dismay and our good fortune. Although the lobster can grow to 45 pounds or so, we usually get them at 1¼ to 1½ pounds. The flesh is so marvelous that I prefer to eat it freshly boiled with no embellishment at all, although I have provided some other preparations in this book.

Other shellfish are equally spectacular, which accounts for the enormous popularity of shrimp. But our experience with scallops is strange. Since we eat only the muscle and rarely see scallops in their beautiful shells, our minds seem to envision shell and seafood as two separate things, the one a crimped, pretty shell found on beaches and the other a round, white bit of meat that resides only in seafood shops. Somehow, that division deprives us of the kind of beauty that can be appreciated in clams, oysters, and mussels still in their shells, peaking through a pasta or a paella.

Then there are the squid, with their "outer skeleton" (called a quill, which is on the inside of the animal) resembling a cartilaginous shoehorn. To overcome a long-standing aversion to this fine seafood, restaurants and recipe writers started calling squid by its Italian name—calamari—even when it was used to prepare, say, a Greek or a Mexican dish. Although novices in cooking squid may hesitate to tackle it, the great surprise about this intriguing shellfish is how easy it is to prepare, quick to cook, and extraordinarily versatile as well as delicious. Despite soaring popularity, squid retains its good value, a seafood with little waste and a reasonable price. Squid are now widely available nationwide, thanks to a vigorous industry here supplemented by Asian producers that send this seafood to stores cleaned and frozen.

OTHER PHYSICAL DIFFERENCES

In addition to being flat or round, having its shell outside or in, being firm or delicate, the seafood available to us has other differences that you should keep in mind. Bone structure varies greatly. The fish, like flounder, that you nearly always see filleted—that is, the flesh removed from the bone—is sold that way for good reason: the bone structure is uncomplicated, allowing the flesh to come off easily and without any annoying, almost impossible-to-remove "flesh bones" not attached to the fish's spinal column. Striped bass and snappers are so good to serve whole because they, too, have skeletons that allow for easy filleting after they are cooked. Fish like shad (which is prized for its roe) have much more complicated skeletal configurations. It takes an expert to fillet them, and they require patience from anyone who eats them unfilleted. Another variation: some fish, like salmon, will fillet quite easily but have pinbones, a line of large bones that are left behind along one side of the fillet. However, most of these are easily removed with fingers, needle-nose pliers, or tweezers; if necessary, they can be cut out.

Another point to keep in mind is rarely mentioned but has an impact on guidelines offered in this book and elsewhere about how much fish to buy per serving when you prepare whole fish. Fish have heads that vary considerably in size. The big head on a striped bass means less edible fish per pound when you're buying a whole fish, compared to, say, purchasing a whole trout, which is small-headed.

Also, since some fish are more beautiful than others, consider aesthetics when deciding whether to serve the fish whole or filleted or prepared some other way. All snappers are gorgeous, all trout are handsome, but whiting (I think) are rather unattractive, although their sweet, tender flesh suits me just fine. I remember the time I substituted a whole whiting in a recipe that called for whole trout and then could hardly look at the big-headed, skinny thing. The solution is not to ignore this otherwise delicious fish, but to remember to cut off its head before preparing or serving it. Some fish, too, like mackerel, have delicate skin that makes fine eating along with the flesh, while the skin of other fish is tough, relatively unpalatable, or unattractive.

SUBSTITUTIONS

In general, substitutions are a simple matter and, if you follow a few guidelines, almost always work out well. One full-flavored, firm fish—tuna or marlin, for instance—will serve roughly as well as another. Except for the lucky ones among us who live right in one of the nation's seafood centers, the fish available on any given day will always be a matter of the relatively few specimens the local fish shop happened to get in during the predawn hours of a particular morning. That means limited choice. So please use the Seafood Selection Guide on page 45 and the information in the glossary on pages 511 to 555 to help you substitute and experiment with abandon. In fish cookery, the mistakes are few and rarely serious; the rewards are too plentiful to number.

6

The "Cuts" of Commercial Seafood

I'll never forget the first time I tried to prepare a recipe that called for a "dressed" fish. Since I had no idea what that meant, and before I could find out, I began to imagine the fish bedecked like a seductive sea nymph. I then leafed through various cookbooks and found two different definitions: one, a fish with head and tail on; the other, a fish with head and tail removed. So rather than leave you wondering what to do, I am providing you with an illustrated guide, relying in part on information from a Washington, D.C.–based supermarket chain, Giant Food, Inc., that has been one of the first supermarkets to offer its customers pamphlets containing shopping hints and nutritional advice.

BUYING FINFISH

WHOLE The fish is intact, just as it comes from the water, guts and all.

DRAWN OR HEAD ON The fish is cleaned, with scales (if any), gills, and entrails removed.

DRESSED OR PAN-DRESSED The fish is cleaned as above, with head, tail, and/or fins removed *according to the customer's wishes.* A dressed fish, therefore, may be no different from a "head on" fish. Or it may have a tail but no head or no head and no tail. It is up to you to spell out what you want.

SPLIT FOR BROILING The fish is cleaned and cut in half lengthwise or butterflied so that the halves remain attached but lie flat.

Drawn or head on: *scaled and gutted*

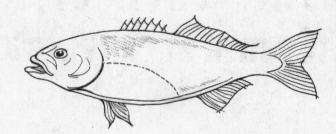

Dressed and pan-dressed: *scaled, gutted, and gills removed; head, tail, and fins may be removed*

Sliced into steaks: *cross-sectional cuts through the backbone, usually 1 inch thick, after fish is dressed*

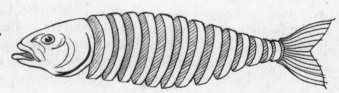

Filleted: *fleshy sides of fish are cut from skeleton*

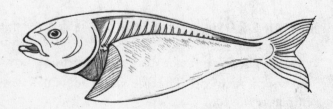

CUTS OF COMMERCIAL FISH

FILLETS The sides of the fish are cut away from the ribs and backbone, producing two elongated pieces. Fillets are often, but not always, boneless, depending upon the bone structure of the original fish. For example, whitefish, shad, carp, and rainbow trout will have fine pinbones in their fillets. Likewise, a salmon fillet may have a single line of large bones, depending on where the fillet was cut.

STEAKS A headless, tailless fish is cut crosswise through the backbone and ribs. Steaks from very large fish, such as swordfish and tuna, are usually boneless because the flesh is first cut from the skeleton and then sliced.

SURIMI Sometimes called "imitation seafood," surimi is processed from real fish. To a fish paste made from fresh pollock (a cod harvested in the cold, unpolluted waters off Alaska), salt, other seasonings, and shellfish flavorings are added to create a low-cost imitation of crab or lobster meat. Surimi is always fully cooked and sold frozen or previously frozen. It is usually available as seafood sticks (Sea Legs is a popular brand) and as salad chunks, both of which can be cut into various lengths and shapes. Surimi can be used as is in salads and hors d'oeuvres or added to hot dishes at the last moment.

BUYING SHELLFISH

SHRIMP Since shrimp are highly perishable, most shrimp are sold frozen or previously frozen. Much to the consumer's advantage, they are frozen right after harvest so that you end up with the freshest possible product. Shrimp sold "fresh"—that is, never frozen—are often treated with sulfites to prevent discoloration. These preservatives can trigger allergic-type reactions in people prone to asthma.

In the market, you are likely to find headless shrimp, which are raw shrimp in the shell (usually previously frozen and defrosted); raw shrimp that have been peeled (either with or without their tail shells removed) and deveined (sold frozen and previously frozen); shrimp cooked in their shells (both frozen and not); and shrimp that have been peeled, deveined, and cooked (both frozen and not). Fully cleaned shrimp packed in salted water are also sold in vacuum-sealed cans.

Shrimp are sold and priced by size: the bigger they are, the fewer you get and the more they cost per pound. Shrimp range from the smallest "salad" shrimp, with 70 to 90 shrimp per pound, to the largest "colossal" shrimp, with fewer than 10 per pound.

SQUID Most markets now only carry small, cleaned, skinned, and gutted squid that have had the tentacled head portion separated from the tubelike body. These are nearly always sold frozen or previously frozen, having been "processed" here or in far-off lands like Taiwan and shipped frozen solid in large bags.

CRABS These are sold whole in hard and soft shells, as pasteurized claws or crabmeat that has been removed from the shell, and as fully cooked and frozen claws or legs. Hard-shell blue crabs are available throughout the year. They may be sold already steamed, seasoned, and ready to eat. Soft-shell crabs are fresh crabs that have recently molted—that is, they have shed their hard shells—and have shells soft enough to eat after the crab is cleaned and cooked (see pages 344, 354, and 468). They are available fresh and alive from May to September and may also be sold frozen the rest of the year.

Pasteurized crabmeat, sold year round, is fresh shelled crab that has been cooked, vacuum-sealed, and heated to kill bacteria so that it will keep—if left unopened and refrigerated—for about 6 months. However, once opened, it should be used within 2 to 3 days. It can be frozen, although this will change its texture.

Crab claws are usually sold fully cooked, fresh in season, and frozen or previously frozen year round. A nutcracker is needed to crack the shell so that the meat can be extracted.

LOBSTER Most inviting are the live lobsters now found swimming in tanks in many supermarkets and fish stores. Three categories of size are generally available. Most weigh about 1¼ pounds, and each one is considered a single portion. Large lobsters weigh more than 1½ pounds. And extra-large lobsters weigh 2¼ pounds or more. Lobster lovers insist that females have more meat. To determine the sex of a lobster, look on its underside at the two small swimmerets near where the tail meets the body. If the swimmerets are soft and feathery, it's a female; if they're hard, it's a male.

Lobster tails are also available frozen, both raw and fully cooked in the shell, and as raw lobster meat without a shell.

CLAMS Quite a few varieties are sold commercially, but the three you are most likely to find are the small littlenecks, which are great whole in a soup or paella; the medium cherrystones, which are commonly steamed or eaten raw on the half shell; and the large, tougher chowder clams, which are usually chopped and used in soups or in recipes calling for minced clams. Clams are sold alive in their shells and as shelled fresh clam meat packed in plastic tubs or glass jars. Whole and minced clams as well as smoked clams are also sold in vacuum-sealed cans.

MUSSELS Most mussels on the market nowadays are "cultured"—that is, they have been raised on a farm. The result is a nearly grit-free, unpolluted product that requires no elaborate precooking preparation. Another advantage to farmed mussels is that you get more meat for your money: at least 30 percent of the weight is meat in farmed mussels as against only about 15 percent in the wild variety. When taken out of water, live mussels will open but should close when iced and agitated. If you are uncertain about an open mussel, squeeze the shell halves together; if the animal is alive, the shell will remain shut. In addition to fresh mussels in their shells and fresh mussel meat, you may purchase smoked mussels, which are sold in vacuum-sealed cans.

OYSTERS Most oysters are sold live in the shell or, because they are so challenging for the home cook to open, already shucked or on the half shell. Two types are generally available: eastern and Pacific. Eastern oysters may be small and used for stewing or large and used for frying. Pacific oysters, nearly all of which are farmed, have less flavor and less salt than the eastern varieties but are usually larger. Oysters are commonly named for the region from which they are harvested.

SCALLOPS Although scallops have two shells like clams and oysters, the shells are rarely seen because only the muscle that holds the shells together is eaten. Just a few of the more than 400 species of scallops are sold. The smallest and often the cheapest are fast-maturing calico scallops harvested from the Carolinas to the Gulf of Mexico. Nearly as small are the bay scallops harvested close to the shores of, primarily, New England and Long Island. Largest are the Atlantic sea scallops harvested farther out to sea and usually an inch or more in diameter.

7

Buying the Best Seafood

When I walk into a store that has a well-designed and properly displayed seafood counter, I can feel my whole being grin, a reaction that until recently was evoked only by beautiful displays of fruits and vegetables. For me, trays of meat or poultry are not as inviting as an attractive and colorful array of various kinds of fish and shellfish. Many cities—not only coastal cities like New York, San Francisco, and Boston, but also inland and midwestern cities like Durham, North Carolina, and Minneapolis and St. Paul—have one or more well-stocked seafood shops. And throughout the country, supermarkets have put in full-service seafood counters with knowledgeable people behind them who not only know their fish and shellfish, but also know how to turn customers on to their wares by offering fresh, well-displayed, and carefully handled seafood.

Fish and shellfish are highly perishable items, so how they are displayed and handled can make a big difference in the quality of the product you buy. Here are some guidelines gleaned from years of personal shopping experience, a study of seafood manuals that the industry provides for commercial vendors, and an excellent consumer publication, *Seafood Savvy*, written for the Cornell Cooperative Extension Service by Ken Gall, a seafood safety specialist with the New York Sea Grant Extension Program (see page 58 for ordering information).

To get the best in seafood, all you have to do is use your senses and good sense. You have a right to quality seafood—nothing but the best, considering how much you are paying for it—and the more often consumers insist on top quality, the more likely every fish buyer will get it.

YOUR NOSE KNOWS

When you walk into a fish store or approach a fish counter, you should not be assaulted by a "fishy" or unpleasant odor. Fresh fish should smell like the sea (if that's where it came from) or clean and sweet. And a shop that is properly maintained, offering only fresh seafood and maintaining high standards of sanitation, should smell equally inviting, like a fresh sea breeze. Likewise for the fish you buy. Do not buy any seafood that has a fishy or, worse, an ammonia-like odor, a sure sign that the fish is well past its prime. If in doubt, ask the fishmonger to rinse under cold water the fish that you are considering buying and then to let you smell it. If this is not permitted, accept the wrapped fish, open the package then and there, and, if the contents have an off-putting odor, return the package immediately to the fishmonger. Incidentally, when buying prepackaged seafood, sniff the package. You can often smell bad seafood right through the wrapping.

LOOK AT THE DISPLAY

Even if the fishmonger is not very artistic in arranging his or her wares, there are some fundamental principles of display—a kind of seafood seller's etiquette—that help to ensure a top-quality product. The single most important factor is temperature. Fresh seafood should always be kept at temperatures as close to 32°F as possible, and frozen seafood should be kept at temperatures below 0°F. Whole fish should be practically buried in crushed ice, with only the eyes, snout, and mouth showing. Live mussels, clams, crabs, and oysters can sit on crushed ice as long as the water from the melting ice is able to drain away. Other shellfish, fish fillets, and fish steaks should be surrounded by, but not directly touch, ice or be stored in a well-refrigerated display case.

A good fish store will keep most of its wares in a commercial cooler or freezer, putting on display only the amount likely to be sold within the next few hours. Cooked seafood should be stored in trays that are clearly separated from raw seafood. And a good fishmonger will use disposable gloves or a clean sheet of plastic or wax paper when handling the fish to reduce the spread of contaminating organisms that foster spoilage.

HOW MUCH FISH SHOULD YOU BUY?

We live in a country that is embarrassed by its riches—or should be. Affluence has driven us to consume much more of the costly high-protein foods than we need or that is good for our health and longevity. That goes for seafood as well as for red meat and poultry. Current nutritional recommendations call for an adult serving size of 3 ounces of cooked fish or shellfish, 2 ounces for a small child. Rather than overdose on seafood—or any other protein food, for that matter—serve it with generous portions of vegetables and a starchy food like potatoes, rice, or pasta to round out the meal.

How big a serving of edible seafood you end up with depends on the nature and "cut" you start with. Inevitably, there is water loss and shrinkage when any animal protein food is cooked. Thus, a 4-ounce fish fillet is likely to yield 3 ounces of cooked food. If a fish steak has a central bone or if you are starting with a whole fish, the losses are even greater. It's the same with shellfish. When buying shucked mollusks (mussels, clams, or oysters), you know how much meat you're getting. But when they are still in the shell, it's hard to tell. Among the crustaceans, there is much less loss from shell-on shrimp since the shells weigh very little, but a lobster shell is another story.

This table should help you decide how much of the various forms of fish and shellfish to purchase. It shows the approximate amount of raw seafood needed to serve one adult. The smaller amount listed should yield about a 3-ounce cooked portion when the item in question is prepared according to standard methods. For types of finfish that may have a high water content such as some haddock or cod, the larger amount listed may be needed to produce a 3-ounce cooked portion, whereas for denser fish like tuna and swordfish, the smaller amount should suffice.

Whole fish	¾ pound
Dressed or pan-dressed fish	½ pound
Fish fillets	¼–⅓ pound
Fish steaks with the bone	⅓–½ pound
Fish steaks without the bone	¼–⅓ pound
Live clams and oysters (in the shell)	6–8
Shucked clams and oysters	⅓–½ pint
Live mussels (in the shell)	1 pound
Live lobsters and hard-shell crabs	1–1½ pounds
Cooked lobster meat or crabmeat	¼–⅓ pound
Scallops	¼–⅓ pound
Shrimp, headless and in the shell	⅓–½ pound
Shrimp, peeled and deveined	¼–⅓ pound
Squid, cleaned	¼–⅓ pound

Note: ¼ pound = 4 ounces; ⅓ pound = 5⅓ ounces; ½ pound = 8 ounces; ¾ pound = 12 ounces.

LOOK AT AND TOUCH THE FISH

Chances are fishmongers will not let you handle seafood before you buy it, but you could ask them to do the touching for you or ask for a protective glove and try it yourself.

A *whole fish* should have bright, shiny, metallic-looking skin and, if the fish has scales, the scales should adhere tightly to the skin. The gills should be bright red or pink with little visible mucus or slime. The eyes are not a wholly reliable indicator, but if they are clear, bright, and protruding or at least flush with the head, that is a sign of freshness. As fish age, their eyes cloud and sink into the head. However, eyes can be damaged in harvesting or storage (for example, direct contact with ice will turn them cloudy) and the fish can still be fresh. When pressed with a fingertip, the flesh should be firm and elastic, springing back to its original position.

Fillets and steaks should look firm, moist, and translucent and have no traces of drying or browning around the edges. Avoid fillets and steaks that look dull, dry, or opaque. The muscle (the part you eat) should not gape or separate; and in steaks with bones, the flesh should adhere to the bone. As with whole fish, the flesh should bounce back after being dented with a fingertip. If the fish is sold prepackaged, the package should be tightly wrapped and should not contain excess liquid.

Bivalve shellfish should be taken only from certified waters that have been duly inspected and found free of harmful pollution. You have a right to ask to see the certification label before buying foods like clams and oysters. When purchased alive, clams, oysters, and mussels should be relatively clean, free of debris, and have intact shells. Do not buy dead oysters, clams, or mussels (you cannot tell how long it's been since they expired) or live ones with cracked shells. Except for soft-shell clams, which cannot close their shells completely (but should move when touched), live shellfish either start out tightly closed or will clam up when their shells are tapped or squeezed together. If a mussel with a cracked or broken shell stays shut, it is still alive and okay to use, but discard any with broken shells that won't stay closed.

If shellfish are sold shucked, the meat should look plump and be covered with a liquid that is relatively clear and free of grit. Scallops (infrequently sold alive to ordinary consumers since only a muscle of the animal is eaten) are usually creamy white, but may also come with a light orange, tan, or pinkish hue. They should not look dry or have yellow or brown discoloration around the edges. The same with squid, which are now almost always sold cleaned, skinned, and gutted. The meat should look white, moist, and shiny and should have a sweet sea smell.

Crustaceans—lobsters, crabs, and crayfish—purchased alive should move when handled. The livelier the crustacean, the better. However, those that have been refrigerated may be sluggish (they are, after all, cold-blooded animals). When a lobster is picked up, it should curl its tail tightly beneath it. If you are buying cooked crustaceans in their shells, they should be bright red in color. Shrimp sold raw should have firm flesh, and the shell and meat should not be slippery; mushy shrimp are old. Cooked shrimp in their shells are pink to reddish in color, and the meat should be white with reddish tinges.

Frozen seafood should be solidly frozen and either tightly wrapped in an intact package or encased in a thin layer of ice (see page 7 for the advantages of frozen seafood and page 64 for instructions on ice glazing at home). The flesh should be free of yellow discoloration and show no signs of drying or thawing and refreezing (ice crystals or water stains in the package are telltale). Avoid packages that are above the frost line in the store's display freezer. Packaged frozen seafood may also have an expiration date. Check the date before you buy the fish, and be sure to use it before that date.

Smoked fish should look bright and glossy and show no signs of mold. It should be displayed in a refrigerated case even if it has been vacuum-packed.

OTHER HELPFUL HINTS

Purchase seafood only from a reputable dealer. Avoid roadside stands, especially when buying shellfish, since you have no way of knowing whether they were taken legally from certified waters.

If you buy canned seafood, avoid cans that are dented, and, for the sake of your nutritional well-being, avoid oil-packed products. Instead, buy seafood that is packed in water, tomato or mustard sauce, or natural juices.

If you should get home and discover that the seafood you bought "fresh" from a store really wasn't, call right away and let the fishmonger know. The store should replace the item or refund your money the next time you come in. But more important than protecting one investment, this will keep fishmongers on their toes by letting them know that their customers will buy and eat only the best.

TAKING HOME YOUR "CATCH"

It does little good to purchase fresh seafood if you are going to give it a chance to start spoiling on the way home. If you are buying seafood in a supermarket and you have other shopping to do there or if you have other stops to make, arrange to pick up your fish after you've completed the rest of your shopping. I have on occasion asked the fishmonger to place my purchases in the cooler until I am done shopping, or, in the supermarket, I pick up the seafood at the end, as I would frozen yogurt.

If it is a warm day or if the seafood will be transported in a warm vehicle or if it will take more than about 20 or 30 minutes to get the seafood from the fishmonger to your home refrigerator or freezer, I suggest you bring along an insulated bag or a small cooler with a freezer pack to keep the seafood cold en route.

SEAFOOD SELECTION GUIDE

It is hard to find any two lists—or people—who agree on how to categorize the many kinds of fish now commercially available. What is mildly flavored to one might be regarded as moderately flavored by another. This is also true of texture. What one cook considers a fish with medium-firm flesh another might consider delicate. I have studied the categorizations and combined them with my own culinary experience to come up with the following guide. This is a handy list to have when you consider making substitutions in fish recipes. Generally, the recipe will work best if you choose a substitute fish that is in the same category as the fish in the original recipe. But often, a fish from a neighboring category will make a fine substitute. This is especially true with regard to texture—for instance, when you wish to switch from a firm to a moderately firm fish. I recommend making a photocopy of this chart to take with you when you shop for fish. That way, when the fishmonger does not have the fish that has been specified in a recipe, you'll have a good idea about what would be a reasonable substitute.

	FLAVOR		
TEXTURE	MILD	MODERATE	FULL
Delicate	Flounder	Atlantic pollock	Butterfish
	Haddock	Sea trout	Herring
	Orange roughy	Trout	Sardines
	Sole	Whiting	Shad
	Tilapia		
Medium-firm	Blackfish (tautog)	Carp	Bluefish
	Cod ("scrod")	Catfish	Eel
	Croaker	Mullet	Mackerel
	Halibut	Perch	Pomfret
	Ocean pout	Porgy	Sablefish
	Pike	Salmon trout	Salmon, Atlantic
	Pompano	Sea bass	Salmon, chinook
	Redfish	Smelt	Yellowtail
	Skate	Spanish mackerel	
	Triggerfish	Striped bass	
	Turbot	Tilefish	
	Wahoo	Walleye	
	Whitefish		
Firm	Monkfish	Char	Bonito
	Opakapaka	Grouper	Mako shark
	Pacific rockfish	Mahi-mahi	Marlin
	Wolffish	Red snapper	Sturgeon
			Swordfish
			Tuna

8
Safety Scares: Fish or Foul?

Americans of late have become obsessed with safety. Some earnest folks seem to be striving for a world that is all benefit, no risk. Unfortunately, there is no such thing. Whether the activity is crossing the street, eating fruits and vegetables, or even breathing, there are potential hazards. Eating seafood is no different. The trick in leading a sane, safety-conscious life is to do whatever you can to ensure that the benefits far outweigh the risks. The information that follows is intended to enable you to do just that when dining on seafood. As you read, keep in mind the bottom line: despite the potential hazards, seafood is one of the safest foods on the American table, and its many benefits, as described in Chapter 3, overwhelm any actual or possible risks.

The fate of seafood in recent years has resembled that of a hot-air balloon. No sooner was its reputation inflated and its consumption sent soaring by reports that fish is the way to save our hearts than it was pricked by warnings that those who dined on raw or undercooked fish and shellfish risked infections by parasites, viruses, and bacteria, some of which could cause serious illness. Still, with millions of Americans watching their cholesterol and cutting back on red meat, fish—both raw and cooked—plugged the leak and regained its gradual rise in popularity in the 1980s.

The next puncture hurt a bit more: advisories from various states to limit consumption of fish caught in lakes and rivers contaminated by industrial and agricultural wastes. These cautions joined warnings that some of the nation's favorite saltwater fish, especially tuna and swordfish, could harbor mercury that in rare cases could reach harmful levels.

So fish consumption took another shallow nosedive. Then just as it was beginning to recover, the final blow came—this time a serious stab wound from the highly respected organization Consumers Union. In the February 1992 issue of its publication *Consumer Reports,* the union revealed the grim results of its six-month investigation into the quality, wholesomeness, safety, and identity of the fish American consumers are buying and eating in hopes of improving their health and expanding their culinary repertoire. In a clamshell, the study showed that "much of the fish sold today is barely fit to eat." By the time they reached the consumer, the report said, many of the 113 fish and shellfish samples from 40 markets in the New York and Chicago metropolitan areas already had one foot in the grave. Some were on the verge of being spoiled, others were infested with bacteria (and possibly viruses) from human and animal wastes, still others were contaminated with potentially harmful chemical pollutants and toxic metals. As if that were not damning enough, *Consumer Reports* investigators found that quite a few fish in the 40 markets were mislabeled, sometimes given the name—and the market price—of more expensive species that they resembled (see the fish glossary on pages 511 to 555 for a guide to fish identification). When the investigators queried fishmongers about the source and status (fresh or previously frozen, shipping dates, etc.) of the fish they were selling, many were poorly informed and could give no answer or only wrong answers.

A major problem, Consumers Union concluded (as had numerous members of Congress and public-interest organizations before it), is inadequate and often unenforced safety standards and inspections of fish—from the sea to the shopping cart. Then, after leaving the store, fish may suffer further deterioration in the hands of consumers, most of whom don't realize that fish, like poultry, requires careful handling if it is to maintain whatever quality it has to begin with.

After reading or hearing about the Consumers Union report, countless consumers said, "Enough of this health-conscious hype about fish," and hightailed it to the meat counter for some good, old, reliable—and, they assumed, safer—American beef. But is fish really more of a hazard than other, more commonly consumed sources of animal protein? How common and how serious are the risks, how do they measure up in relation to the known health benefits of eating more fish, and how can informed consumers further improve the benefit-to-risk ratio by means of better selection and handling of the fish they buy?

The good news is that while, in 1992, fish safety and quality left a lot to be desired and improved rules and inspections could deliver a vastly better product to the fish-consuming public, even then the hazards were not nearly as great as many were led to believe. In fact, people were much more likely to become ill after eating chicken or turkey than after eating fish. According to reports made to the national Centers for Disease Control and Prevention, which monitors infectious illness, poultry causes approximately 10 times more reported cases of acute illness *per serving* than does cooked finfish and shellfish. So it is not just that chicken causes more problems because much more chicken than fish is consumed; it is that eating chicken is simply more dangerous. Whereas a consumer of seafood is likely to become ill in 1 in 250,000 servings, a chicken eater succumbs to 1 in every 25,000 servings. To put this another way, seafood is 10 times safer to consume than chicken. Furthermore, most seafood-caused illness results not from ordinary piscine meals placed on American tables, but from the consumption of raw or seriously undercooked fish and shellfish, something people would never consider doing with chicken. So the bottom line is that if seafood is properly prepared—and you will find that all the recipes in this book conform to accepted preparation guidelines—it is 200 times safer than eating chicken.

The second bit of good news is that while improvements in seafood inspection are clearly needed (and, I might add, strongly supported by the seafood industry), it is not true that fish and shellfish leap from water to table with nary a glance from public safety regulators. In 1990, the Food and Drug Administration established an Office of Seafood to oversee the safety of this valuable source of sustenance. The agency has for years inspected imported seafood, which makes up half of our nation's supplies, and has in recent years increased the number of samples it checks, sometimes looking at 100 percent of an imported product. And those coastal states in which bivalve shellfish like clams and oysters are harvested monitor with the FDA the waters where shellfish grow, checking for possible contamination with harmful bacteria, viruses, and environmental toxins. The waters from which bivalve shellfish can be harvested must be certified as safe and the shellfish taken from them shipped to the market with an appropriate certification label, which the consumer has a right to see before purchasing them. And the FDA has announced its intention to extend this safety measure to all seafood—finfish as well as shellfish—by 1995.

The third bit of good news is that when seafood is wisely purchased and properly stored and prepared at home, its nutritional benefits and culinary delights greatly exceed any short-term or long-term risks to health. Even if every slip twixt the sea and the shopping cart were eliminated, you as the consumer still must know how to treat the fish you buy to be sure that you, your family, and your guests consume a wholesome product that will enhance your health as well as delight your palate. I speak to you now through the voice of experience, for I—before I knew better—mishandled the fish I bought (and, at today's prices, few can afford to do that) and ended up with a not-so-tasty dish. (No one got sick, though, nor would they be likely to if the fish was thoroughly cooked.)

I will get to the matter of seafood handling by the consumer shortly (see pages 61 to 68). But first, you should be aware of the actual and potential hazards that have been linked to eating fish and shellfish and how they can be minimized even without further improvements in government regulation of seafood safety.

POLLUTANTS

Unlike domestic animals such as cattle and chickens that are raised in controlled environments on feed of known constituents, most of the fish that reach the American market are wild. No one regulates where they go or what they eat during their lives. As a result, some fish and shellfish travel in waters that are not of the highest quality.

Of course, it is no one's fault but ours that these valuable food animals end up dwelling in polluted waters and consuming contaminated food. Long-standing human carelessness about environmental quality is the cause; and even though in recent years we have been using fewer and fewer of our waterways as garbage dumps, it will be decades before the most serious pollutants have dissipated sufficiently for all who use the water to be completely safe. The reason is that some of the worst actors are persistent chemicals that degrade very slowly, if at all.

PCBs A classic example is PCBs, shorthand for a class of industrial chemicals called polychlorinated biphenyls that were widely used as coolants and lubricants in electrical equipment as well as in the manufacture of such products as adhesives, paints, varnishes, plastics, and copy paper. PCBs found their way into many of the nation's large lakes and rivers through effluent dumped directly into the water or into open landfills by hydroelectric and manufacturing plants. And there they stayed, degrading very slowly and often into compounds that may be even worse. Although their manufacture was banned in 1976, they will be with us for decades. PCBs have been shown to cause cancer in laboratory animals. Although the amounts in food are far lower than those known to be hazardous to animals, PCBs can build up in the body if they are consumed frequently in small amounts. In addition, in studies that were conducted in the early 1980s among more than 8,000 pregnant women, the babies of women who regularly consumed PCB-contaminated fish from Lake Michigan during their pregnancies (despite state advice to the contrary) were found to be significantly smaller and had more subtle cognitive, motor, and behavioral deficits at birth than babies born to comparable women who ate no lake fish. PCB levels have since declined considerably, and a recent study of fish-eating mothers in Wisconsin showed no effect on their babies.

PCBs are stored in the fat and internal organs of fish. They are found primarily in freshwater fish and in some migratory varieties like striped bass and wild-caught salmon that spend part of their lives in contaminated rivers. The larger, older, and fattier the fish, the more PCBs it is likely to accumulate in the course of its lifetime, and in many cases it is only the biggest specimens of a particular species that will exceed the allowable limit of 2 parts per million (2 ppm in the edible flesh) established by the Food and Drug Administration. Still, according to FDA officials who monitor fish contaminants, only rarely do saltwater fish exceed the 2 ppm level for PCBs.

MERCURY However, some of our large saltwater favorites—swordfish, tuna, Pacific halibut, and that up-and-coming table fish, shark—can become contaminated with mercury and other potentially harmful heavy metals like lead and cadmium that pollute seawater. The FDA monitors swordfish, tuna, and other large species for mercury, the most common such contaminant, but rarely finds that anything other than swordfish exceeds the allowable limit. Tuna, contrary to the scare reports that pop up periodically, rarely is found to have mercury levels that exceed FDA limits. According to the National Shellfish Sanitation Program, which keeps track of hazards in bivalve shellfish and certifies waters where they can be safely gathered, mollusks (mussels, clams, and oysters) are more likely than finfish and other shellfish to pick up metal contaminants. Other problems remain: little is known about the long-term effects of periodically consuming very low levels of mercury, and not enough is known about other heavy-metal contaminants like lead and cadmium.

PESTICIDES Here, too, there are major deficiencies in monitoring. Even though DDT was banned more than two decades ago, traces of it remain in the environment and are occasionally found in the fish we eat. This persistent pesticide, in a class of now-banned pesticides called chlorinated hydrocarbons, can accumulate in the bodies of predatory animals like large fish. (DDT was responsible for the near-demise of fish-eating birds like our national symbol, the bald eagle.) But while DDT levels are no longer a concern in the fish that people eat, there is little attention being paid to contamination by the less-persistent pesticides that have replaced it. Nor is there routine monitoring of fish contamination by petroleum products that often pollute commercial rivers and seas.

HAZARDOUS ORGANISMS

Until now, I've been discussing contamination problems that thus far have only rarely been linked to health problems in people who eat fish. Far more common—and, therefore, more worrisome to the consumer—are ailments traceable to bacteria, viruses, parasites, and plant toxins that may cause no harm to the seafood they inhabit but that sometimes can do serious damage to the people who eat these seafoods. For the most part, these are organisms that fish and shellfish acquire from the water they live in, although sometimes food handlers are responsible for "polluting" the seafoods after they have entered the food distribution chain.

Two kinds of agents are primarily involved: natural organisms that share the environment where fish and shellfish are sometimes gathered and organisms that are the result of pollution by human wastes.

PARALYTIC, AMNESIAC, AND NEUROTOXIC SHELLFISH POISONING These disorders are rarely a problem in commercial fish. They are caused by toxins produced by certain kinds of phytoplankton, the microscopic plants that mollusks eat. The phytoplankton responsible for shellfish poisonings are unusual forms of marine algae that may suddenly flourish in previously safe waters. They are responsible for the so-called red tides that sometimes force the closing of shellfish beds in the Northeast. Although they do not always color the water red, red-tide organisms all contain toxins that, though harmless to the bivalves that eat them (mussels, clams, oysters, and scallops), can cause serious illness and even death to people who unwittingly consume them. The toxins, which are *not destroyed by cooking,* can cause numbness and respiratory distress. There is no effective medication, though most affected consumers do recover. The National Shellfish Sanitation Program is responsible for monitoring red-tide organisms and certifying shellfish beds as free of this and other hazards. When red tides "bloom," the beds are closed to harvest and commercial fisherman stay away. The main risk is to people who ignore posted warnings and gather their own mollusks from polluted waters (the toxin does not accumulate in shrimp, crabs, lobster, or finfish).

CIGUATERA Another hazardous toxin produced by microorganisms that some fish eat is ciguatera, and, again, the poison is *not destroyed by cooking.* Ciguatera poisoning results from the consumption of large tropical fish that eat many smaller fish that, in turn, dine on toxin-producing dinoflagellates. These organisms live on and around warm-water reefs and shore areas off the coasts of Florida and Hawaii, in the Caribbean, and in the Gulf of Mexico and are primarily a problem in fish consumed in these areas. The main carriers among food fish are barracuda and large specimens of grouper, red snapper, moray eel, and jacks. Symptoms of ciguatera poisoning, which usually start within 6 hours of eating toxin-containing fish, vary widely in kind and intensity from person to person. They can include tingling sensations in the mouth, intense itching, nausea, vomiting, diarrhea, abdominal pain, muscle aches, blurred vision, and confused sensations of hot and cold (cold feels hot and vice versa). In severe cases, paralysis and convulsions can occur. Although the symptoms can last for months, the illness is rarely fatal. There is no specific treatment, nor, as of this writing, was there a test being used to screen fish for this poison. Most commercial fishermen know which areas to avoid, but when you dine in endemic areas, the best way to avoid ciguatera toxin is to eat only small (that is, young) specimens of the aforementioned fish since these are least likely to contain the poison.

SCOMBROID Still another type of fish poisoning, scombroid poisoning, results not from a microbial toxin, but from the action of usually harmless bacteria that normally live in fish like mackerel, mahi-mahi, swordfish, tuna, bonito, and Pacific amberjack. When the fish are properly chilled after they are caught, there is no problem. But if they are kept in the warm sun or stored at room temperature for hours, the bacteria can convert the amino acid histadine in the fish into histamine, the chemical responsible for most allergy symptoms. The fish do not necessarily show any sign of spoilage, but people who consume histamine in fish and are sensitive to this substance can develop such symptoms as headache, nausea, vomiting, tingling, itching, flushing, and palpitations that may last for several hours to half a day. Once again, after the fish have become contaminated with this histaminelike substance, *cooking does not help* to prevent a reaction, although treatment with antihistamines may reduce the length and/or intensity of symptoms.

INFECTIOUS MICROORGANISMS Now for the most common and readily avoidable problems: hazardous organisms that can be avoided by properly cooking or otherwise treating the fish before eating it. There are two main types of troublesome organisms: bacteria and viruses introduced directly or indirectly by people before or after the fish are caught or shellfish are harvested, and parasites normally present in some fish that can be destroyed by fully cooking or deep-freezing the fish before eating it.

Every food has the potential to cause food poisoning by such bacteria as salmonella, staphylococcus, or clostridium, and fish is no exception. The main culprits are food handlers who fail to practice good hygiene—not washing hands with soap and water after using the toilet, using the same unwashed knife to cut various raw protein foods (especially poultry), failing to clean cutting boards properly after each use, or allowing sneezes or nasal secretions to come into contact with the seafood. The usual symptoms of food poisoning may include nausea, severe vomiting, abdominal cramps, diarrhea, fever, and, in the worst cases, a temporary loss of consciousness. Though not usually life-threatening, food poisoning is sometimes fatal to infants, the elderly, and people with certain chronic ailments.

Fish and shellfish can also pick up bacteria and viruses from human and animal sewage deposited in the water where edible seafood live. Filter feeders like clams and mussels, which extract food from water that filters through them, are especially likely to build up harmful amounts of infectious organisms *if, and only if,* these agents contaminate their watery homes. The levels of organisms in these bivalve mollusks can reach more than a dozen times their concentration in the water, so a little pollution can go a long way in causing human illness if these shellfish are not thoroughly cooked. The most troublesome ailments are caused by the common intestinal bacterium *Escherichia coli* (the cause of traveler's diarrhea) and by the virus that causes infectious hepatitis (hepatitis A). Whereas *E. coli* usually causes a sudden attack of diarrhea and cramps that lasts a few days, hepatitis, a liver infection, can cause a severely debilitating illness that usually starts with malaise, loss of appetite, nausea, vomiting, and fever and then may progress to jaundice that can last for weeks. In some foreign countries where sanitation is often worse than ours, there is also a risk of contracting the once-common scourges of cholera and typhoid from eating contaminated shellfish that is not properly cooked.

I keep saying "properly cooked" because therein lies the answer to safe consumption of filter-feeding shellfish. True, the National Shellfish Sanitation Program monitors contamination levels where shellfish are harvested and certifies those that are safe. But the consumer, whether in a store or restaurant, may be unable to determine for certain that the clams or oysters on the half shell that look so fine and fresh are safe to eat raw. And my collaborator, Rick Flaste, will tell you emphatically from frightening personal experience that when it comes to eating shellfish, it is better to be safe than sorry. Those dozen oysters on the half shell, delicious though they were and ordered at one of New York's finer restaurants, resulted in severe and consciousness-robbing food poisoning the next day. The sudden illness forced him to cancel a long-planned trip to Minnesota, land of some 12,500 lakes where most natives shudder noticeably at the mere mention of eating raw fish.

All the bacteria and viruses involved in the above-described disorders are destroyed by adequate cooking. That means 4 to 6 minutes of steaming (after the liquid boils) or grilling over hot coals. *It is not sufficient from a health standpoint to steam clams and mussels just until they open.* And if you try to steam too many mollusks at one time, they may not all cook thoroughly. Far better to cook them in several batches than to risk illness. Similarly with fish steaks like tuna, where it has become stylish merely to sear them on the outside (which would kill any bacteria present) and barely warm them on the inside. While it is highly unlikely that you would get sick from eating raw, farm-raised salmon, for example (unless it became contaminated after being caught), there is a risk of extending this eating practice to fish that are more likely to become contaminated before they are caught.

Likewise with parasites. *All are destroyed by adequate cooking.* But if you consume fish raw, as in some forms of sushi, sashimi, or seviche, or fish that was lightly smoked without much heat, you could find yourself eating more than you bargained for—like a tapeworm (curable) or, more likely, a pesky roundworm called anisakis (not curable, though not fatal). Fish can become contaminated with roundworms from the infested feces of such marine mammals as whales and dolphins. The parasites are more of a problem on the West Coast than on the East Coast, but there are no guarantees that the fish you buy or order in a restaurant are free of this risk. While most people who dine on raw fish do not become ill as a result, those unlucky souls who do acquire parasites are likely to experience severe abdominal pain and perhaps nausea and vomiting when the worms attach themselves to the stomach lining and intestinal walls, from which only a surgeon's scalpel can remove them.

Any good sushi chef knows three ways to eliminate the risk of consuming parasites along with raw fish. One is to avoid species most likely to be contaminated. Another is to shine a bright light through the fish slices and remove the visible larvae with a tweezer. The third way, the one that is most practical for home consumers of raw fish, is to freeze the fish at below 0°F (preferably at −4°F) for 72 hours or longer to kill the larvae. *Marinating the fish,* even if you use pure vinegar or lime juice, *will not do them in.* Nor will smoking them without heat. However, freezing the fish will work—if your freezer gets cold enough (you must use a freezer thermometer to check it)—and the effects on fish quality will be minimal and well worth the assurance of knowing that your sushi, sashimi, or seviche is safe to eat.

ALLERGIES It would not do to discuss the hazards of eating seafood without mentioning a risk that does not come directly from the seafood itself, but rather from the reactions of some of the people who eat it. For unknown reasons, the bodies of these individuals treat some aspect of the food being ingested as a foreign invader and mount a massive counterattack, which is the allergic reaction.

Allergies to seafood—particularly to one or more forms of shellfish—are less common than most people believe. Only 1 percent of adults have clinically proven allergic reactions to foods. And while shellfish allergies are among the more common triggers of food allergies, many more people are allergic to such foods as nuts, milk, wheat, and eggs. Actually, it is not the food per se, but specific parts of a certain muscle protein, that triggers the allergic reaction. The protein portions that are the culprits in shrimp allergy have been identified, and similar protein sections are found in lobsters, crabs, and other crustaceans, which may explain why people allergic to shrimp also often react to these other shellfish.

For some with food allergies, the risk can be considerable if they should knowingly or unwittingly consume the food that they are sensitive to. Even though for the first several times that they react their symptoms may be limited to a tingling sensation in the mouth or a scratchy throat, future exposure could eventually produce a life-threatening allergic reaction, including a precipitous drop in blood pressure and difficulty breathing. Anyone severely allergic to seafood or any food would be wise to carry a loaded syringe of adrenalin at all times, which could be self-administered or administered by a bystander in the event of an unexpected allergic crisis.

Few people are born with food allergies. More often the allergies develop over the years following repeated exposure to the offending food. Once the reactions start, they often get progressively more severe with each exposure. So if you know that you react to certain shellfish, however mildly, you would be wise to take extreme care and make sure not to consume it again. Always ask the host or chef or clerk at the salad counter about the ingredients before indulging in any dish that could conceivably be made with the seafood in question. And check labels on all packaged foods, especially those made with "imitation" fish (see page 37), before you buy or eat them.

Keep in mind, too, that just because one kind of shellfish has caused a reaction, this doesn't mean that you are allergic to all shellfish or to fish in general. Allergies are usually highly specific, and while you may be allergic to more than one food, in all likelihood you will not be sensitive to an entire class of food. You can be tested for seafood allergy by a qualified allergist, but it could be very dangerous to test yourself by eating small amounts of the suspected culprit.

STRATEGIES FOR SAFETY

As I said at the outset, cooked seafood is probably the safest animal protein food around as far as acute illnesses go, and by following a few precautions, you can make it even safer. Becoming an aware consumer of fish and shellfish can also go a long way to reduce, if not eliminate, any long-term risks that might result from chemical contaminants. Until and unless a well-designed body of nationwide regulations is established and strictly enforced, it is largely up to the consumer to see to it that this otherwise wonderful food provides benefits with few or no risks.

- Buy all your fish and shellfish from a well-established and reputable source. No roadside stands. Get to know your fishmonger. He or she should be able to tell you a lot about the seafood being sold: where it comes from, how fresh it is, whether it was previously frozen, how and how long to keep it at home, and how it can be prepared. Your dealer should be able to produce the certification tag for bivalve shellfish that tells you the animals were gathered in government-tested waters. Also, seafood should be properly displayed: fillets and steaks in separate pans set on and surrounded by ice; whole fish head down and nearly buried in ice; and, above all, all cooked shellfish and fish salads kept completely separate from raw fish. (See pages 40 to 45 for further guidelines on buying fish.)

- Eat a variety of seafood. Variety is not only the spice of life, it is your ticket to a wholesome diet overall. By choosing among seafood of different types and sizes and from various sources, you'll be far less likely to consume potentially hazardous levels of any one pollutant. Make your selections primarily among saltwater fish from differing environments, shellfish of all types, and farm-raised freshwater fish (see pages 511 to 555 for a glossary of fish and their usual sources). Freshwater "wild" fish should be consumed only according to state advisories.

- When eating large or fatty fish, you can reduce your risk of consuming fat-soluble contaminants like PCBs and DDT by removing (before or after cooking) the fattiest parts of the fish: skin, belly flap, lateral line, and any darkly colored parts of the flesh (see the illustration below).

REDUCING THE RISKS

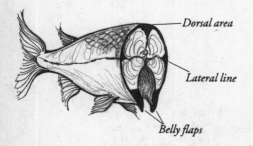 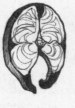 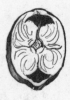

Cutting away the fatty parts of fish (darkened areas) before it is cooked will greatly reduce any residues of chemicals that may be stored in fish's fat depots—the dorsal area, lateral line, and belly flaps—which appear darker or redder than the surrounding flesh.

• If you want to maximize your chances of eating fish uncontaminated by pollutants, there are many options. Flounder and sole and deep-water ocean fish are least likely to be contaminated. Fish that is farm-raised is usually, but not always, more likely to be free of unsavory contaminants than fish caught in the wild near heavily populated shores and coastlines. This is especially true of catfish, which are now widely farmed, allowing their sweet, succulent flavor to emerge unspoiled by pollutants. Fish like pollock and halibut caught in Alaskan waters and orange roughy, which is shipped here frozen from New Zealand, are also likely to be relatively unpolluted. In fact, the pure, natural waters around Alaska account for 58 percent of all commercial fish landings.

• Never eat the liver, brains, eyes, gills, or viscera (intestines, etc.) of any fish. This is where any number of toxic substances may accumulate.

• Heed state advisories about consuming locally caught fish. Depending upon local hazards in fishing waters, a state may caution that fish caught in a particular river, harbor, or lake should not be eaten more often than once a week or perhaps not at all. Women who are pregnant or nursing or who expect to become pregnant in the next few years should avoid eating any fish that might be contaminated with PCBs or mercury. Nor should such fish be given to children under six or anyone with a serious chronic ailment.

• Whether you are buying fish fresh (unfrozen), thawed, or frozen, buy only the freshest fish (see pages 41 to 44). Your nose is your most reliable guide for unfrozen fish: it should not smell unpleasantly fishy. Saltwater fish should have a briny smell, and freshwater fish should smell clean and fresh like cucumbers. Fish that has been wrapped in plastic may acquire a fishy smell, but that should wash away when the fish is removed from the package and rinsed under cold running water. Look, too, for a healthy sheen, intact, moist flesh, and, if the fish is whole, eyes that bulge, skin that is vivid and unblemished, and gills that are red or deep pink (clear eyes are not a reliable guide since exposure to ice can cause the eyes of a perfectly fresh fish to become cloudy).

• Once you get your fish home, store it in its original wrapper, but for no longer than a day, in the coldest part of the refrigerator (away from the door)—ideally at 30°F to 32°F (shelf life is cut in half for every 10°F above that). If you cannot use the fish right away, freeze it in a single layer, if possible. You can safely refreeze previously frozen fish, but it will lose some flavor and texture. However, freezing fish that is marginally fresh is not smart. You're best off cooking it and feeding it to the cat or dog.

• All fish that you eat cooked should be cooked through (though not overcooked). If you are concerned more about safety than overcooking fish, rely on the so-called "Canadian" rule: 10 minutes to the inch on the grill or under the broiler, steamed or boiled, or baked in the oven at 450°F. Add 5 minutes for each inch if a baked fish dish is stuffed or prepared in a sauce. Boil or steam mollusks (mussels, clams, and oysters) for 4 to 6 minutes after the liquid returns to a boil. See pages 82 to 100 for further guidelines on fish and shellfish preparation.

• If you cannot resist the temptation to dine on raw fish (and, I must admit, I sometimes can't), consider making it yourself only after you have stored the fish in the freezer for three or more days at a temperature of 0°F to −4°F. And if clams or oysters on the half shell are your passion (oysters do not, however, make you passionate, regardless of their reputation), ask the dealer to show you the certification tag indicating that the mollusks were obtained from government-inspected waters. Pregnant or nursing women, young children, and people with cancer, liver disease, AIDS, or any other serious chronic ailment that weakens the immune system would be wise to steer clear of all raw or undercooked fish and shellfish.

WANT TO KNOW MORE?

The Food and Drug Administration has established a seafood hotline that consumers can call for information on purchasing, storing, handling, and labeling seafood, on seafood nutrition, on economic fraud, and on almost anything else they might want to know about seafood *except* recipes (and with this book, you'll hardly need those). Seafood specialists can be reached between 12:00 noon and 4:00 P.M. (eastern time) Monday through Friday by calling 1-800-FDA-4010 (in Washington, D.C., dial 205-4314). At other times, callers can select from among 50 or so recorded messages on seafood. In addition, people with access to a touchtone phone and fax machine can have seafood publications faxed to them at any time of the day or night.

Also useful is an excellent handbook, *Seafood Savvy: A Consumer's Guide to Seafood Nutrition, Safety, Handling, and Preparation,* by Ken Gall. To order a copy of this $4.95 publication, write to Cornell Cooperative Extension Publications, The Resource Center, 7 Cornell Business and Technology Park, Ithaca, NY 14850, or call 607-255-2080 to place a credit-card order for the publication.

9
Seafood Etiquette

There are people who can blithely shoot a magnificent animal like a deer or wild turkey without batting an eyelash, and there are others who shudder at the thought of submerging a live lobster in a pot of boiling water or bringing down a clam or oyster by shucking it. At the risk of sounding cavalier, I advise the squeamish to leave the task to others. Or simply avoid those seafoods that must be purchased alive—fresh clams, oysters, mussels, soft-shell crabs, and lobsters—only to die by the hand of the cook.

More than a few people hesitate to boil a live lobster, an animal that is vigorous even to the moment of its demise. I recall my young sons *and* my husband leaving the room when I cooked lobster. But once the dirty deed was done, they certainly enjoyed the edible results. If you wish to minimize the animal's suffering, it is best to cook lobster one or two at a time in a very large pot of rapidly boiling water or in a steamer over a fair amount of boiling water. The more lobsters you put in the pot at one time, the longer it will take them to stop squirming.

When serving shellfish in their shells or whole fish with the bones intact, the considerate host will supply diners with a bowl or two in which to place the shells or bones.

Then there is the matter of eating seafood elegantly. The signature item of the lobster bib should tell you that elegance goes on hold when it comes to eating whole lobsters. Anything goes: fingers, teeth, as well as those skinny little lobster forks designed to help diners extract lobster meat from narrow crevices.

If, at a party, you are offered jumbo shrimp as an hors d'oeuvre, you may certainly hold it like a drumstick to eat it unless you are given a plate and fork and can sit down to eat. Likewise with a miniature seafood kebab.

When eating finfish that are served whole or even fish fillets that may sport an occasional bone, the wise diner looks over the fish and removes visible bones with a fork or knife before taking a mouthful. Should you miss a bone or two that finds its way into your mouth, you can put your napkin to your mouth and deposit the bone in it. But there's nothing wrong, in my view, with using your fingers to remove a bone from your mouth and placing the bone on the edge of your plate or on a napkin for later disposal. When it comes to fish bones, safety should prevail above table etiquette.

Should you accidentally swallow a bone that seems to have lodged in your upper digestive tract, eat a piece of dry bread to help it move down. Even after the bone is dislodged, you may feel as if it is still there for an hour or so.

10
Fish in Your Kitchen

Handling seafood in your home is akin in principle to caring for a fussy houseplant. Just as plants need the right amount of light and water, seafood has to be kept at the right temperature and must not be allowed to dry out. You've gone to a lot a trouble to buy the best seafood. Now maintaining that quality is totally in your hands.

KEEP IT COOL AND CLEAN

Once you get seafood home, your goal should be to get it into the coldest appropriate place as soon as possible. One of the first things I did when I started working on this book was to buy a good refrigerator-freezer thermometer. Fish should be stored in the refrigerator at temperatures as close to freezing (32°F) as possible and in the freezer at below 0°F, and I used the thermometer to identify the coldest parts of my refrigerator and freezer. Then I set those areas aside for my fish. Too many home refrigerators are set to operate near 40°F, a temperature at which seafood quality goes rapidly downhill. Fish held at 32°F keeps twice as long as the same fish held at 42°F.

SEAFOOD STORAGE GUIDE

The National Fisheries Institute suggests these storage guidelines for refrigerated and frozen seafood. They are based on refrigerator temperatures that hover around 32°F and freezer temperatures at or below 0°F. If your seafood is not listed and you are not sure which category it falls into—lean or fatty—consult the table on page 19. The fat quantities listed are the amounts in 3.5 ounces (100 grams) of raw fish. Storage possibilities listed as "Not advised" refer not to safety, but to *quality*—at typical home-freezer temperatures, the quality of these seafoods could suffer.

Product	Never frozen or previously frozen and home-refrigerated	Purchased fresh and home-frozen	Commercially frozen and stored in home freezer
FISH FILLETS/STEAKS			
Leanest fish (2 grams fat or less) Catfish (wild), cod ("scrod"), flounder, grouper, haddock, mahi-mahi, monkfish, ocean perch, ocean pout, orange roughy, pollock, red snapper, rockfish, sea bass, sea trout, sole, tilapia, tuna (yellowfin), turbot, whiting	36 hours	6–8 months	10–12 months
Moderately lean fish (2.1 to 5 grams) Blackfish, bluefish, halibut, mako shark, sea trout, skate, smelt, striped bass, swordfish, sturgeon, tilapia, tilefish, trout (rainbow and sea), tuna (bluefin), wolffish	36 hours	4 months	8–9 months
Fattier fish (6 or more grams) Atlantic mackerel, butterfish, catfish (farmed), herring, lake trout, pompano, sablefish, salmon, shad, smelt (cleaned), Spanish mackerel, wahoo, whitefish	36 hours	4 months	6–8 months
WHOLE FISH (CLEANED)			
Any type	36 hours	Not advised*	8–9 months
SHELLFISH			
Clams, shucked	5 days	Not advised	Not applicable
Crab, king and stone	7 days	9 months	12 months
Crab, snow and Dungeness	5 days	6 months	6 months
Crabmeat, cocktail claws	5 days	4 months	Not applicable

Product	Never frozen or previously frozen and home-refrigerated	Purchased fresh and home-frozen	Commercially frozen and stored in home freezer
Crabmeat, fresh blue	5–7 days	4 months	Not applicable
Crabmeat, pasteurized	6 months	Not advised	Not applicable
Lobster, live	1–2 days	Not applicable	Not applicable
Lobster, tail meat	4–5 days	6 months	8 months
Oysters, shucked	4–7 days	3 months	Not applicable
Shrimp	4 days	5 months	9 months
Surimi (imitation seafood products)	2 weeks	9 months	10–12 months
SMOKED FISH			
Herring	3–4 days	2 months	Not applicable
Salmon, whitefish	5–8 days	2 months	Not applicable

*If your freezer reaches below 0°F and the fish can be well protected against freezer burn and fluctuating temperatures, whole fish can be frozen at home as long as you know it is fresh and has been properly cleaned (see pages 69–71).

If you don't have a thermometer, the coldest part of the refrigerator is usually the meat or vegetable bin or at the back of the open shelves. Refrigerated seafood should be used within a day or two. Consult the table above for a guide to reasonable refrigerator storage times. If you are planning to store the seafood longer than the recommended interval, it is best to freeze it. Or, if you keep it refrigerated, pack it in a container with ice as follows: whole fish can be packed directly on ice, but fillets and steaks should first be placed in sealed, waterproof plastic bags or containers that can be buried in ice; as the ice melts, empty the water and replace the ice, if necessary.

Live shellfish, however, should not be stored directly on ice—the fresh water from the melting ice will kill them by disrupting their water and electrolyte balance. Nor should they be kept in airtight containers such as a closed plastic bag, even if that is how the fishmonger gave them to you. They are, after all, living animals that have to breathe, and they will suffocate when they are enclosed in plastic. Instead, place live shellfish in a shallow dish or pan, and cover them with damp paper towels to keep them from drying out.

You can also shuck bivalves like clams and oysters (which kills them) and store them in their liquor in a closed container set on ice. Use shucked shellfish within a day.

It is important to prevent other foods from dripping on stored seafood and to keep raw seafood from dripping on anything else, especially foods that will not be cooked or reheated before being eaten. I routinely place stored seafood in a pan or pie plate or on a platter with a lip, even if it is in a sealed plastic bag.

TO FREEZE SEAFOOD

Seafood purchased frozen should be placed in your home freezer as quickly as possible, preferably before it has a chance to begin thawing. Seafood purchased "previously frozen" (that is, quickly frozen to a very low temperature by a commercial producer) and thawed can be refrozen at home. Although there may be some loss in quality, it is not a serious loss, and the convenience to the shopper-cook may be worth it. *It is not dangerous to refreeze thawed seafood* as long as it was fresh when it was originally frozen, was properly thawed at refrigerator temperatures, and was not kept in the thawed state longer than 1 to 2 days. However, if you are concerned about quality, you'd be wise not to refreeze seafood that you froze at home and then thawed since the slow process of home freezing can undermine the texture of the seafood.

Raw fish that you are planning to use to make ceviche or such Japanese delicacies as sushi and sashimi *must first be frozen* at a temperature of 0°F to −4°F for at least 3 days to kill any parasites it may contain. It is preferable to use fish that has been commercially frozen since the temperatures of commercial freezers are much lower than those in home freezers.

Before freezing seafood, rinse it quickly under cold running water to remove surface bacteria. Then wrap it tightly in a good-quality plastic wrap to protect it against freezer burn, and place the wrapped seafood in a wrapping of aluminum foil or in a plastic freezer bag, squeezing out as much air as possible before sealing the bag. A close wrap and good seal are especially important now that most freezers are self-defrosting. Seafood is mostly water—70 percent on average—and water loss is a major factor in its deterioration. Fresh mollusks in their shells can be frozen in a sealed plastic bag from which as much air as possible is extracted. Crustaceans like shrimp are best frozen in their shells, also in airtight plastic bags.

You can freeze whole fish and shellfish inside a block of ice, which keeps them from drying out and slows deterioration. Any waterproof container will do as long as you can leave enough room for expansion when the water freezes. If you have the time and patience, you can also mimic the highly effective commercial technique of glazing fish with ice to diminish water loss while the fish remains frozen. This is how it's done: On a tray or baking sheet, place rinsed pieces of fish in a single layer with space between them, and set the tray in the freezer for 1 hour. Then dip the pieces one at a time into a bowl of ice water. The water will form a thin layer of ice on the fish. Place the glazed pieces back on the tray, and return the tray to the freezer. Repeat the glazing process every 15 minutes until you have three or four coatings of ice on the fish. Then package the fish pieces in plastic to protect them from air, and return them to the freezer.

It is a good idea, before freezing seafood, to repackage it in amounts you are most likely to use at any one time. Label each package with the kind and quantity of seafood it contains and the date it was frozen. Seafood cannot be stored indefinitely in the freezer. In fact, it has a limited freezer shelf life. In general, the fattier the fish, the less time it should spend in the freezer. Consult the table on page 62 for suggested freezer storage times. If your freezer is not at 0°F or lower, seafood should not be stored in it for as long as the table indicates. It is not that frozen fish can become dangerous to eat—freezing retards the growth of spoilage organisms—but the quality deteriorates because the fat in fish gradually turns rancid and the flesh dries out.

If possible, store seafood in a freezer that is not opened often, and place it toward the rear of the freezer, where it will be less subjected to temperature fluctuations when the door is opened.

DEFROSTING FROZEN SEAFOOD

Here, again, the goal is to keep the seafood continuously cold. If you defrost it on a countertop, in the hours it will take to thaw completely, the surface of the fish can warm considerably even while the center remains frozen. Therefore, seafood is best defrosted slowly in the refrigerator or quickly in the microwave oven.

When thawing seafood in the refrigerator, be sure to place it on or in a leakproof container so that the juices do not drip onto other foods or the refrigerator shelves. Fillets, steaks, and most shellfish will generally defrost in the refrigerator overnight or in 1 day, but whole fish are likely to take longer—as much as 2 days for a large fish.

If you must hasten the defrosting process, you can thaw well-wrapped (in sealed plastic) frozen seafood under *cold, running water.* Never use warm or hot water. Alternatively, you can enclose frozen seafood in a sealed plastic bag, immerse the bag in pan full of cold water, and place the pan in the refrigerator, allowing 1 to 2 hours per pound of seafood. But do not place seafood in an unrefrigerated container or a sink full of standing water, and avoid prolonged exposure of unwrapped seafood to running water.

The microwave oven provides another quick method of thawing seafood, though great care must be taken to avoid overheating the food so that it starts to cook. Defrost only 1 pound at a time. Place the seafood in a shallow microwave-safe dish, and cover the dish with plastic wrap. Cut some slits in the plastic, or turn back one edge of the wrap to allow the steam to escape. Microwave the seafood on low power (30 percent) for 15 to 30 seconds. Let the seafood stand for 15 seconds. Repeat the process as often as necessary until the seafood is nearly thawed. Then let it stand for another 1 to 2 minutes before you cook it.

STORING COOKED AND SMOKED SEAFOOD

Cooked fish and shellfish are perishable items that must be kept cold. In general, if the seafood was fresh before it was cooked, it will maintain its quality in the refrigerator for about 2 or 3 days after cooking or about 3 or 4 days if it was prepared in a sauce or with an acidic ingredient like tomato, wine, or citrus juice. In general, however, leftovers, whether they are home-cooked, take-out, or from a can, are best used as soon as possible.

Smoked fish and shellfish are also perishable items that must be kept cold. Like raw seafood, if several hours will elapse before it can be refrigerated, place smoked seafood in an insulated container with ice or a freezer pack.

Cold-smoked fish (the kind that is first salted heavily before being smoked at a relatively low temperature) will generally last in the refrigerator for about 3 to 4 days, although some will maintain their quality for about 1 week. Fish prepared in a hot smoker, however, does not have much longer a shelf-life than ordinary cooked fish—about 4 or 5 days in the refrigerator.

Discard any smoked fish that becomes discolored or moldy or develops an unpleasant odor. If you wish to store hot-smoked or cold-smoked fish for longer periods than those recommended above, wrap it well first in plastic wrap and then in heavy-duty aluminum foil, and freeze it at 0°F or less for up to 2 months. Although there may be some loss in textural quality, the convenience of having the smoked fish on hand may be something you'll be thankful for. As with raw seafood, smoked fish should be thawed in the refrigerator. However, you should let smoked fish sit at room temperature for 15 to 30 minutes before it is served to bring out its full flavor.

Cooked fish can be frozen but sometimes with a significant loss in quality in the form of a textural change. In general, fish that is part of a casserole, soup, or stew will freeze with less noticeable effects on gustatory qualities. But don't expect a broiled fillet to emerge from its frozen state in the same delicate condition it went in.

With shellfish, however, I have had considerably more luck, even freezing the meat of steamed mussels and clams to use later as an ingredient in a soup or salad. Try to store cooked shellfish in airtight freezer containers with tight-fitting lids, perhaps enclosing the container in a sealed plastic bag as insurance. I have also been pleased with the results when freezing smoked fish (both hot-smoked and cold-smoked), again taking great care to wrap the fish well to protect it from dehydration.

Keep in mind that regardless of the method of storage—refrigerator or freezer—oilier fish, even when cooked, have a shorter shelf life than low-fat seafood. Unfortunately, few studies have been conducted on proper freezer storage times for cooked fish and shellfish (except for those on commercially frozen fish). So it is wise to err on the conservative side, using such products within 1 to 2 months.

PRE- AND POSTCOOKING SAFETY TIPS

When handling raw seafood, take the following precautions to prevent contamination and to reduce the risk of spoilage once the food is cooked.

- It is always a good idea to rinse seafood quickly under cold, running water before you begin your cooking preparations. This will reduce surface bacteria and slow deterioration.
- Always place marinating seafood in the refrigerator, even if it is only for 15 to 30 minutes. Discard marinades used on raw seafood unless the liquid is thoroughly cooked *after* its use as a marinade.
- Keep the time that raw seafood is unrefrigerated to a minimum. Have everything you need for your recipe ready before you take the seafood out of the refrigerator.
- Wash your hands thoroughly with hot, soapy water both before and after handling raw seafood. Similarly, thoroughly wash all utensils, knives, preparation surfaces, sponges, dishcloths, and towels that have been in contact with raw seafood or exposed to seafood juices. I make it a habit to do this immediately after preparing my seafood lest I forget and risk contaminating food that has already been cooked or that is eaten uncooked. Replace sponges often since it is hard to keep them clean and odor-free, or sanitize them in a bleach solution.
- Sanitation specialists have long recommended the use of nonporous (that is, plastic or Lucite) cutting boards for preparing raw seafood. However, a series of studies conducted by the University of Wisconsin found that wooden cutting boards were less likely to allow contaminating organisms to live and multiply. If you use a nonporous board, be sure to wash it thoroughly with hot, soapy water after each use, and replace boards that become pitted or develop slits that are hard to clean. It is also a good idea to sanitize wooden surfaces periodically with a solution of 2 teaspoons of chlorine bleach and 1 quart of water, then rinse them with clean water. Plastic cutting boards can be sanitized with a bleach solution or by putting them in the dishwasher.

And *never place cooked seafood on the same plate or tray that held raw seafood* unless the plate or tray is first washed with soapy water.

• Avoid leaving seafood, raw or cooked, out of the refrigerator for more than 2 hours, including preparation and table time. Place leftovers in shallow, moisture-proof containers, and refrigerate them as soon as possible. If you are serving seafood as part of a buffet, put out only some at a time, refilling the dish as soon as the contents are consumed.

11
Cleaning and Filleting

These days, most fish shops and fish concessions in supermarkets will prepare the fish any way you wish. But there will be occasions when you may need to clean a fish or fillet it on your own. Catching one yourself usually means that the job is up to you, and then there are the times when you simply change your mind and decide to fillet a fish that you bought whole. Anyway, it's good to have tried these techniques yourself once or twice so that you know enough to evaluate the job done at the store.

PREPARING FISH

CLEANING Most fish require the removal of scales (catfish and monkfish, among others, don't have scales). If you have a scaler (they cost at most a few dollars), by all means use it. Otherwise, a dull knife works well. Scrape against the grain of the scales, from tail to head. Hold the blade at an angle as you go. Scales tend to fly as they come free, so do the job in the sink or outside the house where the few scales that scatter here and there won't make any difference.

A fish must be gutted to avoid off flavors when it is cooked and because it will spoil more quickly with the viscera in it. There are several ways of doing this, but the goal and general approaches for each are similar. The most common method is to open up the belly of the fish by making a slit from the anal vent to the head and remove the entrails with your hands or a kitchen scissors. It is also essential that you cut the gills free with a sharp knife or scissors and discard them; gills contain bacteria and will impart a bitter flavor to cooking liquids. Sometimes even fish that have been cleaned at the store or fish heads sold for making a stock will still have their gills; these must be removed. Carefully wash out the cavity of the fish with cold water to get rid of all blood or any trace of entrails.

To Clean a Fish

Scaling: *With a fish scaler or a dull knife held nearly parallel to the fish, remove the scales by scraping along the sides of the fish from the tail to the head.*

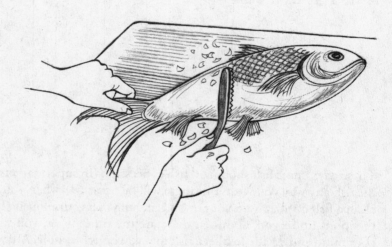

Gutting: *Starting from the anus at the base of the anal fins, slice open the belly, and cut or pull out the innards.*

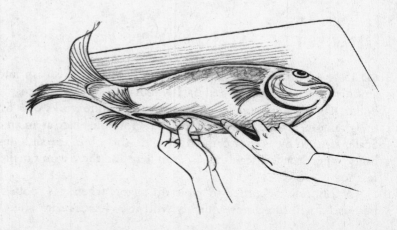

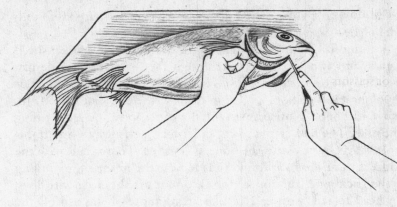

Removing gills: *Lift up the gill covers, and pull out the gills with your fingers or snip them out with a knife or shears.*

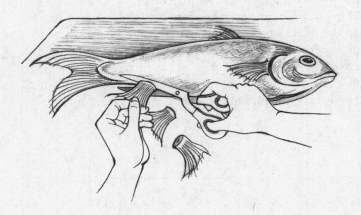

Snipping fins: *With a shears, cut off the anal, pelvic, and pectoral fins, but leave the dorsal fin in place to test for doneness and for ease of deboning if the fish is being cooked whole.*

When I am cooking a whole fish, I like to leave the dorsal fins—the ones on top—intact so that they can be used in testing for doneness, if necessary (a fish is usually cooked through when the fin can be easily pulled free). I also find the dorsal fin a useful guide when I am skinning or filleting a cooked fish. But I use kitchen scissors to cut away the fins on the sides and bottom of the fish.

FILLETING The most crucial aspect of filleting is to use a *very* sharp knife with a long, slender blade—that is, a boning or filleting knife.

To fillet a roundfish (one that would form roundish steaks when sliced crosswise), start with two incisions: cut through the flesh on one side just above the pectoral fin (the "shoulder" or forward fin on the side), and continue the cut along the backbone to just in front of the tail. Cut directly to, but not through, the bone. Notice how, with these incisions, you are defining the size of the fillet. The next step is to cut the fish in such a way as to lift this fillet off whole, staying as close to the bone as possible. To do that, with the fish on its side, start at the incision you made near the head, and, working down from the backbone (the top of the fish), cut off the flesh with long strokes from head to tail, with each stroke lifting more of the fish off the bones. Hold the fish away from the bones as you go, gently so as not to tear it. Little jagged strokes will tend to make a mess of the flesh. Keep an eye on the shape and flow of the bones so that you follow the natural line of the fish. Do not cut the first fillet away completely. It helps to have that first side still slightly attached and in place for support when you turn the fish over to fillet the other side. When the fillets have been removed, cut away any discolored portions. Feel for pinbones, especially near the head, and remove them with needle-nose pliers, tweezers, or your fingernails, or cut them away.

When filleting flatfish like flounder or sole, do the white side first, which is the thinner of the two and more difficult to fillet if you leave it for last.

To Fillet a Fish

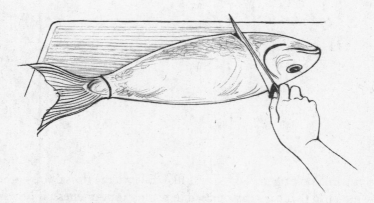

Holding the fish with its back facing you and using a sharp knife, preferably one with a slender blade, make cuts just to the backbone in front of the tail and behind the pectoral fin.

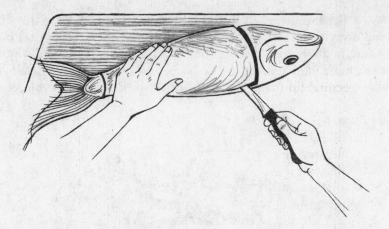

With the knife held horizontally, slice along the top of the fish from head to tail, staying as close to the bone as possible.

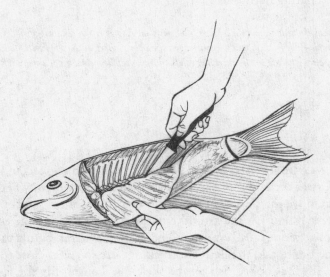

Gradually slice down along the ribs and backbone from the top to the belly of the fish, lifting away the fillet as you go. Leave the first fillet barely attached while you turn the fish over and fillet the other side.

SKINNING A FILLET Place the fillet skin side down on a cutting board with the head end away from you. Take a sharp knife—a chef's knife or a boning knife—and, holding the tail end in one hand, cut into the flesh down to the skin at the tail end. Then cut the flesh free by sawing at an angle along the skin without cutting through it, cleanly lifting the flesh away as you go.

To Skin a Fillet

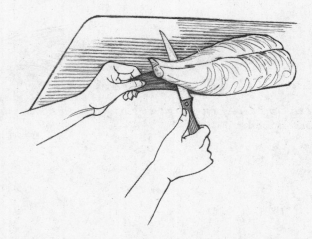

Place the fillet skin side down on a firm, flat surface. At the tip of the tail of the fillet, slice through the flesh just to, but not through, the skin. Then, with the knife held nearly horizontally, slice as close to the skin as possible while holding down the skin with your other hand.

FILLETING A COOKED FISH After a whole fish has been cooked and presented in all its glory at the table, an excellent approach to serving it, whether you've chosen to remove the skin or not, is to slide portions of fish off the bones just as if you were filleting it raw. In other words, first cut along the edges of the flesh at the backbone, head, and tail. Then, using a metal spatula to maneuver between the bones and the flesh and making sure to get as close to the bones as possible, lift the cooked fish off the skeleton. To simplify the task of filleting a cooked fish, only the side of the fish facing you requires much attention. After the cooked fillet is removed from that side, simply remove the bones from the bottom half by grasping the skeleton at the tail and lifting the whole skeleton up and away, severing it at the head end, if necessary.

TO FILLET A COOKED FISH

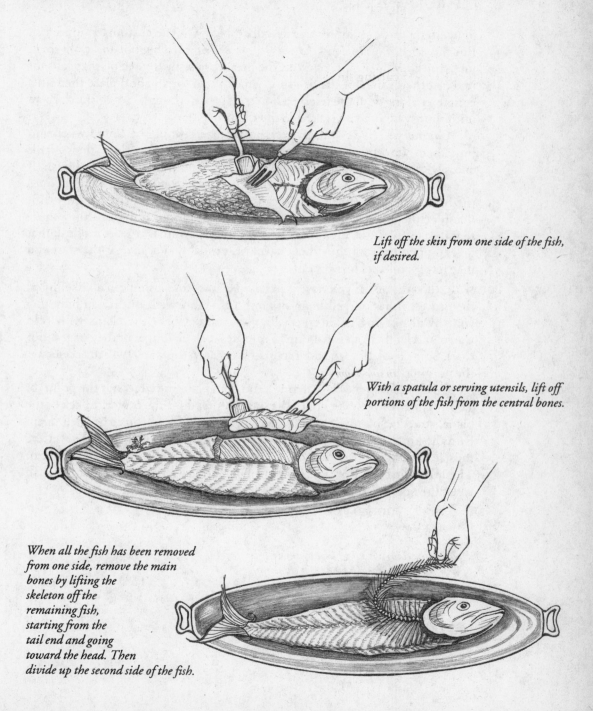

Lift off the skin from one side of the fish, if desired.

With a spatula or serving utensils, lift off portions of the fish from the central bones.

When all the fish has been removed from one side, remove the main bones by lifting the skeleton off the remaining fish, starting from the tail end and going toward the head. Then divide up the second side of the fish.

PREPARING SHELLFISH

Shucking clams and oysters, as described below, is the customary approach. But there are two shortcuts. One is to place them in a big pot and cook them just until they open, then cut out the meat for use in any recipe that calls for it. The other is to have the fish shop shuck them for you and place them in a container along with the reserved liquor. It is best, though, not to shuck them until shortly before you intend to use them.

Caution: All live clams, oysters, and mussels should be closed when you buy them (except for soft-shell clams, which cannot close their shells entirely), indicating that their muscles are taut and they are alive and fresh. If one of them is not closed, tap it or drop it from a height of a few inches onto the countertop; the shock should cause it to shut as a defensive measure. If it doesn't close, discard it. You can also squeeze mollusks shut, discarding those that don't stay shut. After cooking them, the opposite is true. A mollusk that fails to open once all the others have was probably not alive at the start and may have spoiled. Throw it out.

SHUCKING CLAMS If you have purchased clams from a shop, in all likelihood the processor has purged them of sand reasonably well. But if you have dug your own, purging is an especially good idea. Cover the clams with cold water, and let them sit for about 15 minutes (but no longer or they may suffocate). Some cooks like to add ½ cup of vinegar to the water, which accelerates the purging.

To shuck, cup the clam in one hand, and place the edge, not the point, of a clam knife between the lips of the shell. With your fingers on the back of the blade, squeeze sharply inward. Then twist the knife to force the shell open. Run the knife around the edge and the inside of the upper shell to sever the muscle, and loosen the clam from the upper shell without tearing the meat. Then free the clam from the bottom. Do all this over a bowl so that you can catch the liquid, later straining it through cheesecloth for further use.

To Shuck Clams

Holding the clam with the hinge against the lower joint of your thumb, wedge the blade of a clam knife between the shells.

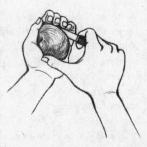

Twist the knife to pry open the hinge. Then move the knife along the inside of the uppershell to sever the muscle.

Loosen or cut free the meat in the lower shell.

SHUCKING OYSTERS Oyster knives are specifically made for this purpose. Unlike shucking clams, here you must enter the shell not with the edge of the knife, but with the sturdy point, which is thrust between the shells under the small lip that protrudes at the hinge. When trying this maneuver, protect the hand holding the oyster with a folded kitchen towel or heavy glove since the possibility of stabbing yourself is real (that's why some oyster knives come with shields at the base of the blade to prevent it from going too far). Twist the knife to force the shell open. Once inside, cut close to the top shell to sever the muscle. Discard the top shell. Then use the knife to loosen the oyster from the bottom shell.

To Shuck Oysters

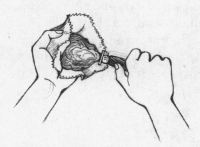
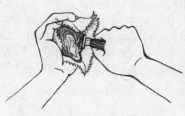
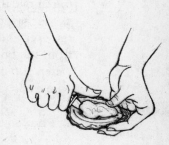

In a heavy cloth, hold the oyster flat side up and with the narrow hinge side facing outward. Wedge the tip of an oyster knife (do not use a paring knife) into the hinge.

Twist the knife to pry open the hinge. Then move the knife along the inside of the upper shell to sever the muscle.

Loosen or cut free the meat in the lower shell.

CLEANING MUSSELS Scrape off any barnacles that may be attached to the outer shells before placing the mussels in a large mixing bowl filled with cold water. Swirl the mussels around vigorously so that they rub against each other, further cleaning the shells. Then remove the mussels from the water, and rinse them in a colander. With a paring knife or fingertips, pull off the woolly beards. Generally, you will save yourself a great deal of work if you buy cultured mussels, ones that have been grown on a farm and arrive at the store clean in the first place, though they still need to be rinsed and debearded at home.

To Debeard Mussels

With a paring knife or fingertips, pull the woolly beard from the flat side of the mussel.

CLEANING SQUID More often than not, squid is sold already cleaned and beheaded. But if you buy squid whole, first separate the head from the body by pulling on the head, which will also remove the innards. Then cut off the tentacles just in front of the eyes, and squeeze the tentacles just below the cut to remove the hard white "beak" inside. Discard the beak, and cut the tentacles into pieces of desired size. From the rest of the head, cut away and discard the eyes and the innards. Pull the hard, translucent, sword-shaped "spine" from the body, and discard it. Then, holding the body under cold running water, slip off the outer speckled skin. Now you are ready to stuff the body whole or slice it into rings or other pieces.

To Clean Squid

Grasp the head of the squid in one hand and the body of the squid in the other, and gently pull them apart.

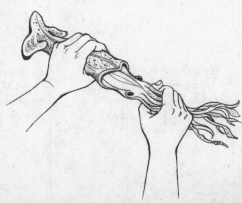

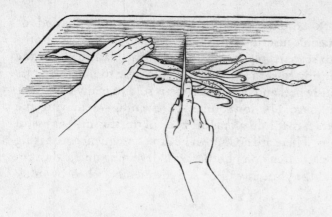

Cut off the tentacle portion just in front of the eyes, and discard the head and innards. Squeeze out the "beak" from the center of the tentacles where they were attached to the head.

Pull out the quill from the body, and pull off the speckled skin. Rinse the body thoroughly inside and out.

Cut the body and tentacles into pieces of desired lengths.

SHELLING AND DEVEINING SHRIMP Everyone has his or her own method for shelling shrimp. Some people just rip at the shell with their fingers, while others tidily snip it off with scissors, placing the point of the blade beneath the shell at the head and cutting toward the tail. A simple little tool that enables the cook to simultaneously peel and devein shrimp is sold in many fish stores and kitchen shops (see page 114 for sources). Deveining—removing the dark-colored digestive tract that runs along the back of the shrimp—is useful only for cosmetic reasons. There are no known health consequences to eating the vein, and, truth to tell, I often don't bother with deveining unless the vein is dark and obvious and the shrimp will be served unembellished by other ingredients.

To Peel and Devein Shrimp

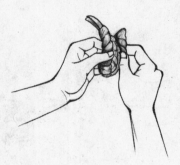

With your fingers, start at the legs of the shrimp, and peel off the shell. If desired, leave the last section and tail attached.

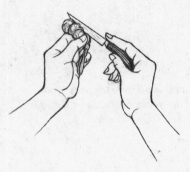

To remove the vein, make a shallow cut with a paring knife along the top side (outer curve) of the shrimp.

Pull out and discard the dark vein (intestinal tract).

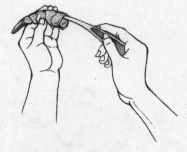

Alternatively, use a shrimp peeler, which loosens the shell and the vein in one step.

CLEANING SOFT-SHELL CRABS Although fishmongers usually do this job for their customers, it doesn't hurt to know how—you just might gather your own someday. It is simple: with a scissors, snip off the eyes, hard mouth parts, and spines along the edge of the shell; then cut away the bottom flap, or apron, of the shell, and lift the side flaps of the carapace to remove the gills.

To Clean Soft-Shell Crabs

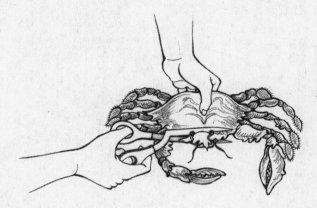

*With a shears,
snip off the eyes.*

*Turn the crab on its back, and
cut away the triangular-shaped
apron.*

*With the crab still on its back,
lift the flaps on each side of the
bottom shell (carapace),
and remove the spongy gills.*

12
Preparation Techniques

This section might be subtitled "How to Overcome Your Fear of Cooking Fish." Many otherwise competent, confident home cooks, comfortable with cooking beef or chicken, become anxious when faced with the prospect of preparing a seafood meal. In a nation that until only recently prided itself on its meat eating, relative unfamiliarity with seafood seems largely to blame for this anxiety because, as you'll see when you read on, seafood preparation is simple, using a wide range of cooking methods that are easy to master and adaptable to almost any environment, from the well-appointed kitchen to the campfire. In preparing seafood, the main objective is to cook the fish or shellfish thoroughly and flavorfully, while retaining its natural moisture. Tenderizing seafood is almost never a problem since almost all fish and shellfish start out tender.

IS IT DONE?

The trick in preparing seafood is to cook it thoroughly without overdoing it. As with meat, where people don't hesitate to say they like it rare or medium or well, "thoroughly" cooked fish is to some extent a matter of taste. My husband won't eat anything that he considers underdone. So clams or mussels steamed just until their shells open, the connoisseur's method (and not advised by safety experts), might as well be raw in his view. And so is tuna cooked medium-rare, as it is in many restaurants today. And yet is he wrong, some kind of philistine? Of course not. As long as the fish or shellfish hasn't reached that chewy or dried-out state, it is not overcooked, just cooked to taste.

In this book, I've tried to find a happy medium: seafood that Richard will eat with pleasure and a reasonable assurance of safety but that still retains its natural moisture and texture. Seafood is usually considered cooked through when it has lost its translucent appearance and has turned more solid look-ing—that is, opaque. Some cooks insist that in many cases fish should remain a little translucent or it will be overcooked. As your familiarity with fish cook-ery increases, that may turn out to be your preference, too. But it is not Richard's, nor, in most cases, is it mine.

In determining how long to cook seafood, it helps to be flexible about some of the standard rules. One is the Canadian 10-minute rule, which sug-gests that you cook fish for 10 minutes per inch of thickness at a high temper-ature (425°F to 450°F in the oven) or, in poaching, after the liquid has begun to boil. Although this rule is helpful, especially to the inexperienced fish cook, it is nothing but a rough guideline, and if you follow it too rigidly, it will give you a false sense of security. For one thing, seafood doesn't come in neatly measured thicknesses; neither is the flesh of the various kinds of fish and shell-fish of the same density. While it doesn't hurt to have the 10-minute rule in mind—and I do refer to it frequently in this book—I think it is silly to be a slave to it.

There are several good ways to tell if fish and shellfish are done to your liking. One way is to check the flesh visually as the seafood cooks. For instance, nobody likes undercooked shrimp, so when you are preparing shrimp, it's a good idea to cook an extra shrimp or two to sacrifice in a test for doneness (that is, opaque all the way through). With finfish, when you think it's close to being done, neatly insert a fork or knife into the thickest part of the fish to see if it is opaque all the way through. Forget the familiar advice to wait until it flakes with a fork; some fish are naturally more flaky than others, and many fish will be overcooked by the time they flake.

There are a couple of other useful indicators. Some accomplished fish cooks like to insert an instant-read food thermometer into the thickest part of the fish when they think it is about done; when the thermometer registers 145°F to 160°F, consider the fish cooked. With a whole fish, thorough cook-ing is usually achieved when a spine from one of the dorsal fins (along the fish's back) can easily be removed by hand.

MAKING IT FLAVORFUL

Like the 10-minute rule, it is also a good idea to reexamine the notion that fish is so naturally good it doesn't need anything special done to it beyond putting it into the broiler, onto the grill, or into a pan with oil or butter. There is some truth in that and a lot of blithe overstatement, too. Sure, a trout pulled right from the stream and grilled over an open fire with no embellishment is going to taste heavenly. But that fillet of flounder or sole that shows up in every fish store will be bland without at least a little help. Moreover, if you don't learn a variety of techniques and seasoning and saucing approaches—even for the most flavorful seafood—you'll be unlikely to eat fish as frequently as it deserves because it will get boring. That's why this book is so varied in its recipes, turning to several different cooking traditions to produce dishes that titillate the taste buds. Fish deserves to be treated like all other food—with creativity and attention to flavor.

THE LOW-FAT APPROACH

Central to all my thinking about seafood is that fish and shellfish must be prepared in a low-fat way, using as little added fat as possible. It strikes me as foolish to take a food as inherently healthful as seafood and diminish its natural benefits with traditional butter or cream sauces or by immersing it in oil. Some basic cooking methods—poaching, steaming, and microwaving among them—lend themselves to recipes that are essentially free of added fat. So does the preparation of seafood soups and stews. Cooks used to be profligate with fat, with countless recipes calling for far more oil or butter than is necessary to produce a successful, flavorful dish. So if you need to soften the leeks and garlic before using them in a soup or sauce, try it with just a teaspoon of oil or butter in a nonstick pan, rather than pouring in the usual 2 tablespoons. And where you need oil to prevent sticking or to aid in browning, spray it on, rather than pouring it in, to create a thin film.

COOKING WITH HERBS

Once you give up the crutch of high-fat cookery, you will start to appreciate natural garden flavors more than ever before, especially the zing of many aromatic herbs. Although my recipes frequently offer the option of dried herbs, these days fresh herbs are widely available year round in most parts of the country and nearly always produce a superior result. If your markets don't stock fresh herbs or it is a hassle to get them when you want them (or you can get them but find them prohibitively expensive), I highly recommend growing your own, especially during the warm months of the year. In winter, many herbs will grow reasonably well on a sunny window ledge. Failing that, summer herbs can be frozen if they are to be integrated into a dish that is then cooked.

Like seafood cooking in general, there are no hard and fast rules about which herbs to use. Parsley, basil, dill, thyme, and tarragon will almost always enhance a seafood dish. Cilantro—an herb that some people love but others despise, saying it has a soapy flavor—is an acquired taste and has been finding new fans every day. For those who admire it, cilantro brings an alluring, exotic accent to a dish, an echo of faraway places like Asia, where it is a staple flavoring. When cilantro is called for in a recipe and you don't want it or can't find it, Italian (flat-leaf) parsley, which is more pungent than the more common curly variety, is a good alternative, with curly parsley a runner-up. The more assertive herbs like rosemary and oregano marry best with seafood strong enough to stand up to them, like tuna or swordfish. Some herbal combinations are naturals: basil or rosemary with thyme, oregano with basil, and chervil with parsley and thyme, for example.

When substituting dried herbs for fresh, generally use half as much as the recipe calls for. In any event, once you become accustomed to using herbs in your seafood cookery, you can have some fun experimenting with them.

SAUCES

Throughout the nation, from spas and restaurants to cookbooks and the test kitchens of big commercial food producers, the drive has been toward lower fat. Commercial cooks are scrambling to respond to consumer demand for a more wholesome diet, but one that doesn't sacrifice the flavors and textures that Americans have long loved. Sauces would seem to offer the greatest challenge to creating low-fat recipes. But I've discovered this is only because we are so used to the old, high-fat ways. As it turns out, there are many low-fat approaches to creating delectable sauces, and I offer them to you in this book.

A common approach is simply to reduce the liquid used in cooking a particular dish to create a sauce, whether it is wine or broth or fruit juice. If a liquid requires thickening, one of the best methods is to use pureed vegetables of one kind or another, as I often do in my recipes. Another approach is to prepare ordinary sauces by using much less fat than is usually called for; you'll be astonished at how unnecessarily freehanded cooks have been with fats and oils. Salsas and vegetable sauces like a fresh tomato sauce are cases in point.

Here, the flavorful ingredients carry the day, making excessive fat—and sometimes any fat—unnecessary.

Vinaigrettes, which traditionally might be made with three parts oil to one part vinegar or lemon juice, needn't be that fatty. I have cut way down on the oil and, instead, amplified the sauce with more juice or wine or even water. The many new nonfat and low-fat products on the market, like nonfat and low-fat mayonnaise, yogurt, and sour cream, have a definite place in this sort of cooking, too. Even though when they are used alone these modified products may lack something in taste, when they are combined with other ingredients, as they are here, you'll be unlikely to miss the flavor once imparted by health-damaging fats.

Other useful cooking ingredients are evaporated skimmed milk and low-fat buttermilk, which can help create creaminess without cream. To keep the milk from breaking down when it is heated, I stabilize it by mixing it with a little cornstarch beforehand. While some traditionalists may deride this approach as somehow fake, in my view there's nothing ersatz about it. The ingredients are genuine, and the results add interest and variety to seafood cookery without adding much, if any, fat.

All these approaches are good examples of how low-fat cookery is not as restraining and dull as its critics would have you think. Instead, it invites invention and a slenderer, healthier you.

13
Basic Cooking Methods

Seafood is ideally suited to many low-fat cooking methods. Here are my favorites.

POACHING

Poaching is simplicity itself and requires no added fat. It involves no more than gently simmering fish or shellfish in a flavorful liquid such as vegetable stock. As with all cooking methods that use liquid or steam rather than surface heat, the process is especially thorough and fast because the moisture is so penetrating. The best fish for poaching have firm, flavorful flesh—salmon, striped bass, snapper, black sea bass, and trout, among others.

For those who have yet to try it, poaching seems to be one of the scariest methods of preparing fish. One reason for this, I think, is that the finished product, if it's a whole fish, is supposed to look professionally gorgeous when it is done. Also, the most efficient way to poach a whole fish (as in the red snapper recipe on page 374) is in an elongated pot called a fish poacher, described on page 89.

But you do not have to own a fish poacher to poach a whole fish.

Alternatives include a roasting pan with a good rack that will enable you to lift out the fish after it is cooked. Or you can create a poaching rack with long, folded strips of foil that are placed crosswise at intervals under the fish and allowed to extend over the edges of the pan, providing handles for lifting the cooked fish. Or you can set the fish on a rack that is first fitted with a long rectangle of doubled cheesecloth and use the edges of the cloth to remove the fish. Or you can wrap the fish itself in several layers of cheesecloth to hold it together.

POACHING WITH CHEESECLOTH

A whole fish, fish steak, or fillet can be wrapped in cheesecloth and a second piece of cheesecloth placed under the fish for support as it is lowered into the poaching liquid and lifted from the pan.

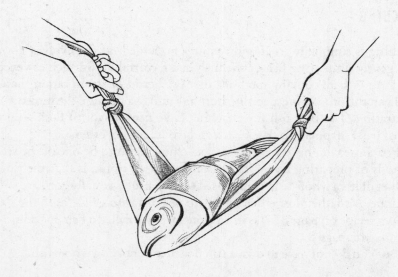

Recipes often instruct you to allow the stock to cool before placing a whole fish in it and then to bring the poaching liquid back up to a simmer. Or recipes may suggest simmering the fish for a period of time and then allowing the stock to cool with the fish resting in it. Both approaches are intended to prolong the time the fish spends in the broth, ensuring that it is permeated by the flavors but without the risk of overcooking it.

When poaching a whole fish, I always prefer to leave the head and tail on. It makes for a more spectacular presentation as well as helping the fish retain its natural juices. But there are times when you may wish to remove the

POACHING IN A FISH POACHER

The rack of the poacher supports the fish, which can be lifted out of the liquid by handles on the rack. Cover the pan while the fish cooks.

POACHING ON STRIPS OF FOIL

Place three or more doubled strips of aluminum foil crosswise under the fish, and extend them over the edges of the pan. Cover the pan while the fish cooks.

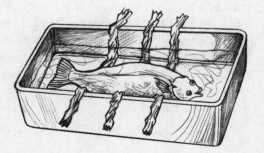

head—if the fish is too big to fit into the poacher or other cooking vessel, for instance, or if you can't get over that unsettling feeling when you see a cooked fish that still looks like a fish. It is your call.

Although it is more dramatic to remove the skin of a whole fish and garnish it before bringing it to the table on a platter, you may prefer to serve it with the skin on. That is up to you, too. It is going to be wonderful no matter what.

Fillets and steaks can be poached in an ordinary covered pan on the stovetop, and when the fish is removed, after perhaps 5 minutes of cooking, the broth can be reduced to serve as the base for a sauce (see the recipe on page 342). In fact, a bonus in poaching is that the leftover broth, perhaps with the addition of some white wine, can be used as a base for making sauces, soups, and many other preparations. If you're not going to use the broth soon, strain it and freeze it.

STEAMING

Steaming has become the favored cooking method among those who are looking for no added fat in their food because it requires none to cook a fish well and quickly. In fact, steamed fish has become the bane of many restaurants whose health-conscious clients order it even when it is not on the menu. The cooking is done entirely, or almost entirely, by the enveloping steam, which keeps the fish moist while penetrating it deeply and rapidly. For fish, the simplest cooking approach is to cover it with vegetables like onions, fennel, and carrots along with, perhaps, a sprinkling of lemon juice or wine, place it on a rack or on a heatproof platter set on a rack above a couple of inches of boiling water, cover the pan tightly, and then steam the fish until it is opaque. The water must be kept at a decent boil throughout so that it creates enough steam, and the lid of the steamer must fit tightly.

But, as with poaching, you do not need a special pot, called a steamer, to steam fish. You can fashion a steamer out of a wide kettle or roasting pan by placing a rack or heatproof platter on pedestals of two or more squat empty cans that have had their lids removed at both ends (tuna cans are perfect).

In general, since the steaming itself adds so little flavor to the fish, I prefer to use this method with seafood that has a distinctive character, such as the tilefish on page 368, avoiding delicate fish like sole and flounder. The exceptions are those recipes with a flavorful accompanying sauce, as in the steamed "scrod" with caper sauce (page 370), where the character of the fish itself is less crucial.

Caution: Steam is deceptively hot, hotter and more penetrating than boiling water, so be careful when you remove the lid of a steamer. Lift it tilted away from you, and protect your hand with an oven mitt or, less preferably, a pot holder.

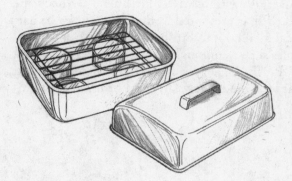

STEAMING IN A ROASTING PAN

Remove the top and bottom lids from 3 or 4 tuna cans, and rest a roaster rack on them. The fish can be placed directly on the rack or on a heatproof platter above boiling water. The pan should be covered tightly while the fish cooks.

Steaming is perhaps the best approach of all for some shellfish such as mussels and clams. While mussels and clams can be steamed in just a cup of water, if ingredients like shallots, herbs, and wine are placed in a pot and a pile of shellfish is added to it, the flavor is all the better. Since only a few of the shellfish are touching the flavoring ingredients at any one time, if you shake the pot a bit, it will help to ensure that none of the mussels or clams are neglected; but it is the steam, not the liquid, that does the actual cooking. The shellfish release their own liquids, which enhance the flavor of the whole dish. The resulting broth, like that in poaching, can be carefully strained, preferably through several layers of cheesecloth to get rid of any sand, and used in other ways. For example, mussel broth might be added to the cooking water for a seafood pasta, and clam broth ("juice") is a common recipe ingredient.

BAKING

Baking is one of the most popular and best ways to cook fish (witness the number of recipes in this book that use it) but, paradoxically, among the most risky. The danger is in its use of dry (and drying) heat. Here, you are submitting fish to high temperatures in an enclosed box—the oven—for 15 to 20 minutes or more. So a great many recipes for baked fish call for some means by which the seafood's natural moisture is retained—a much greater problem with a fillet and a steak than with whole fish encased in its skin. I have wrapped fish in a leafy vegetable, covered it with a variety of sauces, added liquid to the pan, and, on occasion, combined several approaches at once, as in Cindy's Salmon with Honey-Mustard and Tarragon (page 288).

A trendy term at the moment is "roasting," which usually connotes no more than baking a whole, intact fish with relatively little fuss (see the recipe on page 302, for example). The fish is prevented from drying out by its natural wrapping of skin. A typical method is to brush or spray the fish with oil and lay it on a bed of vegetables such as onions and celery, then cook it at a high temperature, 425°F to 450°F. Generally speaking, this method will work best with fish that are at least moderately fatty and firm such as pompano, salmon, or trout.

GRILLING

Probably the hottest—figuratively and almost literally—method for preparing seafood, even by novice cooks, is grilling. Part of its appeal is that the results are nearly always delectable, especially if you invest in a little advance preparation to make sure that the heat does not rob the seafood of moisture and if you keep careful track of the time on the grill to avoid overcooking. Thick (¾ inch to 1 inch), firm-fleshed, and fattier steaks and fillets work best on the grill and need the least attention. Thinner or more delicate fish are best grilled on a bed of foil or greens such as romaine lettuce or cabbage. Or you can use a fine-meshed, well-oiled fish grate, which is also perfect for grilling unskewered shellfish like shrimp and squid. Whole fish are easiest to handle on the grill if they are cooked in a fish holder designed for this purpose (see page 111 for sources).

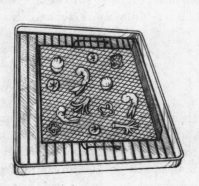

Grilling grate

Grilling basket

Marinating seafood in a flavor-enhancing liquid is a good way to preserve moisture during cooking. Fish is quick to pick up the flavors in a marinade, so most need only 15 to 30 minutes—1 hour at most—in their precooking bath. If your marinade contains a significant amount of vinegar, wine, or citrus juice, keep the marinating time short since the acid will "precook" the fish, turning it opaque and firm before it hits the grill. You'll notice that I use very little, if any, oil in my marinades. Not only does this reduce the calories, it also limits flare-ups that can make the heat uncontrollable and overcook the fish.

As for cooking time, I've found in grilling that the standard Canadian rule of 10 minutes to the inch holds reasonably well for all but the thinnest fish and shellfish, which may need even less time. The trick is to start cooking the fish on a well-heated grill, keeping in mind that if the fish is ice cold it will take a bit longer. To check for doneness, poke a knife or fork into the thickest part of the fish or the section that abuts the bone, and pry the flesh apart just enough to see if it has cooked through. If necessary, fish can be removed from the grill to check for doneness and returned for further cooking. To be sure that especially thick steaks or fillets or whole fish cook through, it is best to cook them over medium-low heat; I also like to cover the grill for at least part of the time.

By placing some soaked and drained wood chips over the hot coals and covering the grill, you can add a variety of smoked flavors to fish. There are also smoking boxes especially designed for grill-top smoking so that the wood chips will not become mixed with the permanent ceramic or lava bricks of the grill (see page 111 for sources).

To keep seafood from sticking to the grill, I routinely brush or spray either the grate or the fish or both with vegetable oil, especially if the seafood is not naturally fatty or has not been in a marinade containing oil. The grate must be clean—cooked-on food particles will cause the seafood to stick—and it should be hot before the food is put on it. The best plan is to heat the grate for several minutes, then brush it with oil.

Warning: If a commercial oil spray is used, you must remove the hot grate from the fire before spraying it.

Fish is best turned only once, and thin fillets may not need any turning, especially if they are cooked with the grill covered. A long or very wide spatula is the ideal turning tool, unless you have a two-sided fish grate that encloses the fish and simply needs to be flipped over to cook the fish on the other side. To get those "gourmet" grill marks on your fish, be sure the grate is oiled and hot before you set the fish on it; diagonal marks are made by placing the fish on the grate at an angle. When cooking a fillet with skin, start it with the flesh side down and turn it only once.

If you have problem with flare-up, keep a mister on hand, and spray some water on the coals, just enough to quench the flame. If you have a gas grill, you might consider replacing the lava bricks with ceramic ones, which are less likely to flare. These are available in most stores that sell grills and other patio equipment.

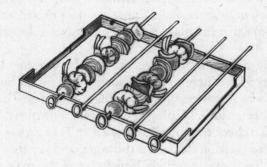

And aficionados of kebabs might consider purchasing a skewer rack that facilitates turning seafood kebabs, which tend to be more fragile than those made with meat. If you choose to use independent skewers, my vote goes to slender wooden ones, which do less damage to fish cubes but which *must* be soaked in water for at least 20 minutes before they are threaded with kebab pieces.

BROILING

Broiling is like grilling but without the added flavor that comes from cooking over coals. This means that many recipes that call for grilling can yield fine dishes under the broiler. The fish is placed 3 to 6 inches from the heat; the thinner it is, the closer it should be. Happily, most broiled fish need not be turned, so the risk of breaking those handsome fillets is much diminished.

Since broiling, like baking, may dry out the fish, marinades or toppings of one kind or another are often used, as in the Broiled Catfish with Mustard on page 335. To minimize added fat, a nonstick broiler tray is useful. Typically, thin fillets will be done in 3 to 4 minutes, and thicker fillets and steaks will take 8 to 10 minutes per inch, depending on how close they are to the heat and the desired degree of doneness. Always preheat the broiler just as you would an oven or grill.

SMOKING

Anyone who grew up loving smoked fish, as I did, has an almost unquenchable desire for it from time to time. Until recently, doing your own smoking at home was difficult, and most of us had to rely on commercially smoked fish. The commercial approach most often is "cold" smoking at temperatures not hot enough to cook the fish. The seafood is usually marinated in brine (that is, a liquid that has been heavily salted) and then smoked at 80°F to 90°F for many hours. But the approach that I and many other people use at home is hot smoking on the range top or on the barbecue grill or even in a wok at temperatures hot enough to cook the fish in just a few minutes (see page 106 for information about my favorite smoker). Here, the heat is doing the cooking, and the smoke is merely a flavoring agent. The result is so potent in flavor that it frequently eliminates the need for much else in the way of ingredients.

You can (and, if you like this sort of flavoring, I would urge you to) purchase a stovetop or backyard smoker designed for this purpose. Or you can add water-soaked wood chips to the briquets of a charcoal grill with a cover or put wood chips in a vented metal container that is then placed on top of the lava or ceramic bricks of a gas grill, which is then covered. Finally, you can smoke fish in a covered wok by placing the wood chips on a strong piece of aluminum foil at the bottom of the wok, setting the fish on a rack that fits inside the wok but sits above the chips, and covering the wok tightly. If the cover does not fit snugly (and few wok covers do), use rolled-up, wet paper towels around the edges of the cover to seal in the smoke.

SMOKING IN A WOK

Place wood chips or sawdust in a wok with a rack and a lid. Place the fish on the rack, and cover the wok.

Seal the edges of the lid with a damp dish towel, taking care to keep the towel inside the edge of the wok and away from the heat.

Caution: If you have an exhaust fan over your range, be sure to turn it on when smoking on the stovetop. Also, if there is a nearby smoke alarm, you'd be wise to disengage it temporarily.

Hot smoking can be accomplished with the addition of little or no fat and still keep the fish moist, with a handsome glaze to it. The flavor is imparted by the burning of sawdust or chips such as hickory, alder, apple, oak, or mesquite. The result is spectacular; after the first time I prepared a smoked bluefish pâté (see page 166), I was possessed by it. I felt the kind of glee that overtakes me whenever I learn something new that I really enjoy. And I made it over and over again, serving it to anyone who came into the house, much to my guests' delight.

Home-smoked fish added to a salad or pasta is often just the flavoring nuance a dish needs to make it extraordinary. A wide variety of fish and shell-fish, from trout to shrimp, emerge from the hot-smoker with new personali-ties. Oilier fish will be moister and often take to the smoked flavor best. Try mackerel, bluefish, eel, salmon, swordfish, and tuna; but even low-fat shell-fish like shrimp and scallops will taste wonderful (see the recipes on pages 134, 264, 382, and 468, for example).

It is important to remember that rapidly smoked seafood has not been preserved and, and like any cooked fish, will begin to spoil after about 4 or 5 days in the refrigerator.

MICROWAVING

Not long ago, no sane cookbook author would have included microwaving as a basic method of seafood cookery. The argument was that if the main benefit of the microwave was speed, why would anyone need it with a type of food that cooked quickly anyway? But it turns out that the microwave does have distinct advantages when it comes to cooking fish. One is that the fish cooks in its own juices yet retains its natural moisture as long as it is not overcooked.

Microwaving works by agitating the molecules within the food, creating friction and, thereby, generating heat. It is like steaming but without the external heat that steam cooking generates. So, here we have a low-fat method of preparing seafood that is fast and especially appealing in warm weather, when you want to keep the kitchen cool.

When microwave ovens were first introduced, many consumers were afraid that microwaves, which are similar to radio waves, might pose some danger from radiation. That has proved not to be so. What danger there is comes from careless handling of the food as it cooks, resulting in steam burns to hands and wrists. Probably, you will find yourself using plastic wrap (as many of the recipes in this book suggest) to cover a dish cooked in the microwave oven. To diminish the likelihood of steam burns, be certain to vent the plastic—that is, leave an opening at a corner of the dish where some of the steam can escape—so that when you lift the wrap to check on or remove the fish, a burst of steam will be less likely to harm you. If you have them, lids made for covering pans and platters in the microwave oven are more convenient and ecologically kinder than plastic wrap. The lids come with a steam vent, they're reusable, and you don't have to worry about having the plastic come in contact with the food (plastic wrap should be kept off the surface of the food to prevent the leaching of substances from the plastic into the dish).

Also, even though microwaves pass right through glass, plastic, or ceramic containers that hold food, all containers will become hot—or at least very warm—as the food inside them heats. Therefore, always use pot holders or mitts when handling these containers just as you would with a pan taken from a conventional oven.

You may notice that several of my microwave recipes call for covering the head and tail of whole fish with pieces of aluminum foil. I know and you know that you are not supposed to put any metal in a microwave oven. But rest assured, the pieces of foil do not create sparks, start fires, or in any way damage the oven *as long as the foil does not touch the sides of the oven.*

Since there are several variables that affect how quickly a microwave oven will cook—from volume and density of the food to power of the oven—it is

an especially good idea to check the fish or shellfish for doneness during the microwaving process. If a range of cooking times is offered, for instance, take a look at the fish when the cooking time reaches the low end of the range and see how things are going. If no range is provided, check 30 seconds to 1 minute ahead just to be sure you're on top of it. There is no reason not to take this sort of care since it is so easy to continue cooking the seafood for an additional 30 seconds at a time until it is done perfectly.

SAUTÉING

Sautéing, a traditional mainstay of fish cookery, plays a relatively small role in this book because, even with the development of excellent nonstick pans, it is a method that too often requires cooking in more oil or butter than I wish to use. I have offered a few sautéed dishes and used extremely little fat in the process, but I am happier using the technique known as oven frying, as in my Oven-Fried Orange Roughy on page 305 and Catfish Sticks on page 306, where that familiar crispy effect is achieved by spraying the fish's coating with just a bit of oil and baking the fish at a high temperature. However, if you prefer stovetop sautéing, be sure to use a heavy pan with a good-quality nonstick surface to minimize the need for added fat.

EN PAPILLOTE

This method—steaming in a casing of parchment or other material—derives its name from the French word for cocoon (butterfly, in French, is *papillon*), and it couldn't be a more appropriate designation for this gentle way of cooking in which food springs to life. The beauty of cooking en papillote is that it allows you to steam fish, using little or no added fat, along with the vegetables and other flavorings that are meant to accompany it. The steam comes from the moisture released by the ingredients, the flavors blending efficiently in what is actually a very primitive cooking contraption.

Most often, parchment is recommended because it inflates as the food cooks, allowing the steam to swirl around the food, and because it looks so dramatic when the packets are served. However, I have never shied away from aluminum foil: it is always around the house, and it is easy to create a seal using foil. The important thing to remember when using aluminum foil is to seal the packet tightly while wrapping the ingredients loosely—leaving some air around them—so that the steam can do its job.

If you are using parchment (see page 112 for sources), there are several ways to create the pouch. One is to cut a large rectangle, say 13 × 15 inches, and fold it in half to form a rectangle that is 13 × 7½ inches. With a scissors, cut from the folded side around the outside edge, forming—as kids do with cutouts—half a heart. Open the heart, place the food on one side of it, then fold the paper over, and crimp it tightly all along the edges to enclose the food, taking special care to roll the point at the bottom several times to secure the seal. If you are using foil, no fancy shape is needed since the foil can be folded over on itself into whatever shape suits your ingredients. But in either case, the packet should be loose enough to allow for expansion created by the steam.

BAKING IN PARCHMENT

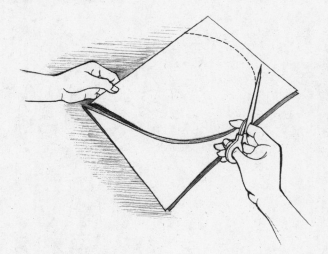

Fold a sheet of parchment paper in half. As if you were making a valentine, cut out a half heart that is at least twice as wide as the fish.

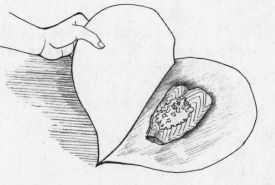

Open the parchment, and place the fish near the fold.

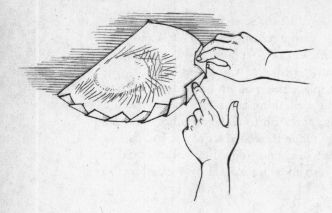

Fold over the parchment so that the edges meet, and, starting from the point, make small consecutive folds along the edge to seal the packet. Be sure to leave some space in the packet.

After the fish is cooked, carefully open the packet, and remove and serve the fish. Or let diners open their own packets.

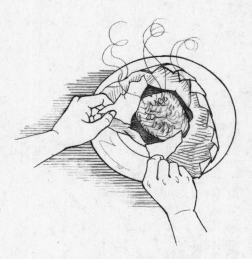

Also remember that when you are cooking en papillote, the food is not served immediately but must sit in its wrappings for several minutes after it is cooked. Even then, the packet should be opened carefully to avoid a steam burn.

14
Cleaning Up the Kitchen and the Cook

My husband, Richard, traces his lack of enthusiasm for fish to the "fishy" odor he remembers permeating his home after his parents cooked fish. In those days, fish was almost always breaded and fried, and it was the frying, not the fish (which was nearly always freshly caught lake fish and not in the least bit fishy), that was the primary source of lingering scents. I feel obliged to repeat what I have said several times already: fresh fish does not smell fishy or foul either before or after it is cooked. And if you stay away from frying and wash your utensils with soapy water soon after using them, you should have little or no problem with unwanted smells.

Still, there may be times when after handling fish you or some of your kitchen equipment reminds you of Hemingway's *Old Man and the Sea*. The antidote is simple. Those of you who saw and recall the movie *Atlantic City* know what it is. Every night, after her stint as an oyster shucker in a restaurant, the character played by actress Susan Sarandon bathed her skin in lemon juice, a natural and harmless neutralizer of fishy odors. But before you invest in a lemon orchard, I must reassure you that you need little more than the moist inside of a squeezed lemon to do the job, both on your hands and your cutting surfaces. Cut the pulpy rind open to form a flat piece, and use it as a wipe.

If you feel a need to refresh the air in your home after cooking fish, any air freshener should do the trick, although I'd opt for one with a citrus scent.

15

Handy Equipment for Seafood Cookery

People who fancy themselves great cooks often claim that they can cook under any condition. They'll make do, they say. Just give them a hot rock or a fire, and they're ready to produce an elegant repast. For most of us, this is a primitive pipe dream. Cooking is immeasurably easier and the results are almost always better when you have the appropriate tools. And this is especially true of fish preparation, which under the right circumstances can be straightforward and effortless. You need to be able to cook and handle fish efficiently and quickly.

As I cook seafood with ever-greater frequency, my own equipment collection grows larger by the day. I delight in finding some new contraption that adds fun to the project. Here are some of the tools that I believe are essential, along with a few I'm fond of but are not necessary. Some ought to be part of any good kitchen, but I mention them here because you absolutely need them for fish cookery, especially nutritious (that is, low-fat) fish cookery.

POTS AND PANS

Since low fat is a primary goal, nonstick pans are indispensable. They allow you to take a recipe that ordinarily might need, say,

2 tablespoons of oil to soften the shallots or sauté the vegetables and reduce that amount—in some cases to as little as 1 teaspoon. Moreover, the Teflon of old has, in recent years, been replaced by much better, longer-lived products. Nonstick pans used to be regarded as disposable items, but these days, if you remember to take care of them (tell the kids not to scrape the bottoms with metal forks and the like), they will last for years. Generally speaking, the more you spend on the pan, the more durable it will be. To make it last longer, the surface of the modern pan has been thickened and toughened, often with microscopic bits of ceramic material, and the best ones come with a 20-year guarantee. As with all pans that don't use some medium like water or steam to distribute the heat evenly, usually the thicker the metal, the better the heat distribution.

Three-quarters of the pots and pans sold in this country now are nonstick. The basic set of sauté pans consists of slope-sided skillets that are 8 inches, 10 inches, and 12 inches in diameter, preferably with lids. You will also need at least a small and a medium-sized nonstick covered saucepan—1 quart and 3 quarts—and a 5-quart or 6-quart Dutch oven or kettle for soups. A helpful but not essential piece of equipment is a 15-inch oval or rectangular nonstick baking pan; a jellyroll pan, for example, is excellent for baking long fillets. Or, if you'd rather not bake fish in metal, a large ovenproof glass or ceramic baking dish is a good choice. There are also the usual, useful uncoated pots and pans, large and small, that most of us already have. But two need mentioning. I find that an ovenproof glass 8 × 12-inch baking dish and/or a large glass pie plate are perfect for many fish chores and are excellent in the microwave oven, too. Also, although you can probably live without an 8-quart to 12-quart kettle, you'll need it if you intend to boil lobsters or steam large quantities of mussels.

KNIVES

Perhaps the worst mistake home cooks make is stinting on their knives. If you can't chop and slice well, cooking becomes unnecessarily frustrating, and you are likely to blame yourself for poor results or just give up on what seems like a tedious chore. The best knives, often expensive but worth every penny, have blades made out of high-carbon stainless steel. They are very sharp and can be sharpened again and again. (Cheap stainless-steel knives can't be sharpened well once they become dull or damaged.) Another thing to consider when purchasing a knife is how it feels in your hand. It should have a comfortable grip and a nice sense of balance and weight. Once you've handled a few knives, you will know which ones feel best for you.

You will need the basic set, graduated in size: paring, utility, and two chef's knives (8-inch and 10-inch blades). Specifically for seafood, it is a good idea also to have a filleting knife, which has a long, thin blade that allows you to stay close to the fish's bone as you remove the flesh. It also will serve you well in removing skin from fillets and in slicing both raw and cooked fish.

Although many people ask their fishmonger to open their oysters and clams for them or they steam them open, it is still a good idea to have on hand a clam knife and an oyster knife. There are several different sorts of knives for these purposes. One kind of clam knife has a thick, rigid blade, sturdier than ordinary knives so that it can withstand the pressure involved in the task. There is another, slightly less sturdy knife designed specifically for littlenecks, which are more fragile than cherrystones and may break when you use that heavier blade. For oysters, one commonly used knife has a short, stubby blade and a hand guard at its base so that when you thrust the knife point into the oyster you won't hurt yourself.

Filleting knife   *Oyster knife*

CUTTING BOARD

You are going to need a cutting board or two. You should have at least one that is large enough to hold the biggest fish you are likely to prepare. You will also want a board large enough to prevent all those fresh herbs I keep talking about from hopping around the kitchen counter like jumping beans as you chop. A good size, if you buy only one board, is about 12 × 16 inches.

Not long ago, I would have recommended purchasing only the plastic cutting boards that have become so popular these days because, presumably, they are more sanitary. And they are, in fact, sanitary enough as long as you wash them thoroughly. But recent research has shown that wooden cutting boards, rather than fostering the growth of bacteria in their rough, porous surfaces, actually contain some as-yet-unknown component that destroys microbes. So now the best advice is that either kind is fine, if you keep them very clean. But if you are not meticulous about cleanup, then a wooden board might actually have an advantage.

TIMER

All cooking is a matter of timing, but this is especially crucial in the quick preparation of fish. So a timer is a must for accuracy. Any timer is better than nothing, but I much prefer the battery-operated digital kind to the wind-up versions since it is precise, easy to read, can be hooked to your clothing, and has a long-lasting beep.

STEAMER

The type of steamer doesn't matter since it is the steam and nothing inherent in the pot (save a rack and a tight-fitting lid) that does the cooking. The one significant problem arises when you want to steam a large fish like the tilefish on page 368. What I've always done in cases like that is to concoct a steamer using a standard covered roasting pan (see the illustration on page 91). Cut out the tops and bottoms of three or four tuna (or similar-sized) cans, place a rack or tray or heatproof platter over them, add an inch or so of water to the bottom of the pan, bring the water to a boil, and you're in business.

FISH POACHER

This is one of those tools people tend to get as gifts and then never use. As a matter of fact, these poachers have never been prominent in my own cooking. But they are useful from time to time, once you give them a try. A poacher is an elongated pot with a rack that sits on the bottom so that a whole beautiful fish can be lifted out without breaking. It is a stunning thing to do. Poachers come in a range of sizes. The one I've seen most often is 18 inches in length, which will snugly accommodate a fish of up to 3 pounds or even a bit larger. That is the size you'll want for four servings. But for larger dinner parties, you may require a larger fish, which makes the 24-inch poacher more practical. And a poacher of that size can be used to prepare smaller fish laid end to end. Poachers come in several materials; they all will do equally well, aluminum as well as copper, differing only in appearance and price.

Fish poacher

It is possible to improvise (as I've had to do when my fish was larger than my poacher), using a roasting pan with a rack (preferably one with handles) placed in it. Or, if you lack a rack, you can fashion one out of foot-long strips of heavy-duty aluminum foil that is doubled or regular foil that is tripled; lay 3 or 4 foil strips across the bottom and up the sides of the roasting pan, set the fish on them, and you should be able to use the ends of the foil to lift up the cooked fish (see the illustration on page 89). Or you can set the fish on a long rectangle of doubled cheesecloth, using the ends of the cloth to lift the fish (see page 88).

SMOKER

I have become enamored of hot-smoked fish, which avoids the saltiness of commercially available cured smoked fish. You can buy all sorts of hot-smokers nowadays, often through mail-order catalogues that cater to outdoor life

Stovetop smoker

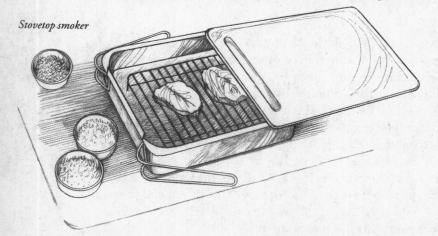

Place wood chips or sawdust in the bottom of the smoker beneath the pan. Set the rack over the pan, place the fish upon the rack, turn on the heat, and, when the wood begins to smoke, close the lid tightly.

and stores that sell patio equipment. The smoker I use most often is a small, handy stovetop version, the Camerons Stovetop Smoker Cooker, available through the Char-Broil catalogue and in many kitchen-equipment stores (see page 111 for sources). It's a simple metal lidded box that contains a tray and a rack. You place sawdust or wood chips of one kind or another under the tray, which smoke furiously when the metal container is heated on the stove. Tightly shut, the smoker both hot-cooks and smokes the fish at the same time. Another smoker I've been using is an oblong box that holds wood chips or sawdust and sits on top of the briquets in my grill. It functions similarly to the range-top version, giving marvelous results. Smoker aficionados use other techniques, including cold smoking with salt, which is a method of curing the fish without cooking it (in the usual sense) with heat. But the two hot-smoked, low-salt methods are the ones I prefer, and I urge you to use them.

FOOD PROCESSOR AND BLENDER

Many of the recipes in this book call for the use of one or the other of these tools. A food processor does more jobs well, like chopping and slicing as well as pureeing solids. A blender is superior for sauces and purees when the goal is to beat some air into the mixture or make the mixture silky smooth. By contrast, some processing chores are done better by hand or with a food mill. (If you've ever tried to make mashed potatoes in a food processor, you have a real sense of the word *glutinous*.) Where once there were just one or two decent brands of processors and blenders, now there are many. The important thing to look for when you shop for one or both of these pieces of equipment is sturdiness. With a food processor especially, once you get one, you're likely to use it all the time as long as you keep it handy and don't stash it away in a difficult-to-reach spot.

MICROWAVE OVEN

Microwaves, a form of energy similar to radio waves, work by agitating the molecules in food and creating heat through the resulting friction. That is why microwaves will pass through plastic without heating it, yet cook the moist food inside the container. Microwave ovens range in power and size. The power might be as low as 400 watts or higher than 700. For some seafood cooking, the difference in cooking time between a low-power and a high-power oven is minimal, perhaps seconds. In larger-volume dishes (a sizable whole fish with several vegetables or a sauce, for instance), the difference in time can be several minutes. So it makes sense to purchase an oven with more power rather than less, but it certainly isn't mandatory since I have successfully prepared excellent fish dishes in my first, now-almost-antique microwave oven—a little, low-power job.

GRILLS

A gas grill is a spectacular implement for cooking seafood outdoors. After decades of fussing with charcoal, I fell in love with the control, flexibility, ease, and neatness of cooking with gas-fired lava or ceramic briquets. Also, since seafood cooks so quickly, it's irksome to sit around waiting longer for the charcoal to get ready than for the food to cook. A gas grill generates a lot of heat after a warm-up of just a few minutes. But if you're happy with a charcoal grill, there's no reason not to use it. Charcoal proponents say that you never get the same flavor from gas-heated briquets, but I find that nicely marinated fish, seared on the gas grill, is as wonderful as fish needs to get. Just as there are advantages to getting a more powerful microwave oven, the gas grills that generate the most heat will sear that salmon steak and everything else better and faster.

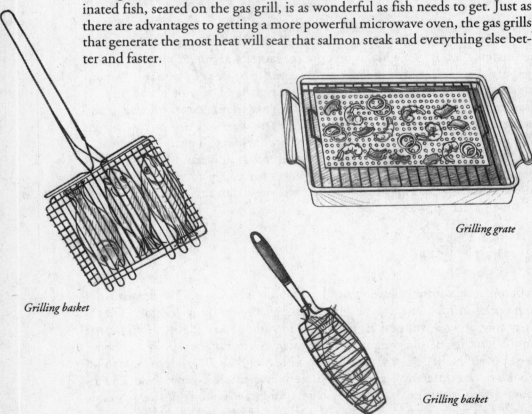

Grilling grate

Grilling basket

Grilling basket

Grilling has generated an industry of clever tools and other paraphernalia. There are four items I want to mention here that are especially handy for fish cookery. An oval grilling basket, hinged at one end, is ideal for grilling a fish and turning it on the grill without breaking the fish. The basket should be heated on the grill first, then removed from the heat (carefully and with pot holders), and sprayed with oil just before placing the fish in it. A grilling grate is a kind of tray with holes in it that sits on top of the grill; it is what you need for small pieces of seafood like shrimp that would otherwise fall through the spaces in the grill rack. Skewers, wood or metal, each have their advocates. The wooden ones are more fragile and need to be soaked for about 20 minutes so that they will not burn (it also helps to wrap bits of aluminum foil around the ends for the same reason). But they are inexpensive, and I prefer them because they are less likely to break up the pieces of fish or impart a metallic flavor to the food. Slender metal skewers, however, do hold bits of fish and vegetables well and last forever. They are also frequently sold these days as part of a nifty kit called a kebab rack, a notched frame that holds the skewers in its notches and allows you to rotate the kebabs easily. Finally, I recommend a broad or elongated spatula to simplify the turning of fish steaks or small whole fish that are not placed in a grilling basket.

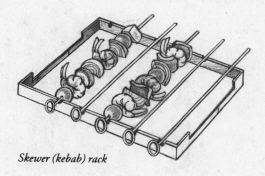

Skewer (kebab) rack

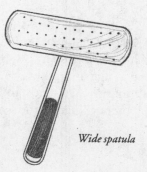

Wide spatula

SMALL FAVORITES

LEMON SQUEEZER OR REAMER One that separates pits from juice is handy. Even handier is one that sits over a measuring cup. If you doubt the need for this tool, take a look at the number of recipes in this book that call for lemon or lime juice, which in my view should always be freshly squeezed.

NEEDLE-NOSE PLIERS OR EYEBROW TWEEZERS Either of these is just the thing for pulling out the thin pinbones that are left behind after many fish have been filleted.

KITCHEN SCISSORS This tool has more uses than most people think, from removing fins to snipping herbs.

METAL SPATULA WITH AN EXTRA-LONG HEAD Turning a fish fillet or whole fish can be risky. This minimizes the danger.

SHRIMP PEELER This bizarre-looking, curved plastic or metal tool is sold through catalogues and in kitchen shops and fish stores. It slips under a shrimp's shell at the top and, with a single thrust, pulls the shell free of the shrimp (usually along with most of the vein). Until you get the knack of it, you are likely to mess up a few shrimp, but if you hate the time-consuming task of peeling shrimp, this inexpensive little tool is worth a try.

Needle-nose pliers

Shrimp peelers

TWO PEPPER MILLS Nearly every serious cook has one mill for freshly grinding black pepper. But many fish recipes call for white pepper, and white pepper that is freshly ground is far superior to the seasoning bought already ground that tends to sit around the kitchen for years losing flavor and potency. Hence, the second mill.

16
Where to Buy It

GRILL EQUIPMENT, HOME SMOKERS, AND WOOD CHIPS

Char-Broil
1037 Front Avenue
P.O. Box 1300
Columbus, GA 31993-2499
Phone: 800-241-8981 for credit-card orders
          404-324-5617 for customer service
Fax: 404-571-6088

A large selection of items: indoor and outdoor grills, stovetop smokers, slow smokers, grilling tools (including those specifically designed for seafood), and wood chips. This is where I found the metal smoker box for my gas grill. Orders are taken 7:00 A.M. to 8:00 P.M. eastern time, Monday through Friday, 8:30 A.M. to 5:00 P.M. Saturday, and 12:00 noon to 5:00 P.M. Sunday.

C.M. International
P.O. Box 60220
Colorado Springs, CO 80960
Phone: 719-390-0505

The Camerons stovetop smoker, made by C.M. International, is available in some kitchen supply stores, department stores, and catalogues, including Char-Broil's, above. If you can't locate one in your area, you can call for a free catalogue and order it directly from C.M. International. The company, by the way, also sells a good selection of wood chips.

Charcoal Companion
7955 Edgewater Drive
Oakland, CA 94621
Phone: 800-521-0505
             510-632-2100 in California
Fax: 510-632-1986

Here is a source for wood chips. Call for a free catalogue or to place an order between 8:30 A.M. and 5:00 P.M. Pacific time.

Luhr Jensen & Sons, Inc.
P.O. Box 297
Hood River, OR 97031
Phone: 800-535-1711
             503-386-3811 in Oregon

This company produces wood chips for smoking. A catalogue costs $3, redeemable with a first order of $20 or more. Call between 7:30 A.M. and 4:00 P.M. Pacific time.

KITCHEN EQUIPMENT, INCLUDING FISH POACHERS AND STEAMERS

The Chef's Catalog
3215 Commercial Avenue
Northbrook, IL 60062
Phone: 800-338-3232 for credit-card orders
             800-967-2433 for customer service

Orders are taken every day, 24 hours a day. Customer service is available Monday through Friday, 9:00 A.M. to 5:00 P.M. central time.

Community Kitchens
1 Community Coffee Place
Ridgely, MD 21685
Phone: 800-535-9901

Orders are taken every day, 7:00 A.M. to 12:00 midnight eastern time. Items are shipped within 48 hours.

Williams-Sonoma/The Pottery Barn
P.O. Box 7456
San Francisco, CA 94120-7456
Phone: 800-541-2233

Williams-Sonoma and The Pottery Barn, separate stores owned by the same parent company, are both good sources of high-quality pots, pans, and other cooking supplies. Williams-Sonoma offers high-end cookware, and The Pottery Barn focuses on less-expensive items. If you don't have these retail stores in your area, you can shop by catalogue. Orders are taken every day, 24 hours a day.

The Wooden Spoon
P.O. Box 931
Clinton, CT 06413
Phone: 800-431-2207

Orders are taken every day from 8:00 A.M. to 12:00 midnight eastern time, fall through spring. Summer hours are 8:00 A.M. to 10:00 P.M.

NONSTICK WOKS

Taylor & Ng
2919 Seventh Street
Berkeley, CA 94710
Phone: 510-849-1000

The Taylor & Ng line of nonstick cookware is sold in department and kitchenware stores across the country. If you can't find what you want in your area, Taylor & Ng does have a mail-order division. Call for a catalogue ($5) between 8:00 A.M. and 5:00 P.M. Pacific time, Monday through Friday.

MICROWAVE ACCESSORIES

Corning/Revere Consumer Information Center
P.O. Box 1994
Waynesboro, VA 22980
Phone: 800-999-3436

A large selection of microwave-safe cookware is offered by Corning. Their Microwave Plus line is made specifically for that purpose. For a free catalogue, call between 8:00 A.M. and 8:00 P.M. eastern time, Monday through Friday.

Ensar Corporation
135 East Hintz
Wheeling, IL 60090
Attn.: Customer Service

The source for a microwave fish cooker (a rectangular pan with rack and see-through lid) and other microwave-safe cookware. Write (do not call) their customer-service division to find out where their products are sold in your area.

PUBLICATIONS

Seafood Savvy by Ken Gall
Information Bulletin No. 104IB226
Cornell Cooperative Extension Publications
The Resource Center
7 Cornell Business and Technology Park
Ithaca, NY 14850
Phone: 607-255-2080 for credit-card orders

This booklet is devoted to the handling and preparation of fish. It is available for $4.95. Send a check for that amount to the above address, making sure to include the number and title of the booklet with your order.

Simply Seafood
1115 NW Forty-sixth Street
Seattle, WA 98107
Phone: 206-789-6506

A superb cooking magazine devoted exclusively to seafood and including information about seafood as well as its preparation. A subscription to the quarterly publication costs $8.95 per year in the United States. Issues can be found at some newsstands and fish markets.

SHRIMP TOOLS

The shrimp peeler/deveiner is an inexpensive item that can be found in many kitchenware stores and seafood markets. One common brand, the Zipout, is made of plastic, and Williams-Sonoma sells a metal one with a handle called the Shrimp-Peel.

THERMOMETERS

Instant-read thermometers for testing the doneness of fish and good-quality refrigerator-freezer and oven thermometers are widely available in kitchenware shops and good department stores. A major producer is Taylor.

ASIAN INGREDIENTS

Many cities across the country have Japanese, Chinese, and Vietnamese grocery stores, and ingredients for Chinese and Japanese-style dishes are often sold in better supermarkets and health-food stores. But if you cannot find the items you need, you can order them by mail. Here are a couple of sources.

Oriental Food Market and Cooking School
2801 West Howard Street
Chicago, IL 60645
Phone: 312-274-2826

The $2 charge for the catalogue will be deducted from the first order.

Oriental Market
502 Pampa Drive
Austin, TX 78752
Phone: 512-453-9058

The catalogue lists only a fraction of what is available from the company. Be sure to ask for anything you don't see in it.

FISH-BROTH CUBES

Knorr brand can be found in most supermarkets. Williams-Sonoma sells dehydrated fish bouillon in packets.

LEAN SAUSAGES

Many supermarkets now carry reduced-fat sausages, the leanest of which are generally made from turkey rather than pork or beef. Try, for example, the Healthy Choice brand. However, there are also at least two mail-order sources.

North Country Smokehouse
P.O. Box 1415
Claremont, NH 03743
Phone: 800-258-4304

Lean smoked sausages, including hot Italian and andouille sausages, smoked turkey, chicken, ham, and other items are produced here. Perishable items are shipped for second-day delivery to assure freshness.

Williams-Sonoma
P.O. Box 7456
San Francisco, CA 94120-7456
Phone: 800-541-2233

A variety of lean sausages, including chicken-and-apple, chicken-and-turkey with sun-dried tomatoes, smoked turkey, and turkey-herb are available only through the catalogue. Phone orders are taken every day, 24 hours a day. Note, however, that sausage orders take 4 to 6 weeks to be filled.

PASTA

Morisi's Macaroni Store
647 Fifth Avenue
Brooklyn, NY 11215
Phone: 718-499-0146

Carrying on a three-generation family business, John Peter Morisi continues to invent fabulous pastas in a host of shapes and flavors. More than 200 varieties are sold. A mail-order catalogue is available. Holiday baskets as well as individual orders of varietal pastas can be shipped anywhere in the United States. To place orders, call between 8:00 A.M. and 5:00 P.M. eastern time, Monday through Friday. Allow 2 to 4 weeks for processing and delivery.

SEEDS FOR GROWING HERBS AND VEGETABLES

Burpee Gardens
W. Atlee Burpee & Co.
300 Park Avenue
Warminster, PA 18974
Phone: 215-674-9633

One of several traditionally reliable sources of seeds, Burpee produces an annual catalogue and accepts credit-card orders by phone Monday through Saturday between 9:00 A.M. and 5:00 P.M. eastern time.

Shepherd's Garden Seeds
30 Irene Street
Torrington, CT 06790
Phone: 203-482-3638
     and
6116 Highway 9
Felton, CA 95081
Phone: 408-335-2080

A selection of excellent seeds, both common and exotic, along with detailed growing instructions are available through an annual catalogue. Credit-card orders are accepted between 9:00 A.M. and 6:00 P.M. (in their respective time zones) Monday through Friday. During the busy season, from January to May, Shepherd's is open until 9:00 P.M. during the week and 9:00 A.M. to 6:00 P.M. on Saturdays.

SMOKED FISH

Ducktrap River Fish Farm, Inc.
57 Little River Drive
Belfast, ME 04915
Phone: 800-828-3825
           207-338-6280

If Ducktrap River smoked fish products are not available at your supermarket, you can get them through the mail. They have nine products, among them smoked mackerel and trout as well as the more common smoked salmon. Call for their brochure.

SPICES AND HERBS

Penzeys' Spice House
P.O. Box 1448
Waukesha, WI 53187
Phone: 414-574-0277

Bulk spices, herbs, seeds, and seasoning mixes are detailed in a large catalogue.

Paula Winchester
Herb Gathering
5742 Kenwood
Kansas City, MO 64110
Phone: 816-523-2653

In addition to dried seasonings, this company sells fresh herbs and herb vinegars.

17

About the Ingredients

Every cook and cookbook author not only has his or her own name for certain ingredients, but an individual way of interpreting ingredients lists. To avoid confusion, I am providing you with the following explanations of potentially misunderstood ingredients.

BLACK AND WHITE PEPPER I specify "freshly ground" because the flavor is much more intense. Anyone who does a fair amount of cooking should consider investing in two pepper mills: one for black peppercorns, the other for white. If you use commercially ground pepper, you may need to use more than the recipes call for.

BREAD CRUMBS I always indicate "fresh" or "dried." Fresh crumbs are made from fresh bread, although they are best made from bread that is a day or two old. Dried crumbs can be made from stale bread or from fresh bread that has been toasted in a slow oven (about 200°F) until the bread has lost all its moisture and is crisp. Or you can lightly toast fresh bread crumbs until they dry out.

CHOPPED OR MINCED HERBS This always means starting with the fresh herb. If dried herbs are an acceptable substitute, the recipe will say so.

CILANTRO Aliases include coriander leaves, fresh coriander, and Chinese parsley. All refer to the pungent herb that, in appearance only, resembles Italian (flat-leaf) parsley (and, to add to the confusion, is usually sold next to parsley). If you are not certain that you are selecting the right herb, smell it or taste one leaf before you purchase the bunch.

DIJON-STYLE MUSTARD I use Grey Poupon brand, which is widely available. But other brands will do.

DRIED HERBS When they are offered as an alternative to fresh herbs, crushing them a bit in a mortar with a pestle or rubbing them between your fingers will enhance their flavor.

FISH BROTH This is also known as fish stock. Homemade broth is preferable (see the recipe on page 179), particularly when it is a main ingredient, as in a soup. But you can also use reconstituted broth made by dissolving Knorr fish-flavored bouillon cubes in boiling water. Or try the dehydrated fish bouillon sold by Williams-Sonoma.

GARLIC Always use fresh garlic. Except in recipes calling for dried seasoning mixes such as cajun seasoning, *never* substitute garlic powder or garlic salt for garlic. Commercially minced or chopped garlic can be used once in a while, but do not make it a habit.

ITALIAN PARSLEY I am referring here to flat-leaf parsley, which has a more intense flavor than the more commonly available curly parsley. However, you can always use curly parsley if that is all you can get.

LEMON AND LIME JUICE Throughout this book, I specify "fresh," which means "freshly squeezed." The bottled kind is a poor facsimile even though it is prepared from the real thing. A reasonable alternative to freshly squeezed juice is to squeeze lemons and limes when they are plentiful and freeze the juice in tiny jars such as the jelly jars one gets in restaurants and on room-service trays. With the cap removed, the juice can be rapidly defrosted as needed in a microwave oven, or it will defrost in about 20 minutes if it is left out at room temperature.

OLIVE OIL This *must* be fresh. Discard oil that smells even a little rancid since it will give your recipe an off flavor. In dressings and marinades, I usually use the darker extra-virgin olive oil since it has the richest flavor. But in cooking (for example, in sautéing onions), the less-expensive, lighter-colored light olive oil will do.

RED PEPPER FLAKES Also known as crushed red pepper, this ingredient refers to the flakes of dried hot chili peppers and is usually available in the spice section of food markets.

RICE VINEGAR Rice vinegar is sometimes called rice-wine vinegar; the two, however, are the same. Seasoned rice vinegar—rice vinegar commercially prepared with added flavorings—is used to prepare the rice for sushi.

SCALLIONS These are sometimes called spring onions or green onions (even though the scallion bulb is as white as new-fallen snow).

SESAME OIL In this book, sesame oil always refers to the dark Asian variety, which is pressed from *toasted* seeds, not the light-colored kind often sold in health-food stores.

TABASCO SAUCE This is the most popular brand of hot pepper sauce. You can substitute other brands, if you choose.

RECIPES

Why No Nutritional Data with My Recipes?

Throughout my professional life, I have been a science and health journalist trained to present information with precision. I have found that much of the nutritional data accompanying recipes these days provide only the illusion of precision. Although a number of readers have requested that I add these data at the end of each recipe, I have refused—and with good reason. It is not possible to provide accurate counts of either calories or fat grams for most recipes; I have seen too many inaccuracies both in computation and in underlying assumptions.

A common source of error is that all the ingredients in a recipe are not necessarily consumed. Much depends on how well a food is trimmed, how much fat is skimmed off or rinsed away, and so forth. With seafood, fat content varies with the season, the temperature of the water in which the fish is caught, whether it is a wild variety or farm-raised, the age of the fish, even the sex of the fish, and where on the fish the portion is cut. And I have yet to see an analysis that takes into account the salt and oil left behind in the water used to cook pasta or the oil used in a marinade that stayed behind in the dish or that burned away during the grilling process. So recipes that list nutritional content in exact numbers are close to meaningless to the person sitting down to a seafood meal.

And just as I deplore the rigidity involved in "dieting," I have always urged people to avoid eating by number. My message is (and always has been) that a well-balanced diet that is low in fat will also be a healthful diet. And if we kill the joy of eating by subjecting it to too much dogma, too many formulas, and interminable calculations, then the powerful movement toward good nutrition will be jeopardized. A calculator may be handy when you are balancing your checkbook, but, as far as I'm concerned, it has no place at the dinner table.

Hors d'Oeuvres and Appetizers: Off to a Grand Start

My favorite foods at parties are hors d'oeuvres. I love sampling a variety of edibles, all the more so if they are nutritionally good as well as good-tasting. More often than not, though, hors d'oeuvres fail nutritionally due to a super-abundance of fatty ingredients. Not so in this book. Isn't it time to abandon the traditional cheese and crackers and fatty chips and dips? At dinner parties, when the hors d'oeuvres are good-tasting and interesting, it always seems that the gathering gets off to an especially warm and friendly start. So it stands to reason that I would pay lots of attention to the hors d'oeuvres and first courses in this book. (In addition to first courses in this section, a number of the entrées can also serve as meal openers, as indicated in the serving yields.)

PICKLED SHRIMP

■

At a celebration of wine and food in San Diego, I unabashedly devoured these marvelous shrimp. With the help of friend and gourmet cook Edie Greenberg of La Jolla, I secured the recipe, compliments of Lois Stanton of Del Mar, California.

Preparation tips: A delicious variation is to use HALF SHRIMP AND HALF SCALLOPS. It is best to cook the shrimp in small batches in order to avoid overcooking some of them. Have a bowl of ice water ready to chill them. Prepare the dish at least 4 hours (or up to 48 hours) before serving it to allow enough pickling time. Toss the mixture several times during the pickling process.

Serving suggestions: Serve the shrimp as an hors d'oeuvre in a shallow bowl with toothpicks, or, for a first course, place the shrimp on individual plates that have been lined with lettuce.

SHRIMP

3½ to 4 pounds MEDIUM OR LARGE
　　SHRIMP, peeled and deveined
　3 large white onions, halved
　　lengthwise and thinly sliced
　　crosswise
　9 bay leaves

DRESSING

　⅔ cup white-wine vinegar
　⅓ cup extra-virgin olive oil
　5 teaspoons celery seeds
　2 teaspoons coarse (kosher) salt

1. Bring a large pot of water to a rolling boil. Add about ½ pound of the shrimp to the pot, and cook them over high heat for 2 minutes or until they just turn pink and opaque. Immediately remove the shrimp from the pot with a large slotted spoon, and transfer them to a bowl of ice water to stop the cooking process. Keeping the water boiling, cook the rest of the shrimp in ½-pound batches in the same manner.

2. After all the shrimp have been cooked, place one-quarter of the shrimp in a layer in a large glass bowl, then one-third of the onions, and one-third of the bay leaves. Repeat the layering process two more times, and top the final layer with the remaining shrimp.

3. In a measuring cup or jar, combine all of the dressing ingredients thoroughly. Pour the dressing over the shrimp mixture in the bowl. Cover the bowl tightly, and refrigerate it for at least 4 hours and up to 48 hours. Toss the mixture from time to time to redistribute the ingredients. Before serving the shrimp, remove and discard the bay leaves. ■

STEAMED SHRIMP

■

10 TO 12 SERVINGS

These shrimp have been a long-standing hit with my guests and family. They are perfect finger-food hors d'oeuvres for fat-conscious eaters because they have no added fat. I thank Nina Simonds and *Gourmet* magazine for making this contribution to my repertoire long before low-fat cooking became popular.

SHRIMP

1 1/2 **pounds** LARGE SHRIMP
  4 **scallions, cut into 1-inch lengths**
  4 **quarter-sized slices gingerroot**
  2 **tablespoons dry sherry**
 3/4 **teaspoon salt**

DIPPING SAUCE

1 1/2 **tablespoons dry mustard (can include 1/2 teaspoon or more hot dry mustard)**
  3 **tablespoons hot water**
  2 **teaspoons dry sherry**
  1 **teaspoon soy sauce**

1. Peel the shrimp, leaving the last section and tail in place. Devein the shrimp, rinse and drain them, and place them in a large bowl.
2. Flatten the scallions and gingerroot by pounding down with your fist on the flat side of a butcher knife or cleaver that has been placed on top of the ingredients. Place the scallions and gingerroot in a small bowl, and add the 2 tablespoons of sherry. Remove the scallions and gingerroot from the bowl, squeezing them over the bowl to extract their juices. Discard the pieces. Add the salt to the sherry, stirring the ingredients until the salt is dissolved. Pour the flavored sherry over the shrimp, and toss the mixture well. Cover the bowl with plastic wrap, and refrigerate the shrimp for 30 minutes or longer.
3. To prepare the dipping sauce, place the dry mustard in a small bowl, and stir in the hot water and the 2 teaspoons of sherry. Let the mixture stand for 10 minutes.
4. While the sauce thickens, arrange the shrimp on a heatproof platter or steamer rack, place the platter or rack in a steamer to which water has been added, and bring the water to a boil. Cover the steamer, and steam the shrimp over the boiling water for 3 minutes. Remove the steamer from the heat, and let the shrimp stand, covered, for another 30 seconds. Remove the shrimp from the steamer to a serving platter.
5. Add the soy sauce to the mustard mixture, and serve the dipping sauce with the shrimp, which can be eaten hot or at room temperature. ■

SPICY SHRIMP

■

This is a wake-up-the-taste-buds appetizer, the hotness of which can be adjusted to taste. Don't be intimidated by the number of ingredients—they're nearly all seasonings. The dish takes only minutes to prepare.

Preparation tips: The recipe can be prepared 1 to 2 days ahead and the shrimp refrigerated in their sauce until shortly before serving. The leftover sauce can be used to prepare a tangy tomato sauce for pasta or rice, or it can be used in a soup that has a tomato base.

Serving suggestion: To temper the hotness of the shrimp, I serve them on round slices of raw zucchini and surround them with steamed broccoli flowerets and cherry tomatoes. The result is an hors d'oeuvre platter that is eye-catching and tasty as well as low in calories.

> 1 **pound** MEDIUM TO LARGE SHRIMP (24 to 32)
> 1 **teaspoon dried basil**
> 1/2 **teaspoon dried oregano**
> 1/2 **teaspoon dried thyme leaves**
> 1 **tablespoon olive oil** *or* **canola oil**
> 2 **teaspoons minced garlic**
> 1 **teaspoon white-wine Worcestershire sauce**
> 2 **tablespoons tomato paste**
> 1/2 **cup dry white wine**
> 1/2 **teaspoon freshly ground black pepper**
> 1/2 **teaspoon salt, or to taste**
> 1/2 **teaspoon cayenne, or to taste**
> 1/2 **teaspoon red pepper flakes, or to taste**

1. Peel the shrimp, leaving the last section and tail in place. Devein the shrimp, if desired, rinse them, and set them aside.
2. Combine the basil, oregano, and thyme in a mortar or heavy bowl, and crush them. Set the herb mixture aside.
3. Briefly heat the olive oil or canola oil in a 3-quart saucepan or deep skillet, add the garlic, and sauté the garlic for 30 seconds.
4. Add to the pan or skillet the Worcestershire sauce, tomato paste, and white wine, stirring the ingredients. Then add the reserved herb mixture and the ground pepper, salt, cayenne, and red pepper flakes. Stir the ingredients to combine them well, and bring the mixture to a boil.

5. Add the reserved shrimp, tossing the shrimp to coat them well with the mixture. Cook the shrimp over medium heat, tossing them occasionally, for 3 minutes or until they turn pink. Remove the pan or skillet from the heat, and, when the shrimp have cooled, refrigerate them in their sauce, taking them out of the refrigerator about 20 minutes before serving them (see "Serving suggestion"). ■

Shrimp

GREEK SHRIMP

A Greek friend, Bill Kutmus of Des Moines, was coming for the weekend, and I decided to welcome him with a meal that would recall his origins. This first course, made with a Greek staple, feta, was such a success that his wife Bonnie said she couldn't wait for the book to be published—she had to have the recipe "now."

Preparation tips: The tomato sauce can be made well in advance, even prepared and frozen for future use. Soak the feta in cold water for 20 to 30 minutes to reduce its saltiness. Greek Shrimp is also wonderful as a topping for pasta—just double the recipe for the sauce. If you have access to scallop shells or small, shallow, ovenproof dishes, you can make individual servings.

SAUCE

- 1 tablespoon olive oil
- 1 medium onion *or* 4 shallots, finely chopped
- 2 teaspoons minced garlic
- 1 16-ounce can tomatoes, drained and juice reserved, chopped
- 2 tablespoons tomato paste
- 1/4 cup chopped fresh parsley
- 2 tablespoons chopped fresh basil
- 1/2 teaspoon salt (optional)

Freshly ground black pepper to taste

SHRIMP

- 1 1/2 pounds MEDIUM-LARGE SHRIMP (about 30), peeled and deveined
- 1 tablespoon fresh lemon juice
- 1/2 pound feta, soaked, drained, and crumbled
- 1 to 2 tablespoons chopped fresh parsley for garnish (optional)

TO PREPARE THE SAUCE

1. Briefly heat the oil in a nonstick skillet that has a lid. Add the onion or shallots, and sauté the vegetable for 2 minutes. Add the garlic, and sauté the vegetables 1 minute longer. Add the remaining sauce ingredients, including the juice from the tomatoes, and stir the ingredients to combine them. Bring the mixture to a boil over medium heat, reduce the heat to low, and simmer the sauce for about 20 minutes. If too much liquid seems to be evaporating, cover the skillet for part of the simmering time.

TO PREPARE THE SHRIMP

2. Heat the oven to 350°F.
3. Place the shrimp in a bowl or on a plate, and sprinkle them with the lemon juice.

4. To assemble the dish, pour about half the sauce into the bottom of a lightly greased shallow baking dish, or divide it among individual baking shells or dishes. Arrange the shrimp in a single layer over the sauce, and pour the remaining sauce over the shrimp. Sprinkle the feta over the top layer of sauce.

5. Place the shrimp in the oven, and bake the dish for 15 to 20 minutes or until the shrimp are just cooked and the cheese has melted. Remove the shrimp from the oven, and sprinkle the dish with the 1 to 2 tablespoons of chopped parsley (if desired). ■

SMOKED SHRIMP WITH RÉMOULADE
■

4 TO 6 SERVINGS

When I first saw these shrimp, I couldn't help blurting out, "Oh, how cute they are!"—neatly curled, bronzed little guys, still wearing their tails. In fact, they are more than cute; they are beautiful, and their smoked flavor is such a change of pace that you will have to keep your guests from eating more than their share. At least that's what happened at my table. I had to remind everyone—emphatically—that there was more food coming.

Preparation tip: It's always a good idea to buy 2 or 3 extra shrimp so that you can remove one during the cooking process and test it for doneness. When you slice into it, look for an even, white coloration throughout. But you must guard against drying out the shrimp by overcooking them.

SAUCE
- 2 tablespoons chopped fresh parsley
- 1 tablespoon minced gherkins
- 1 tablespoon fresh lemon juice
- 1 tablespoon Dijon-style mustard
- 1 teaspoon anchovy paste
- ¼ cup nonfat or low-fat plain yogurt
- ¼ cup nonfat or reduced-fat mayonnaise

Salt to taste
Freshly ground black pepper to taste

SHRIMP
- 2 teaspoons canola oil
- 1 teaspoon minced garlic
- 1 tablespoon fresh lemon juice
- 12 JUMBO SHRIMP (about ¾ pound), peeled with the tails left on and deveined

Vegetable-oil spray

1. Combine all the ingredients for the sauce in a small bowl, and whisk them until they are well blended. Cover the bowl, and refrigerate the sauce until serving time.
2. In a medium-sized mixing bowl, prepare the marinade for the shrimp by blending the oil, garlic, and lemon juice. Add the shrimp, and coat them thoroughly with the marinade. Cover the bowl, and marinate the shrimp in the refrigerator for 20 minutes.
3. Prepare a home smoker according to the manufacturer's directions, place the shrimp in the smoker on a rack sprayed with vegetable oil, and smoke the shrimp. (With the Camerons smoker that I use [see page 106], the shrimp required 12 minutes of stovetop cooking.)
4. To assemble the dish, line the shrimp around the periphery of an attractive platter, their bodies facing in the same direction and their tails point-

ing to the outer rim of the platter. In the center of the platter, place a small bowl of the rémoulade sauce for dipping. ■

HONEYDEW AND SHRIMP SALAD
■   HORS D'OEUVRES FOR 12 OR 8 FIRST-COURSE SERVINGS

Fruit and shrimp go together well. Simplicity itself, this dish can be served on toothpicks (one shrimp and one melon ball per) as an hors d'oeuvre or in dessert dishes on a bed of tangy greens as a first course.

Preparation tip: If you are starting with raw, shell-on shrimp, buy about 48 medium shrimp, peel and, if desired, devein them, and cook them in salted water for about 2 minutes. Chill them immediately.

SALAD
- 1 **medium ripe honeydew, halved lengthwise and seeded**
- 1¼ **pounds COOKED MEDIUM SHRIMP**
- 2 **tablespoons fresh lemon juice**
- **Tangy greens for garnish (for example, arugula or watercress)**

DRESSING
- ½ **cup nonfat or low-fat ricotta**
- 6 **tablespoons buttermilk**
- 1 **teaspoon white-wine vinegar or fresh lemon juice**
- 2 **to 3 tablespoons snipped fresh dill to taste**
- ¼ **teaspoon salt**
- ⅛ **teaspoon freshly ground black pepper**

1. Using a melon baller, scoop out balls of honeydew, and place them in a large bowl. Add the shrimp and the 2 tablespoons of lemon juice, tossing the ingredients to combine them. Refrigerate the mixture until serving time.
2. To make the dressing, add the ricotta and buttermilk to a blender, and puree them. Then add the vinegar or lemon juice, dill, salt, and pepper. Process the mixture for a few seconds at the lowest speed. About 1 hour before serving, remove the melon and shrimp from the refrigerator, and pour the dressing over the mixture, tossing the ingredients to combine them well. Return the salad to the refrigerator.
3. If you are serving this appetizer as a first course, place the greens around the edge of individual small bowls, and, with a slotted spoon, pile the melon-shrimp mixture in the middle of each bowl. If you are serving this dish as an hors d'oeuvre, spear one melon ball and one shrimp on each toothpick, and place the spears on a platter over a bed of the greens. ■

SHRIMP IN EGG CUPS

■

24 HORS D'OEUVRES

It was Easter Sunday, and I was expecting friends for dinner. Easter brings to mind eggs, a tradition in my husband's family, and that in turn reminded me of my long-unused deviled-egg dish—you know the kind, with egg-shaped depressions to hold a dozen stuffed egg halves. Since I have placed yolks on my "rarely" list, I decided to hard-boil a dozen eggs, setting the yolks aside for my spaniel, Max, who, unlike humans, is a true carnivore and does not respond negatively to high-cholesterol foods. Then I devised this colorful and tasty way to stuff the whites.

Preparation tips: Keep in mind that avocado blackens upon long exposure to air, so do not cut it up until shortly before serving time. You can, however, prepare the rest of the dish in advance and even stuff the whites with everything but the avocado. Keep the eggs covered and chilled, and add the avocado within an hour or two of serving time. You can, if you choose, use a commercially prepared cocktail sauce instead of making one.

MAIN INGREDIENTS

12 large eggs
Salt for boiling eggs
24 COOKED, peeled MEDIUM SHRIMP (about $1/2$ pound)
$1/2$ avocado, cut into 1-inch strips

SAUCE

$1/2$ cup strained tomatoes, *or* $1/4$ cup chili sauce and $1/4$ cup ketchup, *or* $1/4$ cup chili sauce and $1/4$ cup canned tomato sauce
2 tablespoons drained horseradish (1 tablespoon if using chili sauce)
2 teaspoons fresh lemon juice
$1/4$ teaspoon Worcestershire sauce
$1/4$ teaspoon Tabasco sauce, or to taste
$1/4$ teaspoon salt (omit if using ketchup or tomato sauce)
$1/4$ teaspoon sugar (omit if using ketchup)

1. Place the eggs in a large saucepan with a lid, and add enough water to cover them. Add about 2 tablespoons of salt to the water to keep the eggs from cracking. Bring the water slowly to a boil, reduce the heat, partially cover the pan, and gently boil the eggs for 15 minutes. Immediately rinse the eggs under cold running water, and set them aside to cool completely. When they are cool enough to handle, carefully peel them to avoid tearing the whites. Slice the eggs in half lengthwise, remove the yolks, and discard the yolks or reserve them for your own or your neighbor's dog (the yolks can be frozen).

2. While the eggs are cooking, combine all the ingredients for the sauce in a small bowl. When the egg-white halves are ready, place about ½ teaspoon of the sauce in the center of each egg half. Lay one shrimp, tail up and aligned toward the narrower part of the egg white, and one strip of avocado in each egg half. Arrange the eggs on a serving platter, cover the platter, and chill the egg cups until serving time. ■

SEAFOOD TABBOULI

■

8 OR MORE SERVINGS

With a luxuriant crop of Italian (flat-leaf) parsley growing on my deck, I was inspired to prepare this tangy treat for summer dinner guests. The hard part was tearing them away from the hors d'oeuvre to get them to the dinner table. Surprisingly, the leftover tabbouli (which I refrigerated, of course) remained delicious for several days, though the spiciness subsided somewhat and the accumulated liquid needed to be drained off.

Preparation tips: The tabbouli can be prepared in advance, with the dressing and the seafood added about 1 hour before serving time. If desired, instead of boiling water, you can use heated Spicy Hot V8 or Bloody Mary mix to soften the bulgur, in which case you should omit the Tabasco sauce and tomato paste in the dressing.

MAIN INGREDIENTS
- ½ cup bulgur, preferably fine-grain
- 1 cup boiling water (see "Preparation tips")
- ½ pound CALICO SCALLOPS *or* BAY SCALLOPS
- 1 cup chopped fresh parsley, preferably Italian (flat-leaf)
- 2 tablespoons chopped cilantro (optional)
- 1 cup seeded, chopped tomatoes
- ¼ cup chopped scallions
- ¼ pound COOKED SALAD (TINY) SHRIMP
- 8 sandwich-sized pitas, preferably whole-wheat, quartered

DRESSING
- ¼ cup fresh lemon juice
- 2 tablespoons olive oil
- 2 tablespoons tomato paste
- 1 tablespoon anchovy paste
- ⅛ to ¼ teaspoon Tabasco sauce, to taste
- ¼ to ⅜ teaspoon freshly ground black pepper, to taste
- ¼ teaspoon salt (optional)

1. Place the bulgur in a heatproof bowl. Add the boiling water, and let the bulgur stand for 30 minutes.
2. In a medium-sized saucepan, bring salted water to a boil. Add the scallops, lower the heat, and simmer the scallops for 2 minutes. Drain them immediately, and set them aside to cool.
3. Pour the bulgur into a colander lined with several layers of cheesecloth or a cotton kitchen towel. Gathering the ends of the cloth or towel together, squeeze out all the liquid from the bulgur. Place the bulgur in a large bowl.

4. To the bulgur, add the parsley, cilantro (if desired), tomatoes, and scallions, and toss the ingredients to combine them well. Set the bulgur mixture aside.

5. In a bowl or small jar that has a tight-fitting lid, add all the dressing ingredients. Whisk or shake the dressing ingredients, and add them to the bulgur mixture, tossing the mixture to coat it evenly with the dressing.

6. Add the reserved cooked scallops and the shrimp to the bulgur mixture, and toss it again gently. Serve the tabbouli with the wedges of pita. ■

Bay scallop

Shrimp

MUSSELS ON THE HALF SHELL WITH AVOCADO SALSA

■

ABOUT 50 HORS D'OEUVRES

Mussel shells are ideal hors d'oeuvre containers, holding a mouthful of food in an attractive black casing. Here, I use mussels steamed open in the microwave oven and served with a coverlet of a guacamole-like salsa.

Preparation tips: The total amount of mussels you will need for this dish will depend on their size. Ask the fishmonger to select the smallest ones. If, for example, you buy small wild mussels, there will be about 25 per pound; with cultured mussels, you may get only 16. Instead of using the microwave oven as described below, you can steam the mussels open in the conventional way—in a heavy pot with perhaps 1/2 cup of wine, 2 teaspoons of minced garlic, and 1 tablespoon of minced shallot for added flavoring. Regardless of how the mussels are cooked, they can be prepared in advance, and the meats removed from the shells and kept chilled or even frozen for later use (also chill or freeze the shells). Then, within hours of serving, the (defrosted) mussel meats should be put back in their half shells and topped with the salsa. Although the finished hors d'oeuvres should be kept chilled, the flavor is best if they are allowed to come to room temperature before they are served.

MUSSELS
 55 **(approximately)** SMALL MUSSELS **(about 3 pounds)**

SALSA
 3/4 **cup finely diced firm but ripe avocado**
 1/4 **cup seeded, finely diced plum (Roma) tomato**
 3 **tablespoons finely chopped red onion**
 3 **tablespoons finely chopped cilantro**
 1 **tablespoon seeded, minced jalapeño (about 1 pepper)**
 2 **teaspoons fresh lime juice**
 1/4 **teaspoon salt**

1. Thoroughly rinse and debeard the mussels. Place half the mussels hinge side down in a glass baking dish or other microwave-safe container. Cover the dish with a microwave lid or with plastic wrap, turning back a small corner of the wrap to vent the steam. Microwave the mussels on high for 5 minutes or until they open. Remove the mussels from the dish with a slotted spoon, pour off the liquid (this can be strained through cheesecloth and frozen for later use), and repeat the process with the remaining mussels. Any mussels that did not open can be returned to the microwave oven for another minute. Discard any mussels that still have not opened.

2. When the cooked mussels are cool enough to handle, remove the meat from the shells, and save one-half of each shell for stuffing. (You may want to save the same half of all the shells so that they can be arranged attractively on a platter in pinwheel fashion.)

3. Prepare the salsa by combining all the salsa ingredients in a small bowl, stirring them gently to mix them well. Try to avoid mashing the avocado.

4. To assemble the hors d'oeuvres, place the meat of one mussel near the narrow end of a half shell. Place 1 level teaspoon of the salsa near the wider end of the shell, covering about half of the mussel meat with the salsa. Repeat the process with the remaining mussels and salsa, arranging the stuffed mussel shells in pinwheel fashion on a serving platter. ■

Mussels

SPANISH-STYLE MUSSELS

■

Sherry gives these mussels a Spanish flair. You could prepare the mussels as a main dish, but I prefer them as a first course, to be followed perhaps by a pasta or rice-based dish. The mussels are especially nice as a dinner-party appetizer because the sauce can be made well in advance and the mussels added 5 minutes before you are ready to serve the dish.

   1 cup diced celery, including some leaves
1$\frac{1}{3}$ cups diced onion
   4 rounded teaspoons minced garlic
   2 tablespoons slivered or sliced almonds, lightly toasted
 $\frac{1}{4}$ cup water *or* fish broth
   2 cups peeled, diced tomatoes
   3 dashes Tabasco sauce
 $\frac{1}{8}$ teaspoon ground coriander
Salt to taste (omit if using salted fish broth)
Freshly ground black pepper to taste
   3 dozen MUSSELS, rinsed well and debearded
   6 tablespoons dry sherry (optional)

1. Place the celery, onion, garlic, almonds, and water or broth in a large saucepan that has a wide bottom and tight-fitting lid. Cook the ingredients in the covered pan over medium heat for several minutes or until the onions are soft. Add the tomatoes, Tabasco sauce, coriander, salt, and pepper to the mixture, cover the pan, and simmer the ingredients for 5 minutes.
2. Add the mussels to the hot sauce, tossing them to coat them well. Cover the pan, and simmer the ingredients for 5 minutes or until the mussels have opened. Discard any mussels that do not open.
3. Serve the mussels in shallow bowls with some of the sauce, adding 1 tablespoon of sherry to each bowl (if desired). ■

OYSTERS OREGANATA

■

12 STUFFED OYSTERS (6 SERVINGS)

I have noticed more than once that people who are reluctant to eat whole oysters or clams, raw or cooked, find them delectable when these mollusks are chopped and mixed with other flavorful ingredients. And so I devised this oregano-flavored version of baked oysters on the half shell for people who were not seafood aficionados. They all loved it.

Preparation tips: The stuffing can be placed in any kind of seafood shell—oyster, large clam, scallop—or in a very shallow baking dish. In the latter case, serve the stuffing with a pâté knife and plain crackers or thin toasts and/or "spoons" made from sliced vegetables like carrots and celery. The stuffed shells can be prepared for baking 1 to 2 hours ahead and stored, covered with plastic wrap, in the refrigerator.

1½ cups RAW OYSTERS, very finely chopped
1½ cups dried bread crumbs
 2 ounces Canadian bacon, finely diced (about ⅓ cup)
¼ cup chopped fresh parsley
 2 teaspoons finely minced garlic
¾ teaspoon dried oregano
Freshly ground black pepper to taste
¼ cup grated Parmesan
12 half shells for stuffing (see "Preparation tips")

Oyster

1. Heat the oven to 400°F.
2. In a medium-sized bowl, combine all the ingredients *except the shells,* stirring the ingredients to mix them well.
3. Using a spoon, fork, or your fingers, divide the mixture among the 12 half shells, gently tamping down the stuffing to make it compact.
4. Place the stuffed shells on a baking sheet, put the sheet in the hot oven, and bake the shells for 10 minutes or until the tops begin to brown. Remove the oysters from the oven, and serve them immediately. (Make sure to provide small dishes and hors d'oeuvre forks.) ■

BAKED OYSTERS WITH SPINACH AND PARMESAN
■

Baked oysters are often prepared with several tablespoons of butter or heavy cream or both. That approach certainly makes for a sumptuous dish. But these days, as we aim for less fat, we're not only getting used to the cleaner taste of the ingredients, we're enjoying it more. These oysters, with their spinach-and-leek topping, aren't just healthy, they are memorable. The only cheese used, Parmesan, is a boon to today's cooks; it is not only relatively low in fat, but, since it packs a lot of flavor, a little goes a long way.

Preparation tip: Many fish shops will shuck the oysters for you, leave them attached to the half shell, and then neatly package them. If you opt to have that done, be sure to cook them soon after you get them home. For instructions on shucking live oysters, see page 77.

Coarse (kosher) salt (enough to form a bed in the baking dish)
16 OYSTERS ON THE HALF SHELL
10 ounces fresh spinach, thoroughly washed but not dried, tough stems removed
1 teaspoon butter
¼ cup chopped leeks, white part only (1 small leek)
¼ cup chopped celery
1 teaspoon fresh lemon juice
¼ cup chopped fresh parsley
Salt to taste
Freshly ground black pepper to taste
¼ cup grated Parmesan
¼ cup fresh bread crumbs
Vegetable-oil spray
Lemon wedges for garnish

1. Heat the oven to 425°F.
2. Into a baking dish large enough to hold all the oysters in a single layer, pour enough salt (to a depth of ¼ inch or so) to create a bed that will keep the oysters level. Place the oysters in the dish, cover the dish, and put it in the refrigerator.
3. Place the wet spinach in a covered saucepan, and cook the spinach until it wilts, about 3 minutes, stirring it once or twice. Drain the spinach in a colander, pressing it gently to remove the excess liquid. Chop the spinach, and set it aside.
4. In a medium-sized deep skillet or sauté pan with a nonstick surface, melt the butter over low heat, and add the leeks and celery. Cook the vegeta-

bles, stirring them, for 3 minutes or until they soften. Add the reserved spinach, the lemon juice, parsley, salt, and pepper to the skillet or pan, and continue to cook the ingredients, stirring them, for about 1 minute.

5. Remove the oysters from the refrigerator, and place an equal amount of the spinach mixture on each (from 1 teaspoon to 1 tablespoon, depending on how large the oysters are).

6. In a small bowl, combine the Parmesan and bread crumbs, and sprinkle this the mixture evenly over the tops of the oysters. Spray each oyster with vegetable oil.

7. Place the oysters in the hot oven, and bake them for 20 to 25 minutes; they should be nicely browned. Serve the oysters with the lemon wedges.

OCTOPUS APPETIZER

You may never have eaten octopus. Neither had I before I made this dish. And was it fun—both to prepare and to consume. And, yes, I had the nerve to serve it to company the first time and was delighted with my guests' response. When purchased raw, octopus is limp and slippery. But as soon as it hits boiling water, it curls up to resemble a pinkish cartoon version of the living animal. If it is available fresh in your area, it deserves at least one try in your kitchen. As an octopus novice, I was guided by the recipes in *Tapas: The Little Dishes of Spain* by Penelope Casas, whence this delightful dish was derived.

Preparation tips: Octopus can be frozen before or after it is cooked. To produce a tender seafood, octopus usually needs to be boiled for about 1 hour. It is wise to test a small piece after about 45 minutes and continue cooking the octopus if it is still not tender. But be careful because it can get mushy if it is overcooked. This appetizer may be prepared in advance through step 7, then baked just before serving time.

OCTOPUS

- 1 **pound RAW OCTOPUS, defrosted if frozen**
- 4 **quarts water**
- 2 **teaspoons canola oil**
- 1/2 **medium onion, peeled**
- 1 **bay leaf**
- 2 **sprigs parsley**
- 1 1/2 **teaspoons salt**
- 4 **peppercorns**

REMAINING INGREDIENTS

- 1/2 **pound potatoes, peeled and cut into 1/2-inch cubes**
- 1 **tablespoon olive oil**
- 1 **red bell pepper, finely diced**
- 1/2 **cup chopped onion**
- 2 **tablespoons minced garlic**
- 1 **teaspoon paprika**
- 1 **bay leaf**
- 1/2 **teaspoon salt, or to taste**
- 1/2 **cup frozen peas, thawed**
- **Greens for lining plates (optional)**

TO PREPARE THE OCTOPUS

1. Tenderize the octopus by gently pounding it with a mallet or by slapping it hard against the bowl of the sink about 10 times. Set the octopus aside.
2. Combine all the remaining ingredients under the octopus heading in a large pot that has a lid. Bring the ingredients to a boil, and add the reserved octopus. When the liquid returns to the boil, reduce the heat, cover the pot, and simmer the octopus for about 1 hour (see "Preparation tips") or until it is tender but not mushy.

3. Remove the octopus to a bowl. Strain the cooking liquid, *saving 1 cup of the liquid.* When the octopus is cool enough to handle, rub off its loose skin with your fingers, and cut the tentacles and body into 1-inch pieces. Place the octopus back in the bowl, and set the bowl aside.

TO PREPARE THE APPETIZER

4. Heat the oven to 350°F.

5. Place the 1 cup of reserved octopus cooking liquid in a small saucepan that has a lid. Add the potatoes, bring the ingredients to a boil, reduce the heat, cover the pan, and simmer the potatoes for 10 minutes or until they are just tender. *Do not drain the potatoes.*

6. In a nonstick skillet, heat the olive oil, add the red bell pepper, onion, and garlic, and sauté the vegetables over medium-low heat for 3 minutes or until the onion is tender.

7. Add the reserved octopus, and sauté the ingredients for another 1 to 2 minutes.

8. Remove the skillet from the heat, and add the paprika, bay leaf, the reserved potatoes and their cooking liquid, salt, and peas. Transfer the mixture to an ovenproof baking dish.

9. Place the dish in the hot oven, and bake the octopus in the uncovered dish for 15 minutes. To serve, remove the bay leaf, and divide the appetizer among 6 small plates lined with the greens (if desired). ■

Octopus

BAKED-CLAM APPETIZER

18 STUFFED CLAMS (6 SERVINGS)

Having been reared by a father who saved everything, I was a recycling enthusiast long before the flower children of the 1960s raised our consciousness about squandering resources and the country realized it had a monumental garbage crisis. So I have had clamshells (I boiled them to remove all traces of fishiness) in my cupboard for years, ready to use for this simple yet fancy-looking hors d'oeuvre. I even got to use my old deviled-egg dish to serve the clams buffet style.

Preparation tips: If you start with a dozen cherrystone clams, you can use their shells as the serving containers. The stuffed shells, covered with plastic wrap and refrigerated, can be prepared hours in advance for baking. If you already have a supply of clean shells for stuffing, this recipe can be made with canned minced clams (I use the Progresso brand or Gorton's).

3/4 cup MINCED CLAM MEAT (**from about 12 cherrystone clams**)
1/2 cup dried bread crumbs
1/4 cup grated Parmesan
1/4 cup finely chopped red bell pepper
 3 tablespoons finely chopped scallions
1/2 teaspoon freshly ground white pepper *or* black pepper
 1 tablespoon olive oil
18 small clamshell halves

1. Heat the oven to 375°F.
2. In a medium-sized bowl, combine all the ingredients *except the oil and clamshells,* tossing the ingredients with a fork to mix them thoroughly. Add the olive oil, and toss the mixture again to distribute the ingredients evenly.
3. With a fork or your fingers, divide the clam mixture among the shells, gently pressing it to compact it lightly.
4. Place the stuffed shells on a baking tray, place the tray in the hot oven, and bake the shells for 12 minutes or until the tops just begin to brown. Serve the baked clams immediately. ■

SURIMI AND SALSA DIP

■

ABOUT 2 CUPS

For every cook, there comes a time when he or she must rely on a dish prepared from ready-made ingredients that require no cooking. Here's one that takes only a few minutes to throw together and was a big cocktail-party hit.

Serving suggestion: This can be eaten with sturdy tortilla chips or plain crackers, but I prefer it spooned into mini-pitas.

$\frac{1}{2}$ **pound SURIMI STICKS (imitation crab legs)**
$\frac{1}{2}$ **cup mild *or* hot commercial salsa (chopped if chunky)**
$\frac{1}{4}$ **cup finely chopped onion**
  2 **tablespoons chopped cilantro, or to taste**
  2 **tablespoons chopped fresh parsley, preferably Italian (flat-leaf)**
  1 **tablespoon fresh lime juice**
  1 **teaspoon seeded, finely minced green chili *or* 1 tablespoon seeded, minced jalapeño (omit if using hot salsa)**
$\frac{1}{4}$ **teaspoon freshly ground black pepper (optional)**

1. Quarter the surimi sticks lengthwise, then cut them crosswise into $\frac{1}{4}$-inch dice. Place the surimi pieces in a medium-sized bowl.
2. Add the remaining ingredients to the bowl, stirring the mixture to combine the ingredients thoroughly. ■

TOMATOES STUFFED WITH ZUCCHINI-SCALLOP SALSA

■   32 HORS D'OEUVRES OR 8 SERVINGS

I tend to be one of those gardeners who assume that half their plants won't grow and so put in twice too many. Well, this time all eight of my plum tomato plants "took" and produced abundantly. This versatile, attractive invention was one way I found to put the tomatoes to good use.

Preparation tips: The tomato halves are best filled close to serving time. Be sure to drain the salsa first. In fact, you can make the salsa without the scallops several hours ahead of time and then drain it and use the liquid for poaching the scallops. If your scallops are on the large side, halve or quarter them before poaching them.

Serving suggestions: These stuffed tomatoes can be served as a first course (4 halves per person) on a bed of greens such as arugula or curly lettuce. Or the salsa can be made with ¾ cup of chopped tomatoes and served by itself (not stuffed in tomatoes) over leafy greens as a first-course salad. Or, if the scallops are diced, the salsa can be eaten with tortilla chips, crackers, or toasted wedges of pita.

  16 **small fresh plum (Roma) tomatoes**
   ¾ **cup diced, unpeeled zucchini (about ¼-inch dice)**
   ¼ **cup thinly sliced or chopped scallions, including some green tops**
   2 **or more tablespoons chopped cilantro, to taste**
   1 **tablespoon seeded, minced jalapeño**
   2 **tablespoons red-wine vinegar**
   1 **teaspoon olive oil**
   ¼ **teaspoon salt**
   1 **pound BAY SCALLOPS (see "Preparation tips")**
Leafy greens for serving (optional)

1. Slice off a thin disk from the stem ends of the tomatoes, and discard the disks. Halve the tomatoes lengthwise, and remove and *save the pulp*. Also, *save any tomato juices* in a 2-quart saucepan that has a lid. Place the tomato shells flesh side down on a platter lined with paper towels, and put the platter in the refrigerator.

2. Coarsely chop the reserved tomato pulp, and put it in a medium-sized bowl. Add all the remaining ingredients *except the scallops and leafy greens* to the tomato pulp, stirring the ingredients to combine them well. Cover the bowl with plastic wrap, and chill the mixture for about 2 hours.

3. Drain the vegetable mixture, catching the liquid in the saucepan with the tomato juice. Add the scallops to the saucepan, and bring the mixture to a boil. Reduce the heat, partially cover the pan, and poach the scallops for 2 minutes. Remove the scallops from the liquid with a slotted spoon, and set them aside to cool. When they are lukewarm, add them to the refrigerated vegetable mixture. Cover the mixture, and refrigerate it.

4. When you are ready to fill the reserved tomato shells, once again drain the salsa, this time discarding the liquid. Using a small spoon, fill the tomato shells with the salsa, and arrange the tomatoes stuffed side up on a serving platter or on 8 individual plates lined with the leafy greens (if desired). ∎

SCALLOP SEVICHE

■

I have eaten and prepared many versions of seviche, but I always come back to an adaptation of a recipe developed by my *New York Times* colleague and friend, the esteemed chef Pierre Franey. In seviche, raw fish is "cooked" in acid (lime juice). But since the fish is never heated, it is vital to start with sparkling fresh saltwater seafood that comes from a reliable merchant.

Preparation tips: Seviche can be made with other firm fish that are safe to eat raw, such as FLOUNDER, BLACKFISH, or SEA BASS, either alone or in combination with scallops. But avoid using cod or its relatives, which may contain parasites. Note that the seafood must marinate in the lime juice for at least 6 hours or up to 1 day.

Serving suggestions: Seviche is frequently served on individual plates over a leafy green. But I also like to serve it as a help-yourself hors d'oeuvre. If the scallops (or fish) are cut into a small dice before they are marinated, seviche can be scooped up with firm tortilla chips. *Note:* If you are serving the seviche with chips, be sure to drain it well before serving it.

    1 **pound** CALICO SCALLOPS *or* BAY SCALLOPS
    ½ **cup fresh lime juice**
    ½ **cup seeded, finely diced tomatoes**
    ¼ **cup finely chopped red onion**
    2 **teaspoons seeded, minced jalapeño, or to taste**
    ½ **teaspoon minced garlic**
    ¼ **teaspoon cumin**
    ¼ **teaspoon salt**
    ⅛ **teaspoon freshly ground black pepper**
    2 **teaspoons olive oil**
    ¼ **cup chopped cilantro**
Leafy greens for lining plates (see "Serving suggestions")

1. Rinse the scallops, and drain them well. If the scallops are large, cut them into halves or quarters, dicing them into ½-inch pieces. (If you plan to serve the seviche as a "dip" with chips, cut them into ¼-inch pieces.) Place the scallops in a medium-sized bowl, and add the lime juice, tossing the scallops to coat them thoroughly with the juice. Cover the bowl with plastic wrap, and refrigerate it for 6 hours or more, tossing the scallops one or more times while they "cook" in the juice.

2. Meanwhile, in a bowl combine the remaining ingredients *except the cilantro and leafy greens*. About 1 hour before serving time, remove the scallops from the refrigerator, and add the tomato mixture to the scallops, tossing the ingredients to distribute them well. Refrigerate the seviche.

3. Just before serving the seviche, pour off any accumulated liquid, and mix in the cilantro. Using a slotted spoon, serve the seviche on individual plates that have been lined with the leafy greens. ■

Bay scallop

ASIAN SEAFOOD ROLL
■

ABOUT 40 HORS D'OEUVRES

Almost everything I know about Asian cooking I have learned from Norman Weinstein, founder of the Hot Wok cooking school and easily the best Jewish-Chinese cook in my native Brooklyn. Rick and I asked Norman for some special insights on preparing fish Chinese style, using little or no added fat. Norman came back with some fabulous alternatives to battered and deep-fried. This superb make-ahead hors d'oeuvre was among them. The recipe calls for 3 egg yolks, but the amount per person is a fraction of one yolk. And even though there are 2 tablespoons of oil in the ingredients list, very little of that oil gets into the food, especially if you use a nonstick pan to prepare the egg pancakes.

Preparation tips: The rolls can be prepared 3 or 4 days in advance and refrigerated. Or they can be made even earlier and frozen, as long as they are thoroughly defrosted and brought to room temperature before serving. Use at least a moderately firm white fish such as WHITEFISH, WALLEYE (YELLOW PIKE), or BLACKFISH to end up with a roll that holds together when it is sliced. Sheets of nori (dried, pressed seaweed) are sold in Asian markets and in some health-food stores. If you cannot get roasted nori (greenish), unroasted nori can be toasted by passing it over an open flame several times until it takes on a greenish tinge. Or, if the nori is unavailable, it can be omitted from the recipe.

Serving suggestion: For those who like things "hot," serve the seafood slices with wasabi (Japanese horseradish paste—see page 156) or a hot Chinese mustard.

EGG PANCAKES
   3 large eggs
  1/4 teaspoon salt
   2 tablespoons vegetable oil
   5 12-inch squares wax paper

FISH FILLING
   1 pound FIRM-FLESHED FISH FILLETS *or* 3/4 pound FISH FILLETS AND 1/4 pound MEDIUM SHRIMP, peeled
   3 egg whites
   1 teaspoon salt
1 1/2 teaspoons sugar
   1 tablespoon peeled, minced gingerroot
   2 tablespoons dry sherry
   2 teaspoons Asian sesame oil
  1/2 teaspoon freshly ground white pepper
   2 tablespoons cornstarch

REMAINING INGREDIENTS
   4 roasted nori sheets (optional but highly desirable)
  24 matchstick strips raw carrot (about 1/4 × 3 inches)
  20 shreds peeled gingerroot
  16 thin strips scallion greens
Diagonally cut carrot slices for garnish (optional)
Feathered scallion greens for garnish (optional)

1. To prepare the egg pancakes, in a medium-sized bowl, lightly whisk the whole eggs with the ¼ teaspoon salt. Heat a 9-inch skillet—preferably nonstick or well-seasoned cast-iron—and add the vegetable oil, swirling the oil to coat the bottom of the skillet. Pour the excess oil into a heat-proof measuring cup or small bowl. Immediately add ¼ of the egg mixture, swirling the pan to distribute the egg evenly along the bottom as if you were making a crepe. As soon as the surface is set, turn the egg pancake out, cooked (bottom) side up, onto a sheet of wax paper. (If necessary, loosen the edge of the pancake with a rubber spatula before flipping it out.) Repeat the process with the remaining batter, separating the pancakes with sheets of wax paper. Cover the top pancake with wax paper, and set the pancakes aside.

2. To prepare the fish filling, cut the fillets (or the fillets and shrimp) into small pieces, place them into the bowl of a food processor, and puree the fish. Transfer the fish puree to a medium-sized bowl. Mix in the rest of the filling ingredients *except the cornstarch,* stirring in one direction only to combine them thoroughly. Then mix in the cornstarch.

3. To assemble the seafood roll, remove the top piece of wax paper from the egg pancakes, and lift up the top pancake with the piece of wax paper it is resting on. Place the pancake on a flat work surface, cooked side down. Place one nori sheet on the pancake, pressing it gently to help it stick to the pancake. With a knife or scissors, trim away the excess nori. Smear one-quarter of the fish filling over the nori, spreading it evenly like frosting all the way to the edge. Arrange ¼ of the carrot strips, gingerroot shreds, and scallion greens horizontally over the surface of the fish to within 1 inch of the nearest and furthest edges of the pancake. Starting from the edge nearest you, tightly roll the pancake toward the opposite edge. Place the roll seam side down on a heatproof platter that fits in the basket of your steamer. Repeat the process with the remaining pancakes.

4. Bring 1 inch or so of water to a boil in the bottom of a steamer. Place the platter with the seafood rolls in the steamer basket. Cover the steamer, and cook the rolls for 12 to 15 minutes. Remove the steamer basket with the platter in it, and set it aside to cool. When the rolls reach room temperature, chill them in the refrigerator. Slice the chilled rolls into rounds or ovals (by slicing on the diagonal) that are about ⅓ inch thick. Arrange the slices on a platter, garnished (if desired) with diagonally cut slices of carrot and feathered scallion greens. ∎

JAPANESE-STYLE GEFILTE FISH

■

In my party-giving experience, nearly everyone—regardless of race, creed, or color—enjoys gefilte fish. For an ethnic change of pace, I jazzed up the original with some Asian seasonings.

Preparation tips: Gefilte fish can also be made with just one kind of fish—most often WHITEFISH. Asian markets are a usual source of pickled ginger and the Japanese horseradish paste called wasabi. The latter is sold either in a tube or can as a prepared paste or in a small tin as a powder that must be mixed one to one with water.

Serving suggestions: The unmolded fish can be sliced into first-course servings and placed on individual plates on a bed of greens decorated with thinly sliced carrot and a feathered scallion instead of the pickled ginger and wasabi. Or the fish can be cut into bite-sized pieces and served with toothpicks.

2½ pounds FISH FILLETS (I use a traditional mix of 1½ pounds WHITEFISH,
    ½ pound PIKE, and ½ pound CARP), cut into 1-inch pieces
1⅓ cups finely chopped onion
 ½ cup finely shredded carrot
 ¼ cup dried bread crumbs *or* matzo meal
 ½ cup fish broth *or* water
 ¼ cup soy sauce
  3 tablespoons drained white horseradish
  2 tablespoons peeled, grated gingerroot
 ½ teaspoon freshly ground white pepper *or* black pepper
Vegetable-oil spray
Pickled ginger (see "Preparation tips" and "Serving suggestions") for garnish
    (optional)
Wasabi (see "Preparation tips" and "Serving suggestions") for garnish (optional)

1. With a tweezers or needle-nose pliers or fingers, remove as many of the fish bones as possible. Place the fish and onion in the bowl of a food processor (or into a meat grinder), and process the mixture until it forms a coarse paste. Take care not to overprocess the fish. Transfer the mixture to a large mixing bowl.

2. Add all the remaining ingredients *except the vegetable-oil spray and garnishes,* stirring the ingredients to combine them thoroughly.

3. Coat a 2½-quart mold or loaf pan with the vegetable-oil spray. Place the fish mixture into the mold or pan, pressing on the ingredients to eliminate any trapped air. Cover the mold or pan with a sheet of wax paper or parchment.

4. Put several inches of water into a covered kettle large enough to contain the mold or pan. Place a steamer rack in the kettle, and set the mold or pan on the steamer rack. Bring the water to a boil, cover the kettle, and steam the fish for 50 minutes. *Alternatively,* heat the oven to 350°F. Then place the mold or pan in a larger pan, add 1½ inches of boiling water to the larger pan, place the pan in the hot oven, and bake the fish for 50 minutes.

5. To serve, unmold the fish onto a platter or cutting board, and cut it, as desired, into serving pieces. Or serve the fish intact with a knife so that people may help themselves. Serve the fish with mounds of pickled ginger and wasabi (if desired). ■

Whitefish

MINCED FISH BALLS

ABOUT 36 HORS D'OEUVRES

Here is another Asian version of that Jewish favorite, gefilte fish. But these balls are simpler to prepare and lend themselves to other uses such as in a delicate Asian vegetable soup or a more potent hot and sour soup. My friends Stephen and Nancy Tim, botanical specialists and neighbors in Brooklyn, New York, delighted me with this dish years ago, and I pried the recipe from them.

Preparation tips: The ingredients can be varied. For example, the scallions and gingerroot can be omitted. Or ¼ pound of FRESH SHRIMP can be combined with the WHITE FISH in place of, or in addition to, the Canadian bacon. Or, for a more subtle flavor, finely minced ham can be used in place of the Canadian bacon. The fish balls can be prepared completely in advance and frozen for later use.

Serving suggestions: Two dipping sauces are offered, one mild and one hot. Alternatives include the hot mustard sauce on page 129 or the Divine Chinese Dipping Sauce on page 503. Be sure to serve the fish balls with toothpicks or tiny cocktail forks.

FISH BALLS
- 1 pound FILLETS OF ANY WHITE FISH, such as cod ("scrod")
- 2 egg whites, lightly beaten
- 1 tablespoon dry sherry
- 2 tablespoons chopped scallions
- 1 tablespoon peeled, minced gingerroot
- ¼ teaspoon salt, or to taste (if substituting for or omitting the Canadian bacon, use at least ½ teaspoon salt)
- ¼ cup minced Canadian bacon (optional—see "Preparation tips")
- 1 tablespoon cornstarch

DIPPING SAUCE 1
- 2 teaspoons Asian sesame oil
- 2 teaspoons soy sauce

DIPPING SAUCE 2
- 2 teaspoons wasabi powder
- 2 teaspoons water
- 1 tablespoon soy sauce

1. To make the fish balls, make sure all the skin and bones have been removed from the fish. Cut the fillets into 1-inch pieces, and place the fish in the bowl of a food processor. Process the fish, stopping to scrape down the sides of the bowl if necessary, for 1 minute or until the fish forms a paste. Transfer the fish to a mixing bowl.

2. Combine the fish with the remaining ingredients for the fish balls, stirring the ingredients in one direction only until the mixture forms a uniform, glutinous paste. At this point, the mixture can be chilled for later cooking.

3. Bring about 4 cups of water to a boil in a wide-mouth, medium-sized saucepan, then reduce the heat to a simmer. With wet hands, remove about 1 teaspoon of the fish mixture from the bowl, and shape the mixture into a 1-inch ball. (Do not make the balls too large or they will not cook through.) Repeat the shaping process with the remaining fish, wetting your hands from time to time as necessary. After you have prepared about a dozen balls, drop them into the simmering water. Let the balls cook for about 1 minute after they rise to the surface, then, with a slotted spoon, remove them to a platter. Repeat the process until all the fish is cooked.

4. To make the dipping sauces, in a small bowl or cup, combine the ingredients for Dipping Sauce 1, and in a second small bowl or cup, combine the ingredients for Dipping Sauce 2, stirring the latter sauce until the wasabi powder is dissolved.

5. To serve, place the two bowls or cups of dipping sauces and a third container holding toothpicks in the center of a large, colorful platter. Place the fish balls around the sauces and toothpicks. ∎

CALIFORNIA ROLLS

■

ABOUT 60 HORS D'OEUVRES

This is a perfect hors d'oeuvre for sushi lovers who fear raw fish regardless of how carefully it is handled. The only raw ingredients are fresh vegetables. The fish is cooked imitation crabmeat (surimi sticks).

Preparation tips: Although it looks complex and its preparation seems involved, nori-wrapped sushi is not difficult to make. Sixty or more of the bite-sized pieces can be prepared in 1 to 1½ hours from start to finish. The only disadvantage is that the rolls should be made on the day they will be eaten lest they lose texture and flavor. Roasted nori (sheets of seaweed) can be purchased in markets that sell Asian products. If the seaweed you purchase is not roasted, it can be toasted over a gas flame. Sushi vinegar, or seasoned rice vinegar, is now widely available in large supermarkets and Asian markets as well as at many fish counters. Wasabi paste or powder is also available in Asian markets. In order to make rice that has the needed sticky consistency, use short-grain or medium-grain rice, also available in many supermarkets and Asian markets. But Carolina brand "extra-long-grain" rice will work, too. Your work surface must be dry when you are preparing the rolls, or the nori will stick to it and tear.

   1 **cup short-grain or medium-grain (sushi) rice (see "Preparation tips")**
1²/₃ **cups water**
  ¼ **cup sushi vinegar (seasoned rice vinegar)**
Wasabi powder and an equal amount of water, *or* **wasabi paste, to taste**
   1 **carrot, about 8½ inches long**
   1 **small zucchini (about ¼ pound), unpeeled**
  ½ **small, ripe but firm avocado**
  2 **to 3 SURIMI STICKS, 1 ounce each**
   4 **sheets roasted nori**
Fingerbowl containing ¼ cup water *and* **1½ teaspoons rice vinegar**

1. If you are using imported Asian rice, place the rice in a sieve, and rinse it under cold water for 2 minutes or until the water runs clear. Drain the rice thoroughly. Place the rice in a medium-sized saucepan that has a lid. Add the water, bring the ingredients to a boil, reduce the heat to low, cover the pan tightly, and cook the rice for 15 to 20 minutes or until all the water has been absorbed. Remove the pan from the heat, and let the rice stand, covered, for 10 minutes. The rice should have a sticky consistency.

2. Transfer the rice to a large, shallow, nonmetallic bowl. Sprinkle the sushi vinegar over the hot rice, and, with a wooden or plastic spoon, toss the rice with the vinegar to combine the ingredients thoroughly. Set the rice aside while you prepare the remaining ingredients.

3. If you are using wasabi powder, place about 1 tablespoon of the powder in a small bowl along with an equal amount of water, and mix the ingredients until they form a smooth paste. Cover the bowl, and set the paste aside for about 10 minutes to let the flavor develop.

4. Meanwhile, cut the carrot into ⅛-inch to ¼-inch julienne strips (8 inches long, if possible). Place the carrots in a steamer or drop them into a pot of boiling water, and steam or parboil them for 3 minutes or until they are barely tender-crisp. Rinse them under cold water, and set them aside to cool. Cut the zucchini into ⅛-inch to ¼-inch julienne strips, leaving the green peel on each strip. Cut the avocado into ¼-inch julienne strips. Cut the surimi sticks into ¼-inch julienne strips. Set these ingredients aside.

5. Using a clean, *dry*, flat work surface, place a sheet of roasted nori, shiniest side down, on it with the longest side facing you. Place one-fourth of the reserved rice (about ¾ cup) on the nori. Dip the back of a stainless-steel spoon into the liquid in the fingerbowl, and use the back of the spoon to distribute the rice evenly over the nori, leaving about 1 inch of the nori uncovered at the top. Press the rice down as firmly and evenly as possible.

6. With a spoon or fingertip, press a narrow groove lengthwise (left to right) into the rice about 1½ inches up from the edge nearest you. Place a thin streak of wasabi along the entire groove. Then place strips of carrot, zucchini, avocado, and surimi lengthwise around the groove, piecing them as necessary, so that each ingredient forms a line across the nori.

7. With dry hands, roll the nori up as tightly as possible, starting from the edge nearest you. Stop when you come to the end of the rice. Using your fingers, wet the uncovered edge of the nori with the liquid in the finger-bowl, and press the edge onto the roll. Place the roll seam side down on a cutting board. Repeat steps 5, 6, and 7 with the remaining nori sheets.

8. With a sharp knife, slice the nori rolls crosswise, one at a time, into rounds about ½ inch thick. Arrange the rounds, overlapping them slightly, on a large serving platter. ■

TUNA MAKI (SUSHI ROLLS)

■
ABOUT 50 HORS D'OEUVRES

These are such a hit with family and friends that I cannot recommend them too highly. Like the California Rolls on page 160, the instructions for these seem far longer and more complicated than the actual execution. Once you get the hang of making sushi rolls, which is usually accomplished within the first two rolls of the first attempt, you should have little trouble.

Preparation tips: Since these sushi rolls are made with raw fish, the fish should be frozen at −4°F for three days (or longer) to be certain that there are no parasites. Make sure to buy top-quality fish, and wrap it well before freezing it so that the quality will be maintained. The use of short-grain or medium-grain rice is important in achieving the sticky consistency needed for the maki pieces to hold together. But Carolina brand "extra-long-grain" rice also works. See page 160 for further information about the ingredients. Be sure your work surface is dry, or the nori will stick to it and tear. If you expect your diners to be timid about the hotness of wasabi, leave it out of the maki and serve it on the side, or rely on the dipping sauce, below.

ROLLS
  1 **cup short-grain or medium-grain (sushi) rice (see "Preparation tips")**
1²/₃ **cups water**
¼ **cup sushi vinegar (seasoned rice vinegar)**
  4 **teaspoons wasabi powder and 4 teaspoons water, *or* 4 teaspoons wasabi paste, or to taste**
⅓ **pound (approximately) raw TUNA, frozen for 3 days (see "Preparation tips")**
  4 **sheets roasted nori (approximately)**
Fingerbowl containing ¼ cup water and 1½ teaspoons rice vinegar
Pickled ginger (optional)

DIPPING SAUCE (OPTIONAL)
  2 **tablespoons soy sauce**
  2 **teaspoons wasabi paste, *or* 2 teaspoons wasabi powder and 2 teaspoons water**

1. To prepare the rolls, place the rice in a sieve if you are using imported Asian rice, and rinse it under cold water for 2 minutes or until the water runs clear. Let the rice drain thoroughly. Place the rice in a medium-sized saucepan that has a lid. Add the 1²/₃ cups water, bring the ingredients to a boil, reduce the heat to low, cover the pan tightly, and cook the rice for 15

to 20 minutes or until all the water has been absorbed. Remove the pan from the heat, and let the rice stand, covered, for 10 minutes. The rice should be sticky.

2. Transfer the rice to a large, shallow, nonmetallic bowl. Sprinkle the sushi vinegar over the hot rice, and, with a wooden or plastic spoon, toss the rice with the vinegar to combine the ingredients thoroughly. Set the rice aside while you prepare the remaining ingredients.

3. If you are using wasabi powder, place it in a small bowl, and stir in the 4 teaspoons of water to form a paste. Set the wasabi aside.

4. Slice the tuna into ⅓-inch strips that are as long as possible (they do not have to be any longer than 7 inches, and it is okay if some strips are short since they can be pieced together).

5. Nori sheets are typically 8 × 7 inches. With a scissors, cut them in half to form sheets that are 4 × 7 inches. Working with one half-sheet at a time, lay the nori, shiniest side down, on a clean, *dry,* flat working surface so that the longest side is closest to you. Place a slightly heaping ⅓ cup of rice on the nori. Dip the back of a stainless-steel spoon into the liquid in the fingerbowl, and use the back of the spoon to distribute the rice evenly over the nori, leaving about 1 inch of the nori uncovered at the top. Press the rice down as firmly and evenly as possible.

6. With a finger, make an lengthwise indentation across the nori about 1 inch from the edge nearest you. Smear some of the wasabi across the indentation (see "Preparation tips"). Place a strip or strips of the tuna in a single line over the wasabi to form a straight line from one edge of the nori to the other.

7. With dry hands, roll the nori up as tightly as possible, starting from the edge nearest you. Stop when you come to the end of the rice. Using your fingers, wet the uncovered edge of the nori with the liquid in the fingerbowl, and press the edge onto the roll. Place the roll seam side down on a cutting board. Repeat this process with the remaining nori sheets. If you will not be serving the maki immediately, transfer the rolls to a platter, cover them with plastic wrap, and chill them until about 20 minutes before serving time.

8. With a sharp knife, slice the nori rolls crosswise, one at a time, into rounds about ¾ inch to 1 inch thick. Arrange the rounds rice side up on a serving platter, leaving a space in the middle.

9. To prepare the dipping sauce (if desired), in a small, shallow bowl, combine the sauce ingredients. Place the bowl in the center of the serving platter along with a second bowl containing the pickled ginger (if desired). Serve the maki at or near room temperature. ■

WAVES OF TUNA

■

These quick-cooking hors d'oeuvres are served on skewers, which makes them an ideal finger food at a party. They also look more difficult to prepare than they are, and guests will be suitably impressed by your ability to make the tuna into wriggly ribbons.

Preparation tips: In this recipe, I think a long marination time is best. I recommend putting the tuna into the marinade 6 to 12 hours before cooking it. Don't worry if you cannot make 4-inch-long slices of tuna or if your slices break apart; they can be strung together when you place them on the skewers and still come out looking like a single wavy ribbon. The skewers can be prepared an hour or so before guests arrive, but do not cook the tuna until serving time. Hoisin sauce is a thick, sweetened condiment that is sold (as are bamboo skewers) where other Asian ingredients can be found.

MARINADE

- 2 tablespoons reduced-sodium soy sauce
- 2 tablespoons rice vinegar
- 2 tablespoons hoisin sauce
- 1 teaspoon minced garlic
- 1 teaspoon peeled, minced gingerroot
- ¼ teaspoon red pepper flakes

SKEWERS

- 1 pound TUNA
- 36 thin bamboo skewers, about 4 to 6 inches long
- Vegetable-oil spray
- 4 teaspoons toasted sesame seeds

1. To make the marinade, combine all the marinade ingredients in a shallow, nonmetallic pan such as a glass baking dish or large pie plate.

2. To prepare the skewers, slice the tuna into strips ⅛ inch thick and about 4 inches long (see "Preparation tips"). Place the tuna strips into the marinade one at a time so that they lie flat in the dish in one or two layers. Gently press the strips into the marinade so that all the pieces are coated with it. Cover the dish with plastic wrap, and refrigerate it for 6 hours or longer.

3. Place the skewers into a tall glass or jar, and cover them with water. They should soak for at least 20 minutes, but they can soak for hours, if that is more convenient.

4. Spray the rack of a broiler pan with vegetable oil, and, if you are planning to cook the tuna right away, heat the broiler.

5. When you are ready to make the hors d'oeuvres, remove the tuna from the refrigerator. Taking a skewer from the glass or jar, thread one tuna

strip onto the skewer to form a wavy ribbon. Repeat the process with the remaining tuna. Each strip should be pierced several times; or, if you must thread the strips using shorter pieces together, be sure that each piece is pierced at least twice so that it does not droop on the skewer. If you wish, this step can be done in advance: place the threaded skewers on a platter, cover the platter with plastic wrap, and chill the tuna until you are ready to cook it.

6. Place the skewers on the greased broiler rack, and place the rack about 4 inches from the heat source of the hot broiler. Broil the skewers for 1½ minutes. Check the tuna to make sure it is cooked (when they are done, the strips should look like cooked chicken breast, having lost their translucent quality). If necessary, broil the skewers for another 30 seconds.

7. As soon as the skewers are removed from the broiler, sprinkle them with the toasted sesame seeds. Serve the tuna ribbons on their skewers. ■

SMOKED-WHITEFISH APPETIZER
■
                                                            4 SERVINGS

A gift of a whole smoked whitefish prompted me to try some simple experiments. This is one of the happy results. It should work as well with any fleshy smoked fish.

½ **pound SMOKED WHITEFISH**
1 **cup frozen green peas, parboiled for 1 to 2 minutes**
¼ **cup finely chopped red onion**
1 **tablespoon white-wine vinegar, or to taste**
8 **plum (Roma) tomatoes**
Lettuce *or* other leafy greens for lining plates

1. Remove and discard the skin from the fish. Carefully bone the fish, separate it into coarse flakes, and place it in a medium-sized bowl.

2. Add the peas, onion, and vinegar, and toss the ingredients to combine them well.

3. Halve the tomatoes lengthwise and scoop out the pulp. Stuff the fish mixture into the tomato shells. To serve, line individual dishes with the lettuce or greens, and arrange the stuffed tomatoes on top. ■

SMOKED-BLUEFISH PÂTÉ

■

24 HORS D'OEUVRES OR 2 CUPS

Most traditional pâtés rely heavily on saturated fats to give them moisture and texture. This one gets its buttery taste from the moderate amount of healthful oils in bluefish, and it gets its body from a mere ⅓ cup of low-fat ricotta. It is exciting proof that low-fat cooking can result not only in wonderful flavor, but in richness, too. I've prepared this pâté so often and have watched others prepare it, too, that I've come to the conclusion it always turns out great.

Preparation tips: See page 95 for information about home smoking. Both the fresh or smoked bluefish fillets and the finished pâté can be frozen for later use. I have even frozen the pâté in a well-covered mold and, after thawing, have unmolded it as an attractive self-serve spread. In some parts of the country, it is possible to buy bluefish already smoked, in which case purchase only 1 pound (which is what the 1¼ pounds in the recipe will shrink to after smoking).

Serving suggestions: Although the recipe calls for spreading the pâté on rounds of toast, it can also be served in a bowl as a "dip" for pieces of celery and large, diagonally cut slices of carrot. Or it can be molded and served in small wedges. To do that, spray a small, attractive mold with vegetable oil, pack the pâté into the mold, and refrigerate the pâté until it is well chilled. When you're ready to serve the pâté, partially submerge the mold in a pot or bowl of warm water to loosen the pâté, and invert the mold on a platter. Tap the mold gently to encourage the pâté to slide out intact.

1¼ **pounds BLUEFISH FILLETS**
⅓ **cup "lite" or part-skim ricotta**
1 **tablespoon fresh lemon juice**
½ **teaspoon salt**
½ **teaspoon freshly ground black pepper**
1 **tablespoon drained horseradish**
2 **tablespoons chopped shallots**
1 **tablespoon Worcestershire sauce**
¼ **cup finely chopped scallions, white and green parts**
24 **thinly sliced, toasted rounds French bread *or* crackers**
12 **cherry tomatoes, halved lengthwise**

Bluefish

1. Prepare a stovetop or other hot-smoker according to the manufacturer's directions, and smoke the fish. Depending on the thickness of the fillets, the process should take 15 to 20 minutes.

2. Remove the fish from the smoker, let it cool slightly, and, if the fillets were cooked with their skin on, remove and discard the skin. Break the fish into chunks, and place them in the bowl of a food processor. Add the ricotta, lemon juice, salt, pepper, horseradish, shallots, and Worcestershire sauce. Process the mixture until it forms a fairly smooth pâté (but do not overprocess it to a paste).

3. Transfer the mixture to a mixing bowl, and blend in the scallions. Chill the pâté until it has become firm.

4. To serve, spread 2 teaspoons of the pâté on each toast round or cracker, and top each round with half of a cherry tomato. ■

SMOKED-FISH SPREAD
■

ABOUT ½ CUP

This delicious spread can be the basis of a wonderful low-fat hors d'oeuvre or a light lunch. Or it can be used as a sandwich filling, dressed with lettuce and sliced tomato.

Serving suggestions: For an attractive, easy-to-eat hors d'oeuvre, the spread can be stuffed into hollowed-out cherry tomatoes or hollowed plum tomatoes halves or leaves of Belgian endive. It can also be served alongside toasted wedges of pita or unsalted crackers.

¼ **pound** SMOKED WHITEFISH *or* CHUB, **skinned and carefully deboned**
2 **tablespoons finely chopped red onion**
2 **tablespoons finely chopped celery**
2 **tablespoons nonfat mayonnaise**
1 **tablespoon finely chopped fresh parsley**

In a small bowl, mash the fish into a coarse paste. Stir in the remaining ingredients, mixing them thoroughly. Chill the spread until close to serving time. ■

SUPER SALMON LOAF WITH RED PEPPER PUREE

■

6 TO 8 SERVINGS

Fish loaves are among the most beautiful of appetizers: a thin slice accompanied by a colorful sauce can signal a terrific meal. Usually fish terrines are made with a lot of cream, which renders them light and airy. What I've done here is to use reduced-fat ricotta, egg whites, and the magic of the food processor to create lightness without excess calories and fat. The red pepper puree is very versatile and can be served either warm or chilled.

Preparation tip: In cooking the vegetables for the red pepper puree, it is important to cover the pan very tightly and to make sure that the liquid does not boil away. This would result in burned vegetables and a harsh sauce. If the liquid is about to evaporate, quickly add 1 to 2 tablespoons of water.

Serving suggestions: Place some pepper puree on the plate and a slice of salmon loaf over it. For added color, garnish the fish with a sprig of dill.

SALMON

1 pound SKINLESS SALMON FILLET
1 cup "lite" or part-skim ricotta
2 egg whites *and* 1 whole egg
2 tablespoons fresh lemon juice
1/8 teaspoon Tabasco sauce
1/2 teaspoon salt, or to taste
Freshly ground black pepper to taste
1/8 teaspoon nutmeg, preferably freshly grated
2 tablespoons chopped dill
2 tablespoons thinly sliced scallions
1/4 pound SMOKED SALMON (NOVA), cut into 1/2-inch dice
Vegetable-oil spray

RED PEPPER PUREE

3 cups chopped red bell pepper (about 1 pound)
1/2 cup coarsely chopped onion
1 teaspoon chopped garlic
2 tablespoons water
2 tablespoons dry white wine
2 tablespoons fresh lemon juice
1 tablespoon apple-cider vinegar
1 teaspoon sugar
Several dashes cayenne, or to taste
Salt to taste (optional)
Freshly ground black pepper to taste

1. Heat the oven to 350°F.
2. In a food processor, process the fresh salmon until it is somewhat chopped. Add the ricotta, egg whites and whole egg, lemon juice, Tabasco sauce, salt, pepper, and nutmeg, and puree the mixture until it is smooth. Transfer the salmon mixture to a large bowl.
3. Add the dill, scallions, and smoked salmon, and stir the mixture to blend the ingredients well.

4. Lightly coat an 8 × 4 × 2½-inch loaf pan with the vegetable-oil spray. Transfer the salmon mixture to the pan, and cover the pan with aluminum foil, sealing the pan well around the edges. Place the loaf pan into a larger pan, and pour hot water into the outer pan to reach halfway up the smaller pan. Place the pans in the middle of the hot oven.

5. Bake the loaf for 50 minutes or until its internal temperature reaches 145°F to 150°F on an instant-read thermometer.

6. When the loaf is done, remove the inner pan from the outer one, pour off any excess liquid that may have accumulated around the loaf, and chill the loaf for several hours in the pan.

7. While the loaf cools, prepare the red pepper puree. Place all the puree ingredients in a saucepan that has a tight-fitting lid. Cover the pan tightly, and simmer the vegetables for 30 minutes. Check after 20 minutes to be sure that there is adequate liquid left in the pan (see "Preparation tip").

8. Pour the red pepper mixture into a food processor or blender, and puree the vegetables until they are very smooth.

9. Before serving the salmon, unmold the loaf, and slice it thinly. Serve each slice over 2 or 3 tablespoons of red pepper puree. ■

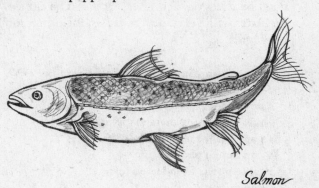

Salmon

SALMON MOUSSE

■

Mousse is traditionally prepared in ways that are neither heart-healthy nor figure-enhancing. But this simple version, firmed up with gelatin, is kind to your body. It is ideal for parties because it can be prepared a day or two ahead and kept refrigerated until serving time. I have used canned salmon here to make the dish both accessible and affordable. If you have a food processor, the preparation is a snap.

Preparation tips: I like to make this in a mold—a fish shape is ideal—and turn it out onto a platter for serving. But if unmolding makes you nervous, the mousse can also be chilled in one or more shallow bowls (pie-plate height) and scooped out by individual diners with a pâté knife or with sliced raw vegetables.

Serving suggestions: The mousse can be served as a spread with crackers, small rounds of bread or toast, or "spoons" of vegetables such as diagonally sliced carrots, leaves of Belgian endive, or sections of celery. It is especially good on slices of cucumber. Or it can be cut in wedges and served salad style on plates with vegetable garnishes, including something nippy like watercress or arugula.

  1 **6-ounce can Spicy Hot V8** *or* **tomato juice** *or* **V8**
1/2 **cup cold water**
  2 **envelopes unflavored gelatin**
30 **ounces (approximately)** CANNED SALMON
3/4 **cup "lite" or part-skim ricotta**
3/4 **cup nonfat plain yogurt**
  3 **tablespoons fresh lemon juice**
1/4 **cup minced scallions**
  2 **tablespoons snipped fresh dill** *or* **2 teaspoons dried dill**
  2 **tablespoons chopped fresh parsley**
  1 **teaspoon paprika (include** 1/4 **teaspoon hot paprika, if available)**
1/2 **teaspoon freshly ground white pepper**
1/4 **teaspoon salt (optional)**
Vegetable-oil spray

1. Place the V8 or tomato juice and the cold water in a small bowl or saucepan. Sprinkle the gelatin over the liquid, and let the gelatin stand for several minutes to soften. In the microwave oven or on the stove, gently heat the mixture until the gelatin is dissolved. *Do not let the gelatin get too hot.* Set the mixture aside to cool.

2. Remove and discard the skin from the salmon. Remove the bones, and either crush them (fingers work well) and return them to the salmon or discard them. Place the salmon into the bowl of a food processor or, if a food processor is not available, into a large bowl.

3. Add all the remaining ingredients *except the gelatin mixture and vegetable-oil spray.* Process the mixture until it is very smooth. If you are not using a food processor, beat the ingredients with an electric mixer until the mixture is smooth. Add the dissolved gelatin mixture to the salmon mixture, and briefly process or beat the mixture again to combine all the ingredients well.

4. Spray a 6-cup mold with the vegetable-oil spray, transfer the salmon mixture to the mold, and chill the mousse for 1 hour or until it is firm. The mousse can remain in the mold, or it can be unmolded onto a flat platter and garnished. Keep the mousse chilled until shortly before serving time. ■

SESAME-SALMON STRIPS

■

6 SERVINGS

These Chinese-flavored slivers of salmon make tasty hors d'oeuvres that go well with bland crackers or thinly sliced pumpernickel. Or you can serve them on an hors d'oeuvre plate all by themselves.

SALMON
½ pound SALMON FILLET
Vegetable-oil spray (optional)
  2 tablespoons lightly toasted sesame seeds
  2 tablespoons chopped scallion greens

MARINADE
  2 tablespoons reduced-sodium soy sauce
  2 tablespoons dry sherry
  1 tablespoon rice vinegar
  1 teaspoon Asian sesame oil
  1 teaspoon sugar
  ⅛ teaspoon red pepper flakes, or to taste

1. Using your fingernails, a needle-nose pliers, or tweezers, pull out any remaining bones in the salmon fillets. Slice the salmon crosswise on the diagonal into slices about ¼-inch thick. The slices can be left whole, but if you intend to serve them with crackers or minibread, cut the slices in half down the middle. Place the salmon pieces in a shallow bowl or non-metallic baking dish.

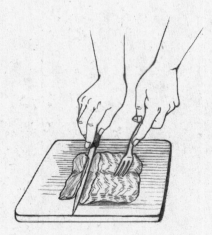

2. In a jar that has a tight-fitting lid, combine all the marinade ingredients, and shake the jar to combine them well. Pour the marinade over the salmon pieces, lifting the pieces gently to coat them on all sides with the marinade. Cover the bowl, and chill it for 30 minutes or longer, gently turning the pieces in the marinade at least once.

3. If possible, place the broiler rack about 4 inches from the heat source. Heat the broiler for about 5 minutes.

4. Meanwhile, remove the salmon from the marinade, and set the slices down on a double sheet of paper towels to absorb any excess liquid. Place the salmon slices in a single layer on a nonstick baking sheet or a baking sheet that has been sprayed with the vegetable oil. Then place the salmon under the broiler for about 1 minute or until the fish is cooked through— 2 minutes maximum. Carefully transfer the salmon strips to a heated serving platter, overlapping the pieces only slightly. Sprinkle the salmon with the sesame seeds and scallions. ■

SALMON-ASPARAGUS BUNDLES

■

These are so lovely to look at, it's almost a shame to eat them—until you taste the first one. The colorful bundles are ideal for a party because they can be made ahead. Have no fear about "wasting" the bottoms of the asparagus. They can be steamed and eaten with the leftover dill sauce or used as an ingredient in a salad or stir-fry.

MAIN INGREDIENTS
24 **thin asparagus spears**
½ **pound (approximately) thick**
  SALMON FILLET, with or without
  skin (enough to make 12 thin
  diagonal slices about 1½ to 2
  inches wide at the widest point)
Salt to taste (optional)
Freshly ground black pepper to taste

SAUCE
¼ **cup nonfat plain yogurt**
1½ **tablespoons snipped fresh dill**
1 **tablespoon raspberry vinegar, *or***
  1 tablespoon fresh lemon juice
  and ½ teaspoon sugar
1 **teaspoon Dijon-style mustard**
¼ **to ⅜ teaspoon sugar (add only if**
  using unsweetened vinegar)

1. Cut off 3½-inch lengths from the flower end (tip) of the asparagus spears. Steam the tips over boiling water for 3 minutes or until they are barely tender-crisp. Rinse them immediately under cold water, and set them aside to cool.
2. Using your fingernails, a needle-nose pliers, or tweezers, remove all the pinbones from the salmon. With the fillet skin side down and using a sharp knife, cut 12 thin crosswise slices on the diagonal, leaving the skin behind if the fish has not been skinned. The slices should be thin but not so thin that they fall apart.
3. Place the broiler rack about 6 inches from the heat source, and heat the broiler.
4. Using one slice of salmon for every two asparagus tips, align two asparagus tips at the narrowest end of the slice of fish, and wrap the fish around the middle of the two spears (as if bundling a sheath of wheat). Repeat the wrapping process with the remaining asparagus spears and salmon slices. Sprinkle the bundles with salt (if desired) and pepper.
5. Arrange the salmon-asparagus bundles seam side down on a greased ovenproof baking tray. Place the tray under the hot broiler, and broil the bundles for 3 minutes or until the fish is just cooked through on the bottom side. Remove the tray from the broiler, and, when the bundles have cooled enough to be handled, transfer them carefully to a serving dish, arranging them pinwheel style. Chill the bundles until serving time.

6. Meanwhile, make the sauce by placing all the sauce ingredients in a small bowl and whisking them until they are well combined. Chill the sauce until serving time. Before serving, spoon some of the sauce over the fish part of the bundles. Place the remaining sauce in a small dish (with a small spoon) in the center of the serving dish. ■

HONEYDEW BELTED WITH LOX
■

16 HORS D'OEUVRES OR 8 SERVINGS

You may be familiar with the traditional Italian appetizer of melon wrapped with prosciutto, a very salty ham sliced paper-thin. This is a seafood adaptation. Nova Scotia salmon (also known as Nova salmon), is far less salty yet offers a color and textural contrast that turns honeydew into a luscious hors d'oeuvre.

1 **small ripe honeydew**
1 **tablespoon fresh lime juice**
16 **thin slices** NOVA-STYLE SMOKED SALMON **(about ½ pound), each slice about 1 to 1½ inches × 4 inches**
Freshly ground black pepper to taste
1 **tablespoon snipped fresh dill (optional)**

1. Cut the honeydew into quarters lengthwise (through the stem and flower ends), remove the seeds, and cut away the rind. Slice each quarter into 4 wedges, again from end to end, and sprinkle the wedges with the lime juice.
2. Wrap a slice of salmon around the middle of each melon wedge, and place the wedges on individual plates (2 per person) or on a serving platter. Sprinkle the melon and the salmon lightly with the pepper and (if desired) dill before serving the dish. ■

CAVIAR ON SWEET POTATO
■

ABOUT 72 HORS D'OEUVRES

Nanette Porcelli, who has an excellent catering service called Simply Delicious in Saugerties, New York, served a version of this colorful, surprisingly delicious, and delightfully easy hors d'oeuvre at my friend Betty Marks's 65th birthday celebration.

Preparation tips: You do not need to break your budget on beluga; ANY KIND OF "CAVIAR" will do in this recipe. Be sure to cook the potatoes just until they are done (if they are overcooked, they will be too soft to slice) and well enough in advance to chill them completely before they are peeled and sliced. However, the yogurt mixture and caviar should be added just before serving. In place of yogurt and sour cream, you can use 3/4 cup of nonfat yogurt that has been well drained through a yogurt strainer or cheesecloth.

  2 **pounds sweet potatoes** or **yams (preferably 4 long, straight potatoes), each about 1 1/2 inches in diameter**
 1/4 **cup nonfat plain yogurt (see "Preparation tips")**
 1/4 **cup nonfat sour cream**
  1 **2-ounce jar BLACK CAVIAR**

1. Steam the potatoes over boiling water in a covered pot for 20 minutes or until they are just cooked. *Do not let the potatoes get mushy*. Rinse the potatoes under cold running water for 1 to 2 minutes to stop the cooking and loosen the skin. Let the potatoes cool, and refrigerate them for at least 1 hour.
2. Remove the potatoes from the refrigerator, peel them, and slice them into 1/4-inch-thick rounds. On a flat serving platter, arrange the rounds, making sure that there is a little space between them.
3. In a small bowl combine the yogurt and sour cream. Place 1/2 teaspoon of the yogurt mixture in the 12 o'clock position on each potato round. Then place 1/4 teaspoon of the caviar just beneath the yogurt mixture at the 6 o'clock position. Serve the hors d'oeuvres immediately. ■

A Celebration of Soups

Soups have just about everything going for them. Nutritionally, almost nothing is wasted—you get out what you put into the pot (although vitamin C might dissipate if a soup is simmered too long). Soups are filling enough to satisfy the appetite without delivering as many calories as a solid meal does. In fact, several studies have shown that eating soup helps people lose weight. Soups are adaptable enough to be first courses or complete meals that can be prepared with almost no added fat. Soups are generally easy to prepare, and this is especially so of many seafood soups, in which the fish or shellfish require little cooking. Soups even have psychological benefits: we all feel better on a drizzly, chilly day when our bellies are filled with a warm, wonderful soup; on a steamy, hot day, dining on a chilled soup hits the spot.

But beyond nutrition, convenience, and uplift, seafood soups happen to be among the most wonderful ever devised—abundant in flavor as well as beautiful. For the grandest start, I urge you to prepare your own fish broth (stock), and I offer a recipe for it in this section. Fish broth is most often the base for seafood soups. The preparation is a snap, the broth freezes well, and it is much better than the bottled clam juice usually suggested as a substitute. Lacking a homemade broth, you can sometimes get away with dehydrated fish bouillon reconstituted with boiling water. As with clam juice, however, be wary of the salt content. If you use these substitutes for a homemade broth, I recommend not adding salt until you've tasted the finished soup.

As you become a veteran at seafood soups and go on to improvise on your own, just remember to choose fish that are at least moderately firm (see the chart on page 45) so that they won't fall apart in the simmering liquid. The best seafoods for soups include all the shellfish and the roundfish that produce thick, firm fillets, including monkfish, catfish, blackfish, mahi-mahi, tilefish, shark, sea bass, tilapia, and rockfish. But steer clear of oily fish like mackerel when preparing soups because the fish oils can give the soup too strong a flavor.

FISH BROTH

■

6 CUPS

Fish broth and clam juice are often used interchangeably in recipes (as is occasionally the case in this book). But clam juice is a poor substitute for the genuine, mild broth you'll get from preparing this recipe. I can't urge you too strongly to prepare the broth in as large a quantity as your freezer space will allow. It's quicker and easier than you may think. Fish broth, according to many accomplished chefs, needs only 20 minutes of cooking. Some even say it is harmed by cooking it any longer. No salt is added in this recipe because fish broth is an ingredient, not something meant to stand alone. If salt were to be added now, you would lose control of just how much was being added to the dish in which it is later used.

Preparation tips: Many fish stores will give you fish heads and bones for free (especially if you are a regular customer); others sell them cheap. Be sure to scrape along the underside of the backbone to remove any residual organ tissue, which can give the broth an off flavor. Since fish broth is easily frozen, you may want to double the recipe. If you double it, there is no need to also double the fish trimmings—3 to 3½ pounds will suffice. I like to freeze the broth in varying quantities, from ½ cup to 1 quart, so that I have on hand the precise amount that each recipe requires. The frozen broth can be defrosted in a microwave oven, in the refrigerator, or in a saucepan over low heat.

2½ pounds FISH BONES, with heads, gills, and organ tissue removed (see "Preparation tips")
  2 cups coarsely chopped onion
  1 cup thinly sliced celery
  1 bay leaf
  8 sprigs parsley
  3 sprigs fresh thyme *or* ½ teaspoon dried thyme leaves
1½ cups dry white wine
 10 peppercorns
  3 whole cloves
  6 cups water

1. Place all the ingredients in a large pot. Bring the mixture to a boil, reduce the heat, and simmer the broth for 20 minutes.
2. Let the broth cool in the pot. Then pour it through a fine-meshed strainer. Pour the broth into one or more containers, and refrigerate or freeze it. ■

CATFISH GUMBO

■

4 TO 6 SERVINGS

Okra arrived in the Americas as a stowaway from Africa; slaves carried its seeds hidden in their hair. The slaves called this unusual vegetable "ngombo." Hence the name *gumbo* for the soup in which it is a vital ingredient. Okra has for too long remained an obscure vegetable outside the South, and it is high time it emerged from its regional and ethnic limits. For here is a food loaded with nutrients, low in calories, and delicious. It is rich in calcium and cholesterol-lowering soluble fiber (it is the fiber that makes okra the essential ingredient in gumbo). With salad and bread, this thick, hearty soup is easily turned into a satisfying main-dish meal.

Preparation tips: Start the rice while the soup is simmering in step 2. If fish broth is unavailable, chicken or beef broth can be substituted. As with most soups, this one not only tolerates advanced preparation, but is the better for it. It also freezes well.

   2 **teaspoons olive oil** *or* **canola oil**
   1 **cup chopped onion**
   2 **teaspoons minced garlic**
   1 **seeded, minced jalapeño, or to taste**
   1 **cup chopped celery**
   1 **cup chopped green bell pepper**
   1 **16-ounce can tomatoes, drained and juice reserved, cut into** $1/2$**-inch dice**
   3 **cups fish broth**
   1 **bay leaf**
 $1/2$ **teaspoon dried thyme leaves**
 $1/2$ **teaspoon salt, or to taste**
 $1/4$ **teaspoon freshly ground black pepper, or to taste**
 $1/2$ **teaspoon Tabasco sauce** *or* $1/8$ **teaspoon cayenne, or to taste**
 $3/4$ **pound fresh okra, tops trimmed (or 10 ounces frozen okra, defrosted), cut into** $1/2$**-inch slices**
   1 **cup corn kernels, fresh or frozen (optional)**
   1 **pound** CATFISH FILLETS, **cut into 1-inch pieces**
 $1^1/2$ **cups hot cooked rice**
Chopped cilantro *or* **fresh parsley for garnish (optional)**

1. Briefly heat the olive oil or canola oil in a 4-quart or larger saucepan that has a lid, preferably a pan with a nonstick surface. Add the onion, garlic, jalapeño, celery, and green bell pepper. Sauté the vegetables for about 5 minutes.

2. Add the tomatoes with their juice, broth, bay leaf, thyme, salt, ground pepper, and Tabasco sauce or cayenne, and stir the ingredients to combine them well. Add the okra, and mix it in gently. Bring the soup to a boil, reduce the heat, cover the pot, and simmer the soup for about 10 minutes.

3. Add the corn (if desired) and the catfish, and simmer the soup for another 5 minutes or until the catfish is just cooked through. Remove the bay leaf.

4. To serve the gumbo, place ¼ cup to ⅓ cup of the cooked rice in each bowl, ladle the gumbo over the rice, and garnish each serving with the cilantro or parsley (if desired). ∎

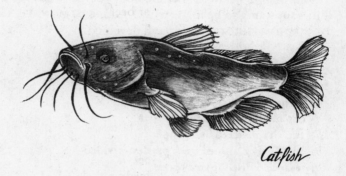

Catfish

MONKFISH GUMBO

Having discovered the culinary, gustatory, and nutritional beauty of okra in midlife, I have been trying to make up for lost time by cooking frequently with this calcium- and fiber-rich vegetable. Upon finding bargains in both sea-fresh monkfish and garden-fresh okra on a Saturday, I devised this thick, hearty soup (some would say it's a stew) that can serve as the main dish at dinner or, with bread, a complete lunch.

Preparation tips: I use browned flour as a no-fat substitute for roux, which is traditionally used to thicken soups, stews, and some sauces. To prepare browned flour, sprinkle a thin layer of flour on a cookie sheet, and bake it for 1 hour in a 325°F oven. Let the flour cool, and store it in a tightly closed jar. The soup can also be made with 1 pound of MONKFISH and ½ pound SMALL OR MEDIUM SHRIMP, peeled and deveined.

    2 teaspoons olive oil
    1 cup chopped onion
    2 teaspoons minced garlic
    ¾ cup chopped green bell pepper
    ¾ cup chopped red bell pepper
    ½ cup finely chopped fresh parsley, divided
    ¾ teaspoon dried thyme leaves
    1 teaspoon salt, or to taste
    ½ teaspoon Tabasco sauce, or to taste
    ¼ teaspoon cayenne, or to taste
    4 cups fish broth
    2 cups diced fresh plum (Roma) tomatoes
    2 tablespoons browned flour (optional—see "Preparation tip")
    ¼ cup cold water
    ¾ to 1 pound okra, stems trimmed, cut crosswise into ½-inch pieces
    1½ pounds MONKFISH, cut into 1-inch cubes
    2 cups hot cooked rice

1. Briefly heat the olive oil in a nonstick kettle or Dutch oven. Add the onion, and sauté it over medium-low heat, stirring it often, for 3 minutes. Add the garlic, and cook the vegetables for another 30 seconds. Add the green bell pepper, red bell pepper, ¼ cup of the parsley, the thyme, salt, Tabasco sauce, and cayenne, and cook the ingredients, stirring them often, for 3 minutes.

2. Add the broth and tomatoes, stir the ingredients, and bring the mixture to a simmer.

3. Meanwhile, place the browned flour (if you are using it) in a small bowl, and stir in the cold water, whisking the mixture to form a smooth paste. Gradually add the flour mixture to the simmering broth, stirring the ingredients constantly. Cook the broth mixture over medium-low heat for 20 minutes.

4. Add the okra to the simmering broth, and cook the vegetable for 5 minutes. Stir in the monkfish (or monkfish and shrimp—see "Preparation tips"), and cook the soup for another 5 minutes or until the fish is just done. Sprinkle the soup with the remaining parsley.

5. To serve the gumbo, place about ⅓ cup of hot rice in each bowl, and ladle the gumbo over the rice. ■

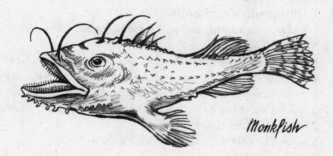

Monkfish

POTATO, CORN, AND MONKFISH SOUP

■

Two starchy vegetables in one dish? Of course, say the devotees of *Jane Brody's Good Food Book,* a celebration of the foods rich in complex carbohydrates (starches). This lean soup with an Italian flair will stick to your ribs (but not your midriff) without straining your budget. Monkfish was originally billed as "poor man's lobster." Although its price has risen with its popularity, it is still far cheaper than lobster and a reasonable substitute in a soup.

Preparation tip: In place of monkfish, you can use any firm-fleshed mild fish such as **CATFISH** or **COD** or even **SMALL SHRIMP** or **SCALLOPS.**

    2 teaspoons canola oil
    1 cup chopped onion
    1 tablespoon minced garlic
    1 tablespoon seeded, minced jalapeño (about 1 pepper)
    3 cups chicken broth
    1 pound small red potatoes, unpeeled, cut into ³/₄-inch cubes
    1 16-ounce can tomatoes, drained and juice reserved, coarsely chopped
    ½ pound green beans, trimmed and cut into ³/₄-inch pieces
    ½ pound zucchini, halved lengthwise and cut into ¹/₂-inch pieces
    2 cups corn kernels
    1 pound **MONKFISH**, cut into 1-inch cubes
    1 tablespoon chopped fresh basil *or* 1 teaspoon dried basil
    2 teaspoons chopped fresh thyme leaves *or* ³/₄ teaspoon dried thyme leaves
    2 teaspoons chopped fresh oregano *or* ³/₄ teaspoon dried oregano leaves
    ½ teaspoon salt (optional)
    ¼ teaspoon freshly ground white pepper
    2 tablespoons chopped fresh parsley for garnish

1. Briefly heat the canola oil in a soup pot or Dutch oven, preferably one with a nonstick surface. Add the onion, and sauté it for 1 to 2 minutes. Add the garlic and jalapeño, and sauté the vegetables 1 minute longer.
2. Add the broth, potatoes, and tomatoes with their juice. Bring the mixture to a boil, reduce the heat to medium-low, and simmer the mixture for 7 minutes. Add the green beans, and simmer the mixture for 3 minutes. Add the zucchini, and simmer the mixture for another 3 minutes. Add all the remaining ingredients *except the parsley,* and simmer the soup for 5 minutes. Serve the soup garnished with the parsley. ■

LEEK, FENNEL, AND MONKFISH SOUP

■

Leeks are a glorious vegetable all winter long. I often use them as an ingredient to "sweeten" Brussels sprouts and Swiss chard. But they are best known in soups like leek and potato soup or vichyssoise, the cold pureed version of same (see, for example, the soup on page 217). But for a lighter and, I think, tastier base for fish, I used fennel in place of potato.

Preparation tips: Like children, leeks love the dirt and require care in removing the sand between their layers. If you are using small or medium leeks, slice them crosswise, place the slices in a colander, and rinse them thoroughly under cold running water. If your leeks are large, first cut them lengthwise in quarters almost to the root end, and, whisking the cut ends like a feather duster, rinse the leeks under running water one at a time. If it is available, purchase a fennel bulb that has some of its feathery leaves attached.

   1 **tablespoon butter** *or* **margarine**
   4 **cups sliced leeks (about 4 medium-large leeks), white and tender
      light-green parts only**
   3 **cups sliced fennel bulb (sliced crosswise—halve or quarter the
      slices if the bulb is large)**
   7 **cups fish broth (preferably)** *or* **chicken broth**
  1/2 **teaspoon dried thyme leaves**
  1/2 **teaspoon freshly ground white pepper, or to taste**
Pinch cayenne (optional)
Salt to taste (omit if using salty broth or broth cubes)
   1 **pound** MONKFISH, **cut into 1-inch pieces**
   2 **tablespoons chopped fennel feathers (leaves) for garnish (optional)**
Plain croutons for garnish

1. Melt the butter or margarine in a large nonstick saucepan (at least 4 quarts) or Dutch oven that has a lid. Add the leeks, cover the top of the pan with a sheet of wax paper, and cover the pan tightly. Over medium-low heat, "sweat" the leeks for 5 minutes, removing the lid and wax paper to stir the vegetable twice.
2. Add the fennel, replace the wax paper and lid, and continue sweating the vegetables for 2 to 3 minutes or until the fennel is barely tender.
3. Add the broth, thyme, ground pepper, cayenne (if desired), and salt (if you are using it). Bring the liquid to a boil, reduce the heat to medium, and add the monkfish. Simmer the soup for 3 to 5 minutes or until the fish is just cooked through.
4. Serve the soup sprinkled with the fennel leaves (if desired) and croutons. ■

MANHATTAN-STYLE HALIBUT CHOWDER

■   6 MAIN-DISH SERVINGS OR 8 FIRST-COURSE SERVINGS

Chowder is a popular, simple soup that can nourish body and soul. When it is made Manhattan-style (that is, tomato-based without milk or cream), as in this recipe, it is also a dieter's delight that can easily become a satisfying lunch when it is served with whole-grain bread. Manhattan-style chowders are so named because they first appeared there in the 1930s, in Italian restaurants. I made this chowder with Alaskan halibut steaks that were sold frozen. My version (even enjoyed by tasters not keen on fish) is based on a recipe from the Alaska Seafood Marketing Institute.

Preparation tips: The chowder can be prepared in advance and reheated or frozen—as long as you do not overcook the fish at the outset. If you start with halibut steaks, first remove the skin and then cut the flesh off the bone before cubing it. You can halve this recipe, if you wish, using a 14-ounce to 16-ounce can of tomatoes.

- 1 tablespoon olive oil *or* canola oil
- 1½ cups chopped onion
- 1 tablespoon minced garlic
- 2 cups julienned carrots, with strips about 1½ inches long
- 2 cups diagonally sliced celery (about 3 ribs)
- 1 28-ounce can tomatoes, drained and juice reserved, coarsely chopped
- 2 cups chicken broth
- 4 tablespoons (¼ cup) chopped fresh parsley, divided
- ½ teaspoon dried thyme leaves
- ½ teaspoon dried basil
- ½ teaspoon salt, or to taste
- ¼ teaspoon freshly ground black pepper, or to taste
- ⅛ teaspoon cayenne (optional)
- 2 pounds HALIBUT STEAKS *or* 1½ pounds skinless HALIBUT FILLETS

1. Briefly heat the olive oil or canola oil in a large saucepan (4 to 5 quarts) with a nonstick surface and a lid. Add the onion, and sauté it over medium heat for about 2 minutes. Add the garlic, and sauté the vegetables 1 minute longer. Add the carrots and celery, and sauté the vegetables for about 5 minutes, stirring them often.

2. Add the tomatoes and their juice, broth, 2 tablespoons of the parsley, thyme, basil, salt, ground pepper, and cayenne (if desired). Bring the mixture to a boil, reduce the heat to medium-low, cover the pot, and simmer the mixture for 20 minutes.

3. Meanwhile, cut the halibut into boneless and skinless 1-inch cubes. Add them to the vegetable mixture, stirring the ingredients just enough to cover the fish with the broth. Cover the pot, and simmer the chowder for another 5 minutes or until the fish is just cooked through. Serve the chowder sprinkled with the remaining 2 tablespoons of the parsley. ∎

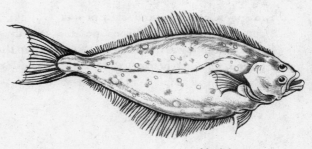

Halibut

STORMY-NIGHT FISH SOUP

■

A December storm with the ferocity of a hurricane (but none of its distinction) gave rise to this dish. Since no one was willing to go out shopping in the driving rain and winds exceeding 50 miles an hour, I made this hearty, bone-warming, yet simple-to-prepare soup from what was already in the house. The delicious leftovers were used for lunch in the days that followed.

Preparation tips: Broccoflower is, as you might have guessed, a cross between broccoli and cauliflower and is pale green in color. You can substitute either or both its genetic parents to prepare this soup. You can use almost any moderately firm boneless white fish, alone or in combination.

2	teaspoons canola oil *or* butter *or* margarine
1½	cups chopped onion
1	tablespoon minced garlic
1	tablespoon seeded, minced jalapeño (about 1 pepper)
1½	cups diced celery
2	cups diced carrots
1½	cups diced bell peppers (green *or* red *or* both)
8	cups fish broth
1	cup dry white wine
2	tablespoons balsamic vinegar
1	tablespoon fresh thyme *or* 1 teaspoon dried thyme leaves
1	tablespoon chopped fresh basil *or* 1 teaspoon dried basil
1	teaspoon salt, or to taste
½	teaspoon freshly ground white pepper
2	cups peeled, diced all-purpose potatoes *or* boiling potatoes
4	cups broccoflower flowerets (see "Preparation tips")
2½	pounds moderately firm WHITE FISH FILLETS (for example, cod ["scrod"] and tilapia), cut into bite-sized cubes

1. Briefly heat the oil or butter or margarine in a soup kettle, preferably one with a nonstick surface. Add the onion, garlic, and jalapeño, and sauté the vegetables for 2 minutes, stirring them often.
2. Add the celery, carrots, and bell peppers, and sauté the vegetables for another 2 minutes.
3. Add the broth, wine, vinegar, thyme, basil, salt, and ground pepper, and stir the ingredients. Bring the mixture to a boil, reduce the heat, and simmer the soup for 10 minutes.
4. Add the potatoes, and simmer the soup for another 10 minutes.
5. Add the broccoflower and fish, and simmer the soup for 5 minutes or until the vegetables are just tender and the fish is cooked through. ■

Cod

Tilapia

CURRIED TUNA AND POTATO CHOWDER

■

You may think it a travesty to put fresh tuna in a spicy soup. But just wait until you taste this zippy chowder, which I consider one of my best creations in the soup department. By using evaporated skimmed milk to "cream" it, I keep the fat and calorie count low but the flavor high. As with other curries, fruit—in this case, fresh apple—provides a delightful balance for the seasonings in the soup.

Preparation tip: In this soup, the starch from the potato helps to stabilize the evaporated skimmed milk. But if you are concerned about the milk separating when it is heated, you can dissolve 1 tablespoon of cornstarch in 2 tablespoons of the milk and stir this mixture into the rest of the milk before it is added to the soup.

> 2 teaspoons olive oil *or* canola oil
> 1 cup chopped onion
> 1 tablespoon minced garlic
> 1 tablespoon seeded, minced jalapeño (about 1 pepper)
> 1 cup diced celery
> 2 teaspoons curry powder
> 1/2 teaspoon hot curry powder *or* an additional 1/2 teaspoon curry powder
> 1 teaspoon cumin
> 1 teaspoon paprika
> 1 teaspoon salt, or to taste (can be omitted if using salted broth)
> 3 cups fish broth (preferably unsalted)
> 1 cup water
> 1 1/2 pounds potatoes, peeled and cut into 1/2 inch cubes
> 1 12-ounce can evaporated skimmed milk (see "Preparation tip")
> 1 pound TUNA, cut into 1/2-inch cubes
> 1 cup cooked or frozen and thawed peas
> 1 small red unpeeled apple, finely diced, for garnish

1. Briefly heat the olive oil or canola oil in a soup kettle or Dutch oven, preferably one that has a lid and a nonstick surface. Add the onion, and sauté it for 2 minutes. Add the garlic and jalapeño, and sauté the vegetables for another minute. Add the celery, curry powder, hot curry powder, cumin, paprika, and salt (if using), and sauté the ingredients 1 minute longer.
2. Stir in the broth and water, and bring the mixture to a boil. Add the potatoes, reduce the heat, partially cover the pot, and simmer the mixture for 10 minutes.

3. Add the evaporated milk (see "Preparation tip"), and bring the mixture up to a boil. Add the tuna, and, when the ingredients just reach the boiling stage, reduce the heat, and simmer the chowder in the uncovered pot for 4 minutes. Add the peas, and cook the chowder 1 minute longer.

4. Serve the chowder piping hot, topping each serving with the diced apple. ■

Tuna

MANHATTAN-STYLE CLAM CHOWDER
■

6 TO 8 SERVINGS

As a child, I had a strong preference for the creamy New England–style clam chowder. Little did I know then that when it is well prepared, the far-less-caloric Manhattan-style chowder offers strong competition. In this recipe, the lean Canadian bacon provides only a bit of fat but lots of flavor.

Preparation tips: I make this chowder with whole fresh clams, using both their meat and their natural juice in the soup. But you can also prepare this dish with canned clams—you'll need about 2 14-ounce cans. Unfortunately, one of the best brands, Progresso, comes in 10½-ounce cans, but you can manage with just 2 of these. The chowder lends itself to advance preparation and reheating, but if you freeze it, the potatoes may become mushy.

>   1 **cup water**
>   2 **dozen** CHOWDER CLAMS *or* **large** CHERRYSTONE CLAMS, **well scrubbed,** *or*
>   **1½ cups** CANNED MINCED CLAMS, **juice reserved (see "Preparation tips")**
>   2 **ounces Canadian bacon, finely chopped (about ⅓ cup)**
>   1 **pound potatoes, peeled and cut into ⅓-inch dice**
>   1⅔ **cups diced onion**
>   1 **cup diced celery**
>   1 **28-ounce can tomatoes, drained and juice reserved, coarsely chopped**
>   2 **cups clam juice (reserved from the clam cooking liquid)**
>   1 **bay leaf**
>   1 **tablespoon finely chopped fresh parsley**
>   1 **tablespoon sugar**
>   ½ **teaspoon dried thyme leaves**
>   ½ **teaspoon freshly ground black pepper**

1. If you are using fresh clams, place the water and the clams in a large kettle with a lid. Bring the liquid to a boil in the uncovered pot, then lower the heat to medium, cover the kettle, and cook the clams until they open. With tongs or a slotted spoon, remove the clams from the liquid as they open (discard any that have not opened after 7 minutes of steaming). *Reserve all the liquid.* When the clams are cool enough to handle, remove the meat from the shells. (If the shells are intact and nice-looking, you can separate the halves, boil the shells in water to remove all traces of fishiness, then dry and store them for use as hors d'oeuvre containers—see, for example, Baked Clam Appetizer on page 148.)
2. Finely chop the clam meat, and set it aside (refrigerate the clams if you will not be using them within ½ hour). You should have about 1½ cups

of chopped clams, but a little more or less will not matter. If you are using canned clams, drain them, set them aside, and *reserve the liquid.*

3. Strain the clam juice from the cooked live clams through several layers of cheesecloth or a fine-meshed sieve into a 2-cup measuring cup, and set the juice aside. If necessary, add water to make 2 cups of liquid.

4. To prepare the chowder, in a 5-quart or 6-quart pot or Dutch oven with a nonstick surface, cook the Canadian bacon for about 1 minute, stirring it constantly.

5. *Except for the reserved clams,* add all of the remaining soup ingredients, including the reserved tomato liquid. Bring the chowder to a boil, reduce the heat to medium-low, and simmer the chowder for 15 minutes.

6. Add the reserved clams, simmer the soup for another 15 minutes, remove the bay leaf, and serve the chowder. ■

NEW ENGLAND–STYLE CLAM CHOWDER
■

Before I converted to low-fat dining, creamy New England–style clam chowder was one of my favorite soups. In developing recipes for this book, I found that I could prepare a delicious, low-fat chowder that more than passed muster with an old friend, Daniel Sullivan, who grew up in New England on the traditional, creamier version. This kind of chowder was developed by New Englanders who, using their ample supply of dairy products, modified a basic French recipe.

Preparation tips: You can use either steamed fresh clams or canned clams or a combination of the two. Fresh clams can be steamed at any time, their meat removed from the shells and frozen and the clam liquor strained and frozen in a separate container. Be sure to reserve all the liquid from the canned clams and/or the clam liquor from steamed fresh clams; you may also need additional bottled clam juice or fish broth. Since the clam liquid as well as the Canadian bacon are salty, I find no need to add salt to this soup.

> 2 dozen CHOWDER CLAMS *or* 4 dozen LITTLENECK CLAMS, well scrubbed, *or* 3
>   6$^{1}/_{2}$-ounce cans MINCED CLAMS *or* 2 10$^{1}/_{2}$-ounce cans minced clams (see
>   "Preparation tips")
> 2 teaspoons olive oil
> 3 ounces Canadian bacon, minced (about $^{1}/_{2}$ cup)
> $^{1}/_{2}$ cup finely chopped onion
> $^{1}/_{2}$ cup finely chopped celery
> $^{1}/_{4}$ cup chopped scallions, including some green tops
> 1 teaspoon minced garlic
> 3 cups clam juice (see "Preparation tips") *or* clam juice and fish broth
> 3 cups water
> 2 pounds potatoes, peeled and cut into $^{1}/_{3}$-inch dice
> 2 cups corn kernels
> $^{1}/_{3}$ cup finely chopped fresh parsley
> 1 teaspoon dried thyme leaves
> $^{1}/_{4}$ teaspoon freshly ground black pepper, or to taste
> 2 tablespoons cornstarch
> 1 12-ounce can evaporated skimmed milk, divided

1. If you are using fresh clams, place them in a large kettle that has a lid. Steam the clams in the covered pot for 5 minutes, or until they open. Remove the clams from the liquid as they open (discard any that have not opened after 7 minutes of steaming), *reserving all the liquid.* When the clams are cool enough to handle, remove the meat from the shells.

2. Chop the clam meat into small pieces, about 1/3-inch cubes, and set the clams aside (refrigerate the clams if you will not be using them within 1/2 hour). If you are using canned clams, drain them, *reserving the liquid,* and set them aside.

3. Strain the clam juice from the cooked live clams through several layers of cheesecloth or a fine-meshed sieve into a 4-cup measuring cup, and set the juice aside. Chill the clam liquid if it will not be used right away.

4. To prepare the chowder, briefly heat the olive oil in a kettle or Dutch oven that has a nonstick surface. Add the Canadian bacon, onion, celery, scallions, and garlic, and sauté the ingredients over medium-low heat for 5 minutes or until the vegetables are soft.

5. If you have less than 3 cups of reserved clam liquid, add bottled clam juice or fish broth to make 3 cups, then add this liquid to the kettle along with the 3 cups water. Bring the ingredients to a boil, add the potatoes, and cook the mixture for 10 minutes.

6. Add the reserved clams, corn, parsley, thyme, and pepper, and simmer the chowder 8 minutes longer.

7. While the chowder simmers, place the cornstarch in a small bowl, and add 1/4 cup of the evaporated milk, whisking the mixture until it is smooth. Pour the remaining milk into a small saucepan. Add the cornstarch mixture, and heat the milk, stirring it often, until it begins to thicken. Add the thickened milk to the chowder, stirring the mixture well, and simmer the chowder 5 minutes longer. ∎

CONCH CHOWDER

■

Conchs (pronounced "konks") are marine snails that live in those large spiral shells that people in the tropics and subtropics sometimes use to decorate their yards. Cool-water conchs live along the Atlantic seaboard.

Preparation tips: Conchs (also known as scungilli) are nearly always sold cleaned (peeled) and fully cooked. But check the label since some are only partially cooked and may need further boiling to soften the meat. **WHELK** can be substituted for conch.

1 tablespoon olive oil
2 ounces Canadian bacon, diced (about ⅓ cup)
1 cup chopped onion
1 teaspoon minced garlic
1 pound COOKED, peeled CONCH, coarsely chopped
1 teaspoon fennel seeds
¼ teaspoon red pepper flakes
2 cups water
3 cups fish broth, *or* 2 cups clam juice and 1 cup water
2 cups tomato juice
1 28-ounce can tomatoes, drained and juice reserved, coarsely chopped
2 carrots, cut into ⅓-inch dice
½ cup coarsely chopped celery
2 large potatoes, peeled and cut into ½-inch cubes
2 tablespoons finely chopped fresh thyme *or* 1 tablespoon dried thyme leaves
Freshly ground black pepper to taste
Salt to taste
½ cup dry sherry
½ cup chopped fresh parsley

Conch

1. Briefly heat the olive oil in a nonstick Dutch oven or soup pot that has a lid. Add the Canadian bacon, onion, and garlic, and cook the mixture, stirring it, for about 1 minute, taking care not to burn the garlic. Add the conch, fennel seeds, and red pepper flakes, and sauté the mixture, for another minute.

2. Add the water, broth (or clam juice and water), and tomato juice. Bring the ingredients to a boil, cover the pot, and simmer the mixture for 20 minutes. Add the tomatoes with their juice, carrots, celery, potatoes, and thyme. Bring the chowder back to a gentle boil, reduce the heat, partially cover the pot, and simmer the chowder for 25 minutes, stirring it several times.

3. Season the chowder with the ground pepper, and taste the chowder before adding the salt. Remove the pot from the heat, stir in the sherry, and, before serving it, sprinkle the chowder with the parsley. ■

SMOKED-SWORDFISH CHOWDER

■

6 SERVINGS

It is well worth putting the Mercedes-Benz of fish steaks into this chowder, which can easily be a main dish for lunch or a light supper. Swordfish holds up nicely when it is diced, and the smoking enhances its flavor without drying out the fish.

Preparation tips: The chowder can also be made with other types of fish that are firm-fleshed, such as **SHARK, MONKFISH, MARLIN,** or **TUNA.** Or you can use **LEFTOVER COOKED FISH** or even **RAW DICED FISH.** If you use the latter, add the fish in step 3 after the potatoes have cooked for 6 minutes.

   1 **pound** SWORDFISH **(see "Preparation tips")**
Salt (optional)
Freshly ground black pepper
Wood chips for smoking
   2 **teaspoons olive oil**
   2 **ounces Canadian bacon, finely diced (about** $\frac{1}{3}$ **cup)**
   2 **cups finely chopped onion**
   6 **cups fish broth**
1$\frac{1}{2}$ **pounds all-purpose potatoes, peeled and cut into** $\frac{1}{2}$**-inch dice**
   1 **cup diced red bell pepper**
   2 **cups cooked corn kernels**
 $\frac{1}{4}$ **teaspoon freshly ground black pepper, or to taste**
 $\frac{1}{4}$ **cup chopped cilantro** *or* **fresh parsley for garnish**

1. Sprinkle the swordfish lightly with the salt (if desired) and pepper. Place the swordfish on the rack of a stovetop smoker into which the wood chips have been placed, and, following the manufacturer's instructions, smoke the fish for about 12 minutes. Remove the fish from the smoker, and place it on a cutting board. Remove any skin from the fish, and cut the fish into $\frac{1}{3}$-inch dice. Put the fish aside.
2. Briefly heat the olive oil in a Dutch oven or a 3-quart or 4-quart saucepan. Add the Canadian bacon and onion, and sauté the ingredients over low heat for 15 minutes or until the onion begins to turn golden.
3. Add the broth, and bring the mixture to a boil. Reduce the heat, and simmer the ingredients for 5 minutes. Add the potatoes, bring the mixture back to a boil, then reduce the heat, and simmer the ingredients for 8 minutes. Add the red bell pepper, corn, and the reserved fish, bring the mixture to a boil, reduce the heat, and simmer the ingredients 3 minutes longer.
4. Season the soup with the ground pepper, and serve it piping hot, garnished with the cilantro or parsley. ■

OYSTER STEW

The oysters I use for this soup are raised in certified waters on an oyster farm in South Bend, Washington. Since these oysters are sold in fish markets and at supermarket fish counters already shucked and freshly packed in half-pint plastic containers, preparing this tasty, low-fat soup is hardly more difficult than flipping a lid.

Preparation tips: If you must shuck the oysters yourself, see page 77 for instructions. For those not as fond as I am of chopping by hand, the onion, mushrooms, and celery can be chopped in a food processor. But be careful not to overdo it; you should end up with distinct pieces, not a puree. In this recipe, a little cornstarch is used to stabilize the milk. This will allow you to heat and reheat the soup without fear of having the milk separate.

1 **pint SHUCKED OYSTERS with their liquid**
2 **teaspoons olive oil** *or* **canola oil**
1 **cup finely chopped onion**
1 **cup finely chopped mushrooms (¼ pound)**
½ **cup finely chopped celery (1 large stalk)**
2 **cups fish broth**
½ **cup water**
1 **pound potatoes, peeled and cut into ½-inch dice**
1 **bay leaf**
½ **teaspoon dried thyme leaves**
¼ **teaspoon hot paprika,** *or* ½ **teaspoon sweet paprika and** ⅛ **teaspoon cayenne**
1 **tablespoon cornstarch**
1 **tablespoon plus 1 cup skim milk, divided**
1 **tablespoon fresh lemon juice**
¾ **cup diced red bell pepper**
¼ **cup chopped fresh parsley**
¼ **teaspoon salt, or to taste (optional)**
¼ **teaspoon freshly ground black pepper**
¼ **cup sliced or minced scallions**

1. Drain the liquor from the oysters into a bowl. Into another bowl, strain the liquor through a sieve lined with several layers of cheesecloth to remove any sand. Rinse the oysters under cold running water, and, if they are large, cut them in half or quarters. Recombine the liquor and the oysters, and set them aside.

2. Briefly heat the olive oil or canola oil in a soup pot or Dutch oven, preferably one with a nonstick surface. Add the onion, mushrooms, and celery, and sauté the vegetables, stirring them often, for 5 minutes or until they are soft.

3. Add the fish broth and water, and bring the mixture to a boil.

4. Add the potatoes, bay leaf, thyme, and hot paprika (or sweet paprika and cayenne), and, when the mixture returns to a boil, reduce the heat to low, and simmer the ingredients for 10 minutes.

5. While the mixture simmers, in a small bowl combine the cornstarch with the 1 tablespoon of skim milk, stirring the ingredients until they are combined. Add the 1 cup of skim milk, stirring the ingredients well.

6. When the potatoes are barely tender, add the milk mixture to the pot. Stir in the reserved oysters and their liquor, the lemon juice, red bell pepper, parsley, salt (if desired), and ground pepper. Bring the stew nearly to a boil, lower the heat, and simmer the stew for 5 minutes or just long enough to cook the oysters. Before serving the stew, remove the bay leaf, and stir in the scallions. ■

KALE, POTATO, AND MUSSEL SOUP

■

Kale is a much underappreciated vegetable, probably used more by gardeners and caterers to form eye-catching displays than by consumers attracted to its rich green color, slightly nippy flavor, and health-saving nutrients. Since kale is an assertive vegetable, it needs a distinctive seafood to stand up to it. So I chose mussels along with a flavorful broth, leeks, potatoes, and carrots, to create a low-calorie, nutrient-packed, colorful, satisfying soup.

Preparation tips: The mussels can be steamed and removed from their shells and the broth strained well in advance of preparing the soup. In fact, the cooked mussel meat and the broth can be frozen in separate containers. You can wash the leeks after they are sliced by placing them in a colander under cold running water, stirring them around a bit, then draining them thoroughly. Kale, which can be gritty, is best washed in a sink full of cold water.

    3 pounds MUSSELS, preferably small ones
   1/2 cup dry white wine
    2 tablespoons minced shallots
    2 teaspoons minced garlic
    2 teaspoons olive oil
 1 1/2 cups thinly sliced leeks
   1/3 cup finely chopped celery
    2 teaspoons minced garlic
 2 1/2 cups chicken broth
 2 1/2 cups unpeeled red new potatoes, cut into 1/2-inch dice
    1 cup carrots, cut into 1/4-inch dice
    1 teaspoon white-wine Worcestershire sauce
   1/4 teaspoon Tabasco sauce
   1/4 teaspoon freshly ground black pepper
    1 pound kale, thoroughly washed, stems removed
    2 cups (approximately) mussel cooking liquid

1. Debeard and rinse the mussels well, and place them in a large, squat pot (6 quarts or more) that has a tight-fitting cover. Pour the wine over them, and sprinkle them with the shallots and garlic. Bring the ingredients to a boil, reduce the heat, cover the pot tightly, give it a shake, and steam the mussels for 5 minutes or until the mussels open.
2. Remove the pot from the heat. When the mussels are cool enough to handle, remove the meat from the shells, discarding the shells and any mus-

sels that did not open. Strain the cooking liquid through several layers of cheesecloth. Reserve the mussels (if they are large, you may want to cut them in half at this point) and the cooking liquid (you should have about 2 cups). Wash and dry the pot.

3. Briefly heat the olive oil in the clean, dry pot. Add the leeks, celery, and garlic, and sauté the vegetables, stirring them often, over medium-low heat for 5 minutes, taking care not to let them burn.

4. Add the chicken broth, and bring the mixture to a boil. Add the potatoes, carrots, Worcestershire sauce, Tabasco sauce, and pepper. Let the mixture return to a boil, reduce the heat, cover the pot, and simmer the vegetables for 5 minutes.

5. While the vegetables are simmering, cut the kale into 1-inch-square pieces. When the vegetables are done simmering, add the reserved mussel cooking liquid, and bring the mixture back to a simmer. Add the kale, cover the pot, and simmer the soup for another 5 minutes.

6. Add the reserved mussel meat, and simmer the soup for 30 seconds or until the mussels are just heated through. Serve the soup piping hot. ∎

Mussels

CARROT AND LEEK SOUP WITH SHRIMP

■   4 SERVINGS

This is an especially simple carrot-soup recipe, both hot and sweet. It's the shrimp that make it extraordinary.

Preparation tip: Although the ingredients list specifies peeling and deveining the shrimp, the deveining part, as I've noted elsewhere, is purely a cosmetic—not a health—issue and is an instruction you can disregard when you are using small or medium shrimp, as is the case here.

Serving suggestion: If possible, serve the soup in shallow soup plates; it looks best if the shrimp do not sink out of sight.

    1 teaspoon canola oil
    1 cup sliced leeks (white and tender green parts only),
       well washed and drained
1½ pounds carrots, thickly sliced
    5 cups canned or homemade chicken broth
  ¼ cup "lite" or part-skim ricotta
  ⅛ teaspoon nutmeg
Salt to taste, divided
Freshly ground black pepper to taste, divided
  ¼ teaspoon Tabasco sauce
    1 tablespoon brandy
    2 teaspoons butter *or* margarine
  ¾   pound MEDIUM SHRIMP, peeled and deveined (see "Preparation tip")
  ¼ cup chopped fresh parsley

1. Heat the oil in a large nonstick saucepan that has a lid. Add the leeks, and cook them over low heat for 3 minutes or until they wilt. Add the carrots and broth, and cover the pan. Bring the ingredients to a boil, reduce the heat, and simmer the mixture for 30 minutes.
2. With a strainer or slotted spoon, remove the vegetables from the pot, reserving the liquid. Place the vegetables, along with the ricotta, nutmeg, salt, and pepper, in a food processor or blender jar along with 1 cup of the soup liquid. Process the ingredients until they are smooth.
3. Add the puree to the remaining liquid in the pot along with the Tabasco sauce and brandy, whisking the ingredients to blend them well. Check the soup for seasoning and thickness. If the soup is too thick, thin it with some broth or water. Set the soup aside, and keep it warm.

4. Heat the butter or margarine in a nonstick skillet, and add the shrimp. Sprinkle the shrimp with the salt and pepper. Sauté the shrimp for about 1½ minutes on each side.

5. To serve, ladle the soup into individual bowls or soup plates. Arrange several shrimp in each bowl or plate, and sprinkle each serving with 1 tablespoon of the parsley. ■

RED LENTIL SOUP WITH SCALLOPS

■

This soup was inspired by one served at the glamorous Hudson River Club in downtown Manhattan. It is an ingenious invention because it takes a healthful, humble soup and dresses it up with minimal fuss: the addition of scallops as a garnish. In this recipe, I use of one of my favorite pieces of equipment, the stovetop smoker, to cook the scallops, thus adding a little of the traditional smoky flavor to the lentil soup.

Preparation tips: If you don't have a smoker, you can grill or broil the scallops. Or, instead of scallops, a single SMOKED SHRIMP per serving (see page 134) is also fine. If you intend to use canned rather than homemade broth, be wary of the low-salt brands. Most have little flavor. It is better to use the old standby versions, unless you know you have a salt problem, and add no salt to the soup as it cooks. The lentil soup can be prepared a day ahead through step 3, then refrigerated for 1 or 2 days or frozen. On serving day, cook the scallops, and finish preparing the soup.

SOUP

- 2 teaspoons olive oil
- 1 cup coarsely chopped onion
- 1 tablespoon minced garlic
- 1 cup coarsely chopped celery
- 1 cup coarsely chopped carrots
- 2½ cups red lentils, picked over and carefully rinsed
- 6 cups chicken broth, homemade or canned (see "Preparation tips")
- 2 cups water
- 2 bay leaves
- 2 sprigs thyme *or* ½ teaspoon dried thyme leaves
- 1 tablespoon red-wine vinegar
- ¼ cup water *or* additional broth (if needed)
- ¼ cup chopped fresh parsley

SCALLOPS

- 12 to 15 large SEA SCALLOPS, cut in half crosswise
- 2 teaspoons olive oil
- 1 teaspoon freshly squeezed lemon juice

Salt to taste

Freshly ground black pepper to taste

1. To prepare the soup, heat the olive oil in a large nonstick soup pot or Dutch oven. Add the onion to the pot, and cook it, stirring the vegetable, until it begins to wilt. Add the garlic, and cook the vegetables 1 minute longer, taking care not to burn the garlic.

2. Add all the remaining soup ingredients *except the vinegar, 1/4 cup of water or broth, and parsley* to the pot, bring the ingredients to a boil, lower the heat, and simmer the mixture for 35 minutes.

3. Remove the pot from the stove, discard the bay leaves, and ladle some of the soup into a food processor or blender jar. Puree the soup until it is smooth, and pour it into a large bowl. Repeat the process until all the soup has been pureed. Return the pureed soup to the pot, and set the pot aside.

4. To prepare the scallops, set up a stovetop smoker according to the manufacturer's directions. Place the scallops in a small bowl, toss them with the oil and lemon juice, and sprinkle them lightly with salt and pepper. Smoke the scallops for the appropriate length of time (in my Camerons stovetop smoker, this procedure takes 6 minutes), then remove them from the smoker. Set them aside.

5. Bring the soup back to a gentle boil, stirring it often to prevent sticking. Stir in the vinegar. The soup should be thick, but if it seems too thick, stir in the ¼ cup of water or additional stock. Remove the soup from the heat, and ladle it into soup plates at once.

6. Carefully arrange 3 scallop halves on each serving of soup. Sprinkle the soup with the parsley before serving it. ∎

SPICY TOMATO SOUP WITH GROUPER

■

4 TO 6 SERVINGS

This sprightly, interestingly textured soup is easy to prepare and can be a meal in itself.

Preparation tips: I used grouper here because its firm, meaty texture is particularly suited to soups and chowders and it is often a good buy. But it's your call. Any firm fish, from MONKFISH to SWORDFISH, will do. The soup can be made more elegant and varied by adding, with the fish, a few large SHRIMP or MUSSELS in their shells. Check the liquid in the pot from time to time. If the lid does not fit tightly, you may have to add up to 1 cup of water in step 3.

1 tablespoon olive oil
1 cup chopped onion
½ cup chopped celery
1 cup peeled potatoes, cut into ½-inch dice
2 teaspoons minced garlic
1 teaspoon ground coriander
⅛ teaspoon cayenne
2 cups tomato juice *or* V8 *or* Spicy Hot V8
2 cups fish broth *or* chicken broth
1 cup dry white wine
1 tablespoon white-wine Worcestershire sauce
⅛ teaspoon Tabasco sauce
1 pound GROUPER, cut into 1-inch cubes
½ cup chopped fresh parsley, preferably Italian (flat-leaf)
1 cup croutons made from 2 slices whole-wheat bread, cut into ½-inch cubes and toasted, for garnish (optional)

1. Heat the olive oil in a 4-quart wide-bottomed saucepan that has a lid and preferably a nonstick surface, and add the onion, celery, and potatoes. Cook the vegetables over medium heat, stirring them, for 3 minutes.
2. Add the garlic, coriander, and cayenne, and cook the ingredients, stirring them, for another 2 minutes, taking care not to burn the garlic.
3. Add the juice, broth, wine, Worcestershire sauce, and Tabasco sauce. Bring the ingredients to a boil, reduce the heat, cover the pot, and simmer the mixture gently for 15 minutes.
4. Add the fish, cover the pot, and simmer the soup for another 5 minutes or until the fish is cooked through. Remove the pot from the heat, and stir in the parsley. Serve the soup hot, garnished with the croutons (if desired). ■

PORTUGUESE FISHERMAN'S STEW

■

Beans and potatoes give soup a lovely texture and heartiness that add substance to a light fish like cod. While there are many versions of Portuguese Fisherman's Stew (and I have yet to discern any common thread other than tomatoes, broth, and fish), I based my recipe on one offered by the Colorado/Nebraska Dry Bean Commission. Its members will be happy to note that I doubled the amount of beans that the commission suggested in its version.

  1 **tablespoon olive oil**
2½ **cups thinly sliced medium onions**
  2 **tablespoons minced garlic**
  1 **16-ounce can stewed tomatoes, including the juice**
  3 **cups chicken broth**
  3 **cups water**
  2 **16-ounce cans Great Northern beans *or* cannellini (white kidney beans)**
  2 **bay leaves**
1½ **teaspoons dried thyme leaves**
 ½ **teaspoon salt, or to taste, *plus* salt for sprinkling on the fish**
 ¼ **teaspoon freshly ground black pepper *plus* pepper for sprinkling on the fish**
1¼ **pounds COD ("SCROD") FILLET, cut into 1-inch chunks**
  1 **tablespoon fresh lime juice *or* fresh lemon juice**
  1 **pound potatoes, peeled and cut into ⅓-inch dice**
  2 **tablespoons chopped fresh parsley for garnish (optional)**

1. Briefly heat the olive oil in a Dutch oven or 5-quart or 6-quart pot, preferably one with a nonstick surface. Add the onions and garlic, and sauté them over medium-low heat, stirring them often, for 7 to 10 minutes or until the onions start to turn golden, taking care not to burn the vegetables.
2. Add the tomatoes with their juice, broth, water, beans, bay leaves, thyme, the ½ teaspoon of salt, and the ¼ teaspoon of pepper. Bring the ingredients to a boil, reduce the heat, and simmer the mixture in the uncovered pot for 30 minutes.
3. Place the fish in a shallow bowl or pie plate, and sprinkle it with the lime or lemon juice, salt, and pepper. Set the fish aside.
4. Add the potatoes to the pot, and continue to simmer the stew for 10 minutes.
5. Gently add the reserved fish to the pot, and simmer the stew for another 3 minutes. Remove the bay leaves. Serve the soup hot, sprinkled (if desired) with the chopped parsley. ■

SHARK SOUP

■

I seem to have a predilection for Chinese-style soups. I concocted this one by using, among other ingredients, a rich homemade chicken broth and a piece of shark that I had stashed in the freezer. It makes an excellent first course.

Preparation tips: Be sure to start soaking the mushrooms before you begin to prepare the soup. Any firm-fleshed fish, such as MONKFISH, MARLIN, or SWORDFISH, can be used in place of shark.

- ¼ cup dried Chinese mushrooms
- 2 teaspoons canola oil
- ½ cup sliced onion
- 1½ teaspoons minced garlic
- 1 teaspoon peeled, minced gingerroot
- 6 cups chicken broth
- 2 tablespoons reduced-sodium soy sauce, or to taste (depending upon saltiness of the broth)
- ½ teaspoon freshly ground white pepper
- ¾ pound mustard greens, tough stems removed, leaves cut into 1 × 2-inch pieces
- ½ cup thinly sliced yellow bell pepper
- ¾ pound SHARK FILLET, sliced ¼-inch thick and then cut into 1 × 2-inch-long strips
- 1 teaspoon Asian sesame oil, *or* ½ teaspoon Asian sesame oil and ½ teaspoon hot chili oil
- ¼ cup thinly sliced scallions, including some green tops

1. Place the mushrooms in a small saucepan, add enough water to cover the mushrooms, and bring the ingredients to a boil. Turn off the heat, and let the mushrooms soak for 5 to 10 minutes or until the mushroom caps are soft. Drain the mushrooms, cut the caps into thin strips, and discard the stems. Set the mushroom strips aside.
2. Briefly heat the canola oil in a kettle or Dutch oven. Add the onion, and cook it over medium-low heat for 1 minute. Add the garlic and gingerroot, and cook the vegetables for 30 seconds.
3. Add the broth, soy sauce, and ground pepper, and bring the mixture to a boil.
4. Add the mustard greens, yellow bell pepper, the reserved mushroom strips, and the shark, and cook the soup for about 5 minutes. Remove the soup from the heat, and stir in the sesame oil (or the sesame oil and chili oil) and scallions. ■

SHREDDED SURIMI SOUP

■

Soup is the usual first or second course in Far Eastern meals, a custom we would do well to adopt since studies have shown that soup enhances meal satisfaction and reduces the number of calories diners are likely to consume at one sitting. Like most Western soups, this Chinese-style dish can be prepared in advance and reheated at serving time.

Preparation tips: This soup can be made with all chicken broth or all fish broth. You can also use fish bouillon cubes. Although I use shredded surimi here, you can use real **CRABMEAT**.

  6 cups chicken broth
  2 cups fish broth
  1 scallion, cut into 1-inch lengths
  3 quarter-sized slices gingerroot
  ½ pound slender asparagus, sliced diagonally into 1-inch lengths
  1 tablespoon dry sherry
  1 teaspoon Asian sesame oil
  ¼ teaspoon freshly ground white pepper
  1 egg, beaten
  4 teaspoons cornstarch
  4 teaspoons cold water
  ½ pound SURIMI, cut into 1-inch shreds
  4 scallions, cut into 1-inch shreds
  2 tablespoons minced cilantro for garnish (optional)

1. Add the chicken broth, fish broth, scallion pieces, and gingerroot to a large saucepan. Bring the ingredients to a boil, reduce the heat, and simmer the broth for 15 minutes. Then remove the scallions and gingerroot with a slotted spoon and discard them.
2. Add the asparagus to the simmering broth, and cook them for 1 minute.
3. Stir in the sherry, sesame oil, and pepper.
4. Add 1 tablespoon of the hot broth to the beaten egg, then slowly drizzle the egg into the soup, stirring it as you pour.
5. Place the cornstarch in a small dish, and add the cold water, stirring to dissolve the cornstarch. Gradually add the cornstarch mixture to the soup, stirring the ingredients, and simmer the soup for 30 seconds.
6. Stir in the surimi, and simmer the soup for another 30 seconds or until it is piping hot.
7. Sprinkle the scallion shreds into the soup before serving it. Serve the cilantro on the side (if desired), to be added by the individual diners. ■

HOT AND SOUR FISH SOUP

Most of the recipes I've seen for this soup call for pork, which usually adds more in the way of texture and substance to the soup than flavor. Fish can accomplish the same thing but in a more healthful fashion.

Preparation tips: Although other fish will do, I've found that orange roughy and catfish hold up especially well during the cooking. Wild mushrooms of any kind are more flavorful than ordinary button mushrooms and, in general, more interesting in this soup. They are now widely available (Carnation, for instance, sells shiitake in supermarkets in small packages—3.5 ounces, which is close enough to the ¼ pound stipulated here) but are relatively expensive, and domestic, cultivated mushrooms can serve the purpose well. Spinach is a good substitute for the Chinese cabbage.

½ **pound THIN FISH FILLETS (for example, ORANGE ROUGHY, CATFISH, or FLOUNDER)**
1 **tablespoon dry sherry**
4½ **cups canned or homemade chicken broth, divided**
¼ **pound sliced fresh shiitake, *or* ¼ pound sliced fresh domestic mushrooms, *or* 4 dried Chinese mushrooms, soaked and cut into slivers, plus ¾ cup sliced fresh domestic mushrooms**
1 **tablespoon reduced-sodium soy sauce (use regular soy sauce if the broth is unsalted)**
¼ **cup rice vinegar**
½ **to ¾ teaspoon freshly ground white pepper, to taste**
3 **tablespoons cornstarch**
1½ **cups thinly sliced Chinese cabbage**
¼ **pound snow peas, ends snipped and halved diagonally**
1 **teaspoon Asian sesame oil (can include some hot sesame oil *or* chili oil)**
2 **tablespoons chopped scallion for garnish**

1. Slice the fish fillets diagonally into pieces ¼ inch thick and 1½ inches square. Place the fish in a bowl, and toss it with the sherry. Cover the bowl, and refrigerate the fish while preparing the rest of the soup.
2. In a large saucepan, bring 4 cups of the broth to a boil, reduce the heat, add the mushrooms, and simmer the ingredients for 3 minutes. Add the soy sauce, vinegar, and pepper, and bring the mixture back to a simmer.
3. Place the cornstarch in a small bowl, blend in the remaining ½ cup of broth, and add this slowly to the soup, stirring the ingredients constantly until the mixture thickens.

4. Add the reserved fish, the cabbage, and the snow peas to the soup, bring the soup back to a simmer, and cook the soup 1 minute longer. Stir in the sesame oil.

5. To serve the soup, ladle it into shallow bowls, and sprinkle each serving with the chopped scallion. ∎

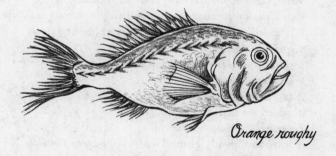

Orange roughy

SHREDDED-SCALLOP AND SNOW PEA SOUP

After my guests stopped singing the praises of this soup, they asked, "But what's in it?" No one guessed that the seafood was scallops that had been cooked until they fell apart into thin shreds.

Preparation tips: I have made this with equal success using bay or sea scallops. Since the latter nearly always cost more, if you are watching your budget (or making the soup for a mob), there's no reason not to use bay scallops. While the scallops cook, prepare the remaining ingredients, which are simply added to the boiling broth along with the shredded scallops. No further cooking is necessary. In keeping with Chinese technique, all the ingredients, except the scallions, are also cut into shreds. You may prepare this soup through step 4, bringing the liquid back to a boil and completing the soup just before serving it.

　5　**to 6 cups chicken broth, preferably lightly salted**
　1　**to 2 cups water (or enough to bring the broth to 7 cups)**
　2　**large cloves garlic, sliced lengthwise 1/8-inch thick**
　4　**quarter-sized slices gingerroot**
　1　**pound SCALLOPS (see "Preparation tips")**
　1　**tablespoon cornstarch**
　2　**tablespoons cold water**
　2　**tablespoons dry sherry**
　1　**teaspoon Asian sesame oil**
1/4　**teaspoon freshly ground white pepper, or to taste**
　2　**ounces Canadian bacon, cut into 1-inch-long slivers (about 1/3 cup)**
1/4　**pound snow peas, trimmed and cut diagonally into 1-inch-long slivers**
　3　**thin scallions, diagonally sliced, including the green tops**

1. Add the broth and the 1 to 2 cups of water to a kettle that has a lid, and bring the liquid to a boil.
2. Add the garlic, gingerroot, and scallops. When the ingredients return to a boil, reduce the heat, cover the pot, and simmer the contents for 1 hour.
3. Remove the pot from the heat, and, with a strainer or slotted spoon, transfer the scallops to a bowl or large platter, *reserving the broth*. Remove and discard the garlic and gingerroot. When the scallops are cool enough to handle, shred them between your fingers, and return the scallop shreds to the reserved broth.

4. Place the cornstarch in a small bowl, add the 2 tablespoons of cold water, and whisk the ingredients until the mixture is smooth. Stir the cornstarch mixture into the broth.

5. Bring the liquid back to a boil, reduce the heat, and simmer the soup for 1 minute. Add all the remaining ingredients, heat the soup for 1 minute, and serve it. ■

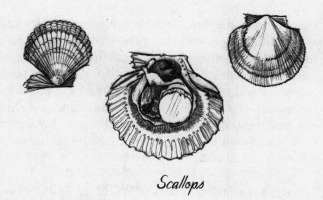

Scallops

SKATE SOUP WITH GREENS
■

I wanted to add a little color to an especially gray, dismal winter day, so I put together this simple soup, bright in flavor and appearance. It has an almost Asian quality—light yet tasty—that makes it an elegant first course. Skate, which is related to the ray, has beautiful lean and delicate white flesh that becomes rippled as soon as it hits the hot broth.

Preparation tips: If the skate you purchase is still attached to its cartilage, use a sharp filleting knife or chef's knife, and, holding the blade almost horizontal to the central cartilage, cut the flesh from the cartilage one side at a time. The broth can be homemade or prepared from fish-broth cubes; if you opt for the cubes, use only 3 cups of broth, and add 1 cup of water to keep the salt content reasonable. This dish may be made in advance, in which case you should not add the fish until you reheat the soup before serving it. Since the fish cooks in a few minutes, you risk breaking up its beautiful corrugated flesh if you cook it first and then reheat it.

Serving suggestion: If desired, place a mound of cooked, cut-up capellini (very thin spaghetti) in each bowl before adding the soup.

Skate

1 SKATE **wing (1 to 1¹/₂ pounds, about ³/₄ pound without the cartilage)**
1 **tablespoon olive oil**
1 **cup chopped onion**
1 **tablespoon minced garlic**
³/₄ **pound mustard greens, large ribs removed and leaves coarsely chopped into**
    2 × 1-inch pieces
³/₄ **cup chopped red bell pepper**
¹/₈ **teaspoon red pepper flakes**
4 **cups fish broth (see "Preparation tips")**

1. Use a sturdy knife with a long blade to prepare the skate. Cut the flesh from the cartilage (see "Preparation tips"), discard the cartilage, and slice the fish with the "grain" into 1¹/₂-inch pieces. Set the fish aside.
2. Briefly heat the olive oil in a large nonstick saucepan or Dutch oven. Add the onion and garlic, and sauté the vegetables for 3 minutes.
3. Add the mustard greens, red bell pepper, and red pepper flakes, and sauté the ingredients, stirring them often, for 3 minutes or until the greens are wilted.
4. Add the broth, and bring the mixture to a boil. Add the reserved fish, reduce the heat, and simmer the soup for 5 minutes or until the fish is just cooked through. ∎

SEAFOOD GAZPACHO

■

I consider gazpacho one of the greatest creations of the culinary world. Adding seafood to it simply enhances its beauty and provides a mild-tasting contrast to the spicy soup. Even those who are not vegetable lovers enjoy this.

Preparation tips: Although I prefer to chop half the vegetable ingredients by hand so that the soup has a fair number of crunchy, albeit tiny, pieces, many cooks these days use a food processor for the entire vegetable portion of the recipe. If you choose the latter course, which is considerably faster, take care not to overprocess the vegetables. The soup can be prepared 1 to 2 days in advance, but do not add the seafood until shortly before serving time.

1 **large cucumber, peeled, halved lengthwise, and seeded, divided**
2 **large tomatoes, halved and seeded, divided**
1 **red bell pepper, halved, cored, and seeded, divided**
1 **medium onion, halved, divided**
2 **cups tomato juice**
¼ **cup red-wine vinegar**
1 **tablespoon fresh lemon juice**
2 **teaspoons extra-virgin olive oil (optional)**
1 **tablespoon crushed garlic**
2 **teaspoons seeded, minced jalapeño**
¼ **teaspoon salt (optional)**
¼ **teaspoon freshly ground black pepper, or to taste**
1 **pound** COOKED MEDIUM SHRIMP *or* COOKED BAY SCALLOPS *or* LUMP CRABMEAT
¼ **cup chopped cilantro for garnish (optional)**

1. Finely chop half of the cucumber, one of the tomatoes, half of the red bell pepper, and half of the onion, and place the chopped vegetables in a large bowl. Cut the remaining half a cucumber, tomato, half a red bell pepper, and half an onion into large chunks, and place them in the container of a blender or food processor.
2. Add the tomato juice to the blender or food processor, and process the vegetables until they are pureed. Pour the puree into the bowl containing the chopped vegetables.
3. Add all the remaining ingredients to the bowl *except the seafood and cilantro.* Stir the soup to combine the ingredients well. Cover the bowl with plastic wrap, and refrigerate the soup thoroughly until serving time.
4. Before serving the gazpacho, add the shrimp or scallops or crabmeat. Offer the cilantro as garnish (if desired) when you serve the soup. ■

VICHYSSOISE WITH SMOKED SALMON

6 SERVINGS

I have made a low-fat version of vichyssoise many times and have always found it appealing, especially in warm weather. But a little dressing up, with bits of smoked salmon, works wonders for this old standby, imparting new personality and flavor. In this version, I have lowered the fat content even more than usual by using mostly evaporated skimmed milk rather than only low-fat milk.

Preparation tip: Of the methods offered here for pureeing the soup—food mill, blender, or food processor—the first produces in the best texture. If you use a blender or food processor, the soup will still taste great, but the look and feel will be more glutinous.

1 **cup thinly sliced leeks, white parts only, well washed and drained**
2 **teaspoons butter** *or* **margarine**
4 **cups peeled and thinly sliced new potatoes (about 1 1/2 pounds)**
4 **cups homemade chicken broth** *or* **low-salt canned broth**
1/8 **teaspoon nutmeg**
1/4 **cup nonfat or low-fat milk**
12 **ounces evaporated skimmed milk**
Salt to taste
Freshly ground white pepper *or* **black pepper to taste**
1/8 **to** 1/4 **pound NOVA-STYLE SMOKED SALMON, cut into** 1/4**-inch strips 1** 1/2 **inches long**
2 **tablespoons snipped fresh dill for garnish**

1. In a medium-sized nonstick saucepan that has a lid, sauté the leeks in the butter or margarine until the vegetable is tender but not brown.
2. Add the potatoes, broth, and nutmeg, bring the ingredients to a boil, reduce the heat, partially cover the pan, and simmer the mixture for 30 minutes.
3. With a food mill, blender, or food processor, process the soup until it is smooth, and pour it into a large serving bowl or tureen. Allow it to cool unrefrigerated until it is no longer steaming. Stir in the milk, evaporated milk, salt, and pepper. Cover the bowl or tureen, and chill the soup.
4. To serve the vichyssoise, ladle individual portions of the soup into shallow soup plates, equally distribute the smoked salmon over the top of each serving, and sprinkle each portion with the dill. ■

COLD 'N' CREAMY MUSSEL SOUP

■

4 SERVINGS

Although I was hurrying to leave for a summer weekend in the country, I could not resist the magnificent mussels that the fish vendor had brought that morning to my local farmers' market. The mussels were wild, small, and so fresh that they still smelled of the sea. So I hastily rinsed and debearded them, threw them in a kettle with a little water, and steamed them. As soon as they were cool enough to handle, I removed the mussel meat from the shells, strained the cooking liquid, froze some of each, and took the rest with me to use in several dishes. This soup, then, combined with the fresh tarragon growing abundantly in my garden, took but a few minutes to prepare.

Preparation tips: If small mussels are not available, you may want to cut the meats in half or thirds. In place of yogurt, you can use buttermilk; if you do this, use less of the mussel cooking liquid—just enough to achieve the desired consistency. Fresh tarragon has a hint of anise which can be enhanced by the Pernod. But for those not crazy about anise, the tarragon is probably all that is needed.

> 2 **pounds SMALL MUSSELS (about 48, less if they are large)**
> 2/3 **cup water**
> 2 **cups nonfat or low-fat plain yogurt**
> 2 **to 3 teaspoons Dijon-style mustard, to taste**
> 1 **teaspoon sugar**
> 1/4 **teaspoon freshly ground white pepper, or to taste**
> 6 **teaspoons (2 tablespoons) chopped fresh tarragon, divided**
> 1 1/2 **teaspoons Pernod (optional)**
> 1 1/2 **cups seeded and finely diced cucumber (if waxed, peel the cucumber before dicing)**

To Debeard Mussels

With a paring knife or fingertips, pull the woolly beard from the flat side of the mussel.

1. To prepare the mussels, debeard (see page 78) and rinse them well, and place them in a large pot that has a lid. Add the water, cover the pot, and, over high heat, steam the mussels for 5 to 7 minutes or until they open and are just cooked. They should be tender.
2. With a slotted spoon, remove the mussels from the pot, and set them aside to cool. Strain the cooking liquid through several layers of cheese-cloth, and *reserve 1 cup* (the rest can be frozen for other uses). Remove the mussel meat from the shells, and discard the shells.
3. To prepare the soup, in a large bowl whisk the yogurt until it is smooth, then stir in the reserved mussel liquid, the mustard, sugar, pepper, 4 tea-spoons of the tarragon, and (if desired) the Pernod. Add the reserved mussels. Refrigerate the soup until serving time (it should be served chilled).
4. When you are ready to serve the soup, remove it from the refrigerator, and stir in the diced cucumber. Ladle the soup into shallow bowls so that the mussels can be readily seen. Top each serving with ½ teaspoon of the remaining tarragon. ■

CHILLED CORN AND CRAB CHOWDER
■

This is an ideal dish for the end of summer, when the markets and roadside stands are teeming with fresh vegetables and the temperature says, "No hot food, please."

Preparation tips: If lump crabmeat is unavailable or too rich for your budget, SURIMI (either as seafood sticks or salad pieces) will do just fine. You can also use frozen corn kernels in place of fresh corn.

Serving suggestion: With a hearty whole-grain bread and a green salad, this thick, tangy soup makes a perfect light, refreshing meal.

    2 teaspoons canola oil
    2 ounces Canadian bacon, finely chopped (about ⅓ cup)
    1 cup finely chopped onion
    1 cup finely diced red bell pepper
    ¾ cup finely chopped celery
    1 tablespoon seeded, minced jalapeño (about 1 pepper)
    2 teaspoons minced garlic
    1 teaspoon ground cumin
    6 cups chicken broth
    1 bay leaf
    2 heaping cups corn kernels (cut from about 4 medium ears)
    ¼ teaspoon freshly ground white pepper
    1 cup nonfat or low-fat plain yogurt
    1 pound LUMP CRABMEAT or SURIMI, cut into bite-sized pieces
    2 tablespoons chopped cilantro or chopped fresh parsley, or to taste
Additional chopped cilantro or chopped fresh parsley for garnish (optional)

1. Heat the canola oil briefly in a nonstick soup pot or Dutch oven. Add the Canadian bacon, and sauté the bacon, stirring it often, for about 2 minutes. Add the onion, and sauté the ingredients for about 3 minutes. Add the red bell pepper, celery, jalapeño, garlic, and cumin, and sauté the mixture 2 minutes longer.
2. Add the broth, bay leaf, corn, and ground pepper. Bring the ingredients to a boil, reduce the heat, and simmer the mixture for 20 minutes. Remove the pot from the heat, and discard the bay leaf. Set the mixture aside to cool until it is lukewarm.
3. Place the yogurt in a small bowl. Add some of the liquid from the pot to the yogurt, stirring the ingredients well. Then pour the yogurt back into

the pot, and stir the mixture until the yogurt is well integrated with the other ingredients. Add the crabmeat or surimi, stirring the chowder gently, then add the 2 tablespoons of cilantro or parsley. Chill the soup until serving time. Before serving the soup, garnish each portion with the additional cilantro or parsley (if desired). ■

COLD SPINACH AND SEAFOOD SOUP

■

6 SERVINGS

A casual summer supper at my friend Beatrice Jacoby's lovely house in Brooklyn, New York, opened with this superb dish that prompted me to say, "I'd like to know what else we'll be eating tonight before I devour the rest of this soup!" Beatrice, a good friend and cook par excellence, parted with the recipe, which I modified by reducing the fat and adding cooked mussels.

Preparation tips: Although in this soup I prefer the color contrast and texture offered by mussels, it can also be prepared with **COOKED BABY CLAMS, SHRIMP** (small or halved), **BAY SCALLOPS,** or **SURIMI.** If you are using salted broth, taste the soup before adding more salt. If you are using nonfat yogurt (as I always do) and prefer a thicker consistency for the finished product, consider draining the yogurt through cheesecloth or a yogurt strainer for 15 to 30 minutes before whisking it into the soup. To cook the mussels, see page 140 or 246.

    1 10-ounce package frozen chopped spinach
 4½ cups chicken broth, divided
    1 tablespoon olive oil
    5 scallions, thinly sliced, including some green tops
 1½ teaspoons minced garlic
Salt to taste (optional)
Freshly ground black pepper to taste
Pinch nutmeg (optional)
    2 cups nonfat or low-fat plain yogurt
 ¾ pound COOKED MUSSELS *or* other seafood, cut into bite-sized pieces

1. In a medium-sized saucepan, add the spinach and ½ cup of the broth, and cook the ingredients for about 5 minutes. Drain the spinach, *reserving the broth.* Set the spinach aside.
2. Briefly heat the olive oil in a large saucepan or Dutch oven, preferably one with a nonstick surface. Add the scallions, and sauté the vegetable for about 2 minutes. Add the garlic and the reserved spinach, and sauté the vegetables for 1 minute longer.
3. Add the remaining 4 cups of broth, the reserved spinach broth, salt (if desired), pepper, and nutmeg (if desired), bring the mixture to a boil, reduce the heat, and simmer the soup for about 10 minutes.
4. Transfer the soup to a large bowl, and let the soup cool down until it is lukewarm. Then stir in the yogurt, whisking it until the soup is smooth.
5. Before serving the soup, add the cooked mussels or other seafood. ■

Salads Bar None

If you have been as fortunate as I with friends and enjoy nothing better than having good company around you, especially at mealtime, main-dish salads are almost an essential part of your life. Since they can frequently be made in advance for groups large and small, they can give you the luxury of enjoying that aperitif and predinner conversation without jumping up every minute to tend the stove. Seafood salads, particularly those made from shellfish, are satisfying as main courses, the seafood adding substance and protein (but few calories) to vegetables or pasta. But you don't need much seafood to satisfy even the heartiest of appetites, so salads are an ideal way to obtain seafood's healthful benefits while keeping costs down.

In this section, I think I had the most fun experimenting with the dressings—the light vinaigrettes, the low-fat basil buttermilk, and a sparkling hot-mustard dressing among them. Once you've tried several, don't hesistate to use a dressing designed for one salad (if you're especially fond of that dressing) on another, related dish.

CURRIED SHRIMP SALAD

■
4 FIRST-COURSE SERVINGS OR 2 MAIN-DISH SERVINGS

This is a perfect I-have-no-time-or-energy-to-cook dish, especially suitable for a warm summer day when the heat of the curry can help to cool you down. I devised the low-fat recipe based on one distributed by the Grand Union Company, a supermarket chain.

Preparation tips: CRABMEAT or a mixture of SHRIMP AND CRABMEAT can be used in place of the shrimp. The curry powder is cooked in a bit of oil to reduce its rawness. You can do this in a microwave oven or in a pan on the top of the stove, or you can skip the step entirely and simply add the curry (without oil) to the yogurt.

DRESSING

1 teaspoon canola oil *or* olive oil
1 teaspoon curry powder (can include some hot curry powder)
1/3 cup nonfat or low-fat plain yogurt
1/2 teaspoon peeled, finely minced gingerroot
1/4 teaspoon salt
1/8 teaspoon freshly ground black pepper

SALAD

1 cup coarsely chopped COOKED SHRIMP
1/3 cup raisins
1/4 cup diced celery
1/4 cup coarsely chopped dry-roasted peanuts
4 tablespoons (1/4 cup) chopped scallions, including green tops, divided

1. To prepare the dressing, in a small skillet (or in a small bowl in the microwave), heat the canola oil or olive oil, add the curry powder, and cook it for about 30 seconds. Transfer the mixture to a small bowl, add the yogurt, gingerroot, salt, and pepper, and whisk the ingredients to combine them well.
2. To prepare the salad, in a medium-sized bowl, combine the shrimp, raisins, celery, peanuts, and 3 tablespoons of the scallions. Add the dressing, and toss the salad to combine the ingredients well. Before serving the salad, sprinkle it with the remaining 1 tablespoon of scallions. ■

MEXICAN SHRIMP SALAD

6 TO 8 FIRST-COURSE SERVINGS OR 4 MAIN-DISH SERVINGS

Colorful and low in calories, the lime juice and cilantro give this salad a light Mexican flavor.

MARINADE/DRESSING
- ¼ cup fresh lime juice
- 2 tablespoons olive oil
- 3 tablespoons chopped cilantro
- 1 jalapeño, seeded and finely chopped
- 1 teaspoon minced garlic
- ½ teaspoon salt

SALAD
- 1¼ pounds MEDIUM OR LARGE SHRIMP, peeled and deveined (if necessary)
- Vegetable-oil spray
- 6 cups or more torn salad greens
- 2 medium tomatoes, cut into 8 wedges each
- 1½ cups broccoli flowerets, steamed 4 to 5 minutes
- ½ pound asparagus, steamed 5 minutes (optional)
- ½ to 1 red bell pepper, cored, seeded, and cut into ¼-inch strips
- ½ to 1 cup corn kernels

1. To prepare the marinade/dressing, add all the marinade/dressing ingredients to a jar that has a tight-fitting lid. Cover the jar, and shake it to mix the ingredients well.
2. To prepare the salad, place the shrimp in a nonreactive bowl, and pour *half* of the marinade/dressing over them, tossing the shrimp to coat them well. Cover the bowl, and chill the shrimp for 30 minutes or longer.
3. Heat a broiler or grill. Away from the heat, spray a slotted broiler pan or fish grate with the vegetable oil.
4. Remove the shrimp from the marinade, discard the marinade, and place the shrimp on the pan or grate. Broil or grill the shrimp for about 2 minutes or until they are just done. Transfer the shrimp to a clean bowl, and chill them until shortly before serving time.
5. Line a large serving platter or individual salad plates with the salad greens, and arrange the shrimp and the remaining salad ingredients on the greens in a decorative manner. Serve the salad drizzled with the remaining marinade/ dressing. ■

SHRIMP SALAD WITH SNOW PEAS

■

6 FIRST-COURSE SERVINGS OR 3 TO 4 MAIN-DISH SERVINGS

This colorful, versatile salad can be used as a first course at dinner, as a light main course, or even as a picnic lunch.

DRESSING
- 3 tablespoons rice vinegar *or* lime juice
- 2 tablespoons dry sherry
- 1 tablespoon soy sauce
- 1 tablespoon Asian sesame oil
- 1 tablespoon minced garlic (3 large cloves)
- 1 teaspoon peeled, grated gingerroot
- 1/4 teaspoon red pepper flakes

SALAD
- 4 to 8 dried Chinese mushrooms
- 1 pound MEDIUM-LARGE SHRIMP (26 to 30 per pound)
- 1 dried red chili pepper
- 1/2 teaspoon salt
- 1/3 cup dry white wine
- 1/2 red bell pepper, cored, seeded, and cut into slivers
- 1/2 pound snow peas, ends and strings removed, steamed for 1 minute, and chilled
- 1/3 cup sliced scallions, including green tops
- Salad greens for lining plates
- 1 tablespoon lightly toasted sesame seeds for garnish

1. To prepare the dressing, add all the dressing ingredients to a small jar that has a tight-fitting lid, cover the jar, and shake it to mix the ingredients thoroughly. Chill the dressing until serving time.
2. To make the salad, place the mushrooms cap side down in a small saucepan. Add enough water to cover them completely. Bring the water to a boil, and simmer the mushrooms for about 5 minutes. Remove the pan from the heat, and set the mushrooms aside to cool.
3. Put the shrimp in a medium-sized saucepan. Add the chili pepper, and sprinkle the shrimp with the salt. Add the wine and enough water to just cover the shrimp. Bring the liquid to a boil, reduce the heat to medium-low, and cook the shrimp for 2 to 3 minutes or until they turn pink. Drain the shrimp, discard the chili pepper, and set the shrimp aside to cool. Peel and, if you wish, devein the shrimp. Chill them.

4. Drain the cooled mushrooms, and cut the caps into thin slivers, discarding the tough stems.

5. At serving time, in a large bowl combine the reserved shrimp, the mushrooms, red bell pepper, snow peas, and scallions. Shake the dressing, and add it to the shrimp mixture, tossing the salad ingredients to coat them well with the dressing. Place the salad greens on a serving platter or on individual plates, top them with the salad, and sprinkle the salad with the sesame seeds. ■

LOBSTER AND SHRIMP SALAD IN BASIL BUTTERMILK

4 TO 6 SERVINGS

The miracle of buttermilk is a subtle one: it seems so rich yet is low in fat and calories. I use it to create a light-textured, delicate, but zippy dressing.

DRESSING

- ½ cup buttermilk
- ½ cup nonfat or reduced-fat mayonnaise
- 1 tablespoon Dijon-style mustard
- 3 tablespoons fresh lime juice
- 1 cup loosely packed basil leaves

Salt to taste

Freshly ground black pepper to taste

SALAD

- 2 tablespoons plus 1 teaspoon salt, divided
- 2 LOBSTERS (about 1¼ pounds each)
- 1 pound LARGE SHRIMP, peeled and deveined
- 1 bay leaf
- 12 peppercorns

Mixed greens, such as arugula and romaine lettuce

- 1 medium green bell pepper, cored, seeded, and sliced crosswise into ¼-inch rounds
- 1 medium yellow bell pepper, cored, seeded, and sliced crosswise into ¼-inch rounds
- 1 small red onion (about ½ pound), thinly sliced crosswise
- 2 medium tomatoes, cored and quartered
- 2 tablespoons chopped scallions for garnish

1. To prepare the dressing, add all the dressing ingredients to the container of a food processor or blender, and process them until the basil is finely chopped. Transfer the dressing to a bowl or jar, cover it, and chill it until you complete the salad.

2. To prepare the salad, add 4 quarts of water to a large pot, bring the water to a boil, add the 2 tablespoons salt, and place the lobsters in the water head first. Bring the water back to a boil, reduce the heat, and simmer the lobsters for 12 to 14 minutes. Remove the lobsters from the pot, and set them aside to cool.

3. Meanwhile, place the shrimp in a small saucepan with just enough water to cover them. Add the bay leaf, peppercorns, and the 1 teaspoon salt. Bring the water to a boil, reduce the heat, and simmer the shrimp for about 2 to 3 minutes or until they are just cooked. Drain the shrimp, and set them aside to cool. Discard the bay leaf and peppercorns.

4. Remove the meat from the claws and tail of the reserved lobsters, and cut the meat into bite-sized chunks. Place the lobster meat and the reserved shrimp in a large bowl, and add ¾ cup of the dressing, tossing the ingredients.

5. Line 4 individual plates with the greens. Arrange the green bell pepper, yellow bell pepper, and onion around the edge of each plate, and place 2 wedges of the tomato on either side. Mound some lobster and shrimp in the center of each plate. Before serving the salad, drizzle the remaining dressing over the vegetables, and garnish each plate with a sprinkling of the scallions. ■

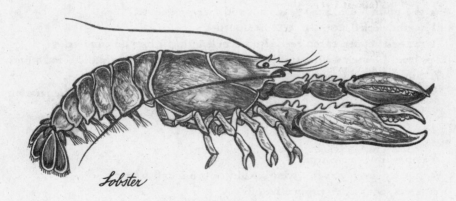

Lobster

Shrimp

SPIRAL-PASTA SALAD WITH SHRIMP AND SUGAR SNAPS
■
6 SERVINGS

You may already know of my passion for those wonders of modern plant genetics—sugar snap peas. They are easy to grow, quick to cook, and, like snow peas, have an edible pod but larger peas than snow peas. They are lovely additions to a pasta salad.

Preparation tips: If sugar snaps are unavailable, you can substitute blanched snow peas or small broccoli flowerets or even green beans cut into 1 1/2-inch lengths and steamed tender-crisp. COOKED MUSSEL meats, SURIMI pieces, or even rings of COOKED SQUID could replace the shrimp. If you are preparing the salad well in advance of serving it, chop the basil as close to serving time as possible, and add it along with the dressing.

SALAD
  1 **pound spinach rotini** *or* **comparable pasta**
  3/4 **to 1 pound sugar snap peas, ends and strings removed**
  1 **pound peeled,** COOKED MEDIUM SHRIMP
  1 **red bell pepper, cored, seeded, and cut lengthwise into julienne strips**
Tops from 1 bunch scallions, sliced into 1/3**-inch pieces,** *or* 1/2 **cup sliced red onion**
  1/2 **cup crumbled feta**
  1/2 **cup finely chopped fresh basil (about** 2/3 **cup packed leaves—see "Preparation tips")**

DRESSING
  1/4 **cup white-wine vinegar**
  1/4 **cup dry sherry** *or* **white wine** *or* **chicken broth** *or* **fish broth**
  1 1/2 **tablespoons extra-virgin olive oil**
  1 **tablespoon Dijon-style mustard**
  2 **teaspoons anchovy paste** *or* 2 **anchovies, minced**
  2 **teaspoons finely minced garlic**
  1 **teaspoon white-wine Worcestershire sauce**
  1/2 **teaspoon salt (optional)**
  1/2 **teaspoon freshly ground black pepper**

GARNISHES (OPTIONAL)
Lettuce leaves for each plate (about 12)
Sliced tomatoes
Sliced cucumber
Sliced mushrooms

1. Place the pasta in a large pot of boiling water to which some salt and oil have been added. Cook the pasta according to package directions or until it is just tender (mushy pasta will fall apart in a salad). Drain and rinse the pasta, and place it in a large nonreactive bowl to cool.
2. While the pasta cooks, bring some water to a boil in a saucepan, and add the sugar snap peas. When the water returns to a boil, reduce the heat to medium-low, and cook the sugar snaps for 2 to 3 minutes or until they are tender-crisp. Immediately drain them, rinse them under cold running water, and set them aside to cool.
3. When the pasta has cooled, add to the bowl the reserved sugar snaps, shrimp, red bell pepper, and scallions or onion. Toss the ingredients gently. Then add the feta and (if you will be serving the salad soon) basil, and toss the ingredients again.
4. To prepare the dressing, combine all the dressing ingredients in a small bowl, whisking them until the oil is emulsified. If you are not planning to serve the salad within the next hour or so, set the dressing aside, and refrigerate the salad mixture. Close to serving time, whisk the dressing again, pour it over the salad, add the basil (if this was not done in step 3), and toss the salad gently.
5. To serve, you may line each plate with the lettuce leaves before placing several scoops of the salad on top of them, and place slices of tomato, cucumber, and mushrooms along one side of the plate. ■

PASTA, PESTO, AND PESCE SALAD

■

My young friend Kris Kim inspired the following salad idea by tossing pesto with spinach fusilli, a macaroni perfectly designed to hold this thick sauce. The green-on-green effect was surprisingly lovely. I chose to highlight it with a pale color (shrimp or scallops) and a red (cherry tomatoes).

Preparation tips: You can also use a combination of **SHRIMP AND SCALLOPS.** The remaining ingredients can be prepared while the pasta water is brought to a boil and the pasta cooks. If you prepare the pesto prior to cooking the shellfish, you can use 2 tablespoons of chicken or fish broth in place of the shellfish cooking liquid.

SALAD

- 1 pound spinach fusilli *or* similar pasta
- 1½ pounds MEDIUM SHRIMP, peeled and deveined, *or* 1½ pounds BAY SCALLOPS *or* CALICO SCALLOPS
- ¾ cup dry white wine
- 3 tablespoons fresh lemon juice
- Salt to taste (optional)
- Freshly ground black pepper to taste
- ½ cup sliced scallions, including green tops
- 1 pint cherry tomatoes, halved

PESTO

- 1 tablespoon chopped garlic
- ¼ teaspoon salt
- 2 tablespoons olive oil
- 2 tablespoons shellfish cooking liquid *or* broth (see "Preparation tips")
- 2 cups firmly packed fresh basil leaves
- ¼ cup pine nuts *or* walnuts
- ½ cup grated Parmesan

1. Place the pasta in a large pot of boiling water to which some salt and oil have been added. Cook the pasta according to package directions or until it is al dente. Drain and rinse the pasta, place it in a large bowl, and cover the bowl to keep the pasta warm.

2. While the pasta cooks, prepare the shrimp or scallops by combining the wine, lemon juice, salt (if desired), and pepper in a medium-sized saucepan. Bring the mixture to a boil, and add the shrimp or scallops. Return the mixture to a boil, reduce the heat to medium-low, and simmer the shellfish for 2 to 3 minutes or until they are just cooked. Drain the shrimp or scallops, and *reserve all the cooking liquid.*

3. To prepare the pesto, place the garlic, the ¼ teaspoon of salt, olive oil, and 2 tablespoons of the reserved shellfish cooking liquid (or broth) into the container of a food processor or blender. Process the mixture until it is smooth. Add the basil leaves and pine nuts or walnuts, and blend the

mixture until it is smooth, periodically stopping the machine to scrape down the sides of the container and redistribute the ingredients. Add the Parmesan, and blend the ingredients until they are well combined.

4. When the pasta is ready but still warm, toss it with the pesto.

5. Add ¾ cup (or more, if a thinner dressing is desired) of the reserved shell-fish cooking liquid to the pasta, and toss the ingredients to combine them well. Check the seasonings, adjusting them, if necessary.

6. Add the scallions, tomatoes, and the reserved cooked shrimp or scallops, and gently toss the salad. Serve the salad slightly cool or at room temperature. ■

SHRIMP ASPIC WITH DILL

■

6 TO 8 FIRST-COURSE SERVINGS OR 4 MAIN-DISH SERVINGS

I confess, after I emerged from a Jell-O–filled childhood, I steered clear of gelatinized salads for years. Then I discovered through a Cranberry Salad Mold from Ocean Spray and a Tomato-Seafood Aspic that my husband made (see *Jane Brody's Good Food Book* for both) how much I was missing. Here is low-fat treat that is lovely as a luncheon main dish or a first course at dinner.

Preparation tips: CRAB, SURIMI (imitation crabmeat), or **COOKED SCALLOPS** can be used in place of the shrimp. For simpler preparation, after step 3 you can pour the entire gelatin mixture into the mold or bowl, then place the shrimp on the top, pushing them in just flush with the surface of the gelatin mixture. When the salad is unmolded, the shrimp will be at the bottom.

      6 ounces (3/4 cup) V8
      1 envelope (1 tablespoon) unflavored gelatin
      1 cup nonfat plain yogurt
      1 to 2 tablespoons fresh lemon juice, to taste
      1 to 2 tablespoons sugar, to taste
  1 1/2 tablespoons snipped fresh dill *or* 2 teaspoons dried dill
      1 tablespoon snipped fresh chives *or* finely chopped scallion
      1/4 teaspoon salt, or to taste
      1/8 teaspoon cayenne
  Several dashes Tabasco sauce, or to taste
      1 cup peeled, seeded, and diced cucumber
  Vegetable-oil spray
      1/2 pound peeled, deveined, and COOKED MEDIUM SHRIMP
  Salad greens (for example, watercress) for garnish
  Cherry tomatoes for garnish

1. Place the V8 in a small saucepan. Sprinkle the gelatin on top, and allow the gelatin to soften for 5 minutes. Gently heat the mixture, stirring it once or twice, just enough to dissolve the gelatin (*do not let the mixture get hot*). Remove the pan from the heat, transfer the mixture to a medium-sized bowl, and let the mixture cool to lukewarm.
2. To the cooled juice-and-gelatin mixture, add the yogurt, lemon juice, sugar, dill, chives or scallion, salt, cayenne, and Tabasco sauce. Stir the mixture to combine the ingredients well, then stir in the cucumber.
3. Spray a mold or shallow bowl with the vegetable oil.

4. Arrange the cooked shrimp in a decorative manner on the bottom of the mold (and along the sides, if you are using a shallow bowl), and pour in a small amount of the gelatin mixture, just enough to fill in the spaces between the shrimp. Chill the mold or bowl for about 20 minutes or until the mixture is firm enough to hold the shrimp in place, and then add the remaining gelatin mixture. Cover the mold or bowl with plastic wrap, and chill the mixture for about 2 hours or until it is firm.

5. To unmold the aspic, hold the mold or bowl in a large pan of tepid water for 10 to 30 seconds, shaking the mold or bowl gently to loosen the aspic. Place a flat platter over the mold or bowl, and invert the aspic onto the platter. Cut the aspic into wedges. Arrange the salad greens and tomatoes on individual salad plates, and top each plate with a wedge of the aspic. ▪

MOLDED SCALLOP SALAD

6 TO 8 SERVINGS

This attractive make-ahead dish is practically fat-free. Only the avocado contributes a bit of fat, happily the heart-sparing monounsaturated kind. I first prepared this salad for friends I invited to brunch on a warm summer day. It would be equally suitable for lunch or even as a first course for dinner (serving probably 10 to 12).

Preparation tips: Be sure to cook the scallops far enough in advance so that they have a chance to cool thoroughly before being added to the salad mixture. There are no set rules about the vegetables used. Choose those you like best as long as they can be cut into bite-sized slivers or slices.

Serving suggestions: Wedges of the molded salad can be served simply on a bed of leafy greens, or you can compose a minisalad of vegetables on individual plates, place a wedge of the molded salad in the middle, and serve the dish with a mild vinaigrette for the vegetables. Crusty whole-grain bread would round out the meal nicely.

SCALLOPS
- ½ cup fish broth
- ¼ cup dry white wine *or* dry sherry
- 2 tablespoons fresh lemon juice
- 1 teaspoon minced garlic (optional)
- ½ teaspoon freshly ground white pepper
- 1 pound BAY SCALLOPS *or* CALICO SCALLOPS, rinsed and drained

REMAINING INGREDIENTS
- 1 11½-ounce can V8 Picante, *or* 1 6-ounce can Spicy Hot V8 *or* Bloody Mary mix and 1 6-ounce can tomato juice
- 2 envelopes (2 tablespoons) unflavored gelatin
- ¾ cup nonfat plain yogurt
- ¾ cup nonfat sour cream
- 2 tablespoons fresh lemon juice
- 1 teaspoon white-wine Worcestershire sauce
- 1 teaspoon Pernod (optional)
- 2 dashes Tabasco sauce
- 2 teaspoons sugar
- 1 teaspoon paprika (can include ¼ teaspoon hot paprika)
- ¼ teaspoon freshly ground white pepper
- ¼ cup chopped fresh parsley, preferably Italian (flat-leaf)

1 tablespoon chopped fresh tarragon (omit if unavailable—do not substitute dried tarragon)

½ cup inch-long slivers red bell pepper

½ cup thin crosswise slices celery

⅓ cup inch-long slivers red onion *or* white onion, *or* thinly sliced scallions

Vegetable-oil spray

¼ firm but ripe avocado, peeled and slivered lengthwise

½ cup peeled or scored cucumber, sliced ⅛ inch thick

1. To prepare the scallops, place all the scallop ingredients *except the scallops* in a small (2 quart) saucepan. Bring the ingredients to a gentle boil, and cook them for 1 minute. Add the scallops, bring the ingredients back to a boil, and simmer the scallops for 2 to 3 minutes (use the lesser time if the scallops are very small) or until they are just cooked through. Drain the scallops immediately, place them in a shallow bowl, and refrigerate them until they are cool.

2. Place the V8 (or the V8 or Bloody Mary mix and tomato juice) into a small saucepan. Sprinkle the gelatin on top, and allow the gelatin to soften for 5 minutes. Gently heat the mixture, stirring it once or twice, just enough to dissolve the gelatin *(do not let the mixture get hot)*. Set the mixture aside.

3. In a large bowl, combine the yogurt, sour cream, lemon juice, Worcestershire sauce, Pernod (if desired), Tabasco sauce, sugar, paprika, and and the ¼ teaspoon of ground pepper. Mix or whisk the ingredients to combine them thoroughly. Then stir in the cooled gelatin mixture, the parsley, and tarragon, and mix the ingredients again. Set the mixture aside to thicken slightly (about 20 minutes at a cool room temperature, about 10 minutes in the refrigerator).

4. To the thickening mixture, add the red pepper, celery, onion or scallions, and the reserved scallops, mixing the ingredients to distribute them evenly. Spray a 6-cup shallow mold with vegetable oil. Arrange the avocado slivers in an attractive pattern along the bottom of the mold. Carefully ladle out the salad mixture on top of the avocado, spreading the mixture evenly in the mold. Arrange the cucumber slices over the salad mixture, barely pressing them into the mixture. Cover the mold with plastic wrap, and refrigerate it for 1 hour or until it is firm.

5. To unmold the salad, fill the sink or a large basin with *lukewarm* water. Hold the mold in it for 10 to 15 seconds, taking care not to let the water reach the top of the mold. Place a flat platter larger than the mold over the top of the mold, and invert the mold onto the platter. Gently shake the platter and mold if the salad does not drop out immediately. If the salad is still stuck in the mold, repeat step 5. ∎

SOUTHWESTERN SCALLOP SALAD

■

6 FIRST-COURSE SERVINGS OR 3 MAIN-DISH SERVINGS

I devised this colorful salad to start the grilled-fish meal I was serving one summer night. The southwestern flavorings—jalapeño, cilantro, and lime—should cool down any hot day.

Preparation tips: If you substitute shrimp for the scallops, start with 1 1/4 pounds fresh **MEDIUM SHRIMP,** and peel and (if you wish) devein them before cooking them. The rest of the salad and the dressing can be prepared while you reduce the wine and poach the seafood.

SALAD
- 1 cup dry white wine
- 8 to 12 whole black peppercorns
- 1 pound SEA SCALLOPS, sliced in half crosswise if large
- 2 cups diced plum (Roma) tomatoes
- 1 cup diced celery
- 1/3 cup finely chopped red onion
- 1 small jalapeño, seeded and minced
- 2 tablespoons chopped cilantro

Salad greens for lining plates

DRESSING
- 2 tablespoons fresh lime juice
- 1 tablespoon dry white wine
- 1 tablespoon extra-virgin olive oil
- 1/4 teaspoon salt, or to taste

Freshly ground black pepper to taste

1. To make the salad, place the wine and peppercorns in a 3-quart saucepan or 10-inch skillet. Bring the wine to a boil, reduce the heat to medium, and cook the wine until it is reduced by about half.
2. Add the scallops, and poach them for 5 minutes (if using shrimp, poach them for 2 to 3 minutes or until the shrimp turn pink—see "Preparation tips"). Drain the scallops immediately, and set them aside to cool. Remove and discard the peppercorns.
3. In a bowl, combine the rest of the salad ingredients *except the greens.* Add the reserved scallops, and chill the salad until shortly before serving time.
4. To make the dressing, combine all the dressing ingredients in a small jar that has a tight-fitting lid, and set the dressing aside. Shortly before serving the salad, shake the dressing well, and pour it over the salad, tossing the ingredients gently but thoroughly.
5. To serve the salad, line 6 individual salad plates or 3 dinner plates with the greens, and divide the salad among the plates. ■

CURRIED CORN AND SEAFOOD SALAD

■

4 SERVINGS

During the dog days of summer, I frequently find myself dining on the cold leftovers of once-hot dishes. A refrigerator raid on a curried corn-vegetable side dish convinced me that it would be a wonderful base for a seafood salad. My tasters agreed.

Preparation tips: Although I first made this salad with the meat from two small **LOBSTERS**, I have since found that it works well (and is easier to prepare and costs less) with steamed **MUSSELS** (meat from about 3 pounds), **SURIMI** (imitation crabmeat), boiled **SHRIMP,** or steamed **SCALLOPS.** So feel free to choose your favorite, most accessible seafood. You can start with leftover cooked corn, or you can substitute 2½ cups of frozen corn kernels for out-of-season preparation.

4 medium-sized ears of corn, shucked
1 tablespoon butter *or* margarine
½ cup sliced scallions, including green tops
1 teaspoon curry powder
Salt to taste (optional)
Freshly ground black pepper to taste
2 tablespoons finely chopped cilantro
1½ cups COOKED SEAFOOD, cut into bite-sized pieces (see "Preparation tips")
4 plum (Roma) tomatoes, cut into ½-inch pieces

1. Cut the corn kernels from the cobs, and set the kernels aside (you should have about 2½ cups).
2. In a large skillet, melt the butter or margarine over medium heat. Add the scallions and curry powder, and sauté the ingredients, stirring them, for 1 minute. Add the reserved corn kernels, salt (if desired), and pepper, and cook the mixture, stirring it often, for 4 minutes (1 minute, if you are starting with corn that has already been cooked). Remove the pan from the heat, and transfer the corn mixture to a large bowl.
3. Stir the cilantro into the hot corn mixture, then set the corn aside to cool. When the mixture is nearly at room temperature, add the seafood and tomatoes. Toss the salad gently to combine the ingredients well. Serve the salad lightly chilled or at room temperature. (If the salad has been refrigerated until serving time, take the chill off of it by warming it in a microwave oven for about 1½ minutes.) ■

WILD RICE AND SCALLOP SALAD

■   4 TO 6 SERVINGS

Wild rice (which really isn't rice, but a grass) is now being cultivated in Minnesota and California. If you are lucky enough to be in the Twin Cities area (Minneapolis/St. Paul), you may want to visit one of the local supermarkets, where wild rice is sold in 1-pound packages for less than half the price usually charged for this nutty, nutritious grainlike food.

Preparation tips: Tiny SALAD SHRIMP can be used in place of the scallops. For efficiency, prepare the rest of the salad while the rice cooks. It is best not to add the dressing more than a few hours before serving the salad since the rice acts like a sponge. You can substitute chopped fresh mint for the basil.

SALAD

1 cup wild rice (about 6 ounces)
2 cups chicken broth *or* fish broth *or* vegetable broth
1/4 cup (approximately) water, if needed
1 pound BAY SCALLOPS
1 tablespoon fresh lemon juice
Salt to taste
Freshly ground black pepper to taste
1 cup thinly sliced celery (about 2 stalks)
4 plum (Roma) tomatoes, seeded and cut into 1/2-inch dice
1/2 large green bell pepper, cored, seeded, and cut into 1/3-inch dice
1/2 cup thinly sliced scallions, including some green tops (about 4 scallions)

DRESSING

3 tablespoons white-wine vinegar
2 tablespoons olive oil
2 tablespoons finely chopped basil (about 8 large leaves)
1 teaspoon minced garlic
2 teaspoons Dijon-style mustard
1/4 teaspoon salt, or to taste
1/4 teaspoon freshly ground black pepper, or to taste

1. To prepare the salad, combine the wild rice and broth in a medium-sized saucepan that has a lid, and bring the mixture to a boil. Reduce the heat to low, cover the pan tightly, and simmer the rice for 35 minutes, checking after 25 minutes to see if the ¼ cup of water is needed. When the rice is tender, remove the pan from the heat, and, if necessary, drain the rice. Set it aside to cool.

2. Rinse and drain the scallops. Sprinkle them with the lemon juice, salt, and pepper, and place them on a steamer rack over a small amount of boiling water. Cover the steamer, and steam the scallops for 5 minutes. Remove the rack from the heat, and let the scallops cool.

3. Combine the cooled rice and the cooled scallops in a large bowl with the rest of the salad ingredients.

4. To prepare the dressing, place the dressing ingredients in a small jar that has a tight-fitting lid, shaking the jar to combine the ingredients thoroughly.

5. Within a few hours of serving, pour the dressing over the salad, and toss the salad to mix the ingredients well. ■

MOROCCAN SEAFOOD SALAD

6 SERVINGS

This salad is an ideal summer supper or buffet offering—colorful, tasty, and easy to prepare.

Preparation tips: Although Moroccan salads are often made with chicken, there is no reason why you cannot use a firm seafood like small SHRIMP, BAY SCALLOPS, or SURIMI instead. If you are using sliced surimi sticks, do not add them until the salad has been dressed and tossed; too much tossing will cause the surimi to fall apart, and you'll end up with shreds rather than chunks.

SALAD

- 4 cups bite-sized broccoli flowerets
- 3/4 cup thinly sliced scallions, including green tops (about 6 slender scallions)
- 1 medium red bell pepper, cored, seeded, and diced
- 1/4 cup currants *or* raisins
- 3/4 pound bite-sized COOKED SEAFOOD (see "Preparation tips")
- 3 cups chicken broth
- 1 1/2 cups couscous
- 1/4 cup chopped fresh parsley
- 1/2 teaspoon dried thyme leaves
- 1/4 cup coarsely chopped pecans or other nuts (optional)

DRESSING

- 2 tablespoons fresh lemon juice
- 2 tablespoons extra-virgin olive oil
- 1 teaspoon curry powder (can include 1/4 teaspoon hot curry powder, or to taste)
- 1/2 teaspoon freshly ground black pepper
- 1/8 teaspoon red pepper flakes, or to taste

1. Steam the broccoli flowerets for 5 minutes, then immediately refresh them under cold running water. Place the broccoli in a large bowl.
2. Add the scallions, red bell pepper, currants or raisins, and seafood (except surimi sticks) to the bowl. Set the bowl aside.
3. Bring the broth to a boil in a medium-sized saucepan that has a tight-fitting lid. Add the couscous, parsley, and thyme, and cook the mixture for *30 seconds*. Remove the pan from the heat, cover it, and let the mixture stand for 5 minutes.
4. Meanwhile, prepare the dressing by combining all the dressing ingredients in a bowl or in a jar that has a tight-fitting lid. Whisk or shake the dressing until the oil is emulsified.

5. When the couscous is done, add it while it is still hot to the vegetable mixture in the bowl, and toss the ingredients to combine them well. Add the dressing, and toss the mixture to combine the ingredients well. If you are using sliced surimi sticks, add them to the bowl now, and toss the mixture gently to distribute the surimi evenly throughout the salad.

6. Cover and chill the salad for 1 hour or longer. Before serving the salad, sprinkle it with the chopped nuts (if desired). ▪

PASTA SALAD WITH MUSSELS
■

This salad not only has mussels—it has muscles! It packs a wallop that had me and my tasters coming back for more.

Preparation tips: The mussels and salad ingredients can be combined and the dressing can be made in advance, but they are best mixed together within hours of serving. The salad is especially good when prepared with a flavorful pasta such as the Roquefort-flavored one from Morisi's Macaroni Company (see page 116 for ordering information). But plain macaroni works well, too. Try to use a macaroni shape that has some substance to it, like cresta di gallo.

MUSSELS
- 2 tablespoons chopped onion
- 8 peppercorns
- 1 bay leaf
- 2 sprigs parsley
- 1/2 cup dry white wine
- 2 pounds MUSSELS, well rinsed and debearded

SALAD
- 3/4 pound macaroni, cooked al dente and cooled
- 1 medium zucchini, halved lengthwise and thinly sliced crosswise
- 1 red bell pepper, cored, seeded, and cut into 1/2-inch dice
- 3 scallions, including some green tops, sliced 1/4 inch thick

Greens for lining plates

DRESSING
- 3/4 cup buttermilk
- 1/4 cup nonfat or reduced-fat mayonnaise
- 1 tablespoon olive oil (omit if using reduced-fat mayonnaise)
- 1/2 cup packed fresh parsley leaves
- 1 teaspoon chopped garlic
- 1/2 teaspoon salt, or to taste
- 1/4 teaspoon red pepper flakes
- 1/4 teaspoon freshly ground black pepper

1. To prepare the mussels, in a large kettle that has a tight-fitting lid, combine all the ingredients for the mussels, bring the mixture to a boil, cover the pot, and cook the mussels over medium-high heat, shaking the pot once or twice, for 5 minutes or until the mussels have opened and are just cooked through. Remove the pan from the heat, and let the mussels cool. When the mussels are cool enough to handle, discard any mussels that did not open. Remove the mussel meat from the shells, and discard the shells and the cooking mixture (or strain the liquid, and save it in the refrigerator or freezer for another use).
2. To prepare the salad, in a large mixing bowl, combine the mussels with the all the salad ingredients *except the greens*.
3. To prepare the dressing, combine all the dressing ingredients in the bowl of a food processor, and process them for a few seconds or until they are well mixed and the parsley is chopped. If you prepare the dressing manually, whisk together the buttermilk, mayonnaise, and oil (if using). Chop the parsley and mince the garlic, and add them to the buttermilk mixture with the remaining dressing ingredients, stirring them to combine them well.
4. Pour the dressing over the salad, and toss the salad to coat it thoroughly with the dressing. Serve the salad chilled or at room temperature over a bed of the greens. ■

MUSSEL AND SQUID SALAD
■

Lovers of squid and mussels can rejoice, for it's almost impossible to gain weight eating them as long as they are prepared—as they are in this dish—using only a little oil. The salad looks more complicated than it is, but the cooking technique is simple and the time spent preparing it brief.

Preparation tip: The various elements of the salad can be prepared well ahead, but don't assemble the salad until 15 to 30 minutes before serving time because the greens will wilt.

MUSSELS
- ¾ **cup dry white wine**
- 8 **whole peppercorns**
- 3 **whole cloves**
- 4 **sprigs parsley**
- 1 **bay leaf**
- 3 **pounds MUSSELS, well rinsed and debearded**

SQUID

- 1 **pound cleaned SQUID**
- 1½ **cups water**
- ¼ **cup dry white wine**
- ¼ **teaspoon salt**

SALAD
- 3 **tablespoons fresh lemon juice**
- 1 **tablespoon olive oil**
- 2 **teaspoons Dijon-style mustard**
- ½ **teaspoon salt, or to taste**
- ½ **teaspoon freshly ground black pepper, or to taste**
- 1 **large or 2 small fennel bulbs, thinly sliced crosswise and halved (about 3 cups)**
- ½ **cup halved and thinly sliced red onion**
- ¼ **cup coarsely chopped dill**
- 3 **plum (Roma) tomatoes, sliced crosswise**

Crisp, sharp greens, like arugula or watercress, for lining the platter or plates
- 2 **ripe tomatoes, quartered, for garnish**

TO PREPARE THE MUSSELS

1. Combine all the ingredients for the mussels in a large nonreactive saucepan that has a tight-fitting lid, cover the pan, and bring the mixture to a boil over medium-high heat.
2. Shaking the pot once or twice, steam the mussels for 5 minutes after the liquid boils or until the mussels have opened and are cooked through. Remove the pan from the heat. Drain the mussels, discard any that have not opened, and allow the rest to cool.
3. Remove the mussel meat from their shells, and discard the shells. Any remaining beards can now be plucked free and discarded. Chill the mussels, covered, until you are ready to prepare the finished salad.

TO PREPARE THE SQUID

4. Cut the squid bodies into $1/2$-inch rings. Cut the tentacles into $1 1/2$-inch lengths. Remove the fins, and, if they are large, cut them in half. Set the squid aside.
5. Combine all the ingredients for the squid *except the squid* in a 2-quart saucepan, and bring the ingredients to a boil. Add the reserved squid. When the liquid returns to the boil, remove the pan from the heat, drain the squid, transfer it to a bowl, and allow the squid to cool. Cover the bowl with plastic wrap, and chill the squid until you are ready to assemble the salad.

TO ASSEMBLE THE SALAD

6. Prepare the dressing by placing the lemon juice, olive oil, mustard, salt, and pepper in a small bowl and whisking the ingredients vigorously to blend them.
7. In a large bowl, combine the reserved mussels, the reserved squid, fennel, onion, dill, and sliced plum tomatoes, and gently toss the ingredients. Pour the dressing over the salad, and lightly toss the salad.
8. Arrange the greens on a large serving platter or on individual plates. Mound the salad in the center of the platter or plates, and garnish the salad with the tomato wedges. ■

NEW POTATO AND CLAM SALAD

■

4 SERVINGS

A "new" potato is any kind of potato that is harvested during the first nine months of the year. Its skin is thin and its flesh firm, making it ideal for salads because it does not need to be peeled and, after cooking, holds up well when tossed. Here is a delightful way to use new potatoes, one that I devised when my market offered littleneck clams from Maine for $1.69 a pound.

Preparation tips: If fresh clams are not available or convenient, you can substitute about 17 ounces of **CANNED CLAMS** (but be sure to *reserve the liquid*). Since the main ingredients are virtually fat-free, I was more liberal than usual with the olive oil in the dressing. However, if you want to reduce the amount of oil further, use only 1 tablespoon. For maximum flavor, since the potatoes should be tossed with the dressing while they are still warm, it is best to cook the clams first and then prepare the dressing, perhaps while the potatoes cook.

SALAD

- 4 pounds LITTLENECK CLAMS (see "Preparation tips")
- 2 pounds small red potatoes (about 1½ inches in diameter), unpeeled
- 1 red bell pepper, cored, seeded, and cut into ½-inch pieces
- 1 cup thinly sliced celery
- ¼ red onion, peeled and slivered lengthwise

Greens for garnish (optional)
Sliced cucumber for garnish (optional)
Sliced tomato for garnish (optional)

DRESSING

- ¼ cup fresh lemon juice
- ¼ cup clam liquid (see "Preparation tips")
- 2 tablespoons olive oil (see "Preparation tips")
- 2 teaspoons Dijon-style mustard
- ¼ cup minced fresh parsley
- 1 tablespoon minced fresh basil *or* 1 teaspoon dried basil
- 1 teaspoon minced fresh tarragon *or* ½ teaspoon dried tarragon
- ¼ teaspoon salt
- ¼ teaspoon freshly ground black pepper, or to taste

1. Rinse the clams under cold running water to remove any outer grit. Place them in a large kettle that has a tight-fitting lid, cover the kettle, and cook the clams over medium-high heat for 6 to 7 minutes, shaking the pot occasionally. With a slotted spoon, remove the opened clams from the kettle, reserving the liquid, and set the clams aside to cool. If any clams have not opened, steam them 1 to 2 minutes longer, discarding those that still do not open. Strain the clam liquid through several thicknesses of cheesecloth, and set it aside. When the clams are cool enough to handle, remove and reserve the meat, discarding the shells.

2. Cut the potatoes lengthwise into quarters. Steam them over boiling water for 8 to 10 minutes or until the potatoes are just tender.

3. While the potatoes are steaming, prepare the dressing by adding all of the dressing ingredients to a small bowl or a jar that has a tight-fitting lid and whisking or shaking them until they are well combined. When the potatoes are done, transfer them to a large bowl, add about half the dressing, and toss the ingredients well. Set the bowl aside until the potatoes have cooled to lukewarm.

4. When the potatoes have cooled add the reserved clams, red bell pepper, celery, and onion to the bowl. Drizzle the remaining dressing over the salad, and toss the salad.

5. To serve the salad, if desired line a large platter or 4 individual plates with the greens. Arrange slices of cucumber and tomato along the edge of the platter or plates, and heap the salad in the middle. ∎

CRAB, CANTALOUPE, AND CASHEW SALAD

■
8 TO 10 FIRST-COURSE SERVINGS OR 4 TO 6 MAIN-DISH SERVINGS

Although the combination may sound odd, shellfish and fruit go well together. Try this colorful dish, and see for yourself.

Preparation tips: If crabmeat is unavailable or too expensive, you can use SURIMI (imitation crab) sold as sticks (cut them into ½-inch pieces) or salad pieces. This salad can also be made with COOKED SHRIMP instead of crab, honeydew or papaya instead of cantaloupe, and dry-roasted peanuts in place of cashews. All the ingredients can be prepared ahead and chilled, but dress the salad shortly before serving it.

SALAD

- 1 pound CRABMEAT, broken into bite-sized pieces
- 1 medium cantaloupe, cut in half and seeded
- 1 cup sliced or diced celery
- ½ cup sliced scallions, including some green tops
- ¼ cup golden raisins (preferably) or dark raisins
- ¼ to ½ cup coarsely chopped cashews, to taste

DRESSING

- ¾ cup nonfat plain yogurt
- 1½ teaspoons curry powder (can include ½ teaspoon hot curry powder)
- 2 tablespoons finely chopped shallots or mild onion
- 1 tablespoon fresh lime juice or fresh lemon juice

1. Place the crabmeat in a large bowl, and remove any bits of shell or cartilage.
2. Scoop out the cantaloupe with the small end of a melon baller, or cut the melon into ½-inch cubes. Add it to the crabmeat along with the remaining salad ingredients *except the cashews.* Chill the ingredients until shortly before serving time.
3. Add all the dressing ingredients to a small bowl, whisking the ingredients to combine them well.
4. Shortly before serving time, add the cashews and dressing to the salad, and toss the salad gently to combine the ingredients. ■

SURIMI AND SUGAR SNAP SALAD

■
8 SERVINGS

This salad more than held its own at a summer buffet supper that included grilled smoked sausages and burgers. It is attractive as well as delicious and lends itself to variations depending upon season and availability of the vegetables.

Preparation tips: The salad and the dressing can be prepared in advance, but do not combine them until shortly before serving time. If you use canned black beans, be sure to rinse them.

Serving suggestions: As a main dish for lunch or supper, this salad is stunning served on a bed of leafy greens and garnished with wedges of tomato and avocado.

SALAD
  1 **pound sugar snap peas, ends trimmed and strings removed**
  1 **pound** SURIMI CHUNKS
  1 **large red bell pepper, cored, seeded, halved crosswise, and cut lengthwise into julienne strips**
  3 **stalks celery, thinly sliced crosswise**
1²/₃ **to 2 cups cooked black beans (see "Preparation tips")**
  2 **cups cooked corn kernels**
¹/₂ **cup thinly sliced red onion**
  1 **tablespoon seeded, minced jalapeño, or to taste**

DRESSING
¹/₃ **cup fresh lime juice**
  2 **tablespoons olive oil**
  1 **tablespoon orange juice**
  2 **teaspoons white-wine vinegar**
¹/₂ **teaspoon cumin**
¹/₂ **teaspoon hot chili powder,** *or* ¹/₂ **teaspoon mild chili powder and** ¹/₈ **teaspoon cayenne**
¹/₂ **teaspoon salt, or to taste**
Freshly ground black pepper to taste
  1 **cup loosely packed cilantro leaves, chopped**

1. In a medium-sized saucepan, bring enough water to a boil to cover the sugar snap peas. Add the peas, reduce the heat to medium, and cook the peas for 4 minutes. Immediately drain and refresh the peas under cold water. Set the peas aside to cool.
2. Cut the surimi chunks into 1-inch pieces, if necessary, and place them in a large bowl. Add the red bell pepper, celery, black beans, corn, onion, and jalapeño. When the peas have cooled to lukewarm, add them to the salad mixture. Toss the ingredients to combine them well. Cover the bowl with plastic wrap, and chill the salad until shortly before serving time.
3. To prepare the dressing, in a jar that has a tight-fitting lid, add all the dressing ingredients *except the cilantro*. Cover the jar, and shake the jar to combine the ingredients well. Shortly before serving time, add the cilantro to the jar, and shake the jar again.
4. Pour the dressing over the salad, and toss the salad to coat it with the dressing. ■

HAWAIIAN FISH AND FRUIT SALAD

■

A recipe card that I picked up at a supermarket fish counter inspired this dish, which was a huge hit among my guests one pleasantly warm summer evening. I kept the theme Hawaiian by using mahi-mahi along with tropical fruits and coconut. Mahi-mahi used to be called dolphin fish, but so many people confused it with the acrobatic mammal that this beautiful blue and gold saltwater fish is now widely known by its Hawaiian name. Although coconut contains saturated fat, it is used here in moderate amounts.

Preparation tips: Those not adept at cracking coconuts may use canned coconut milk and dried shredded coconut that has been soaked in hot water—to soften it—and then drained. Coconut milk can be prepared from fresh coconut by pureeing about ½ cup of coconut water with ½ cup of coconut pieces and then straining the resulting "milk." Meaty, firm alternatives to mahi-mahi include SWORDFISH, TUNA, or MARLIN. The fish, fruits, and dressing can be prepared in advance and kept chilled. But the salad is best assembled just before serving time.

Serving suggestions: Nice accompaniments may include a minted salad of sugar snap peas or green beans and a rice salad. Or you could start the meal with a cold soup and serve both courses with hearty breads.

FISH
- 2 **pounds** MAHI-MAHI **in pieces 1 inch thick**
- ⅓ **cup orange juice**
- 1 **tablespoon soy sauce**
- 1 **tablespoon Asian sesame oil**
- 1 **teaspoon peeled, grated gingerroot**
- ⅛ **teaspoon cayenne**

Vegetable-oil spray

Mahi-mahi

DRESSING
- ⅓ **cup nonfat plain yogurt**
- ⅓ **cup coconut milk (see "Preparation tips")**
- ⅓ **cup mandarin orange juice (reserved from the oranges listed in the salad ingredients),** *or* ⅓ **cup orange juice and 1 teaspoon sugar**

SALAD
- 2 **cups bite-sized chunks fresh pineapple**
- 2 **cups cantaloupe balls or bite-sized pieces**

2 11-ounce cans mandarin oranges packed in light syrup, drained and juice reserved

1 cup red grapes (optional)

⅔ cup fresh or dried and softened shredded coconut (see "Preparation tips")

Fresh greens for lining plates (optional)

2 kiwis, peeled and quartered lengthwise for garnish (optional)

1 cup pecan pieces *or* cashew pieces

TO PREPARE THE FISH

1. Rinse and pat dry the mahi-mahi. Slice away the skin, if any, and cut the fish into 1-inch-thick strips. Place the strips in one layer in a shallow bowl or nonreactive pan.

2. In a small bowl, combine all the remaining ingredients for the fish *except the vegetable-oil spray,* and pour this mixture over the fish, turning the pieces of fish so that all its sides are coated with the marinade. Cover the bowl or pan with plastic wrap, and refrigerate the fish for 1 hour or longer, turning the fish at least once.

3. Heat a grill or broiler. Remove the hot grate, spray it with the vegetable oil, and return the grate to the grill or broiler. Remove the fish from the marinade, and place the strips on the grill or in the broiler. Grill the strips of fish for about 4 minutes (or broil them for 3 minutes) on one side, then turn them over and grill (or broil) them 3 to 4 minutes longer on the second side. *Note:* If the fish is less than 1 inch thick, reduce the cooking time. Set the fish aside to cool. When it is cool, chill it while you prepare the remaining ingredients. When the fish is cold, cut the strips into 1-inch cubes.

TO PREPARE THE DRESSING

4. Combine all the dressing ingredients in a small bowl or a jar that has a tight-fitting lid, and whisk or shake the ingredients well. Chill the dressing until serving time.

TO ASSEMBLE THE SALAD

5. In a large bowl, combine the pineapple, cantaloupe, mandarin oranges, grapes (if desired), and coconut, tossing the ingredients to distribute them evenly. Add the fish cubes and the dressing, and toss the ingredients gently.

6. Serve the salad on individual plates that have been lined with the greens and garnished with the kiwis (if desired). Offer the nuts for individual use. ■

CHINESE-STYLE TUNA SALAD

■

Having succumbed to a bargain on fresh tuna sold in chunks too thick to grill, I decided to try them sliced, marinated, and quickly broiled for a salad. This is the wonderful, colorful result.

Preparation tips: The marinade/dressing can be prepared in advance, and the tuna can be marinated and broiled up to a day ahead. But avoid marinating the fish for longer than 1 hour because it may get too soft. Its texture is best if the fish is cooked on a grate, if you have a grate fine enough so that the pieces won't fall through. Five-spice powder is usually available wherever Asian ingredients are sold as well as in many supermarkets. If it is unattainable, you can make it yourself by grinding together 1/8 teaspoon each of anise, cinnamon, cloves, fennel seeds, and, if available, Sichuan peppercorns. The salad vegetables can be varied to taste. Options include steamed asparagus, diagonally sliced carrots, sugar snap peas, or raw strips of bell peppers (especially the colorful ones).

MARINADE/DRESSING

- 1/4 cup orange juice
- 1/4 cup fresh lemon juice *or* fresh lime juice
- 1/4 cup cup water
- 1/4 cup soy sauce, preferably reduced-sodium
- 4 teaspoons Asian sesame oil
- 2 teaspoons minced garlic
- 2 teaspoons peeled, minced gingerroot
- 1/2 teaspoon mustard powder
- 1/2 teaspoon five-spice powder
- 1/8 teaspoon cayenne *or* 1/4 teaspoon red pepper flakes (optional)

SALAD

- 1 pound TUNA STEAKS, sliced into 1/3-inch-thick strips
- Vegetable-oil spray
- Lettuce leaves *or* arugula *or* watercress
- 4 plum (Roma) tomatoes, sliced crosswise
- 1/4 pound snow peas, ends and strings removed, raw or steamed for 1 minute
- 1/4 pound broccoli flowerets, steamed 4 to 5 minutes
- 2 tablespoons diagonally sliced scallions, including green tops
- 1 to 2 tablespoons chopped cilantro *or* chopped fresh parsley

1. In a 12-ounce or larger jar that has a tight-fitting lid, combine all the marinade/dressing ingredients, shaking them well.
2. Place the tuna slices in a shallow bowl, and sprinkle them with about 1/3 cup of the marinade/dressing, turning the fish pieces to coat them well with the marinade. Cover the fish with plastic wrap, and refrigerate it for 30 minutes.

3. Heat the broiler (or grill). Remove the hot broiler pan (or fish grate), and spray it with the vegetable oil. Drain the fish well, place the pieces in a single layer on the pan (or grate), and broil or grill them for about 2 to 2½ minutes or until they are just done. Remove the fish pieces from the pan (or grate), and chill them until shortly before serving time.

4. On a large serving platter or on 4 individual salad plates, arrange the lettuce or arugula or watercress along with the fish slices, tomatoes, snow peas, and broccoli. Sprinkle the salad with the scallions and cilantro or parsley. Chill the salad until serving time.

5. Shortly before serving the salad, shake the remaining dressing well, and drizzle about ¼ cup of it (1 tablespoon for each individual plate) over the salad, saving any remaining dressing for another use. ■

Tuna

FRESH TUNA AND VEGETABLE SALAD

■

6 SERVINGS

In this salad, the tuna is almost as easy to prepare as opening and draining the canned variety. My recipe is derived from one offered by the West Coast Fisheries Development Foundation.

Preparation tips: This salad can also be made with **HALIBUT, SHARK,** or **ALBACORE TUNA.** You can use any salad vegetables, raw or steamed, that you desire as long as you balance the color and texture and do not overwhelm the fish. The dressing can be prepared, the tuna cooked, and the vegetables steamed a day ahead.

DRESSING
- ¼ cup fresh lime juice
- ¼ cup white-wine vinegar
- 2 tablespoons olive oil
- 2 teaspoons soy sauce
- 4 teaspoons Dijon-style mustard
- 4 teaspoons fresh thyme leaves, chopped, *or* 1 teaspoon dried thyme leaves
- 4 teaspoons chopped basil leaves *or* 1 teaspoon dried basil
- 1 tablespoon minced garlic

SALAD
- 1½ pounds TUNA STEAKS, about 1 inch thick
- ½ lemon, sliced
- ½ onion, sliced
- 1 bay leaf
- 5 to 10 black peppercorns

Lettuce *or* similar greens
- 2 to 3 cups small broccoli flowerets, steamed 4 to 5 minutes or until tender-crisp
- 3 carrots, sliced diagonally and steamed 4 to 5 minutes or until tender-crisp
- 4 plum (Roma) tomatoes, sliced lengthwise
- ½ pound sugar snap peas *or* snow peas, ends and strings removed and steamed tender-crisp (5 minutes for sugar snaps, 1 to 2 minutes for snow peas)
- ¼ red onion, peeled and slivered lengthwise
- ⅓ cup crumbled feta

1. To a jar that has a tight-fitting lid, add all the dressing ingredients, combining them well. Set the dressing aside (chill it if it is not going to be used within a few hours).

2. Place the tuna in a skillet that has a cover and that is large enough to hold the fish in a single layer. Add just enough water to barely cover the fish. Scatter the lemon, onion slices, bay leaf, and peppercorns over and around the fish. Bring the water to a boil, reduce the heat, cover the skillet, and simmer the fish for 8 minutes or until it is just cooked through. Drain the fish, and let it cool. Then cut it into 3/4-inch pieces. Chill the fish.

3. About 2 hours before serving time, shake the dressing to combine the ingredients thoroughly, and toss the tuna with *half* the dressing. Return the fish to the refrigerator.

4. Shortly before serving, arrange the lettuce or greens on a large platter or on 6 individual plates. Place the tuna in the middle of the platter or plates, and arrange the remaining vegetables in a decorative manner around the tuna. Shake the remaining dressing, and drizzle it over the vegetables. Sprinkle the entire salad with the feta. ■

PESCE PRIMAVERA PASTA SALAD

■
FOR A CROWD—20 TO 30 SERVINGS (ABOUT 10 QUARTS)

Pasta salads often leave a lot to be desired. They frequently lack color and are usually saturated with a high-fat dressing. This one avoids both pitfalls. The vegetables make for a colorful dish, and the dressing is relatively low in fat. For the "pesce," I use marlin, a large game fish with a steaklike consistency.

Preparation tips: Any fish with a similar meaty or firm consistency—SWORD-FISH, TUNA, even MONKFISH—should work well here. The fish can be grilled or broiled, but in either case it should be cooked enough in advance to allow for thorough chilling before it is cut into bite-sized pieces. I use a combination of colorful flavored pastas, including a hot-chili pasta, which adds an extra kick to the salad. When I prepare a recipe like this, I get all the main components ready in advance and combine them shortly before serving time. That way the dressing doesn't "disappear" into the pasta, and the vegetables maintain their crispness.

FISH

2½ **pounds MARLIN**
  ½ **cup dry sherry** *or* **white wine**
  1 **tablespoon olive oil**
  1 **tablespoon balsamic vinegar**
  2 **teaspoons minced garlic**
  ½ **teaspoon freshly ground black pepper**
  ¼ **teaspoon salt, or to taste**

Marlin

SALAD

  6 **cups bite-sized broccoli flowerets**
  4 **cups carrots in round slices about ⅛ inch thick**
  ¾ **pound green beans, ends trimmed and cut into 1-inch lengths**
  2 **large red bell peppers, cored, seeded, and cut into ½-inch dice**
  2 **large green bell peppers, cored, seeded, and cut into ½-inch dice**
  1 **large red onion, cut into ⅓-inch dice**
  2 **15-ounce cans kidney beans, drained and rinsed**
  2 **cans small pitted black olives (total 12 ounces drained weight)**
2½ **pounds pasta (see "Preparation tips")**

DRESSING

  2 **cups grated Parmesan**
  1 **cup nonfat plain yogurt**
  ¼ **cup fresh lemon juice**
  2 **tablespoons balsamic vinegar**
  2 **tablespoons olive oil**

2 tablespoons finely minced garlic
1 tablespoon Dijon-style mustard
1 teaspoon red pepper flakes
1 teaspoon salt, or to taste
1 teaspoon freshly ground black pepper, or to taste
1/2 cup chopped fresh basil
1 cup chopped fresh parsley, preferably Italian (flat-leaf)
1 1/2 cups (approximately) pasta cooking liquid

1. Rinse the marlin, pat it dry, slice it into strips 1/2 inch thick, and place it in a small nonreactive pan or shallow bowl. In a small bowl, combine all the remaining fish ingredients, mixing them well, and pour them over the fish, lifting or turning the strips so that the marinade coats both sides. Chill the fish, covered, for 30 minutes, turning it once.

2. Heat the broiler or grill. Place the strips of fish on a baking tray (or a fine-meshed grilling grate). Broil the fish for about 3 minutes (or grill it for 4 to 5 minutes) or until it is just cooked through. Let the fish cool, and then chill it.

3. Separately (to avoid overcooking any one ingredient) steam the broccoli, carrots, and green beans for about 5 minutes each or until they are tender-crisp. As each vegetable is done, rinse it under cold running water, drain it, and place it in a very large bowl (5 quarts). Add the red bell peppers, green bell peppers, onion, beans, and olives. Toss the ingredients to combine them, cover the bowl, and chill the mixture until just before serving time.

4. To a large kettle of rapidly boiling water to which some salt and vegetable oil have been added, add the pasta, preferably in batches. Cook the pasta according to package directions until it is al dente. (Take care not to let the pasta get too soft, or it will break apart when the salad is tossed.) Drain the pasta, *reserving 2 cups of the cooking liquid,* and rinse the pasta under cold running water. Place the pasta in a very large bowl, cover it with plastic wrap, and chill it until just before serving time.

5. To prepare the dressing, in a medium-sized bowl, stir together all the dressing ingredients *except the pasta cooking liquid.* Stir in the reserved pasta cooking liquid 1/2 cup at a time until the dressing reaches the consistency of a thick, cold, creamed soup (usually 1 1/2 cups of the liquid will do).

6. Just before serving time, transfer the pasta to a very large basin, plastic tub, or kettle (a 16-quart canning kettle will work fine). Add the dressing to the pasta, and toss the pasta until it is thoroughly coated with the dressing. Add the vegetables, and toss the ingredients to mix them well. Slice the cold fish into 3/4-inch pieces, and gently toss them in. ■

RED AND GREEN FISH SALAD

■

A bountiful crop of cherry tomatoes and green beans in my Woodstock, New York, garden inspired this tangy salad.

Preparation tips: If you are feeling flush, the salad can be made with fresh lump CRABMEAT (picked over) or COOKED SMALL TO MEDIUM SHRIMP. Or you can use SURIMI salad pieces or ANY COOKED FISH that breaks into pieces but does not totally fall apart when tossed in a salad. If you prefer, the fish can be cooked in a microwave oven. Marjoram, like rosemary, is an herb with a very distinctive flavor, especially when it is used fresh, and may not be to everyone's liking. You may want to taste it before adding it to the salad.

SALAD

- 1 pound COD ("SCROD") FILLET, about ¾ inch thick
- Cayenne to taste
- Salt to taste (optional)
- Freshly ground white pepper to taste
- ¾ pound green beans, ends trimmed and cut into 1-inch lengths
- ½ cup thinly sliced red onion
- 1½ cups cherry tomatoes, halved through the stem end
- Lettuce or other greens

DRESSING

- ¼ cup fresh lime juice
- 1 tablespoon raspberry vinegar or other mild vinegar
- 1 tablespoon olive oil
- ¼ cup finely chopped cilantro, or to taste
- 1 tablespoon chopped fresh marjoram leaves or 1 teaspoon dried marjoram (optional)
- 1½ teaspoons seeded, minced jalapeño
- ½ teaspoon salt
- ½ teaspoon freshly ground black pepper

1. Heat the broiler. Sprinkle the fish with the cayenne, salt (if desired), and ground pepper. Place the fish in a shallow baking pan, place the pan in the hot broiler so that the fish is about 4 inches from the heat, and broil the fish for about 3 minutes. Carefully turn the fish, and broil it on the other side 3 minutes longer. (If you are using a microwave oven, follow the instructions for your unit, or see page 471.) Transfer the fish to a platter to cool.

2. Steam the green beans over boiling water for 5 minutes or until they are tender-crisp, or cook them in boiling water for about 2 minutes. Rinse them immediately under cold water, drain them, and place them in a bowl to cool.

3. Meanwhile, to a large nonreactive bowl, add all the dressing ingredients, combining them well. When the beans have cooled to warm, add them to the dressing along with the onion and cherry tomatoes. Toss the ingredients gently to coat them with the dressing. Transfer the vegetables to a large platter or to individual plates lined with the lettuce or greens.

4. To serve the salad, when the fish has cooled to lukewarm, gently "flake" it, and arrange it on top of the vegetables. ■

Cod

SQUID-INK PASTA AND SURIMI SALAD

■

4 SERVINGS

Squid ink, the black defensive secretion of this marine animal, has become a popular flavoring and coloring for pasta. Here, the black squid-ink (or calamari) pasta becomes a wonderful backdrop for creamy white surimi (imitation crabmeat)—or, if you like, real crabmeat—and glistening green snow peas. The result is a tangy main-dish salad good any time of year but especially nice on a warm summer day.

Preparation tips: Squid-ink pasta is available in gourmet food shops and by mail from Morisi's Macaroni Company (see page 116). Surimi (salad chunks or sticks cut into bite-sized pieces) is colorful, tasty, and economical, but for a fancier (and costlier) version of this salad, you could use real CRABMEAT.

SALAD

- ¾ pound squid-ink pasta (macaroni or fettucini cut into 2-inch to 3-inch lengths—see "Preparation tips")
- ½ pound snow peas, ends trimmed and strings removed
- ½ cup thinly sliced scallions, including tender green tops
- ¾ pound SURIMI, cut into bite-sized pieces (see "Preparation tips")

DRESSING

- 2 tablespoons rice vinegar *or* fresh lemon juice
- 1 tablespoon olive oil
- 1 tablespoon soy sauce
- 1 teaspoon Asian sesame oil
- ½ teaspoon white-wine Worcestershire sauce
- 1½ teaspoons peeled, finely minced gingerroot
- 1 teaspoon finely minced garlic
- ¼ teaspoon freshly ground black pepper
- ⅛ teaspoon cayenne *or* red pepper flakes, or to taste

1. Place the pasta in a large pot of boiling water to which some salt and oil has been added. Cook the pasta according to package directions until it is al dente. Drain the pasta, rinse it immediately under cold water, drain the pasta again thoroughly, and place it in a large bowl.
2. While the pasta is cooking, to a small bowl or a jar that has a tight-fitting lid, add all the dressing ingredients. Whisk or shake the dressing, and pour it over the cooked pasta.
3. Add the snow peas to a medium-sized saucepan of boiling water, and blanch the peas for 1 minute. Rinse the peas immediately under cold water.
4. Add the peas to the pasta along with the scallions and surimi. Toss the ingredients to mix them well. Chill the salad until serving time. ■

BLACKFISH AND BLACK BEAN SALAD
■

4 TO 6 SERVINGS

This is a salad with a Mexican flair. It is simple, nutritious, colorful, and tasty.

Preparation tip: If you are preparing this dish in the summer and don't wish to heat up the kitchen, the fish can be cooked in a microwave oven. Follow the timing recommended for your microwave oven, adjusted for the thickness of the fillets. Small pink beans can be used in place of the black beans.

SALAD
- 1 pound BLACKFISH FILLET
- Cajun seasoning (see page 424) *or* freshly ground black pepper to taste
- Vegetable-oil spray
- 1 2/3 cups cooked black beans (1 14-ounce *or* 16-ounce can, drained and rinsed)
- 2/3 cup 1/2-inch pieces red bell pepper
- 2/3 cup 1/2-inch pieces green bell pepper
- 1/2 cup sliced celery
- 1/3 cup diced red onion
- 2 tablespoons chopped cilantro
- Salad greens

DRESSING
- 3 tablespoons fresh lime juice
- 2 tablespoons olive oil
- 2 tablespoons red-wine vinegar
- 1 tablespoon seeded, minced jalapeño (about 1 pepper)
- 1 teaspoon minced garlic
- 1/4 teaspoon salt, or to taste

1. Heat the broiler (see "Preparation tip").
2. Sprinkle the fish generously on both sides with the Cajun seasoning or ground pepper, and spray it on both sides with vegetable oil. Put the fish on the rack of the broiler pan, and broil the fish for 4 minutes on each side. Transfer the fish to a platter or cutting board, and let the fish cool.
3. In a measuring cup or small jar that has a tight-fitting lid, combine all the dressing ingredients, and set the dressing aside.
4. In a large bowl, combine the beans, red bell pepper, green bell pepper, celery, onion, and cilantro.
5. When the fish has cooled, break it or cut it into bite-sized pieces. Add the fish to the bean-vegetable mixture.
6. Stir the dressing, and add it to the salad, tossing the ingredients gently.
7. Serve the salad on a bed of the salad greens. ■

SMOKED-TUNA SALAD

■

4 SERVINGS

My brother Jeffrey, a fisherman and fish enthusiast, gave me a stovetop smoker for my birthday, urging me to cook all kinds of fish in it. But it took a year and the impetus of this book before I would give it a try. Oh, what I had been missing! Smoking adds no fat to food, just distinctive flavor. And the smoked flavor of tuna, a fish with an appealing density, comes through in this pungent salad as clearly as if it were smoked pork or beef. A hearty, crusty loaf of bread would make this salad a satisfying meal.

Preparation tips: Different types of home smokers will require different procedures. The tuna can be smoked and the dressing prepared in advance and both set aside in the refrigerator. Or the whole salad (except the greens) can be prepared ahead. If you have no smoker, MARINATED TUNA that is broiled or grilled will work well (see the recipe on page 443). Or other, store-bought, already SMOKED FISH, such as trout, will make good substitutes for the tuna.

SALAD

1 pound TUNA STEAKS
2 tablespoons fresh lemon juice
Salt to taste
Freshly ground black pepper to taste
1 pound medium boiling potatoes
   or all-purpose potatoes, peeled
   and quartered
Mixed greens such as arugula and
   lettuce

DRESSING

1/2 cup nonfat or low-fat plain
   yogurt
1/4 cup nonfat or reduced-fat
   mayonnaise
1/4 cup chopped pickle
1/2 cup chopped green bell pepper
1/2 cup chopped red onion
1/4 cup chopped celery
2 tablespoons fresh lime juice
1/8 teaspoon cayenne, or to taste
2 tablespoons Dijon-style mustard
1/4 cup chopped fresh parsley

1. Sprinkle the tuna with the lemon juice, salt, and pepper. Smoke the fish in a smoker according to the manufacturer's instructions (about 15 minutes in my stovetop Camerons smoker).
2. To a large saucepan, add the potatoes and water to cover, and boil the potatoes for 15 to 20 minutes or until they are just tender. While the potatoes are still warm, cut the quarters crosswise into 1/2-inch pieces.
3. In a medium-sized bowl, combine all the dressing ingredients. Cut or break the smoked fish into small chunks, and add it and the potatoes to the dressing, tossing the ingredients to coat them well with the dressing.
4. Chill the salad. At serving time, arrange the greens on 4 individual plates, and mound some salad in the center of each plate. ■

WARM SMOKED-BLUEFISH SALAD

8 FIRST-COURSE SERVINGS OR 4 MAIN-DISH SERVINGS

When I was testing another smoked-fish recipe, I had to shop for bluefish. Since it was so inexpensive, I bought extra, froze a whole fillet, and waited for the opportunity to use it. One wintry evening in Woodstock, when friends arrived for a casual dinner, I defrosted the fillet and devised this splendid, multicolored, warm salad.

Preparation tip: The bluefish can be smoked up to 3 days before serving it and then refrigerated, or it can be smoked even further ahead and frozen. But it must be gently brought back to room temperature before using it.

 1 **pound skinless** BLUEFISH FILLET
Salt to taste, divided
Freshly ground black pepper to taste, divided
 1 **tablespoon olive oil**
 1 **cup chopped green bell pepper**
 1 **cup chopped red bell pepper**
 2 **cups sliced onion**
 2 **cups sliced fennel**
 1 **tablespoon minced garlic**
 2 **tablespoons fresh lemon juice**
 ¼ **cup dry white wine**
 ¼ **cup chicken broth**
 6 **cups mixed salad greens such as red-leaf lettuce,**
    watercress, and arugula

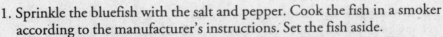

Bluefish

1. Sprinkle the bluefish with the salt and pepper. Cook the fish in a smoker according to the manufacturer's instructions. Set the fish aside.
2. Heat the olive oil in a large nonstick skillet, and add the green bell pepper, red bell pepper, onion, fennel, and garlic. Cook the vegetables, stirring them occasionally, over medium heat for about 10 minutes. Add the lemon juice, wine, broth, salt to taste, and pepper to taste, and bring the mixture to a simmer. Remove the vegetables from the heat, and keep them warm.
3. Arrange the salad greens on individual salad or dinner plates. Place equal portions of the vegetable mixture in the center of each mound of greens. Slice the reserved bluefish into strips about 1 inch thick, and arrange the fish on top of each portion of vegetables. ∎

POACHED FISH SALAD WITH HOT MUSTARD DRESSING
■

4 SERVINGS

British restaurant food has come a long way since my first foray into the English countryside in 1967. I had little trouble during a trip in 1993 finding dishes that would not violate my nutritional and culinary sensibilities. One especially delicious dish—poached salmon on a bed of salad—inspired me to devise my own version.

Preparation tips: The salad can be made with ANY FIRM FISH FILLET OR STEAK that will withstand the rigors of poaching. If you use large steaks with a center bone, the flesh, when cooled, should be removed intact from the bone and served as a boneless fillet. The specific salad ingredients can vary according to taste and availability. If you plan to serve the fish hot, do the first step last.

Serving suggestion: This dish works well either as a room-temperature or a cold salad or as hot fish served on a cold salad base.

FISH
1¼ pounds SALMON FILLET *or* 1½ pounds firm fish steaks (see "Preparation tips")
½ cup fish broth *or* chicken broth
¼ cup dry white wine
¼ cup water
1 tablespoon balsamic vinegar *or* white-wine vinegar
½ teaspoon salt, or to taste
⅛ to ¼ teaspoon freshly ground black pepper, to taste

SALAD (SEE "PREPARATION TIPS")
Red-leaf lettuce *or* any mixture of salad greens
1 medium red bell pepper, cored, seeded, and cut lengthwise into thin strips
4 small plum (Roma) tomatoes, thinly sliced crosswise
4 small cooked red new potatoes, thinly sliced crosswise
¼ cup slivered red onion *or* white onion
¼ pound zucchini, cut into julienne strips, *or* thin, tender-crisp asparagus tips *or* snow peas *or* sugar snap peas
Thinly sliced scallion tops *or* chopped fresh parsley for garnish (optional)

DRESSING
1½ tablespoons sherry vinegar *or* white-wine vinegar *or* red-wine vinegar
1½ tablespoons dry sherry *or* dry white wine
1 tablespoon olive oil
½ to 1 teaspoon English mustard *or* hot horseradish mustard, to taste

1 teaspoon minced garlic
¼ teaspoon salt, or to taste
⅛ teaspoon freshly ground black pepper, or to taste

1. To prepare the fish, remove any pinbones from the fillet with a needle-nose pliers, tweezers, or fingernails. Place the fish in a skillet with a lid and just big enough to hold it in one layer. Combine all the remaining ingredients for the fish, and pour them over the fish. Bring the liquid to a boil, reduce the heat, cover the skillet, and simmer the fish until it is just cooked through (8 to 10 minutes for each inch of thickness). If the liquid does not fully cover the fish, be sure to turn the fish halfway through the cooking time. With a large spatula, carefully remove the fish from the cooking liquid, place it on a platter to cool, and remove the skin and bones from the flesh, if necessary. Divide the fish into 4 portions.
2. Place the lettuce or salad greens on 4 individual plates. Attractively arrange the rest of the salad ingredients on top. Place a fish portion in the center of each plate.
3. To a small jar that has a tight-fitting lid, add all the dressing ingredients. Cover the jar, and shake it well. With a spoon, dribble the dressing over the salad and fish. Sprinkle the fish with the scallions or parsley (if desired). ■

Salmon

SUMMER-SLIM TUNA SALAD

Thanks to the wide use of the canned variety, tuna is by far the most popular fish in this country. And as enamored as I am of fresh fish, I would be a fool to eschew the virtues of processed tuna. Once canned tuna became widely available packed in water instead of oil, my principle objection to it—its high fat content—was removed. Now, the challenge is to use water-packed tuna in ways that enhance its flavor without adding much, if any, fat to the fish. Here is one recipe that does just that.

Preparation tips: To keep the dish from getting watery, be sure to drain the tuna thoroughly by pressing the lid of the opened can against the fish as you pour off the liquid. Then further dry the fish by squeezing it in two layers of paper towels. Seeding the tomatoes and cucumber, as indicated, also helps.

Serving suggestions: The salad can be served on a bed of crisp greens and accompanied by crunchy celery and carrot sticks and a crusty bread. Or it can be stuffed into a pita with sprouts or lettuce to make a delicious sandwich. However, the salad should not be put in or on bread until just before it is to be eaten.

2 6½-ounce cans TUNA PACKED IN WATER, well drained (see "Preparation tips")
⅔ cup low-fat small-curd cottage cheese
2 tablespoons snipped chives *or* garlic chives (optional)
Several dashes cayenne *or* pinch red pepper flakes (optional)
¼ to ⅜ teaspoon freshly ground black pepper, to taste
4 plum (Roma) tomatoes, seeded
1 small cucumber, peeled, halved lengthwise, and seeded
½ cup sliced scallions, including some green tops
Salt to taste (optional)

1. Place the drained tuna in a medium-sized bowl. Add the cottage cheese, chives or garlic chives (if desired), cayenne or red pepper flakes (if desired), and black pepper, and mix the ingredients well, taking care to leave discrete pieces of tuna.
2. Cut the tomatoes into 1/3-inch dice. Cut the cucumber into quarters lengthwise and then slice it crosswise into pieces 1/4 inch thick. Add the tomatoes, the cucumber, and the scallions to the tuna mixture, and toss the ingredients to combine them well.
3. Check the seasonings, adding the salt (if desired) and more pepper. ■

Baked Beauties

Baking has always been a favorite method of preparing fish, in part because it requires the least attention: just heat the oven, place the food in it, and let the heat take care of the rest. The only real concern—and one that is especially important in fish cookery—is the oven's tendency to dry things out. That is why so many of the baked and broiled dishes in this section are shielded in some way: by sauces, foil, or vegetable coatings. Sometimes, though, the oven's hot, drying capability is just right for the job, as in my oven-fried foods (see, for example, the Catfish Sticks on page 306 and the Salmon Croquettes with Dill Sauce on page 310). Then, a very hot oven allows me to prepare a dish with the crispiness of frying but without the added fat (and added calories). There are also many "mixed dishes" in this section—that is, those dishes in which preparation is started on the stovetop but finished in the oven, which helps to meld the flavors and/or brown the top for a beautiful presentation.

SPANISH MACKEREL BAKED IN WHITE WINE

■

When I was on a nature trip with my family in the Gulf of California, our ship encountered a large school of Monterey Spanish mackerel that prompted one of the crewmembers to hop in a skiff and, rod in hand, go after them. We all watched as these spectacular fish, which seemed to fly through the air, practically landed in the skiff unaided. Dinner that night was divine. So when my local fishmonger offered fillets of this mild-flavored mackerel, albeit the Atlantic Ocean species, I was anxious to try them. I adapted a delicious blue-fish recipe devised by the Massachusetts Cooperative Extension Service.

Preparation tips: Alternatives include fillets of BLUEFISH, regular MACKEREL, and SALMON, with the baking time adjusted according to the thickness of the fillet. For 2 pounds of fish, increase the marinade ingredients by about 50 percent, but you don't have to be a slave to exact proportions. Note that the fish marinates for 1 hour.

⅔ **cup dry white wine**
1½ **teaspoons minced garlic**
  2 **tablespoons finely chopped fresh parsley**
  1 **tablespoon finely chopped fresh basil** *or* **1 teaspoon dried basil**
  2 **teaspoons fresh thyme leaves** *or* **1 teaspoon dried thyme leaves**
¾ **teaspoon paprika**
  1 **teaspoon fresh lemon juice**
⅛ **teaspoon salt, or to taste**
Freshly ground black pepper to taste
1¼ **pounds SPANISH MACKEREL FILLETS**

1. To a baking dish large enough to hold the mackerel, add all the ingredients *except the fish,* combining them well. Place the fillets flesh side down in the marinade, and spoon some of the marinade over the skin side. Cover the dish, and place it in the refrigerator. After about 30 minutes, turn the fish over, spoon some marinade over the fish, cover the dish, and chill the fish for another 30 minutes or so.
2. Heat the oven to 400°F.
3. Carefully pour the marinade out of the baking dish, saving some of the herbs to put on top of the fillets. If the fillets have thin tails, tuck them under so that the tail portion approximates the thickness of the rest of the fillet. Bake the fillets in the center of the hot oven for 10 to 15 minutes or until the mackerel is opaque at the thickest part of the fillets. ■

SPANISH MACKEREL WITH FRESH TOMATO AND HERB SAUCE
■
6 SERVINGS

The buttery flesh of this mild-flavored fish is delightful under a tangy, fresh-tasting sauce accented by orange juice. This dish lends itself to company or family meals since it can be prepared in advance for baking. It also has staying power after it is cooked. I savored the leftovers for lunch three days in a row; they heated beautifully in the microwave oven.

Preparation tips: This sauce would suit many kinds of fish, including fillets of ordinary **MACKEREL**, **BLUEFISH**, **TILEFISH**, **OCEAN PERCH**, or **COD** (**"SCROD"**). If fresh herbs are not available, a reasonable facsimile of the sauce can be made with 2 teaspoons of dried basil, 1 teaspoon of dried oregano, and 1 teaspoon of dried thyme leaves. You can set up the fish with its sauce (through step 3) hours in advance. Just keep the dish refrigerated until about half an hour before it is to be baked. The exact baking time will depend upon the thickness of the fillets, measured at their thickest point (15 minutes for a fillet that is ¾ inch thick).

Vegetable-oil spray
2 pounds SPANISH MACKEREL FILLETS
⅔ cup finely chopped onion
½ cup chopped green bell pepper
½ cup chopped red bell pepper
2½ cups chopped tomatoes
2 tablespoons chopped fresh basil (see "Preparation tips")
2 tablespoons chopped fresh oregano (see "Preparation tips")
1 tablespoon fresh thyme leaves (see "Preparation tips")
¼ teaspoon red pepper flakes
¼ cup dry white wine
¼ cup orange juice
½ teaspoon salt, or to taste
½ teaspoon freshly ground black pepper, or to taste

Spanish mackerel

1. Heat the oven to 400°F.
2. Spray the vegetable oil on the bottom of a baking dish just large enough to hold the fish in one layer. Set the fillets, skin side down, in the dish, tucking the tails under the fillets so that the fish will bake evenly.
3. To a large bowl, add all the remaining ingredients, stirring them to mix them well. Distribute the mixture evenly over the fillets.
4. Place the baking dish in the hot oven, and bake the fish for about 15 minutes or until it is just cooked through. ■

TILAPIA FILLETS WITH FENNEL SAUCE

■

4 SERVINGS

Tilapia, slightly firmer and, to my taste, a bit sweeter than flounder, is showing up in stores all across America. Because it breeds so well in fish farms in this country and around the world it is also often a better buy than many other fish. When I prepared this dish one morning (almost on a whim), I tasted it, served it for lunch, and placed the leftovers back in the refrigerator. I tried the leftovers several days later and found that they tasted fine—maybe better than before, having been preserved to some extent by the acid from lemon juice and tomatoes.

Preparation tips: Fish alternatives include OCEAN PERCH, CATFISH, OCEAN POUT, SNAPPER, and COD ("SCROD"). Look for a fennel bulb that has some of its feathery leaves still attached.

> 2 cups chopped fennel bulb (reserve some of the feathery leaves)
> 2/3 cup finely chopped onion
> 1 teaspoon grated lemon rind
> 4 teaspoons fresh lemon juice
> 1 16-ounce can plum tomatoes, drained and juice reserved, coarsely chopped
> Salt to taste, divided
> Freshly ground black pepper to taste, divided
> 1 1/4 pounds skinless TILAPIA FILLETS, in 4 portions
> 1/4 cup chopped fresh parsley
> 2 tablespoons chopped fennel leaves

1. Place the fennel, onion, lemon rind, lemon juice, tomatoes with their juice, salt, and pepper in a saucepan. Bring the ingredients to a boil, reduce the heat, and simmer the sauce for 15 minutes.
2. Meanwhile, heat the oven to 350°F.
3. Sprinkle the fillets with the salt and pepper.
4. Spoon half of the sauce into the bottom of a covered casserole. Place the fillets on top of the sauce, and cover the fish with the remaining sauce. Cover the casserole, and bake the fish for 20 minutes.
5. Before serving the fish, sprinkle the dish with the parsley and fennel leaves. ■

BAKED BLUEFISH IN YOGURT-MINT SAUCE
■

The primary peril in baking fish is that thinner parts of it will dry out before the rest has a chance to cook through. That's why I so often bake fish en papillote—wrapped in a leaf or parchment or foil (see, for example, the recipes on pages 290, 291, and 296). Here, the yogurt mixture placed on top of the fillets does double duty: it adds a tangy flavor and acts as a lid that guarantees delicately moist results.

Preparation tip: Although mint lends a pleasant change of pace to this dish, other fresh or dried herbs would work well, too, including dill, basil, or parsley.

SAUCE
- 1 tablespoon chopped fresh mint (see "Preparation tip")
- 1 teaspoon Dijon-style mustard
- 2 tablespoons fresh lemon juice
- 1 teaspoon minced garlic
- ¼ cup nonfat or low-fat plain yogurt
- Salt to taste
- Freshly ground black pepper to taste

FISH
- Vegetable-oil spray
- 1¼ pounds BLUEFISH FILLETS, in 4 portions

1. Heat the oven to 425°F.
2. To make the sauce, place all the sauce ingredients in a mixing bowl, and whisk the ingredients to blend them well.
3. To prepare the fish, spray a baking pan with the oil, and place the fish in it. Using a rubber spatula, spread the sauce smoothly over the surface of each fillet.
4. Place the pan in the hot oven, and bake the fish for 10 minutes or until it is cooked through. ■

BAKED BLUEFISH IN A MUSHROOM CRUST

■   4 SERVINGS

The mushroom topping in this dish is thick and moist, creating a layered effect that is made all the more appealing by the crisp bread crumbs on the surface. A mystery of fish cookery is that at times 1 to 1¼ pounds of one fish will comfortably feed four, but the same amount of another fish will barely satisfy them. In this case, the puzzle isn't hard to solve: the vegetable-rich topping—which has only a bit of added fat—gives this dish a hunger-satisfying quality as well as a smooth, mellow flavor.

Preparation tips: Since the topping has so much character, it is important to use a fish that does, too. **SPANISH MACKEREL,** for instance, would be a good substitute for the bluefish. Onion can replace the leek. The mushrooms should be minced very finely; and while a chef's knife can do the job, here the food processor does it better and faster. Bluefish fillets vary considerably in thickness, so testing for doneness as the fish cooks is particularly advisable.

TOPPING
- 10 ounces mushrooms, minced (about 1½ cups)
- 2 teaspoons olive oil
- ½ cup minced leek, white part only
- ¼ cup minced celery
- 1 teaspoon minced garlic
- Salt to taste
- Freshly ground black pepper to taste
- 2 tablespoons chopped fresh parsley, divided
- 1 tablespoon fresh lemon juice
- 1 tablespoon Parmesan
- ½ cup fresh bread crumbs
- Vegetable-oil spray

FISH
- 1¼ pounds BLUEFISH FILLETS
- Salt to taste
- Freshly ground black pepper to taste
- Vegetable-oil spray

1. Heat the oven to 400°F.
2. Place the mushrooms in cheesecloth, a dish towel, or a double layer of strong paper towels, and squeeze the mushrooms to remove as much of their liquid as possible. Set the mushrooms aside.
3. Heat the olive oil in a large nonstick skillet, add the leek, celery, and garlic, and cook the vegetables, stirring them, for 1 minute.
4. Add the reserved mushrooms, the salt, and pepper, and cook the mixture, stirring it, for another 2 minutes. Remove the skillet from the heat, and blend in 1 tablespoon of the parsley and the lemon juice.
5. Sprinkle the flesh side of the fish with the salt and pepper.
6. Spray a baking pan with vegetable oil, and place the fish in it, skin side down. Spoon a layer of the mushroom mixture over the surface of the fish, smoothing the mixture as you go.
7. In a small bowl, mix the Parmesan with the bread crumbs, and sprinkle the mixture over the mushroom topping, patting the bread crumbs down to make sure they adhere. Spray the breading with the vegetable oil to help it brown.
8. Place the pan in the hot oven, and bake the fish for 15 minutes or until it is cooked through and the topping is evenly browned. ∎

Bluefish

GROUPER WITH ANCHOVY SAUCE

■

4 SERVINGS

Grouper, like red snapper, is a firm but sweet and flavorful fish that can stand up to a sauce with character. And this sauce has lots of character without being overwhelming.

Preparation tip: Canned anchovies are heavily salted (hence the recommended rinsing), so be sure to taste the dish before adding salt.

Serving suggestion: Because the sauce is too good to leave on the plate, serve the fish with an ample portion of a starchy side dish that will absorb the extra sauce—rice, couscous, or orzo, perhaps.

SAUCE
- 1 tablespoon olive oil
- ½ cup chopped onion
- 1 teaspoon chopped garlic
- 5 anchovy fillets, rinsed, patted dry, and coarsely chopped (about 1½ tablespoons)
- 2 cups canned crushed tomatoes
- ⅛ to ¼ teaspoon red pepper flakes, to taste
- 2 tablespoons balsamic vinegar
- Salt to taste (see "Preparation tip")
- Freshly ground black pepper to taste
- 16 small green pitted olives, rinsed

FISH
- Vegetable-oil spray
- 1¼ pounds GROUPER FILLETS
- Salt to taste
- Freshly ground black pepper to taste
- 2 tablespoons chopped fresh basil for garnish

Grouper

1. Heat the oven to 425°F.
2. To prepare the sauce, heat the olive oil in a large nonstick saucepan, add the onion and garlic, and cook the vegetables for 1 to 2 minutes or until the onion begins to wilt.
3. Stir in the anchovies, then add the tomatoes, red pepper flakes, vinegar, salt (if desired), and pepper. Bring the mixture to a simmer, reduce the heat, and cook the ingredients, uncovered, for 7 minutes. Add the olives, and simmer the sauce 1 minute longer.
4. Spray a baking pan with the vegetable oil. Sprinkle the grouper with the salt and pepper, place it in the pan, and pour the tomato sauce over it.
5. Place the pan in the hot oven, and bake the fish for 10 to 15 minutes or until it is cooked through.
6. Serve the fish from the oven, sprinkled with the basil. ■

TROUT WITH TOMATO-YOGURT CURRY SAUCE

■

In this recipe, trout takes on an Indian flair without added fat, and the sauce can double as the seasoning for an accompanying starch.

Preparation tips: Almost any mild-flavored white fish will work, including CATFISH, TILAPIA, COD ("SCROD"), HALIBUT, TILEFISH, HADDOCK, and GROUPER. You can also use WHOLE TROUT in place of fillets. Garam masala is a popular Indian seasoning mix now sold in many specialty food stores. A reasonable facsimile can be made at home by combining equal amounts of cardamom, cumin, cinnamon, and coriander (say, 1 teaspoon each) with smaller amounts (about 1/4 teaspoon each) of ground cloves and black pepper. Note that the fish marinates for about 20 minutes.

Serving suggestions: Small steamed or boiled potatoes or even baked potatoes would be a lovely accompaniment. Brown rice or basmati rice would also go well with the curried sauce.

FISH
2 large or 4 small BROOK TROUT
   FILLETS (1 to 1 1/4 pounds total) *or*
   fish steaks (see "Preparation tips")
1 1/2 tablespoons fresh lemon juice
Salt to taste (optional)
Vegetable-oil spray

SAUCE
1 cup tomato puree
1/2 cup nonfat or low-fat plain yogurt
2 teaspoons minced garlic
1 teaspoon peeled, minced gingerroot
1/2 teaspoon garam masala (see
   "Preparation tips")
1/4 teaspoon turmeric
1/4 teaspoon salt
1/8 teaspoon cayenne

1. Sprinkle the fish on both sides with the lemon juice and salt (if desired). (If you are using a whole fish, first make 3 diagonal slashes about 1/2 inch deep on each side.) Place the fish in a baking dish that has been sprayed with the vegetable oil.
2. To a medium-sized bowl, add all the sauce ingredients, whisking them to combine them thoroughly. Pour the sauce over the fish. (If you are using a whole fish, put some of the sauce in the fish cavity.) Cover the baking dish with plastic wrap, and let the fish marinate in the refrigerator.
3. After the fish has marinated for 10 minutes, remove it from the refrigerator, and heat the oven to 400°F.
4. After the fish has marinated for 20 minutes, remove the plastic wrap, place the baking dish in the hot oven, and bake the fish for 15 minutes (20 to 25 minutes if you are using a whole fish). ■

SKATE IN CREOLE SAUCE

■

Skate, a scaleless, boneless, bottom-dwelling fish that is related to sharks, is just coming into its own in this country. And what a treat you have in store if you haven't tried it yet. Only the flat, finlike wings of the skate are eaten; and in place of bones, it has a corrugated plate of cartilage that can be filleted away before or after cooking or that diners can easily eat around. In this dish, the latter approach is used (see page 280 for a filleted version).

Preparation tips: Skate is nearly always sold with its tough skin already removed. If the skin has not been removed, ask the fishmonger to clean it for you. For alternatives to skate, try any reasonably thick white fish such as COD ("SCROD"), HADDOCK, or KING MACKEREL, or a meatier fish like SWORDFISH. If a boneless fish is used, reduce the baking time to 15 minutes.

Serving suggestions: Since skate is a delicate white fish, a hefty carbohydrate such as baked or boiled potatoes or a substantial pasta is an ideal companion, especially when some of the sauce from the fish is used to flavor the side dish. For a lighter meal, try white or brown rice. For complementary color and flavor, I serve this dish with steamed green beans tossed with sautéed mushrooms and onions.

SAUCE
- 1 tablespoon olive oil *or* canola oil
- 1 cup finely chopped onion
- 1 cup finely chopped green bell pepper
- 1 cup finely chopped celery
- 1 tablespoon minced garlic
- 1 14-ounce can tomatoes
- 3 tablespoons tomato paste
- 2 tablespoons dry white wine
- 1/2 teaspoon dried oregano leaves
- 1/2 teaspoon dried thyme leaves
- 1/2 teaspoon Tabasco sauce

Generous pinch cayenne, or to taste
Salt to taste (optional)

FISH
- 1 2-pound SKATE wing *or* 2 1-pound wings, skinned (see "Preparation tips")

Salt to taste
Freshly ground black pepper to taste
Vegetable-oil spray
- 1/4 cup chopped fresh parsley

1. Heat the oven to 400°F.
2. To prepare the sauce, briefly heat the olive oil or canola oil in a large non-stick skillet, and add the onion, green bell pepper, celery, and garlic. Sauté the vegetables over medium heat, stirring them often, for about 7 minutes or until they soften.
3. Meanwhile, drain the tomatoes, reserving the juice in a medium-sized bowl, and chop the tomatoes finely.
4. To the bowl with the tomato juice, add the tomato paste, wine, oregano, thyme, Tabasco sauce, cayenne, and salt (if desired), and stir the ingredients to combine them well. When the vegetables have softened, add the chopped tomatoes and the juice mixture to the skillet, stirring the ingredients to combine them. Bring the mixture to a boil, reduce the heat to low, and simmer the sauce, uncovered, for 10 minutes.
5. To prepare the fish, wash and dry the skate, and sprinkle it with the salt and pepper. Spray the vegetable oil lightly on a baking dish just large enough to hold the skate and sauce. Spoon one-third of the sauce into the baking dish, and lay the skate on it. Spoon the remaining sauce over the skate, covering the fish completely. Place the dish in the hot oven, and bake the fish for 20 to 25 minutes (use the lesser time for 1-pound wings).
6. To serve the fish, sprinkle the dish with the parsley, and cut the skate wing through the cartilage (easily done with a spatula) into serving pieces. ■

Skate

BAKED SKATE WITH OKRA

■

Skate, a relative of the ray, doesn't look like anything you've seen before, but don't let that intimidate you. The flesh of the wings is sweet and the cooking easy, as this straightforward recipe demonstrates. To be eaten, the wings must be skinned, which is how fish stores usually sell them. Sometimes the wings are also sold filleted, with the cartilage of the wing removed, which is how I use them here.

Preparation tips: To fillet a skate wing, use a sharp filleting or chef's knife, and, with a sideways motion, slice the flesh off both sides of the cartilage. Alternatives to skate might include 1¼ pounds of fillets of **BLACKFISH, TILE-FISH,** or even **COD ("SCROD")** or **HADDOCK.**

  1 large SKATE wing (about 2 pounds), skinned and filleted (see "Preparation tips")
Salt to taste
Freshly ground black pepper to taste
Vegetable-oil spray
  ¾ pound small okra, stem ends trimmed not quite down to the flesh
  ½ cup diced fresh plum (Roma) tomatoes
  ¾ cup thinly sliced onion
  ½ cup diced dried apricots
  ½ cup fish broth *or* chicken broth
  2 tablespoons fresh lemon juice

1. Heat the oven to 425°F.
2. Sprinkle the skate with the salt and pepper. Lightly spray with the vegetable oil a covered casserole dish that will hold the fillets in one layer. Place the fish in the casserole, and spread the okra over it.
3. In a small bowl, combine the tomatoes, onion, apricots, fish broth or chicken broth, and lemon juice. Spoon this mixture over the okra, distributing the mixture well.
4. Cover the casserole, and place it in the hot oven. Bake the casserole for 20 minutes or until the okra is just tender. ■

ONION-TOPPED WALLEYE

■

4 SERVINGS

Walleye, also known as walleyed pike, is a popular game fish in the upper Midwest; it is also caught commercially with gill nets in the clear, fresh waters of Canada. It has a white, firm, sweet-flavored flesh and is lovely baked or poached. This simple recipe makes for a quick and tasty dinner.

Preparation tips: Alternatives to walleye include CATFISH, ORANGE ROUGHY, or other mild but relatively firm fillets.

1¼ pounds WALLEYE FILLETS
Salt to taste
Freshly ground black pepper to taste
  2 tablespoons Dijon-style mustard
  2 teaspoons honey
  1 large onion, thinly sliced (about 1½ cups)
Paprika

1. Heat the oven to 425°F.
2. Rinse and pat dry the fillets, and sprinkle them on one or both sides with the salt and pepper. Place the fillets in a nonstick or lightly oiled baking dish, tucking under the thin ends.
3. To a small bowl, add the mustard and honey, stirring them to combine them thoroughly. Smear the fillets with the mustard mixture. Then arrange the onion slices, overlapping them if necessary, on top of the fillets. Sprinkle the onions generously with the paprika.
4. Place the baking dish in the hot oven, and bake the fish for 15 minutes or until the fish is opaque through its thickest part. ■

Walleye

BAKED SEA BASS MEXICANA

On the west coast of Mexico, a classic approach to saucing fish is to smother it in tomatoes, onions, and olives, then fire it up with hot peppers. The result is brilliantly colored and offers a startling mixture of textures and tastes.

Preparation tips: The recipe calls for one pickled jalapeño pepper, which is enough to give the dish some spark but not enough to make it really hot. If you like your dishes fiery, add a second pepper. A fresh jalapeño can be used as well, though it may not be quite as hot. **ROCKFISH** can be substituted for black sea bass.

FISH
Vegetable-oil spray
1¹/₄ pounds BLACK SEA BASS FILLETS
  1 tablespoon fresh lime juice
Salt to taste
Freshly ground black pepper to taste

SAUCE
  1 tablespoon olive oil
  2 cups thinly sliced onion
  1 tablespoon minced garlic
  1 28-ounce can Italian plum tomatoes, drained and juice reserved, chopped
  2 tablespoons drained capers
16 Spanish olives (green olives stuffed with pimientos), rinsed
  1 pickled jalapeño, finely chopped (about 1 tablespoon)
  3 tablespoons chopped cilantro *or* Italian (flat-leaf) parsley
  1 teaspoon chopped fresh thyme *or* ¹/₂ teaspoon dried thyme leaves
Salt to taste
Freshly ground black pepper to taste

1. Spray a baking pan with the vegetable oil. Place the fish, skin side down, in the pan, and sprinkle the fillets with the lime juice, salt, and pepper. Cover the fish with plastic wrap, and refrigerate it until the sauce is ready.
2. Heat the oven to 425°F.
3. To prepare the sauce, heat the olive oil in a large nonstick skillet. Add the onion, and cook it over medium heat, stirring it, for about 5 minutes or until the onion begins to take on a touch of color. Add the garlic, and sauté the vegetables for another 2 minutes, taking care not to burn the garlic.

4. Add all the remaining sauce ingredients to the skillet. Bring the sauce to a simmer, reduce the heat to low, and cook the sauce, uncovered, for 7 minutes.

5. Take the fish out of the refrigerator, and remove the plastic wrap. Pour the sauce over the fish, taking care to cover the fillets completely. Place the pan in the hot oven, and bake the fish for 10 minutes or until it is cooked through. ■

Black sea bass

OVEN-STEAMED BASS WITH CRISP VEGETABLES

■

The idea here is to smother fish fillets with colorful vegetables. Even though the heating takes place in the oven, the fish is not baked as much as it is steamed—by the wine, by the juices released by the fish itself, and by the liquid from the vegetables. There is no fat added in this recipe, yet the fish remains delicate and moist while the vegetables emerge tender-crisp.

Preparation tip: If you prefer your vegetables soft, partially cook them first in a steamer or in a pan with a little broth.

Serving suggestion: The liquid that remains after the fish has been cooked is splendid. Try serving the fish over a bed of wild rice, using this broth to moisten the rice. Or strain the liquid, and add it to water used to cook rice for another meal.

> 1 small carrot, sliced paper thin (about $1/2$ cup)
> $1/2$ cup chopped celery
> 1 small red bell pepper, cored, seeded, and sliced in $1/4$-inch julienne strips (about $3/4$ cup)
> 1 small onion, sliced in thin rings (about $1/2$ cup)
> 1 cup dry white wine, divided
> 1 tablespoon fresh lemon juice
> 1 tablespoon peeled, minced gingerroot
> 2 teaspoons minced garlic
> 1 bay leaf

$1 1/4$ pounds BLACK SEA BASS *or* STRIPED BASS FILLETS (skin on)
Salt to taste
Freshly ground black pepper to taste
> $1/2$ teaspoon dried thyme leaves *or*, preferably, 4 sprigs fresh thyme

1. Heat the oven to 425°F.
2. In a mixing bowl, toss together the carrots, celery, red bell pepper, and onion.
3. Pour $3/4$ cup of the wine and the lemon juice into a shallow baking dish large enough to hold the fillets in one layer.
4. Cover the bottom of the dish with the mixed vegetables, sprinkling the vegetables evenly with the gingerroot and garlic. Add the bay leaf.
5. Place the fish flesh side up on a cutting board or platter, and sprinkle the fillets with the salt and pepper.

6. If you are using dried thyme, sprinkle the fish with it. Place the fillets *flesh side down* over the vegetables, and, if you are using fresh thyme, slip the sprigs of thyme under them. Sprinkle the fish with the remaining ¼ cup of the wine.

7. Cover the baking dish tightly with aluminum foil, and bake the fish in the hot oven for 20 minutes or until it is cooked through. Discard the thyme sprigs and the bay leaf, and serve the fish flesh side up with the vegetables spooned over it. ▪

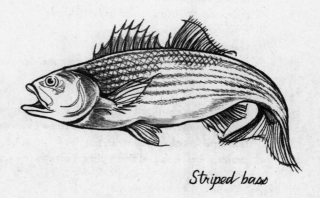

Striped bass

CATFISH WITH MANY HERBS AND SPICES
■

This dish was slightly adapted from a prize-winning recipe in a catfish cooking contest. Steve Smith of Providence, Rhode Island, devised it. It initially attracted my attention early one summer because I happened to have in my window-box garden all the fresh herbs that the recipe called for. But I have since gone out of my way to get the ingredients—even in the dead of winter.

Serving suggestion: These highly seasoned fillets go best with a neutral, starchy side dish such as baked or boiled potatoes, rice, or pasta with just a sprinkling of oil and grated cheese.

SPICE MIXTURE
   1 tablespoon fennel seeds
   1 teaspoon freshly ground black pepper
   3/4 teaspoon paprika
   1/2 teaspoon salt
   1/4 teaspoon ground thyme *or* 1/2 teaspoon dried thyme leaves

HERB MIXTURE
   3 tablespoons chopped fresh basil *or* 1 1/2 teaspoons dried basil
   2 tablespoons chopped fresh oregano *or* 1 1/2 teaspoons dried oregano leaves
   2 tablespoons chopped fresh parsley
   1 tablespoon chopped fresh chives *or* minced scallion greens

FISH
   1 tablespoon olive oil *or* canola oil
   2 teaspoons minced garlic
   2 pounds CATFISH FILLETS
   2 tablespoons fresh lemon juice

1. Heat the oven to 400°F.
2. In a small bowl, combine all the ingredients for the spice mixture. In another small bowl, combine all the ingredients for the herb mixture.
3. In a baking dish large enough to hold the fish in one layer, place the oil and garlic. Sprinkle one-third of the spice mixture over the garlic. Then sprinkle one-third of the herb mixture over the spice mixture.
4. Arrange the fish on top of the spices and herbs, and sprinkle the fillets with the lemon juice. Then sprinkle the remaining spice mixture over the fillets, followed by the remaining herb mixture.
5. Place the dish in the hot oven, and bake the fish for about 10 minutes (less if the fillets are less than 3/4 inch thick at their thickest part). Turn the heat up to broil, and cook the fish in the oven about 1 minute longer. ■

SIMPLY SUPERB SALMON FILLET

■

Salmon warrants minimalist treatment. It would be hard to find a simpler yet more elegant way to prepare it than this, compliments of my devoted friend Margaret Shryer of Minneapolis.

Preparation tip: The fillet can be prepared in advance for baking (through step 3), but keep it covered and chilled.

1¼ **pounds** SALMON FILLET
Vegetable-oil spray
Salt to taste
Freshly ground black pepper to taste
  1 **lemon, very thinly sliced crosswise and seeded**
  1 **large white onion** *or* **yellow onion, very thinly sliced crosswise**

1. Heat the oven to 450°F.
2. Place the fillet skin side down in a baking pan that has been lightly sprayed with the vegetable oil. Spray the fillet with the vegetable oil, and sprinkle it with the salt and pepper.
3. Arrange the lemon slices over the fillet. Top the fillet with the onion slices.
4. Place the pan in the middle of the hot oven, and bake the fish for 20 minutes or until it is just cooked through. ■

CINDY'S SALMON WITH HONEY-MUSTARD AND TARRAGON

■

4 SERVINGS

My sister-in-law Cindy Brody is no slapdash cook. Even with two pre-schoolers underfoot, she manages to prepare imaginative meals at least four nights a week. This is one of her happy creations, pretty enough to serve at the most elegant of dinners. Cindy says that the poaching liquid in the baking pan prevents the fish from drying out even if a sudden child-related crisis should result in keeping the fish in the oven too long.

Preparation tip: The dish can be fully prepared for baking an hour or more ahead and kept covered and chilled. But bring it back to room temperature before placing the pan in the oven.

Serving suggestion: Side dishes like rice pilaf and a green vegetable (for example, asparagus, broccoli, or peas) make a colorful and nutritious meal.

> 2 tablespoons Dijon-style mustard
> 1 tablespoon honey
> 4 SALMON STEAKS, about 1 inch thick
> 4 tablepoons (¼ cup) chopped fresh tarragon, divided
> 4 slices tomato
> 4 teaspoons nonpareil (small) capers
> ¼ cup dry white wine
> ¼ cup water

1. Heat the oven to 400°F.
2. In a small bowl, combine the mustard and honey, and spread the mixture on one side of the salmon steaks. Place the steaks, mustard side up, in a baking pan large enough to hold them in one layer.
3. Sprinkle the salmon with 3 tablespoons of the tarragon. Top each steak with a slice of tomato, and sprinkle the tomato with the remaining tarragon. Scatter 1 teaspoon of the capers over each steak.
4. In a small bowl or measuring cup combine the wine and water, and pour it into the pan around the fish (but not over the fish).
5. Place the baking pan in the hot oven, and bake the fish for about 15 minutes or until it is just cooked through. Using a wide spatula, remove the steaks from the pan to individual plates. ■

BAKED SALMON WITH SCALLION-POTATO TOPPING

■

4 SERVINGS

One of the trendiest dishes appearing in the high-toned restaurants of New York during the early 1990s was fish wrapped in thin slices of potato that had been arranged to resemble scales. This recipe, inspired by that idea, is humbler and far less fussy to prepare, but it still has a wonderful look and flavor to it. It does require fish with a distinctive character, like salmon, tuna, or swordfish, since a less flavorful, less meaty fish would get lost in the potatoes.

TOPPING

- ¾ **pound all-purpose potatoes, peeled and quartered**
- 2 **teaspoons butter** *or* **margarine, divided**
- ½ **cup chopped scallions**
- 1 **teaspoon minced garlic**
- ¼ **cup skim or low-fat milk**

Salt to taste
Freshly ground black pepper to taste

FISH

Vegetable-oil spray
1¼ **pounds** SALMON FILLET
Salt to taste
Freshly ground black pepper to taste
- 1 **tablespoon grated Parmesan**

1. To prepare the topping, in a medium-sized saucepan, boil the potatoes in water to cover for 20 to 25 minutes or until the potatoes are soft.
2. While the potatoes cook, melt 1 teaspoon of the butter or margarine in a small nonstick skillet, and add the scallions and garlic. Briefly cook the vegetables until the scallions have just begun to soften.
3. Heat the oven to 425°F.
4. In a bowl, mash the potatoes with a potato masher or fork, adding the remaining 1 teaspoon of butter or margarine and the milk. Blend in the warm scallion mixture, and add the salt and pepper. Set the potatoes aside.
5. To prepare the fish, spray a baking dish with the vegetable oil, and place the salmon fillet in it. Sprinkle the fish with the salt and pepper. Evenly coat the salmon with the reserved potato mixture, and sprinkle the Parmesan over the potatoes. Spray the potatoes lightly with the vegetable oil to help the top brown.
6. Place the baking dish in the hot oven, and bake the fish for 15 to 17 minutes, depending on its thickness. Then switch the oven to broil, and place the fish under the broiler. Cook the fish for another 2 or 3 minutes or until the potatoes are lightly browned.
7. To serve the fish, use a sharp knife to cut the salmon into 4 portions. ■

STUFFED FLOUNDER WRAPPED IN CHARD

■

4 SERVINGS

When my husband sees me putting in an herb and vegetable garden each spring in soil that barely covers a hillside of slate, he cannot resist remarking, "Hope springs eternal in my baby's breast!" I persist against all odds because every year the garden yields a new surprise. One of the happiest was the crop produced by seeds of Italian chard from Shepherd's Garden Seeds of Torrington, Connecticut. What a fabulous vegetable! Bright-green fungus- and frost-resistant leaves with a slight peppery bite and the tenderness of spinach. The windfall inspired a number of experiments with this tasty, nutritious vegetable, including this winner. I use it here to produce fish rolls that are elegant enough for a dinner party.

Preparation tips: Any thin, mild fillet can be used—SOLE or CATFISH, for example. Or, if you prefer a more flavorful fish, try small fillets of BLUEFISH or MACKEREL. The fish rolls can be made in advance through step 4, then baked 20 minutes before serving time.

³⁄₄ **pound Italian chard** *or* **Swiss chard, divided**
2 **teaspoons olive oil**
¹⁄₃ **cup chopped scallions**
2 **teaspoons minced garlic**
¹⁄₂ **teaspoon salt**
¹⁄₈ **teaspoon red pepper flakes**
Freshly ground black pepper to taste
4 **FLOUNDER FILLETS (about 4 ounces each)**
Vegetable-oil spray

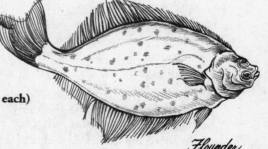

Flounder

1. Heat the oven to 375°F.
2. Select 4 large, whole leaves of chard. Cut off the stems, and, with a sharp knife, shave off any thick part of the center ribs. Set these leaves aside. Chop the remaining chard, and set it aside.
3. In a large nonstick skillet, briefly heat the olive oil, add the scallions, and sauté them for 1 minute. Add the garlic, and sauté the vegetables for 30 seconds. Then add the reserved chopped chard, salt, red pepper flakes, and ground pepper, and sauté the vegetables for about 5 minutes or until the chard is just cooked and reduced in volume.
4. Place the fillets on a work surface. Spread each fillet with one-quarter of the cooked vegetable mixture. Roll up the fillets, starting with the narrowest end. Then wrap one reserved chard leaf around each roll.

5. Spray a baking dish with the vegetable oil. Place the fish rolls in the dish, and spray the rolls with the vegetable oil.

6. Place the baking dish in the hot oven, and bake the fish rolls for 15 minutes (about 5 minutes longer if the fillets are thicker than small flounder). ∎

WRAPPED TILAPIA
∎

4 SERVINGS

While I was developing the recipes for this book, I fell in love with fish farming, which is bringing to cooks everywhere species that were once exotic or restricted to certain regions. Tilapia, an African fish, is one of those. The fillets are thin and boneless, perfect for eat-it-all en papillote preparation.

4 **12 × 15-inch pieces aluminum foil**
4 **skinless TILAPIA FILLETS (about 1¼ pounds total)**
Salt to taste
Freshly ground black pepper to taste
1½ **teaspoons finely minced garlic**
⅓ **cup finely chopped onion**
⅔ **cup chopped tomato**
4 **teaspoons chopped fresh basil**
2 **tablespoons dry white wine**
2 **teaspoons fresh lemon juice**

Tilapia

1. Heat the oven to 425°F.

2. Lay the pieces of foil on a work surface, and place one fillet crosswise in the center of each piece (if space is limited, work with one piece of foil and one fillet at a time). Sprinkle the fillets on both sides with the salt and pepper, placing the side of the fillets that had the skin (the flesh will be slightly darker and probably smoother on the skin side) against the foil.

3. In a medium-sized bowl, combine all the remaining ingredients. Spoon this vegetable mixture over the fillets, dividing it evenly among them. Seal the packets (be sure to leave some space inside them) by folding the long ends together first, then by folding the sides together, and by turning the side folds upward to reduce the risk of leakage (see page 293).

4. Put the packets on a baking tray, place the tray in the hot oven, and bake the fish for 15 minutes. Remove the tray from the oven, and *let the packets sit 5 minutes longer.*

5. To serve the fish, carefully open each packet, and, with a long spatula, lift the fillets with their topping off the foil, and place them on individual plates. ∎

POLLOCK EN PAPILLOTE

■

4 SERVINGS

This is pedestrian pollock dressed for a ball. It's hard to imagine that a dish so straightforward to prepare can look so elegant when served. Pollock, a mild-flavored fish with a pleasing texture, comes to us mainly from the clean waters off Alaska. It is relatively inexpensive and widely available, often sold frozen in supermarkets. I have used chard in other recipes to wrap fish (see page 290, for example), but here the chard is slivered as a colorful, nutritious bedding.

Preparation tips: There are a number of alternatives to the chard, according to taste and availability: bok choy (the green leafy part), mustard greens, collards, Chinese cabbage, or very thinly slivered green cabbage. Other fish possibilities include FILLETS OF COD ("SCROD"), though it is milder in flavor and flakier in texture than pollock. SMALL FISH STEAKS also work well, although they are harder to eat than fillets since the bones and skin would have to be removed by the diner. The fish packets can be set up hours in advance and kept refrigerated until you turn on the oven. The foil cools quickly after the fish is baked, allowing you to open the packets with bare hands.

> 4 12 × 18-inch pieces aluminum foil
> 4 cups finely shredded chard leaves (about ¾ pound) (see "Preparation tips")
> 2 cups thinly slivered sweet onion (such as Vidalia *or* Texas)
> 2 ounces finely chopped Canadian bacon (about ⅓ cup)
> Salt to taste, divided
> Freshly ground black pepper to taste, divided
> 1½ cups seeded, chopped tomatoes
> 2 tablespoons chopped fresh parsley
> 2 teaspoons minced garlic
> 4 thick pieces POLLOCK FILLETS (about 5 ounces each)
> 2 teaspoons fresh lemon juice

1. Place the pieces of foil, shiny side down, on a work surface with the 12-inch side facing you (you may have to do this one piece at a time unless you have a large work area).
2. In a medium-sized bowl, combine the chard, onion, Canadian bacon, salt, and pepper. In a small bowl, combine the tomatoes, parsley, and garlic.
3. Heat the oven to 425°F.
4. Using one-fourth of the chard mixture, create an oblong pile in the center of each piece of foil.

5. Sprinkle both sides of the fish with the salt and pepper, and place *one* fillet on top of each pile of the chard mixture. Sprinkle ½ teaspoon of the lemon juice over each fillet. Arrange a heaping ¼ cup of the tomato mixture on top of each fillet. Working with one packet at a time, bring the shorter ends of the foil together over the fish, and crimp the edges together at the top and sides of the fish, turning the sealed edges several times to eliminate some—but not all—of the unused space inside the packet and to prevent the juices from leaking out. As they are sealed, place the packets on a baking tray large enough to hold all 4 of them.

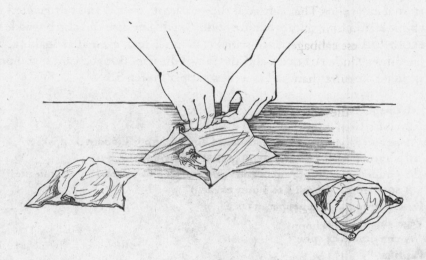

6. Place the baking tray in the hot oven, and bake the fish for 20 minutes. Remove the tray from the oven, and *let the fish rest for 5 minutes.* Then open one packet at a time, taking care to avoid steam burns. With a large slotted spatula, transfer the contents of the packets onto individual plates, leaving behind the juices. ■

ROLLS OF SOLE

■

Sole, a flounder, is an elegant, mild-mannered fish that does well with pungent accoutrements. With a still-ample supply of chard in my garden and a sale on shrimp at my local market, I decided to try a more upscale variant of the Stuffed Flounder Wrapped in Chard (see page 290). The result delighted diners aged 6 to 76.

Preparation tips: The stuffing can be prepared a day ahead. The fillets can be stuffed and rolled hours ahead if they are kept covered and refrigerated until about 20 minutes before they are to be baked. The dish can also be made with FLOUNDER or slender fillets of SNAPPER. Since feta, even after soaking, has a fair amount of salt, I don't add any salt to the fish. But you can, if you prefer, sprinkle the fillets with salt as well as pepper in step 5.

> **1 teaspoon olive oil**
> **2 tablespoons minced shallots**
> **½ pound Swiss chard *or* Italian chard, finely chopped (about 3 cups)**
> **10 ounces peeled, COOKED MEDIUM SHRIMP, divided**
> **½ pound feta, cut into cubes and soaked in cold water for 15 to 30 minutes**
> **8 SOLE FILLETS (about 4 to 5 ounces each)**

Freshly ground black pepper to taste
Vegetable-oil spray

> **⅓ cup dry white wine**

Paprika

> **8 slices large ripe tomato for garnish**
> **8 small basil leaves for garnish**

1. Briefly heat the olive oil in a nonstick skillet, add the shallots, and sauté them for 1 minute. Add the chard, and sauté the vegetables for about 2 minutes or until the chard has wilted. Remove the skillet from the heat, and set the vegetables aside to cool slightly.
2. Heat the oven to 375°F.
3. Slice 4 of the shrimp in half lengthwise, and set them aside. Coarsely chop the remaining shrimp, and place them in a large bowl.
4. Drain the feta, and finely crumble it into the bowl. Add the sautéed chard and shallots, and stir the ingredients to combine them well.
5. Place the fillets on a work surface, and sprinkle them with the pepper. Divide the mixture in the bowl among the fillets, spreading it over the fillets and patting it down. Starting from the narrow end, roll up each fillet, and secure the roll with toothpicks. Repeat the procedure with the

remaining fillets. Place the fish rolls in a shallow baking dish that has been sprayed with the vegetable oil. Pour the wine into the dish. Sprinkle the fish lightly with the paprika.

6. Cover the baking dish with aluminum foil, sealing the foil around the edges. Place the dish in the hot oven, and bake the fish for about 15 minutes.

7. While the fish bakes, arrange the tomato slices on a serving platter or on individual plates, and place a basil leaf on each slice. When the fish is done, remove each roll with a slotted spatula and place one roll at the edge of each tomato slice. Top each roll with a shrimp half before serving it. ▪

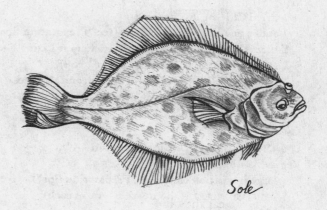

Sole

BAG O' BLUEFISH
■

Bluefish, a popular northeastern sport fish, is often discarded by fishermen who simply enjoy a good fight. But what a wonderful fish it is. Bluefish is now at a premium in the market. Like mackerel, it is a full-flavored fish that is good source of health-promoting omega-3 fatty acids. This experiment with bluefish resulted in a meal, completed with rice, that was colorful and so tasty that everyone ate the tender skin on the fish without even realizing it.

Preparation tips: If bok choy is unavailable, you can substitute Chinese cabbage (4 leaves for wrapping and several more for slivering), Swiss chard, or lettuce. The vegetables in the stuffing can be varied according to taste and availability. Be sure to seal the foil packets tightly, leaving some space inside the packets so that the fish and vegetables steam properly.

STUFFING
   6 **dried Chinese mushrooms**
   4 **stalks bok choy from 4 leaves (see "Preparation tips"), slivered**
   1 **carrot, cut into matchstick slivers (about 1 cup)**
   1 **medium zucchini, slivered (about 1 cup)**
   ½ **large red bell pepper, cored, seeded, and slivered**
   2 **scallions, including green tops, slivered**

FISH
   4 **12 × 15-inch pieces aluminum foil**
Vegetable-oil spray
   4 **large leaves bok choy (see "Preparation tips")**
   4 **BLUEFISH FILLETS (about 4 to 5 ounces each)**
Freshly ground white pepper to taste
   2 **tablespoons peeled, slivered gingerroot**
   1 **tablespoon slivered garlic**

SAUCE
   2 **tablespoons soy sauce**
   1 **tablespoon sherry**
   2 **teaspoons Asian sesame oil**

1. Place the dried mushrooms in a small saucepan with water to cover by 1 inch. Bring the water to a boil, remove the pan from the heat, and let the mushrooms soak for 15 minutes. When the mushrooms are soft and cool enough to handle, cut the caps into slivers, discarding the tough stems.

2. Heat the oven to 400°F.

3. Spray the dull side of the foil with the vegetable oil. Place one of the leaves of bok choy in the center of each piece of foil. Sprinkle the fillets with the ground pepper, and place one fillet in the middle of each leaf of bok choy. Divide the gingerroot and garlic among the fillets.

4. Align the mushrooms and all the remaining stuffing ingredients lengthwise on top of the fillets, distributing the vegetables evenly among the pieces of fish.

5. Combine all the sauce ingredients in a small bowl, and sprinkle one scant tablespoon of the sauce over each piece of fish with its vegetables. Seal the packets (be sure to leave some space inside them) by folding the long ends together over the fish, then crimping the side edges together and turning them upward to reduce the risk of leakage (see page 293).

6. Put the packets in a shallow baking dish, place the dish in the hot oven, and bake the fish for 15 minutes. Remove the baking dish from the oven, and *let the packets sit 5 minutes longer.*

7. To serve the fish, carefully open each packet, and slide the contents onto individual plates. The bok choy leaf should be served with the fish. ∎

HERB-INFUSED RED SNAPPER

■
4 TO 6 SERVINGS

Whole red snapper is such a beautiful fish that it is best prepared in a way that shows it off—as baking does. Snapper, a mild-flavored fish, takes well to herbs.

Preparation tips: These fish will look their best if the heads remain on, but they can be removed if they will not fit in your baking pan. Note that the fish should marinate for 1 hour.

Serving suggestion: Baked potatoes are a satisfying accompaniment. The potatoes can be put in the hot oven about 30 to 40 minutes (depending on size and type) before you plan to bake the fish, which should take about 25 minutes.

MARINADE
- ½ cup dry white wine
- 3 tablespoons fresh lemon juice
- 2 tablespoon dry sherry
- 1 tablespoon olive oil
- ¼ cup finely chopped shallots
- ¼ cup finely chopped fresh parsley
- 2 tablespoons snipped dill
- 1 tablespoon minced garlic
- 2 teaspoons white-wine Worcestershire sauce
- ½ teaspoon salt, or to taste
- ⅛ teaspoon freshly ground black pepper

Red snapper

FISH
- 2 small WHOLE RED SNAPPERS (about 1⅓ pounds each), cleaned
- ½ cup mixed fresh herbs (for example, sprigs of parsley, dill, tarragon, and thyme)

Vegetable-oil spray

1. In a small bowl or measuring cup, combine all the ingredients for the marinade. Set the marinade aside.
2. Cut three ½-inch-deep diagonal slices on each side of each fish. Stuff ¼ cup of the mixed herbs into the cavity of each fish. Place the fish in a large nonreactive pan. Pour the marinade over the fish, gently lifting the fish to be sure that some of the marinade gets underneath. Cover the pan with plastic wrap, and chill the fish for about 1 hour.

3. Heat the oven to 425°F.

4. With the vegetable-oil spray, grease a baking dish large enough to hold both fish. Remove the fish from the marinade (reserve the marinade, if you wish), and place them in the baking dish, if possible with both heads at the same end. Take care to keep the herb stuffing inside the fish, and spoon some of the chopped herbs from the marinade over the top of the fish. Place the pan in the middle of the hot oven with the heads of the fish facing the back of the oven, and bake the fish for about 25 minutes.

5. To serve the fish, remove the fillets carefully from the bones using a metal spatula (see page 74 for instructions). If desired, simmer the marinade for several minutes, and offer it on the side. ∎

BAKED WHOLE FISH WITH CLAMS
■

The presentation of this dish elicited "Oh, that's beautiful" from my guests. With or without heads and tails, whole fish can look sensational. The flavorings, inspired by a recipe distributed by Grand Union supermarkets, helped a lowly, inexpensive fish like mackerel (the fish I used) rise to new heights. Incidentally, when mackerel is fresh, it has none of the fishiness commonly associated with an oily fish. And keep in mind that the oil consists of the healthful omega-3 fatty acids.

Preparation tips: Although I originally prepared this dish with 2 large MACK-EREL, there are any number of choices: BLUEFISH, RED SNAPPER, STRIPED BASS, SEA BASS, SEA TROUT, CROAKER, or MULLET, among others. The dish can be made with 2 small fish weighing about 1¼ pounds each before cleaning, or with 1 fish weighing 2½ pounds before cleaning, or with 1 fish weighing 2 pounds after cleaning and dressing (that is, with head and tail removed). The dish can be prepared several hours before baking, covered, and refrigerated. Remove the baking dish from the refrigerator about 20 minutes before you plan to bake it.

Serving suggestions: The juices in the baking dish are lovely spooned over wide egg noodles or rice or a baked potato. A green or red vegetable would make a colorful addition to the plate, and a crusty bread would complete the meal.

    2 small WHOLE FISH (about 1¼ pounds each), cleaned, *or* 1 whole fish (about 2½ pounds), cleaned, *or* 1 2-pound cleaned, dressed fish (see "Preparation tips")
    1 dozen LITTLENECK CLAMS
    1 teaspoon dried rosemary
    1 teaspoon dried oregano leaves
Salt to taste
Freshly ground black pepper to taste
Vegetable-oil spray
    ¼ cup fresh lemon juice
    ¼ cup fish broth *or* chicken broth *or* clam juice
    2 teaspoons minced garlic
    2 tablespoons chopped fresh parsley

1. Heat the oven to 450°F.

2. Rinse the fish under cold running water, and dry it thoroughly inside and out. With a sharp knife, make three or four deep diagonal slashes on each side of each fish.

3. Thoroughly scrub the clams under cold running water, and set them aside.

4. Crush the rosemary into a coarse powder in a mortar with a pestle, then combine it with the oregano. Rub some of the herb mixture into the slashes in the fish, and place the rest in the fish cavities. Lightly sprinkle the fish inside and out with the salt and pepper.

5. With vegetable-oil spray, lightly grease a baking dish large enough to hold the fish and clams. Place the fish in the dish, and surround it with the reserved clams, placing the hinged end of the clams toward the bottom of the dish so that the clams will open facing upward.

6. In a small bowl or measuring cup, combine the lemon juice and broth or clam juice, and pour the mixture over the fish and clams. Sprinkle the fish and clams with the garlic, and spray the whole dish lightly with the vegetable oil.

7. Place the baking dish in the hot oven, and bake the fish for 20 to 25 minutes or until the fish is cooked and the clams have opened.

8. Sprinkle the dish with the parsley. Serve the fish either by cutting through the bone or by filleting it off the bone with a metal spatula (see page 74). Divide the clams among the plates, and spoon the pan juices over each serving; or serve the juices on the side in a gravy dish (see "Serving suggestions"). ▪

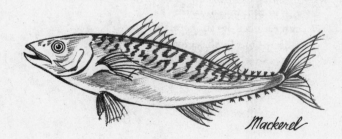

Mackerel

ROASTED WHOLE BLUEFISH WITH CAPER DRESSING

■

"Roasted" fish has been showing up recently on restaurant menus around the country. Although it sounds esoteric, it's just fish that has been baked with its skin on at a high temperature. Since this method is suitable for most whole fish that have at least a moderate oil content, you may wonder why you have never done this before. Bluefish, a relatively inexpensive fish that looks impressive when roasted, is used here because its oil helps to keep it moist.

Serving suggestions: You may serve this roasted fish with its skin on or off. The crisp, chewy skin from the upper side of the fish is flavorful and attractive. That same crisp skin, however, makes it a bit more difficult to slide the fish neatly off the bone for serving. An alternative serving method is to slice the fish through the bone into thick steaks.

FISH
- ½ **cup sliced carrots**
- ½ **cup sliced scallions, white and green parts**
- 1 WHOLE BLUEFISH (2½ **to 3 pounds), cleaned, head and tail intact, and gills removed**

Salt to taste
Freshly ground black pepper to taste
- ½ **cup chopped fresh basil**

Vegetable-oil spray
- 2 **tablespoons chopped chives for garnish (if serving the fish without its skin)**

DRESSING
- ¼ **cup nonfat mayonnaise**
- ¼ **cup reduced-fat mayonnaise**
- 2 **tablespoons fresh lemon juice**
- 1 **tablespoon chopped fresh parsley**
- 1 **tablespoon small capers, drained**

1. Heat the oven to 425°F.
2. Spread the carrots and scallions on the bottom of a baking dish in an elongated fashion, about the shape of the fish. Sprinkle the fish inside and out with the salt and pepper, stuff the cavity with the basil, and spray the fish with the vegetable oil. Loosely wrap the head and tail of the fish with aluminum foil, set the fish in the baking dish on top of the vegetables, and place the dish in the hot oven. Bake the fish for 30 minutes or until it is cooked through.
3. While the fish is baking, to a small bowl, add all the dressing ingredients, blending them well.
4. Remove the fish from the oven. Leaving behind the carrots and scallions, carefully lift off the skin with a paring knife. Sprinkle the fish with the chives. (Or, if you prefer, leave the skin on, and omit the chives.)
5. Use a metal spatula to remove serving portions of the fish from the bones (in effect, filleting it). When all the fish has been removed from the top side, grasp the skeleton at the tail, and remove and discard it. Cut the remaining fish into portions. Serve the dressing on the side. ∎

OVEN-FRIED SCALLOPS WITH TARTAR SAUCE

■

4 SERVINGS

This method of oven frying—heating the baking tray first and then cooking the breaded scallops under the broiler—has important advantages. The scallops don't have to be turned because the breading on the bottom as well as the top will brown, and the crisp scallops require little oil to cook. The tried-and-true marriage of scallops and tartar sauce is ideal especially since in this recipe the tartar sauce is low in fat, too.

SAUCE
- 2 tablespoons minced gherkins
- 1 tablespoon minced shallots
- 1 teaspoon minced garlic
- 1 tablespoon minced capers
- 1 teaspoon minced fresh parsley
- 1 teaspoon Dijon-style mustard
- ¼ cup nonfat or reduced-fat mayonnaise
- ¼ cup nonfat plain yogurt

SCALLOPS
- ½ cup dried bread crumbs
- 2 tablespoons grated Parmesan
- 1 teaspoon salt
- Freshly ground black pepper to taste
- 1 egg white
- 1 pound BAY SCALLOPS
- Vegetable-oil spray

1. Combine all the ingredients for the sauce in a small bowl, cover the bowl with plastic wrap, and set the sauce aside.
2. Line a baking tray with aluminum foil, shiny side down, and heat the tray under the broiler, about 6 inches from the heat source, for 4 to 5 minutes.
3. Meanwhile, on a platter, blend the bread crumbs, Parmesan, salt, and pepper. Set the platter aside.
4. Lightly beat the egg white in a bowl large enough to hold all the scallops. Place the scallops in the bowl, and toss them until they are evenly coated with the egg white. Then roll the scallops in the bread-crumb mixture, shaking off any excess breading.
5. Remove the hot baking tray from the broiler, and spray it with the vegetable oil. Place the scallops on the tray, spray them with the vegetable oil, and return the tray to the broiler. Broil the scallops for 4 to 5 minutes or until they are browned and cooked through.
6. Serve the scallops with the tartar sauce on the side. ■

OVEN-FRIED ORANGE ROUGHY

■

4 SERVINGS

Those of us with fond memories of freshly caught fish breaded and pan-fried have a real treat in store with this recipe for the health-conscious 1990s: all the joys of breaded and fried with almost none of the fat. I thank my friend Margaret Shryer, a gourmet cook who watches the fat, for this one. As both Margaret and I have discovered, this dish is as suitable for company as it is for a quick family supper.

Preparation tips: The fillets can be soaked in the salted milk for 1 hour or longer, but be sure to keep them chilled. The fillets can also be breaded in advance of baking, again kept chilled until shortly before they are to be cooked. Suitable alternatives to orange roughy include any mild-flavored skinless fillets such as HADDOCK or COD ("SCROD"), but be sure to adjust the baking time according to the thickness of the fillets.

1 **cup skim or low-fat milk**
1 **teaspoon salt**
1¼ **pounds ORANGE ROUGHY FILLETS in 4 pieces**
⅔ **cup dried bread crumbs**
¼ **cup grated Parmesan**
¼ **teaspoon ground thyme** *or* **crumbled dried thyme leaves**
Vegetable-oil spray

1. Heat the oven to 450°F.
2. Combine the milk and salt in a shallow bowl or pan. Add the fillets, and coat them well with the milk.
3. In a second shallow bowl or pan, combine the bread crumbs, Parmesan, and thyme. Remove the fillets one at a time from the milk, and dip them into the crumb mixture, coating them thoroughly. Place the breaded fillets in a baking pan that has been sprayed with the vegetable oil. Spray the fillets with the vegetable oil.
4. Place the pan in the middle of the hot oven, and bake the fillets for 12 minutes or until they are just baked through. ■

Orange roughy

CATFISH STICKS

■

If you, like me, are of a certain age, chances are your childhood meals often consisted of fish sticks—a handy-to-store, easy-to-prepare child pleaser (especially since the fish was mild and tender and the breading did much to disguise its presence). Well, far be it for me to argue with a successful and potentially nutritious product. But when I make my own fish sticks, I use whole pieces of a recognizable fish, and I bake them instead of frying them in oil.

Preparation tips: I've also tried these with COD ("SCROD") with equal success, and I suspect that any reasonably thick white fish fillet, such as ORANGE ROUGHY, would work as well. If you're concerned about getting food on the table fast, you can set up the breaded fish for baking well in advance, cover it lightly with plastic wrap, and chill it until shortly before baking time. But keep in mind that it will take a while to get the oven heated to 450°F—longer than it takes to set up the fish.

FISH
Vegetable-oil spray
1 pound thick CATFISH FILLET
½ cup nonfat or low-fat milk
¼ teaspoon salt, or to taste

BREADING
½ cup dried bread crumbs
¼ cup grated Parmesan
½ teaspoon dried oregano leaves
½ teaspoon dried basil
½ teaspoon paprika
¼ teaspoon freshly ground pepper

1. Heat the oven to 450°F.
2. Spray a baking tray with the vegetable oil.
3. Cut the fillets down their length into 1-inch-wide strips, then cut the strips into sections about 3 inches long.
4. Combine the milk and salt in a shallow bowl large enough to hold all the fish. Add the fish, turning the strips in the milk to coat them on all sides.
5. In a second shallow bowl, place all the breading ingredients, combining them well. Remove one piece of fish at a time from the milk, and roll it in the breading mixture. Place the fish on the greased baking tray. Repeat this process with the remaining pieces of fish, aligning them on the tray so that there is some space between each piece. Spray the breaded fish lightly with the vegetable oil.

6. Place the tray in the middle of the hot oven, and bake the fish sticks for 5 minutes or until they have turned golden brown on the bottom. Remove the tray from the oven, and, with a spatula, carefully turn the fish sticks over. Return the tray to the oven for another 3 minutes or until the fish sticks are brown on the other side. *Note:* If your oven heats from the top and bottom, it may not be necessary to turn the fish sticks to brown them on both sides. ∎

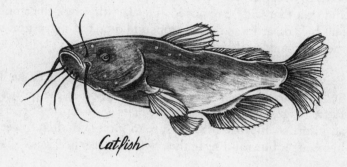

Catfish

SWEET PEPPER FISH CAKES

■   8 FIRST-COURSE SERVINGS OR 4 MAIN-DISH SERVINGS

Fish cakes as a main dish or an appetizer can be dressed up with sauces or served as is—even to children who may otherwise resist fish. The ingredients used to make these fish cakes amount to a well-balanced mini-meal in a single patty: a combination of fish, several garden vegetables and herbs, and potato and bread crumbs to give the cakes body.

Preparation tips: The recipe calls for ¾ pound of boneless fish. If you are starting with fish steaks, however, purchase 1 pound to make up for the bones and skin that will be removed. To spare the cook the trouble of flipping the half-baked patties so that the tops will brown, I suggest serving the cakes with their browned undersides facing up.

Serving suggestions: Try these fish cakes with reduced-fat Tartar Sauce (page 304); or, to achieve a more elegant look, place the patties over Red Pepper Puree (page 168), and garnish the plate with a sprig or two of fresh herbs. For an informal approach that is sure to please children, place the fish cakes on hamburger buns and serve them with tartar sauce, salsa, or ketchup.

1 **large baking potato (about ½ pound), peeled and quartered**
1 **teaspoon olive oil**
1 **cup minced onion**
½ **cup minced celery**
½ **cup minced red bell pepper**
1 **teaspoon minced garlic**
¾ **pound skinless, boneless WHITE FISH (for example, POLLOCK, COD ["SCROD"], or HADDOCK)**
½ **cup finely ground fresh bread crumbs**
2 **tablespoons Dijon-style mustard**
2 **tablespoons chopped fresh basil *or* 2 teaspoons dried basil**
1 **tablespoon white-wine Worcestershire sauce**
¼ **teaspoon Tabasco sauce**
1 **whole egg *or* 2 egg whites, lightly beaten**
Salt to taste
Freshly ground black pepper to taste
Vegetable-oil spray

1. Place the potato in a medium-sized saucepan with salted water to cover, bring the water to a simmer, and cook the potato for 15 minutes or until it is tender. Drain the potato, transfer it to a large bowl, and mash it.

2. Heat the olive oil in a medium-sized nonstick skillet, and add the onion, celery, red bell pepper, and garlic. Cook the vegetables over medium heat, stirring them, for about 3 minutes, taking care not to burn the garlic. Add the vegetables to the bowl, and let them cool.

3. Finely chop the fish in a food processor or by hand, and add the fish to the bowl along with all the remaining ingredients *except the vegetable-oil spray.* Cover the bowl, and refrigerate it for 30 minutes.

4. Heat oven to 400°F.

5. Spray a heavy, nonstick baking tray with the vegetable oil. With moistened hands, form the fish mixture into 8 patties, using about 1/3 cup of the mixture for each cake. Take care to make the patties smooth on top and bottom so that they will brown evenly. Place the patties on the baking tray.

6. Place the tray in the hot oven, and bake the patties for 20 minutes or until they are cooked through and are nicely browned on the bottom. Serve the patties bottom side up. ∎

Pollock

Haddock

SALMON CROQUETTES WITH DILL SAUCE

■

4 SERVINGS

Salmon croquettes were one of my mother's specialties and a childhood favorite of mine. Here, I've kept the flavor of my mother's version but eliminated the added fat by baking them in the oven instead of frying them. And I serve them with a nonfat-yogurt sauce.

Preparation tips: These patties can be prepared in advance, chilled, and then baked just before being served. Or the patties can be baked in advance and reheated in the oven or microwave oven. The sauce, too, can be prepared ahead and kept covered and chilled. But it should be brought to room temperature before it is served.

CROQUETTES

14^1/$_2$ **ounces** CANNED SALMON, **thoroughly drained**
  ^{1}/$_2$ **cup cooked mashed potatoes** *or* ^{3}/$_4$ **cup fresh bread crumbs**
  ^{1}/$_2$ **cup finely chopped celery**
  ^{1}/$_2$ **cup shredded carrots**
  ^{1}/$_3$ **cup finely chopped onion**
  ^{1}/$_4$ **cup finely chopped red bell pepper** *or* **green bell pepper**
  2 **egg whites, lightly beaten**
  2 **tablespoons finely chopped celery leaves (optional)**
  2 **teaspoons fresh lemon juice**
  1 **teaspoon white-wine Worcestershire sauce**
  ^{1}/$_4$ **teaspoon freshly ground black pepper, or to taste**
Vegetable-oil spray

SAUCE

  ^{1}/$_2$ **cup nonfat plain yogurt**
  1 **tablespoon snipped fresh dill** *or* 1 **teaspoon dried dill**
  ^{1}/$_2$ **teaspoon Dijon-style mustard**
  ^{1}/$_2$ **teaspoon sugar**
  ^{1}/$_4$ **teaspoon salt, or to taste**
  ^{1}/$_4$ **teaspoon freshly ground black pepper, or to taste**

1. To prepare the croquettes, place the salmon in a large bowl, and mash it well—skin, bones, and all. Add all the remaining ingredients for the croquettes *except the vegetable-oil spray,* and combine them thoroughly.
2. Heat the oven to 400°F.
3. Place a nonstick baking tray large enough to hold 8 croquettes in the oven.
4. Form the croquette mixture into 8 round or oval patties, using about 1/3 cup of the mixture for each cake.
5. When the baking tray is hot, remove it from the oven, and spray it with the vegetable oil. Place the patties on the hot tray, and place the tray in the hot oven. Bake the patties on one side for 10 minutes or until they have browned on the bottom. Then remove the tray from the oven. Using a wide spatula, carefully turn the patties over, and return the tray to the oven. Bake the patties on the other side 5 to 8 minutes longer or until the second side has browned lightly and the patties feel somewhat firm.
6. While the patties bake, add all the sauce ingredients to a small bowl, whisking or stirring the ingredients to blend them thoroughly. Serve the patties hot with the room-temperature sauce on the side. If desired, the sauce can be warmed in a microwave oven for about 15 seconds. ■

CLAM-STUFFED ACORN SQUASH

■

Come the first fall-like days and I begin to crave winter squash. Combined with a garden's windfall of tomatoes and basil, the arrival of acorn squash at the farmers' market called for a new invention. I first prepared this dish early one chilly September morning and, after one taste, could not resist having it for breakfast—and again later for lunch.

Preparation tips: The recipe can be prepared with either fresh steamed clams or minced canned clams (if you use the latter, try to get the Progresso brand or Gorton's, which to me are superior to all others I've tried). For efficiency's sake, the filling should be prepared while the squash bake (see step 3).

      2 **acorn squash (about 1 pound each)**
Vegetable-oil spray
      1 **teaspoon olive oil *or* canola oil**
    ⅓ **cup finely chopped onion**
      1 **teaspoon minced garlic**
      1 **cup (approximately) COOKED CHOPPED CLAMS (from 2 dozen fresh littlenecks)
          or 1 10½-ounce (or slightly larger) can minced clams, drained**
      1 **scant cup chopped fresh tomatoes**
      1 **scant cup fresh bread crumbs**
    ¼ **cup finely shredded Parmesan**
      2 **tablespoons chopped fresh basil *or* 2 teaspoons dried basil**
    ¼ **teaspoon freshly ground black pepper, or to taste**

1. Heat the oven to 350°F.
2. Cut each squash in half lengthwise, and scoop out and discard the seeded center (a grapefruit spoon is ideal for this task). Spray the cut sides of the squash lightly with the vegetable oil, and place the squash halves, cut side down, on a nonstick baking tray. Bake the squash in the hot oven for 30 minutes. Then remove the tray from the oven, but *do not turn the oven off.*
3. While the squash bake, prepare the filling. Briefly heat the olive oil or canola oil in a deep nonstick skillet, add the onion and garlic, and sauté the vegetables for 1 minute or until they just soften. Remove the pan from the heat, and stir in the clams, tomatoes, bread crumbs, Parmesan, basil, and pepper, mixing the ingredients to combine them well.
4. When the squash are done, remove them from the oven, and turn them cut side up. (If necessary, cut a very thin slice from the underside so that the squash sit straight on the tray.) Divide the stuffing mixture among the

four squash halves, mounding the stuffing into the center cavities. Return the squash to the hot oven, and bake them for 15 minutes or until the stuffing has browned lightly. ■

Clams

SEAFOOD CREPES

■

Filled pancakes, from blinis to tortillas, are popular in almost every culture. This recipe, combining the French crepe with a curry-flavored fish-and-vegetable filling, focuses more on taste and texture than on national boundaries.

Preparation tips: Almost ANY FIRM FISH STEAK will work in this recipe. If you use a nonstick crepe pan or slope-sided skillet, you will need very little butter or other fat. I prefer to unwrap one end of a cold or frozen stick of light butter and wipe the hot pan with it. Both the crepes and the filling can be prepared in advance and chilled separately until they are needed.

CREPES (8 PANCAKES)
1 large egg
Pinch salt
1/2 cup all-purpose flour
5 ounces (1/2 plus 1/8 cup) nonfat or low-fat milk
2 teaspoons (approximately) butter *or* margarine
10 8-inch squares of wax paper

Vegetable-oil spray

FILLING
1 teaspoon olive oil
1/4 cup finely chopped onion
1/4 cup finely chopped celery
1 teaspoon minced garlic
1 1/2 teaspoons curry powder (can include 1/2 teaspoon hot curry powder)
1 1/2 tablespoons all-purpose flour
1 1/4 cups nonfat or low-fat milk *or* evaporated skimmed milk
1 teaspoon fresh lemon juice
1/2 pound (trimmed weight) skinless MAKO SHARK *or* comparable firm fish steak, cut into 1/3-inch dice
1/2 cup corn kernels, cooked or raw
1/2 cup thawed frozen peas (preferably tiny peas)
1/4 teaspoon salt, or to taste
1/8 to 1/4 teaspoon freshly ground black pepper, to taste

TO PREPARE THE CREPES

1. In a mixing bowl, whisk together the egg and salt. Alternately whisk in some of the flour and some of the milk until all the flour and milk have been added to the bowl and the batter is smooth.
2. Heat a 7-inch or 8-inch crepe pan or slope-sided skillet (preferably one with a nonstick surface), and grease it lightly with the butter or margarine (see "Preparation tips"). Add 2 tablespoons of batter to the pan, immedi-

ately swirling the batter by tipping the pan gently so that the batter completely covers the bottom of the pan. Cook the crepe over moderately high heat for about 30 to 40 seconds, then flip it, and cook it for 15 seconds on the other side. Turn the crepe out onto one of the squares of wax paper. Repeat this process with the remaining batter, greasing the pan only as necessary (if at all). The cooled crepes can be stacked, separated by the squares of wax paper. The stack can be covered and chilled until you are ready to fill the crepes.

TO PREPARE THE FILLING

3. Briefly heat the olive oil in a medium-sized saucepan or deep skillet, add the onion and celery, and sauté the vegetables, stirring them often, for about 2 minutes or until they soften. Add the garlic, curry powder, and flour, and cook the ingredients over low heat, stirring them, for another minute.

4. Gradually stir in the milk, whisking the ingredients to prevent lumps. Cook the mixture over low heat, stirring it often, for 5 minutes or until it thickens to the consistency of heavy cream.

5. Add the lemon juice, fish, corn, peas, salt, and pepper, and cook the mixture, stirring it occasionally, for 3 minutes or until the fish is just cooked through. Remove the pan from the heat, and let the mixture cool to lukewarm. It can then be covered and chilled or used immediately.

TO ASSEMBLE THE CREPES

6. Heat the oven to 350°F.

7. Separate the crepes from the wax paper, and place them on a work surface with the side you cooked second facing upward. (If space is limited, you can work with one crepe at a time.)

8. Using approximately ⅓ cup of filling for each crepe, place the filling in an off-center strip that ends about ½ inch from each side of the crepe. Starting with the edge nearest you, fold the crepe over to form a roll, and place the roll seam side down in a shallow baking pan that has been sprayed with the vegetable oil. Repeat this step with the remaining crepes.

9. Bake the crepes for 10 minutes (15 minutes, if the filling was chilled). ∎

MAKO SHARK BURRITOS

■

4 TO 8 SERVINGS

Shark is ideal for these tortilla rolls because when shark is cooked, it has the consistency of meat and can easily be cut into a small dice. The result is a burrito with substance. And the leftovers are good even cold.

Preparation tips: Any firm fish steak such as SWORDFISH or TUNA could be used instead of shark, albeit at a higher price. The sauce can be made a day or so ahead, or even sooner if you wish to freeze it. The filling can be prepared and the burritos rolled hours ahead of baking and kept chilled. But bring them back to room temperature before adding the sauce and baking them.

SAUCE
- 1 28-ounce can whole tomatoes, drained
- ½ cup chopped onion
- 2 tablespoons seeded, minced jalapeños (about 2 peppers)

BURRITOS
- 1 pound MAKO SHARK STEAKS *or* other firm steaks
- Hot chili powder to taste
- Salt to taste
- ½ cup finely chopped red onion
- ⅔ to ¾ cup *cooked* black beans, drained and rinsed
- 1 cup finely shredded Monterey Jack, preferably jalapeño-flavored
- 2 to 4 tablespoons chopped cilantro, divided (optional)
- 8 10-inch flour tortillas

1. Heat the oven to 425°F.
2. To make the sauce, add all the sauce ingredients to the container of a blender or food processor, and process the ingredients until they reach the consistency of a smooth puree. Set the sauce aside.
3. To make the burritos, sprinkle the shark steaks liberally with the chili powder and salt. Put the fish in a shallow baking dish, place the dish in the hot oven, and bake the fish for 15 to 18 minutes or until it is just cooked through. Remove the fish from the pan to a cutting board, and, when it is cool enough to handle, cut the fish into ¼-inch cubes. Put the diced fish in a large bowl.
4. To the fish, add the onion, black beans, cheese, and 1 to 2 tablespoons of the cilantro (if desired). Toss the ingredients to combine them well.
5. Heat the oven to 350°F.

6. To soften the tortillas, heat a 10-inch or 12-inch skillet, and place 1 tortilla in it for about 5 seconds on each side. Place the softened tortilla on a flat work surface. Spread ½ cup of the fish mixture in a strip across the middle of the tortilla. Roll the tortilla over the filling, and place the burrito seam side down in a greased baking pan large enough to hold all 8 burritos. Repeat this step with the remaining tortillas.

7. Pour the reserved sauce over the burritos. Place the baking pan in the hot oven, and bake the burritos for 15 minutes or until they are heated through. If desired, sprinkle the remaining cilantro over the burritos before serving them. ∎

Mako shark

SEAFOOD "SHEPHERD'S" PIE

■

4 TO 6 SERVINGS

I fondly remember shepherd's pie from my heavier meat-eating days (it was one of my husband's favorites) and decided that the basic construction of the dish would stand up well to fish. I was very pleased with the outcome, which amounts to a one-dish meal, needing only a green salad to complete it.

Preparation tips: Note that you'll need 1 12-ounce can of evaporated skimmed milk for this recipe. The vegetables can be varied to taste, but try to stick with those that come in, or can be cut into, small pieces. I use the potato liquid to cook the fish because it adds flavor and saves work.

TOPPING
  1 pound baking potatoes *or* all-purpose potatoes, peeled and cut into chunks
  1 teaspoon butter *or* margarine
  1 teaspoon finely minced garlic
  1/4 teaspoon salt
  1/8 teaspoon freshly ground black pepper
  1/4 cup evaporated skimmed milk

MAIN INGREDIENTS
  1 pound boneless, skinless WHITE FISH (for example, HALIBUT, COD ["SCROD"], BLACKFISH, ORANGE ROUGHY)
  4 teaspoons cornstarch
  1 cup evaporated skimmed milk, divided
  1/2 cup fish broth *or* clam juice
  1 teaspoon mustard powder
  1/8 teaspoon cayenne, or to taste
  1/8 teaspoon freshly ground black pepper, or to taste
  2 teaspoons olive oil *or* canola oil
  3/4 cup finely chopped onion
  1/2 cup finely diced celery
  2 teaspoons minced garlic
  1 cup sliced mushrooms
  1 cup diced red bell pepper
  1 cup frozen peas, thawed (preferably tiny peas)
  1 cup cooked corn kernels
Paprika

1. To prepare the topping, in a medium-sized saucepan, cook the potatoes in salted water to cover for 12 minutes or until the potatoes are soft but not crumbly. With a slotted spoon, remove the potatoes to a bowl, but *reserve the potato cooking liquid.* Mash the potatoes, working in the butter or margarine, garlic, salt, and pepper. Then add 1/4 cup of the evaporated milk, combining the ingredients well. Set the potato mixture aside.

2. Heat the oven to 350°F.

3. To prepare the pie, cut the fish into 1 1/2-inch pieces, and place the pieces in the saucepan with the reserved potato liquid. Bring the liquid to a boil, reduce the heat, and simmer the fish for 5 minutes. Drain the fish, and set it aside to cool while you prepare the remaining ingredients.

4. Place the cornstarch in a medium-sized bowl, and add 2 tablespoons of the evaporated milk, stirring the mixture until the cornstarch is dissolved. Add the remaining evaporated milk, fish broth or clam juice, mustard powder, cayenne, and ground pepper, mixing the ingredients to combine them well. Set the milk mixture aside.

5. Briefly heat the olive oil or canola oil in a large nonstick skillet. Add the onion and celery, and sauté the vegetables, stirring them often, for 3 minutes. Add the garlic, mushrooms, and red bell pepper, and sauté the vegetables for another 3 minutes. Stir the milk mixture once again, and add it to the skillet. Cook the mixture over medium heat, stirring it occasionally, until it begins to thicken significantly.

6. Add the peas and corn to the skillet, and cook the mixture 1 minute longer. Remove the skillet from the heat.

7. Flake the reserved, cooled fish, and add it to the skillet, stirring the ingredients gently to combine them. Transfer the mixture to a 2-quart casserole. Distribute the reserved potato mixture over the fish filling (this is easiest to do if you make potato patties with your hands and arrange them so that they barely overlap). Sprinkle the potato topping generously with the paprika.

8. Place the casserole in the hot oven, and bake the pie for 20 minutes. If you wish, you may then place the casserole under the broiler for 2 minutes to brown the top. ∎

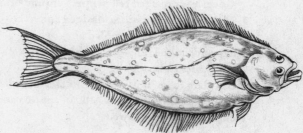

Halibut

PAELLA

■

Paella, a Spanish rice casserole, can be rendered heart- and figure-healthy with just slight alterations in traditional preparation techniques. In preparing it for a crowd, I double the recipe and bake it in a very large, heavy casserole (no lid is necessary).

Preparation tips: Note that there are three kinds of shellfish in this recipe: clams, mussels, and shrimp. You can, if you wish, use cut-up **LOBSTER** or **LOBSTER TAILS** in place of any of the other shellfish. See page 115 for sources of low-fat sausage. If you have a paella pan, by all means use it. However, the individual ingredients can be prepared in a nonstick skillet and the paella baked in the oven in a 4-quart casserole dish. If your baking dish is not designed for stovetop use, prepare the onion, garlic, and peppers (in step 6) in the skillet, and bring the broth, clam juice, and tomato liquid to a boil in a separate pot; then transfer all the ingredients to the casserole before adding the rice and remaining ingredients.

Serving suggestion: With a salad or a vegetable side dish, paella becomes a complete meal. Top it off with a colorful fruit dessert.

   1 **pound boneless chicken breasts**
Salt to taste
Freshly ground black pepper to taste
   4 **teaspoons olive oil** *or* **canola oil, divided**
  ½ **pound hot (spicy) sausage** *or* **garlic sausage**
1½ **dozen** LITTLENECK CLAMS, **divided**
   1 **dozen** MUSSELS, **divided**
1½ **cups chopped onion**
   1 **tablespoon minced garlic**
   1 **to 2 long, hot chili peppers, seeded and minced, to taste**
   2 **medium red bell peppers, cored, seeded, and cut into** ½**-inch pieces,** *or* **1**
      4-ounce jar roasted red peppers *or* **pimientos, drained and diced**
   1 **14-ounce can tomatoes, drained and** ½ **cup juice reserved, coarsely chopped**
  ½ **teaspoon saffron, crumbled**
   2 **cups uncooked long-grain white rice**
   2 **cups chicken broth**
   1 **cup clam juice (liquor from the steamed clams, above,** *or* **bottled juice)**
  ¾ **pound** MEDIUM OR LARGE SHRIMP, **peeled and deveined**
   1 **cup frozen peas, thawed**

1. Cut the chicken into bite-sized pieces, about ¾ inch, and sprinkle them with the salt and pepper. In a nonstick skillet large enough to hold the chicken in a single layer, heat 2 teaspoons of the olive oil or canola oil. Add the chicken, and cook it, turning it once or twice, for 3 to 5 minutes or just until it loses its pink color and begins to brown. Remove the chicken from the skillet, and set it aside.

2. Slice the sausage into ¼-inch pieces, and cook the pieces in the skillet or in the microwave oven on several sheets of paper toweling. Set the sausage aside.

3. Rinse the clams, and place all but 6 or 8 of them (depending upon how many people you are serving) in a kettle to which ½ inch of water has been added. Cover the kettle, and steam the clams just until they open. Remove the clams with a slotted spoon, reserving the liquid. Remove the meat from the clams, setting it aside, and discard the shells. Strain the liquid through several layers of cheesecloth or a fine sieve lined with paper toweling, and reserve it.

4. Thoroughly rinse and debeard the mussels. Place all but 6 or 8 of them (depending upon how many people you are serving) in a kettle to which ½ inch of water has been added. Cover the kettle, and steam the mussels just until they open. Remove the meat from the mussels, setting it aside, and discard the shells and cooking liquid.

5. Heat the oven to 375°F.

6. In a casserole or Dutch oven (see "Preparation tips"), heat the remaining 2 teaspoons of oil. Add the onion, garlic, and chili peppers, and sauté the vegetables for 2 minutes. Add the red bell peppers or roasted peppers or pimientos, and sauté the vegetables for another 3 minutes. Stir in the tomatoes and saffron. Then stir in the rice, chicken broth, clam juice, and the ½ cup of reserved tomato juice (if you do not have enough reserved liquid, make up the difference with water or additional broth to achieve a total of 2½ cups liquid). Bring the mixture to a boil.

7. Evenly distribute the reserved chicken and sausage pieces on top of the rice mixture. Add the clam meat and mussel meat. Arrange the shrimp over the other shellfish. Then place the uncooked clams and mussels on top.

8. Bake the casserole in the hot oven for 25 minutes. Remove the paella from the oven. Rinse the peas under hot water, and sprinkle them over the casserole. Before serving the paella, remove the clams and mussels in their shells, and set them to one side, then lightly toss the paella to distribute the ingredients. Top each serving with 1 clam and 1 mussel in the shell. ■

SEAFOOD LASAGNA

■

12 TO 16 SERVINGS

Lasagna has undergone a number of wonderful transformations in recent years, inspired by health-conscious cooks looking for alternatives to ground meat and sausage in the filling. Why not seafood? Unfortunately, when most restaurants prepare a seafood lasagna, the idea of a low-fat dish is lost in a gooey cheese sauce. Instead, I use part-skim ricotta mixed with feta, another relatively low-fat cheese, for added flavor and texture. And I add broccoli to make the dish a self-contained meal, needing only a salad to complete it. It is a wonderful make-ahead treat for company since, like other lasagnas, it can be prepared in advance for baking and then frozen.

Preparation tips: This recipe fills two lasagna pans; either or both lasagnas can be frozen for later baking. Since the sauce may be used as the base for many other dishes, you might double the recipe and freeze half. Before assembling the lasagna, to assure an equal distribution of ingredients, it helps to measure the sauce yield and divide that by 8; then measure the seafood-broccoli mixture and the cheese mixture and divide each of them by 4. The noodles are not precooked. They absorb the liquid from the other ingredients and will cook thoroughly in the covered pans.

SAUCE
- 1 tablespoon olive oil *or* canola oil
- 2½ cups chopped onion
- ¾ cup chopped green bell pepper (about 1 medium pepper)
- ¾ cup chopped red bell pepper (about 1 medium pepper)
- 1 to 2 tablespoons seeded, minced jalapeño *or* ¼ to ½ teaspoon red pepper flakes *or* both, to taste
- 1 tablespoon minced garlic
- 70 ounces canned tomatoes (2 35-ounce cans, or 2 28-ounce cans and 1 14-ounce can), juice reserved, coarsely chopped
- 12 ounces tomato paste
- ¾ teaspoon salt
- 1 teaspoon freshly ground black pepper, or to taste

MAIN INGREDIENTS
- 2 pounds cleaned SQUID
- 3 teaspoons olive oil, divided
- 2 pounds SEA SCALLOPS
- 1 pound MONKFISH
- 1 large head broccoli
- 32 ounces part-skim ricotta, *or* a combination of part-skim ricotta and fat-free ricotta
- ½ pound feta, crumbled
- Vegetable-oil spray
- 1 pound lasagna noodles
- ¼ cup grated Parmesan *or* Romano (optional)

TO PREPARE THE SAUCE

1. Briefly heat the olive oil or canola oil in a large nonstick saucepan (about 5 quarts). Add the onion, green bell pepper, red bell pepper, and jalapeño and/or pepper flakes, and sauté the vegetables over medium heat for 3 to 5 minutes or until the vegetables are just soft.

2. Add the garlic, and sauté the vegetables, stirring them, 1 minute longer.

3. Add the chopped tomatoes with their juice, tomato paste, salt, and ground pepper. Stir the ingredients to combine them well. Bring the mixture to a boil, reduce the heat, and simmer the sauce for 50 minutes, stirring it from time to time. You should have about 8 cups of thick sauce.

TO PREPARE THE MAIN INGREDIENTS

4. Cut the squid bodies into narrow rings (about ¼ inch), and cut the tentacles into bite-sized pieces. In a large nonstick skillet that has a lid, briefly heat 1 teaspoon of the olive oil. Add the squid, cover the skillet, and cook the squid for 2 minutes. Drain the squid in a colander, transfer the squid to a large bowl, and set the bowl aside. Wipe out the skillet.

5. Slice the scallops in half crosswise. Heat 1 teaspoon of the olive oil in the skillet. Add the scallops, and cook them, covered, for 3 minutes. Drain the scallops, and add them to the bowl with the squid. Wipe out the skillet.

6. Cut the monkfish into ½-inch cubes. Heat the remaining 1 teaspoon of the olive oil in the skillet. Add the monkfish, and cook it, covered, for 2 to 3 minutes. Drain the monkfish, and add it to the squid and scallops.

7. Cut the broccoli into small flowerets, and thinly slice the tender stems. Steam the broccoli for 3 minutes. Add it to the bowl with the seafood, tossing the ingredients to combine them well. Set the bowl aside.

8. In a medium-sized bowl, mix together the ricotta and feta.

TO ASSEMBLE THE LASAGNA

9. Heat the oven to 350°F.

10. With the vegetable-oil spray, lightly grease two lasagna pans (about 15 × 9 × 3½ inches). Prepare *each pan* as follows: Spread 1 cup of the sauce on the bottom, lay 3 noodles on top of the sauce, then distribute ¼ of the cheese mixture (about 1¼ cups) over the noodles. Spoon ¼ of the seafood-and-broccoli mixture (about 3 cups) over the cheese. Repeat the layering—sauce, noodles, cheese, seafood mixture—ending with a third layer of noodles topped with the remaining 1 cup of sauce. Sprinkle the dish with the Parmesan or Romano (if desired). Seal the pans tightly with aluminum foil.

11. Place the pans in the hot oven, and bake the lasagnas for 1 hour or until the noodles are just tender and most of the liquid has been absorbed. Let the lasagnas stand covered for about 15 or 20 minutes before removing the foil and cutting the lasagnas into serving pieces. ∎

CLAM AND MUSSEL PIZZA

■

8 SLICES, SERVING 4

Here is a delicious low-calorie pizza with a thin, crisp crust and no cheese. Once the crust is made, this is an especially easy pizza to prepare.

Preparation tips: Since the dough will take 2 hours to rise, remember to leave plenty of time for the pizza's preparation. The dough can also be made through step 3, wrapped in plastic, and refrigerated for up to 4 days; or it can be frozen for longer periods. If you freeze the dough, it will need at least 1 hour to thaw before it can be used. A simple alternative to steaming open the mussels is to place them, hinge side down, in a microwave-safe baking dish (with minced garlic and shallots, if desired), cover them with a microwave lid or vented plastic wrap, and microwave them for 5 minutes.

CRUST

- ½ cup warm water (105°F to 115°F)
- 1¼ teaspoons active dry yeast (½ envelope)
- Pinch sugar
- ½ cup whole-wheat flour
- 1 cup all-purpose flour, divided
- 1 teaspoon salt
- 2 teaspoons olive oil
- Vegetable-oil spray
- 1 tablespoon corn meal (optional)

TOPPING

- 2 pounds MUSSELS (small ones, if available), well rinsed and debearded (see "Preparation tips")
- ½ cup water
- 1 teaspoon chopped garlic
- 1 tablespoon minced shallots *or* onion
- 3 teaspoons olive oil, divided
- 2 tablespoons minced garlic
- ⅛ to ¼ teaspoon red pepper flakes, to taste
- 13 ounces (2 6½-ounce cans) CANNED MINCED CLAMS, well drained
- ⅓ cup finely chopped fresh parsley
- 2 tablespoons grated Parmesan

TO PREPARE THE CRUST

1. Place the warm water in a small bowl, and sprinkle the yeast and sugar into the bowl, stirring the ingredients to dissolve them. Let the mixture stand for about 5 minutes or until it begins to bubble.
2. Place the whole-wheat flour, ¾ cup of the all-purpose flour, and the salt in a medium-sized bowl. Stir in the yeast mixture and the olive oil. Form the dough into a ball. Sprinkle some of the remaining all-purpose flour on a sturdy work surface, and turn the dough out onto the floured sur-

face. Knead the dough for about 6 minutes or until it is smooth and satiny, adding as much flour as needed to keep the dough from sticking. The dough should be soft but not moist.

3. Place the dough in a bowl that has been lightly sprayed with the vegetable oil, cover the bowl with a damp dishtowel, and set it in a warm, draft-free place to rise for 2 hours or until the dough has doubled in bulk. Punch down the dough, and place it on a firm work surface.

4. Roll out the dough to form a 13- or 14-inch circle. (The dough will be springy, but it will eventually hold its width.) Transfer the dough to a pizza stone or pan that has been sprinkled with the corn meal (if desired) *or* sprayed with the vegetable oil.

TO PREPARE THE PIZZA

5. Place the mussels in a large pot that has a lid. Add the water, the 1 teaspoon of chopped garlic, and the shallots or onion. Bring the water to a boil, cover the pot, and steam the mussels over medium heat for 5 minutes or until they open. Remove the mussel meat from the shells, and discard the shells and any mussels that have not opened.

6. Heat the oven to 450°F.

7. Brush the dough with 1½ teaspoons of the olive oil. Scatter the 2 tablespoons of minced garlic and the red pepper flakes over the surface of the dough. Then distribute the drained clams and the mussels over the dough. Sprinkle the pizza with the parsley and Parmesan, and drizzle the remaining 1½ teaspoons of the olive oil over the top.

8. Place the pizza in the bottom third of the hot oven. Bake the pizza for 10 minutes. To serve, divide the pizza into 8 slices (a pizza wheel works best for cutting through the crisp crust). ∎

SHRIMP AND ONION PIZZA

■

8 SLICES, SERVING 4

When onions are cooked over low heat for a long time—a method called caramelizing—they become soft, sweet, and delicious, even appealing to those who think they don't like onions. Here, I use caramelized onions as the moist bedding for a low-calorie shrimp pizza that gets added zip from a garnish of anchovies, which provide a nice contrast to the sweet onions. I also used a thin, crisp crust, which better suits both the vegetable and a pizza made without cheese.

Preparation tips: Since the dough will take 2 hours to rise, remember to leave plenty of time for the pizza's preparation. The dough can also be made through step 3, wrapped in plastic, and refrigerated for up to 4 days; or it can be frozen for longer periods. If you freeze the dough, it will need at least 1 hour to thaw before it can be used. Note, too, that the onions must cook for about 1 hour. They can cook and the other ingredients can be prepared while the dough is rising.

CRUST
- ½ **cup warm water (105°F to 115°F)**
- 1¼ **teaspoons active dry yeast (½ envelope)**

Pinch sugar
- ½ **cup whole-wheat flour**
- 1 **cup all-purpose flour, divided**
- 1 **teaspoon salt**
- 2 **teaspoons olive oil**

Vegetable-oil spray
- 1 **tablespoon corn meal (optional)**

TOPPING
- 2 **teaspoons olive oil**
- 2 **pounds onions, halved lengthwise and thinly sliced crosswise**
- 2 **tablespoons dry red wine**
- ¼ **teaspoon dried thyme leaves**
- ½ **pound MEDIUM SHRIMP, peeled and deveined**
- 1 **tablespoon fresh lemon juice**

Salt to taste, divided

Freshly ground black pepper to taste, divided
- 1½ **tablespoons chopped fresh rosemary or 1½ teaspoons crushed dried rosemary, divided**
- 4 **small plum (Roma) tomatoes, cut lengthwise into ¼-inch slices**
- 6 **ANCHOVIES, rinsed and dried**

TO PREPARE THE CRUST
1. Place the warm water in a small bowl, and sprinkle the yeast and sugar into the bowl, stirring the ingredients to dissolve them. Let the mixture stand for about 5 minutes or until it begins to bubble.

2. Place the whole-wheat flour, ¾ cup of the all-purpose flour, and the salt in a medium-sized bowl. Stir in the yeast mixture and the olive oil. Form the dough into a ball. Sprinkle some of the remaining all-purpose flour on a sturdy work surface, and turn the dough out onto the floured surface. Knead the dough for about 6 minutes or until it is smooth and satiny, adding as much flour as needed to keep the dough from sticking. The dough should be soft but not moist.

3. Place the dough in a bowl that has been lightly sprayed with the vegetable oil, cover the bowl with a damp dishtowel, and set it in a warm, draft-free place to rise for 2 hours or until the dough has doubled in bulk. Punch down the dough, and place it on a firm work surface.

4. Roll out the dough to form a 13- or 14-inch circle. (The dough will be springy, but it will eventually hold its width.) Transfer the dough to a pizza stone or pan that has been sprinkled with the corn meal (if desired) *or* sprayed with the vegetable oil.

TO PREPARE THE PIZZA

5. While the dough is rising, briefly heat the olive oil over low heat in a large, nonstick skillet. Add the onions, tossing them so that they are coated with the oil. Stir in the wine and thyme. Cook the onions over *low heat* for about 1 hour, stirring them every 10 minutes or so. *Do not let the onions become charred or crisp.* They should take on an even, golden hue and be soft, sweet, and slightly moist.

6. Heat the oven to 450°F.

7. Place the shrimp in a medium-sized bowl, and toss them with the lemon juice, salt, pepper, and ½ tablespoon of the fresh rosemary (or ½ teaspoon of the dried rosemary).

8. Distribute the onions over the pizza dough. Sprinkle them lightly with the salt and pepper. Arrange the tomato slices over the onions in concentric circles, with their narrow ends pointing toward the center of the pizza. Place the shrimp between the tomato slices (do not worry if the shrimp end up on top of the tomatoes). Scatter the remaining rosemary over the pizza, and sprinkle the shrimp and tomatoes with some salt and pepper. Lay the anchovies over the pizza as if they were the spokes of a wheel.

9. Place the pizza in the bottom third of the hot oven. Bake the pizza for 10 minutes. To serve, divide the pizza into 8 slices (a pizza wheel works best for cutting through the crisp crust). ■

SQUID AND SWEET PEPPER PIZZA

■

8 SLICES, SERVING 4

After repeated unsuccessful attempts to popularize pizza in Japan, Domino's Pizza finally succeeded when it introduced pizza topped with squid, one of that country's favorite protein foods. Here is a garlicky Italian version, more in keeping with American tastes. My husband, a pizza lover, maintains that pizza is not pizza without cheese. So here's one for you, Richard.

Preparation tips: You can prepare this pizza with a ready-made crust, or you can make your own crust (see the recipe on page 326). Ready-made crusts, sold in the refrigerated or frozen-food section of supermarkets, are partially baked and thus ideal for seafood pizzas because they require less oven time. If arugula is not available, you can use mustard greens, kale, or spinach cut into thick shreds.

1 prepared pizza crust *or* pizza dough that bakes in 12 minutes (see "Preparation tips")
Vegetable-oil spray *or* 1 tablespoon corn meal
 2 teaspoons olive oil, divided
 3 teaspoons (1 tablespoon) minced garlic, divided
 ½ yellow bell pepper, cored, seeded, and sliced lengthwise into thin strips
 ½ red bell pepper, cored, seeded, and sliced lengthwise into thin strips
 ½ small zucchini, halved lengthwise, seeded, and sliced lengthwise into thin 3-inch-long strips with skin on each
Salt to taste, divided
Freshly ground black pepper to taste, divided
 ¾ pound small cleaned SQUID, bodies cut into ½-inch rings and tentacle portions cut in half *lengthwise* (cut very long tentacles into 2-inch lengths)
 1 tablespoon fresh lemon juice
 ½ teaspoon dried oregano leaves, crushed
 4 ounces (¼ pound) shredded part-skim mozzarella
20 (approximately) arugula leaves, stem ends removed (see "Preparation tips")
 ⅛ teaspoon red pepper flakes
 2 tablespoons grated or shredded Parmesan

1. Place the pizza crust or prepared pizza dough on a pizza stone or pan that has been sprayed with the vegetable oil or sprinkled with the corn meal.

2. Heat the oven to 450°F.

3. Briefly heat 1 teaspoon of the olive oil in a nonstick skillet that has a lid. Add 1½ teaspoons of the garlic, and sauté the garlic for 30 seconds. Add the yellow bell pepper, red bell pepper, and zucchini, tossing the vegetables to coat them with the garlic. Sprinkle the vegetables with some salt and pepper, and sauté the vegetables over medium heat for 2 minutes, stirring them often. Turn the heat to low, cover the pan, and cook the vegetables, stirring them once or twice, 2 minutes longer or until they are just tender. Transfer the vegetables to a bowl, and set them aside.

4. Wipe out the skillet. Briefly heat the remaining 1 teaspoon of olive oil, add the remaining 1½ teaspoons of garlic, and sauté the garlic for 30 seconds. Remove the pan from the heat, and add the squid pieces, tossing them to coat them well with the garlic. Sprinkle the squid with the lemon juice, oregano, and some salt and pepper, tossing the ingredients until the squid are evenly coated with the seasonings.

5. If you are making your own crust, double over the edge of the dough to form a ½-inch rim. Evenly scatter the mozzarella over the dough or crust to within ½ inch of the edge. Place the arugula over the cheese like the spokes of a wheel, with their stem ends pointing toward the center. Scatter the squid over the pizza. Place the yellow and red pepper strips over the arugula and squid, arranging them like the spokes of a wheel, with one end of the strips pointing toward the center. Arrange the zucchini strips on the pizza like spokes at the hub, with the green side of the zucchini facing upward. Sprinkle the pizza with additional salt and pepper (if desired), red pepper flakes, and Parmesan.

6. Place the pizza in the bottom third of the hot oven. Bake the pizza for 12 minutes or until the crust begins to brown and the squid have just cooked through (overcooking will make them tough). To serve, cut the pizza into 8 slices with a chef's knife or pizza wheel. ■

BROCCOLI AND SCALLOP PIZZA

■

8 SLICES, 4 SERVINGS

My friend Faith Sullivan, a taster for this beautiful dish, thought I should call it Christmas Pizza. The colors—green and white with touches of red—reminded her of her favorite holiday.

Preparation tips: I used a commercially prepared crust for this pizza and was delighted with the result. You can do the same, or you can make your own (see the recipe on page 326).

> 1 prepared pizza crust *or* pizza dough that bakes in 10 to 12 minutes (see "Preparation tips")
> 1 tablespoon corn meal *or* vegetable-oil spray
> 2 teaspoons olive oil, divided
> 3 teaspoons (1 tablespoon) minced garlic, divided
> ½ pound small broccoli flowerets
> ¼ cup water
> Salt to taste, divided
> Freshly ground black pepper to taste, divided
> ¾ pound SEA SCALLOPS, halved crosswise
> 1 tablespoon fresh lemon juice
> 4 ounces (¼ pound) shredded part-skim mozzarella
> ¼ cup coarsely chopped fresh basil (about 8 large leaves)
> 4 small plum (Roma) tomatoes, cut *lengthwise* into ¼-inch slices
> 2 to 3 tablespoons shredded or grated Parmesan, to taste

1. Heat the oven to 450°F.
2. Place the pizza crust or prepared pizza dough on a pizza stone or pan that has been sprinkled with the corn meal or sprayed with the vegetable oil.
3. Briefly heat 1 teaspoon of the olive oil in a large nonstick skillet that has a lid. Add 1 teaspoon of the garlic, and sauté it, stirring it, for 30 seconds. Add the broccoli, toss it to combine it well with the garlic, and sauté the broccoli for 1 minute or until it turns bright green. Add the water, cover the skillet, and cook the broccoli over low heat for 3 minutes or until it is tender-crisp. Sprinkle the broccoli with the salt and pepper, transfer it to a bowl, and set it aside.
4. Wipe out the skillet, add the remaining 1 teaspoon of olive oil, and briefly heat it. Add the remaining 2 teaspoons of garlic, and sauté it, stirring it, for 30 seconds. Remove the pan from the heat, and add the scallops, lemon juice, and a light sprinkling of the salt and pepper, tossing the scallops to coat them well with the garlic and other seasonings.

5. Evenly scatter the mozzarella over the crust or dough to within ½ inch of the edge. Sprinkle the basil over the cheese. Arrange the tomato slices in concentric circles, with their narrow ends pointing toward the center of the pizza. Place the scallops and the broccoli in an attractive pattern on the cheese and tomatoes. Sprinkle the entire pizza with the Parmesan.

6. Place the pizza in the bottom third of the hot oven. Bake the pizza for 10 to 12 minutes or until the scallops are just cooked through and the crust is golden around the edges. To serve, cut the pizza into 8 slices with a chef's knife or pizza wheel. ∎

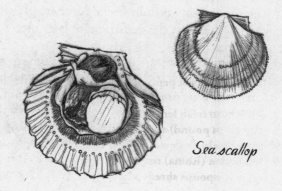

Sea scallop

OYSTER–CORN BREAD DRESSING

■

8 SIDE-DISH SERVINGS

Traditional dressings, like this one, usually come to mind as an accompaniment to turkey, which generally limits their appearance to a couple of times a year. This dressing is cooked outside of any bird and doesn't need one to be enjoyed. It is a spectacular alternative to polenta, potatoes, rice, or pasta as a main-course side dish.

Preparation tips: Be sure to bake the corn bread before you prepare the dressing. Oysters are far better fresh than canned, but they're devilish to shuck (see the instructions on page 77). Fish stores these days are often accommodating enough to shuck fresh ones for you on the spot. Just be sure the work is done over a container so that the oyster liquor can be saved. Once the oysters have been removed from their shells, they should be used within a day or so. Alternatively, in season you can often purchase plastic, dated containers of fresh, shucked oysters that can be frozen for later use.

CORN BREAD
Vegetable-oil spray
1½ cups yellow corn meal, preferably stone-ground
½ cup all-purpose flour
½ teaspoon salt
2½ teaspoons baking powder
1 egg white *and* 1 whole large egg
¾ cup nonfat or low-fat milk

DRESSING
1 tablespoon butter *or* olive oil
1 cup chopped onion
1 cup diced celery
½ cup chopped red bell pepper
1 teaspoon dried oregano leaves
⅛ teaspoon cayenne
12 OYSTERS, shucked and coarsely chopped, liquid reserved
1 egg white *and* 1 whole large egg, beaten
½ cup chicken broth, divided
1 tablespoon white-wine Worcestershire sauce
5 cups coarsely crumbled corn bread (see the recipe, below)
¼ cup chopped fresh parsley
Salt to taste
Freshly ground black pepper to taste
Vegetable-oil spray

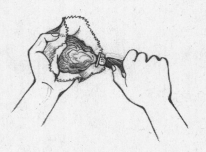

TO PREPARE THE CORN BREAD

1. Place a rack in the center of the oven, and heat the oven to 425°F.
2. Spray an 8 × 8-inch baking pan with the vegetable oil, and place it in the oven while you prepare the batter.
3. In a medium-sized bowl, thoroughly combine the corn meal, flour, salt, and baking powder.
4. In a small bowl, whisk together the egg white and whole egg and the milk, and add them to the corn-meal mixture, stirring the ingredients until they are just combined.
5. Remove the pan from the oven, spread the batter evenly in the pan, return the pan to the oven, and bake the bread for 8 to 10 minutes or until a tester inserted in the center of the bread comes out clean. Remove the pan from the oven, loosen the edges of the bread with a knife, and invert the bread onto a rack. Let the bread cool while you prepare the rest of the dressing. When the bread is cool, crumble it.

TO PREPARE THE DRESSING

6. Heat the oven to 350°F.
7. In a large nonstick skillet, melt the butter or heat the olive oil, and add the onion, celery, red bell pepper, oregano, and cayenne. Cook the vegetables, stirring them, for 3 minutes or until the onion begins to wilt. Transfer the vegetables to a large bowl.
8. To the bowl, add the oysters with their reserved liquid, beaten egg white and whole egg, ¼ cup of the broth, the Worcestershire sauce, corn bread, parsley, salt, and pepper. Combine the ingredients well, and transfer them to a 9 × 13-inch baking dish that has been sprayed with the vegetable oil.
9. Place the dish in the hot oven, and bake the dressing for 45 minutes. Check the dressing after 30 minutes. If it seems too dry, moisten it with the remaining ¼ cup of broth. ∎

TANDOORI FLOUNDER

■

4 SERVINGS

Having just savored the Tandoori Chicken from *Jane Brody's Good Food Gourmet,* I decided to dress up flounder with its spicy, fat-free marinade. The name, incidentally, comes from the traditional cylindrical clay oven called a tandoor, used in India.

Serving suggestion: In keeping with the Indian theme, this fish would go well with a rice pilaf with lentils or with basmati brown rice cooked with finely chopped onion and red and green bell peppers. Any green vegetable or carrots would complete the plate.

MARINADE
- 1 cup nonfat plain yogurt
- 1 small clove garlic, crushed
- 1/2 teaspoon peeled, grated gingerroot
- 1 teaspoon sweet paprika
- 1 teaspoon cumin
- 1 teaspoon coriander
- 1/8 teaspoon cayenne

Salt to taste
- 1/2 teaspoon freshly ground black pepper

FISH

1 1/4 pounds FLOUNDER FILLETS *or* similar THIN WHITE-FISH FILLETS

Vegetable-oil spray

1. In a shallow bowl or glass baking dish, combine all the marinade ingredients, mixing them well. Add the fish, tossing the fillets to coat them thoroughly with the marinade. Cover the bowl or dish with plastic wrap, and put it in the refrigerator for several hours.
2. Place the oven's broiler rack so that the top of the broiler pan will be about 4 inches from the heat.
3. Heat the broiler.
4. Spray a slotted broiler pan with the vegetable oil. Remove the fillets from the marinade, and place them in a single layer on the slotted pan. Place the pan in the broiler, and broil the fish for 3 minutes on one side. Turn the fillets, and broil them for 2 to 3 minutes on the other side. ■

BROILED CATFISH WITH MUSTARD

■
4 SERVINGS

This technique of coating seafood generously with mustard can be used for broiling almost any fish. But it is particularly suitable for catfish, imparting instant character to its mild, sweet flesh. The bonus here is that so little work results in so much flavor.

Preparation tip: Thinner catfish fillets, which are less dense and springy, are better for broiling than thicker pieces of the fish.

Vegetable-oil spray
- 4 CATFISH FILLETS (1¼ pounds total)
- 2 teaspoons canola oil *or* additional vegetable-oil spray

Salt to taste
Freshly ground black pepper to taste
- 2 tablespoons Dijon-style mustard
- 2 tablespoons chopped fresh chives for garnish
- 4 to 8 lemon wedges for garnish

1. Place the broiler rack about 6 inches from the heat source. Heat the broiler.
2. Spray a baking pan with the vegetable oil. Place the fillets in the pan, brush them with the canola oil or spray them with the vegetable oil, and sprinkle them with the salt and pepper. Coat each fillet with 1½ teaspoons of the mustard.
3. Place the pan on the broiler rack, and broil the fish for 5 minutes or until it is done. The mustard will become rich and dark in color but should not burn.
4. To serve, place each fillet on an individual plate, sprinkle the fish with the chives, and garnish each plate with 1 or 2 lemon wedges. ■

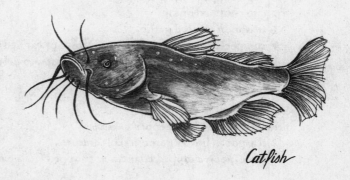

Catfish

BROILED MONKFISH IN ORANGE SAUCE
■

Many people compare the taste of monkfish to lobster, which has always struck me as an exaggeration. It is, however, a sweet fish with a lobsterlike springiness that goes well with this orange sauce. Notice that, at the end of the recipe, 2 teaspoons of butter are added—only ½ teaspoon per serving. This is an echo of the traditional orange sauce, which uses several tablespoons of butter. The trick here is to use real butter (substitutes will tend to add a greasy film to the finished sauce), incorporating it once the sauce is off the heat so that it emulsifies and gently flavors the sauce.

Preparation tips: With monkfish, it is important to be ruthless in removing the dark meat and the membrane around the fillet. Only the pure white flesh has that desirable resemblance to lobster. Timing is important in preparing this dish. Since the sauce takes about 10 minutes to cook, be sure you have all the sauce ingredients ready to go before broiling the fish. Start cooking the sauce as soon as the fish goes into the broiler.

Serving suggestion: A simple, attractive way of serving this dish is to ring the platter or individual plates with halved cherry tomatoes. Rice or a sauce-catching squiggly pasta makes a practical accompaniment.

FISH
1¼ pounds MONKFISH in 4 portions
Vegetable-oil spray
Salt to taste
Freshly ground black pepper to taste

SAUCE
  ½ cup chopped red bell pepper
  ½ cup chopped yellow bell pepper
  ½ cup chopped onion
   1 teaspoon minced garlic
  ½ cup peeled, seeded, and chopped fresh or canned tomatoes
   1 tablespoon chopped fresh basil *or* 1 teaspoon dried basil
  ½ cup orange juice
   2 tablespoons fresh lemon juice
Salt to taste
Freshly ground black pepper to taste
   2 teaspoons butter at room temperature
   1 tablespoon chopped cilantro *or* chopped fresh parsley for garnish

1. Heat the broiler.
2. Spray the monkfish with the vegetable oil, and sprinkle the fish with the salt and pepper (see "Preparation tips" with regard to starting the sauce). Place the fish on the oven's broiler rack, and broil the fish for 10 minutes or until it is cooked through. Remove the fish to a serving platter, and keep it warm until the sauce is done.
3. *While the fish broils,* prepare the sauce. Place the red bell pepper, yellow bell pepper, onion, and garlic in a nonstick saucepan that has a lid. Over low heat, cook the vegetables, stirring them, for 3 minutes, taking care not to burn the garlic. (If you don't have a nonstick saucepan, spray the pan first with vegetable oil, or add 1 teaspoon canola oil or butter to it.) Add the tomatoes and basil, cover the pan, and cook the mixture for another 5 minutes.
4. Add the orange juice and lemon juice, raise the heat to medium, bring the liquid to a boil, and cook the liquid for 2 minutes. Add the salt and pepper.
5. Remove the pan from the heat, and swirl in the butter. Pour the sauce over the fish, and sprinkle the dish with the cilantro or parsley. ∎

At Home on the Range

Today, most cooking is done at the stovetop, the scene of more crimes against good nutrition than anywhere else. For it is here under the guidance of recipes, that you might sauté an ingredient in ¼ cup of oil or boil a cup of heavy cream until it is reduced by half. But the range top is only a source of heat. And, as you look at the variety of cooking methods offered in this section—poaching, steaming, smoking, sautéing—you will find this simple heat source turned to the service of healthful but delicious dining.

For the recipe writer and the home cook, the stovetop has its particular perils. For one thing, ranges can be very different in what they do and how they do it. Many kitchens are equipped with electric ranges, for instance, which heat and cool more slowly than gas; this means that the cook has less control over the temperature and must be especially vigilant (even when the power is turned off, an electric coil can keep cooking food that is left on it since the coil cools down gradually).

As for gas ranges, they are far from equal, some delivering a bonfire and others little more than a flicker. One cook will take forever bringing the liquid in a pan back to a simmer while another will do it in an instant.

For these reasons and others, I find it necessary to offer approximate cooking times in the recipes as well as the phrase "or until it is cooked through." In other words keep your eyes open, and test as you go along. But don't let this task get you tense. Cooking should always be fun.

BRAISED RAINBOW TROUT

■

Fresh whole trout from a nearby farm is a special treat during my summer stays in Minnesota. While I have always had them grilled outdoors with just salt, pepper, and lemon juice, one cold July evening I decided to cook them on the stovetop. This was the happy result.

Preparation tips: If the whole fish will not fit in your skillet, cut off the heads (you can freeze and save the heads, without the gills, to make broth). Half a cup of fish broth can be substituted for the clam juice and water.

Serving suggestions: If you serve 2 whole fish to 4 people, after the fish is cooked you can either cut the 2 fish in half crosswise (into head ends and tail ends), or, for a more elegant service, you can remove the flesh from the bones (see page 74), serving each person a fillet.

  4 RAINBOW TROUT about ³⁄₄ pound each *or* 2 trout about 1¹⁄₄ pounds each
  2 teaspoons olive oil, divided
Freshly ground black pepper
Salt to taste
  ¹⁄₂ cup dry white wine
  ¹⁄₄ cup clam juice
  ¹⁄₄ cup water
Narrow (¹⁄₄ inch) strips zest from ¹⁄₂ lemon
  2 tablespoons fresh snipped dill
1¹⁄₂ teaspoons Dijon-style mustard
  1 teaspoon butter *or* margarine, *or* 1 more teaspoon olive oil
  4 cloves garlic, halved lengthwise

1. Rinse the fish, and dry them thoroughly inside and out with paper towels. Rub the fish with 1 teaspoon of the olive oil, and sprinkle them generously with the pepper.
2. Heat a large, heavy, nonstick skillet that has a lid until it is very hot. Add the fish, and sear them on both sides (about 1 minute per side). Remove the fish to a platter, and sprinkle them with the salt on both sides.
3. While the pan cools, in a measuring cup or bowl, combine the wine, clam juice, water, lemon zest, dill, and mustard. Set the mixture aside.
4. Add the remaining 1 teaspoon of olive oil and the butter or margarine or olive oil to the pan. Add the garlic, and cook it over medium-low heat until it just begins to turn golden.

5. Add the reserved wine mixture to the pan, raise the heat, bring the mixture to a boil, reduce the heat to medium-low, cover the pan, and simmer the mixture for about 10 minutes.

6. Uncover the pan, add the seared fish, basting them with the pan juices and seasonings. Cover the pan, and simmer the fish, basting them from time to time, for 8 minutes or until the fish just turn opaque. Serve the fish topped with the garlic and lemon zest. ∎

Trout

REDFISH BRAISED IN CIDER SAUCE

■

4 SERVINGS

Sweet-fleshed fish is often complemented by sauces that have some sweetness, too. In this dish, attractive redfish fillets (often sold as ocean perch) are braised in a spicy apple cider that serves as both a cooking liquid and a sauce.

Preparation tips: When you reduce a liquid by boiling it (as this recipe requires you to do), the wider the pan used, the better since it allows the steam to escape more quickly. FLOUNDER, SOLE, WEAKFISH, SEA TROUT, or RED SNAPPER work well here, too.

Serving suggestion: Accompany the fish with hefty servings of pasta, potatoes, or rice not only to fill out the meal, but also to absorb the extra sauce.

  1 **teaspoon olive oil**
  4 **tablespoons finely chopped shallots**
  1 **tablespoon peeled, minced gingerroot**
1¹⁄₂ **cups apple cider**
  1 **tablespoon cider vinegar**
  1 **tablespoon lemon zest, cut into 1-inch julienne strips**
  2 **teaspoons unsalted butter (optional)**
1¹⁄₄ **pounds** REDFISH FILLETS, **skin on**
Salt to taste
Freshly ground black pepper to taste
  2 **teaspoons unsalted butter (optional)**
  1 **tablespoon chopped fresh parsley for garnish**

Redfish

1. Heat the olive oil in a large nonstick skillet, and add the shallots and gingerroot. Cook the ingredients for about 1 minute, stirring them constantly.
2. Pour the cider and vinegar into the pan, and add the lemon zest. Bring the liquid to a rapid boil, and continue to boil the ingredients until the volume is reduced to about ¹⁄₂ cup.
3. Sprinkle the fish on both sides with the salt and pepper, and place the fillets in the pan, flesh side down. Reduce the heat to medium, and cook the fish for about 2 minutes. Turn the fillets, and cook them on the other side 2 minutes longer or until they are cooked through. Remove the fish to a platter.
4. If you are using the butter, remove the pan from the heat, and swirl the butter into the sauce until the sauce is smooth.
5. Serve the fish immediately, pouring equal amounts of the sauce over each portion and sprinkling each portion with the parsley. ■

BRAISED RED SNAPPER WITH GINGER

■

4 SERVINGS

Braising is a method of cooking that is halfway between sautéing and poaching—the fish, which are partially covered by a flavorful liquid, are cooked at a low temperature in a covered pot.

Preparation tips: Any sweet-fleshed fish that is firm enough to hold up to the braising process would work here, including ANY MEMBER OF THE SNAPPER FAMILY as well as STRIPED BASS or SEA BASS. To clean the leek before slicing it, cut each leek lengthwise from just above the white base all the way down to the greenish end. Repeat the procedure so that the leek, although still attached at the bottom, is in quarters and flops about like a whisk broom. Run the leek under cold water, meticulously washing away the dirt. Or slice the leek first, then rinse it well in a colander, and let it drain thoroughly.

2 teaspoons olive oil *or* canola oil
1 cup thinly sliced carrots
1/2 cup chopped onion
1 tablespoon peeled, minced gingerroot
1 cup dry white wine
3/4 cup fish broth *or* clam juice
1 1/4 pounds RED SNAPPER FILLETS, cut into 4 portions
1/2 cup thinly sliced leek, white and tender green parts only, well washed (see "Preparation tips")
1 cup chopped fresh or canned tomatoes
Salt to taste
Freshly ground black pepper to taste
2 tablespoons chopped fresh parsley for garnish

1. In a large nonstick skillet that has a lid, briefly heat the olive oil or canola oil, add the carrots, onion, and gingerroot, and sauté the vegetables over medium-low heat for 3 minutes or until the onion wilts.
2. Add the wine and fish broth or clam juice, cover the skillet, and simmer the ingredients for 5 minutes.
3. Place the fish on top of the vegetables, and top the fish with the leek and tomatoes. Sprinkle the fish and vegetables with the salt and pepper. Cover the skillet, and cook the ingredients for 3 minutes. Turn the fish, and continue cooking the ingredients 2 minutes longer. Serve the fish with the vegetables, sprinkling each portion with the parsley. ■

SOFT-SHELL CRABS BRAISED IN WINE

■

4 SERVINGS

Soft-shell crabs, most often blue crabs, are not a separate species that happen to have soft shells, but rather crabs that have just molted their old shell and now have a new, soft, larger one that would harden eventually if left in the wild. The most familiar soft-shell crab recipes are those that have you flour the crabs and then fry them, yielding a lovely crunch and a quick calcium boost but at a fatty price. An old friend, the marvelous Italian-American cook Ed Giobbi, has a different approach that I was eager to try. He prepares a highly flavored braising liquid first and then simply places the crabs in it for a few minutes. The shell is still satisfying, and the cooking liquid becomes a piquant sauce. This is a modification of his method.

Preparation tips: Be sure the crabs are alive when you buy them (live crabs move, albeit slowly when they are ice-cold). Seafood shops are generally happy to clean crabs for their customers, but if this is not the case, see page 81 for instructions on how to do it.

Blue crab

   1 **tablespoon olive oil**
   1 **tablespoon minced garlic**
1½ **cups coarsely chopped tomatoes**
1½ **cups thinly sliced scallions**
   3 **tablespoons coarsely chopped fresh mint**
 ¼ **teaspoon red pepper flakes**
Salt to taste
Freshly ground black pepper to taste
 ¾ **cup dry white wine**
   4 **large or 8 medium SOFT-SHELL CRABS, cleaned (see "Preparation tips")**

1. In a large nonstick skillet that has a lid, heat the olive oil, add the garlic, and cook the garlic, stirring it, for 1 minute, taking care not to let it burn. Add the tomatoes, scallions, mint, red pepper flakes, salt, and pepper. Cover the skillet, and cook the ingredients about 5 minutes.
2. Add the wine, cover the skillet, and simmer the contents for 8 minutes.
3. While the sauce simmers, wash the cleaned crabs, and pat them dry. When the sauce is done, add the crabs to the skillet. Cover the skillet, and cook the crabs for 4 minutes. Turn the crabs, cover the skillet, and cook them 4 minutes longer. Serve the crabs immediately with some of the sauce spooned over each crab. ■

MACKEREL IN WINE SAUCE

■

4 SERVINGS

In this mackerel dish, I adapted the Italian approach to preparing fresh sardines (and if you have the large sardines—actually small herring—available locally, you might give them a try). But I found that mackerel, a more common fish, is well suited to this method of cooking, emerging with uncommon elegance. And while most fish dishes are quick to prepare, this one is especially so—just 10 to 15 minutes from start to finish are required.

Preparation tips: Note that the recipe calls for a lot of fresh basil. Do not substitute the dried herb for the fresh. If you should try this recipe with **FRESH SARDINES,** prepare them by snipping off the fins; then cut off their heads, and clean out the innards through that opening. Crush the garlic by placing it under the broad side of the blade of a chef's knife and pounding against the blade with your fist.

Serving suggestions: Flat noodles such as fettucine are a good accompaniment—they are perfect with the extra sauce—and a garnish of steamed baby carrots will add brightness.

> 1 tablespoon olive oil
> 2 cloves garlic, crushed (see "Preparation tips")
> 4 MACKEREL FILLETS (1¼ to 1½ pounds total)
> 1 cup dry white wine
> ½ cup chopped fresh basil
> 2 cups coarsely chopped fresh (unpeeled) or canned plum (Roma) tomatoes

Salt to taste
Freshly ground black pepper to taste
> 1 bay leaf
> ¼ teaspoon red pepper flakes

1. Heat the olive oil in a large nonstick skillet that has a lid. Add the garlic, and sauté it until it begins to take on color. Remove and discard the garlic, reserving the flavored oil in the skillet.
2. Place the mackerel flesh side down in the skillet, and cook the fish for about 1 minute at medium heat. Turn the fish, and cook the other side 1 minute longer. Holding back the fish with a spatula, carefully pour away the excess fat and liquid.
3. Add the wine to the skillet, bring the wine to a boil, and cook the fish, uncovered, in the wine for 1 minute.
4. Add the basil, tomatoes, salt, pepper, bay leaf, and red pepper flakes. Cover the skillet, and simmer the mixture for 3 minutes. Remove the bay leaf. Serve the fish hot or at room temperature with the extra sauce on the side. ■

SCALLOPS IN FRESH TOMATO SAUCE
■
4 SERVINGS

A bumper crop of cherry tomatoes inspired this basic Italian-style recipe, embellished by fresh herbs and peas. Served over rice, the colors add eye appeal to the tasty dish.

Preparation tips: The vodka and brandy, although they are listed as optional, add a mellow flavor to the dish. You can use one or the other (doubling the amount if you do) or both. The dish can also be prepared with **SQUID** (add them in step 2) and/or **SHRIMP** (add them in step 3) in place of, or in addition to, the scallops. The liquid will almost evaporate in step 2, but the scallops release a lot of liquid in step 3. If you are replacing the scallops with squid and/or shrimp, you may want to cover the skillet during step 2.

Serving suggestion: Serve the scallops over cooked rice or a light pasta like orzo or capellini that has been broken in half before cooking.

  2 teaspoons olive oil
  ³⁄₄ cup finely chopped onion
  1 teaspoon minced garlic
  1 cup sliced mushrooms (optional)
  ½ cup dry white wine
  ¼ cup water
  ¼ cup plus 1 tablespoon finely chopped fresh basil, divided
  1¼ cups cherry tomatoes, halved through the stem end
  ¼ teaspoon salt, or to taste
  ⅛ teaspoon freshly ground black pepper
  ⅛ teaspoon red pepper flakes
  1 cup fresh or frozen and thawed peas
  1 to 1¼ pounds BAY SCALLOPS
  2 tablespoons citron vodka, or 2 tablespoons plain vodka plus ½ teaspoon grated lemon zest (optional)
  2 tablespoons brandy (optional)

1. Briefly heat the olive oil in a large nonstick skillet that has a lid. Add the onion and garlic, and sauté the vegetables, stirring them often, over medium heat for 2 minutes. Add the mushrooms (if desired), and sauté the vegetables 2 minutes longer.
2. Add the wine, water, the ¼ cup of basil, tomatoes, salt, ground pepper, and red pepper flakes. Bring the liquid to a boil, reduce the heat, and simmer the sauce for 10 to 15 minutes. If you are using fresh peas, add them during the last 5 minutes of cooking time in this step.
3. Add the peas (if they are frozen and thawed), scallops, citron vodka or vodka and lemon zest (if desired), and brandy (if desired). Return the mixture to a boil, reduce the heat, cover the skillet, and simmer the ingredients for 1½ minutes. Remove the cover, and simmer the ingredients for another 1½ minutes.
4. Before serving the dish, sprinkle it with the remaining 1 tablespoon of basil. ∎

CURRIED MAHI-MAHI

■

As a graduate student at the University of Wisconsin in the early 1960s, I lived on the cheapest food available. Except on Friday nights, when I took advantage of a local wonder: the Friday night fish fry—all you could eat for $3.50, including dessert! One restaurant went well beyond the traditional deep-fried lake fish and served all manner of seafood, including turtle and dolphin fish, now widely known as mahi-mahi. It is a treat by any name.

Preparation tip: If this dish is prepared in advance to be reheated later in the pan or in a microwave oven, cook it no longer than 5 minutes in step 4.

Serving suggestion: Although Indian curries are traditionally served with an aromatic rice or rice pilaf, with this dish you can also serve mashed or boiled potatoes or a light pasta such as orzo or capellini.

Mahi-mahi

 1 pound MAHI-MAHI FILLETS, skinned and cut into 1-inch pieces
 ¼ teaspoon salt, or to taste
Freshly ground black pepper to taste
 1 tablespoon olive oil *or* canola oil
 ⅔ cup chopped onion
 1 teaspoon minced garlic
 1 teaspoon peeled, minced gingerroot
 1½ teaspoons curry powder (can include
    ½ teaspoon hot curry powder,
    or add ⅛ teaspoon cayenne, or both)
 1½ cups fresh or canned diced tomatoes
 1 tablespoon fresh lemon juice *or* fresh lime juice
 2 tablespoons minced fresh parsley *or* 1 tablespoon minced cilantro

1. Sprinkle the fish with the salt and pepper, and set it aside.
2. In a large nonstick skillet that has a lid, heat the olive oil or canola oil over medium heat, add the onion, garlic, and gingerroot, and sauté the ingredients for 3 minutes or until the vegetables are soft. Add the curry powder (and cayenne, if you wish), and sauté the vegetables 1 minute longer.
3. Stir in the tomatoes and lemon juice or lime juice, and cook the sauce over medium heat, stirring it occasionally, for about 5 minutes.
4. Add the fish to the skillet, combining it well with the sauce. Bring the sauce to a boil, reduce the heat to medium-low, cover the skillet, and simmer the fish for 5 to 7 minutes or until the fish is just cooked through.
5. Before serving the dish, sprinkle it with the parsley or cilantro. ■

SAUTÉED CATFISH IN RASPBERRY-SHALLOT SAUCE

4 SERVINGS

This dish is an illusion. It looks like fish fillets in a cream sauce, but there is no cream in this recipe. Enhanced by raspberry vinegar, the low-fat sauce brings to the common catfish an uncommon elegance.

Serving suggestion: To complement the color and texture of this dish, serve steamed julienned carrots, cooked until they just begin to soften but still have some crunch to them.

FISH
1 1/4 pounds CATFISH FILLETS, cut into
    4 portions
Salt to taste
Freshly ground black pepper to taste
  2 teaspoons olive oil
  2 tablespoons finely chopped fresh
    parsley for garnish

SAUCE
  1 teaspoon cornstarch
  3/4 cup evaporated skimmed milk,
    divided
  1 teaspoon butter *or* margarine
  4 tablespoons finely chopped
    shallots
  1/4 cup raspberry vinegar
Salt to taste
Freshly ground black pepper to taste

1. To prepare the fish, sprinkle the fish with the salt and pepper. Heat the olive oil in a nonstick skillet, add the fish, and cook the fillets over medium heat for 2 minutes on each side or until the fish is lightly browned and cooked through.

2. Remove the fish to a heated platter, cover the fish with aluminum foil to keep it warm, and set the platter aside.

3. To prepare the sauce, place the cornstarch in a small saucepan, add 1 tablespoon of the evaporated milk, and stir the ingredients until the cornstarch has dissolved. Add the rest of the milk to the saucepan, and heat the milk gently over a medium-low heat, but do not allow it to reach a boil. Keep the milk warm over low heat.

4. While the milk warms, melt the butter or margarine in a medium-sized nonstick skillet. Add the shallots, and cook them, stirring them, until they begin to wilt. Add the vinegar, and cook the ingredients until the liquid has completely evaporated.

5. Remove the skillet from the heat, and stir in the heated milk mixture. Add the salt and pepper.

6. To serve the fish, use a slotted spatula to transfer the fillets to individual plates, spoon the sauce over them, and sprinkle them with the parsley. ■

SEA SCALLOP AND MARLIN ESCABECHE

■
8 APPETIZER SERVINGS OR 4 TO 6 MAIN-DISH SERVINGS

I didn't know what an escabeche was before I started this book, but was I glad I learned about it. This method of marinating fish in a pickling liquid is one of many cooking procedures developed through the years as a form of preservation. The escabeche method—introduced to Europe by the Moors in the fourteenth century and then transported to Latin America—is among the most effective and survives today, like cheese and smoked fish, because it tastes so good. An escabeche can last a long time, especially if it has been covered and refrigerated. Certainly, if it is eaten within a week it will taste as fresh as ever.

Preparation tips: I chose scallops and marlin because their firm texture seemed especially pleasing prepared this way. But **ANY FIRM BONELESS SEAFOOD**—skin on or skin off—in any combination that pleases you will work. The fish need not cook completely in the skillet because it will cook further when it is doused in boiling wine and vinegar and then left to sit for a while.

Serving suggestions: Although the fish is enjoyable as a main-dish salad, its sourness may be a bit much for some people who would prefer a small appetizer portion. Either way, a crusty bread is an excellent accompaniment.

  ½ **cup all-purpose flour**
Salt to taste
Freshly ground black pepper to taste
  1 **pound** MARLIN STEAKS, **cut into 1-inch cubes**
  1 **pound** BAY SCALLOPS *or* SEA SCALLOPS **(halved crosswise, if large)**
  1 **tablespoon olive oil**
  1 **cup thinly sliced onion**
  ½ **cup thinly sliced carrot**
  1 **tablespoon minced garlic**
  1 **cup chopped fresh tomatoes**
  4 **thin slices lemon**
  1 **cup white-wine vinegar**
  1 **cup dry white wine**
  1 **teaspoon sugar**
  ⅛ **teaspoon cayenne**
  4 **sprigs fresh thyme** *or* ½ **teaspoon dried thyme leaves**
  1 **bay leaf**
  ½ **cup chopped fresh basil**

1. Place the flour in a shallow bowl, and season it with the salt and pepper. Dredge the marlin and scallops in the seasoned flour to coat them lightly.
2. Heat the olive oil in a large nonstick skillet, add the marlin and scallops, and sauté the seafood for 3 minutes or until they are lightly browned. With a slotted spoon, remove the seafood to a large nonreactive bowl. *Do not wash the skillet.*
3. To the same skillet, add the onion, carrot, and garlic, and briefly cook the vegetables until the onion wilts. Add the tomatoes, lemon, vinegar, wine, sugar, cayenne, thyme, and bay leaf. Bring the mixture to a boil, reduce the heat, and simmer the mixture for 15 minutes.
4. Pour the hot vinegar mixture over the seafood, cover the bowl, and let the seafood marinate for 15 minutes. Remove the bay leaf, sprinkle the escabeche with the basil, and serve the escabeche warm. Or chill the escabeche, and serve the dish cool. ■

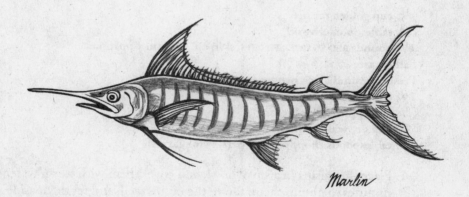

Marlin

SAUTÉED SNAPPER WITH ONIONS AND GOLDEN RAISINS
■

4 SERVINGS

Sweet and sour works as well with fish as it does with meat and vegetables. Although this recipe, which pits vinegar against raisins, takes less than 30 minutes to prepare, the results are glorious.

Preparation tips: I chose snapper here, but ANY FILLET WITH THE SKIN ON (to help hold it together while it is being removed from and then returned to the pan) will be successful. If the fillets are cut into 8 portions after the initial sautéing, this dish can then make an attractive appetizer.

Serving suggestion: Bulgur cooked in chicken broth provides a nice foil for the assertiveness of the onions and raisins. Mashed potatoes would also make an excellent accompaniment.

    ½ cup golden raisins
    1 tablespoon olive oil
1¼ pounds RED SNAPPER FILLETS, skin on, cut into 4 portions
Salt to taste
Freshly ground black pepper to taste
1½ cups onions in ¼-inch slices
    ¼ cup apple-cider vinegar
    ¼ cup dry white wine
    2 tablespoons chopped fresh parsley for garnish

1. Place the raisins in a small bowl, and cover them with warm water for 10 minutes to plump them. Drain the raisins well, and set them aside.
2. Heat the olive oil in a large nonstick skillet that has a lid. Sprinkle the fish with the salt and pepper, place the fish in the pan flesh side down, and sauté the fish about 1½ minutes. Turn the fillets, and cook them for another 1½ minutes. With a slotted spatula, remove the fish to a platter, and set the platter aside.
3. Place the onions in the pan, and sauté them over medium heat, stirring them often, for 10 minutes or until they are soft and lightly browned.
4. Add the vinegar, wine, and the reserved raisins, and cook the mixture, stirring it, for 30 seconds. Add the reserved fish and any accumulated juices. Spoon some of the onions and raisins over the fish, cover the pan, and continue cooking the fish 2 to 3 minutes longer or until the fish is cooked through.
5. Serve the fish smothered with the onions and raisins and topped with a sprinkling of the parsley. ■

LEMONY SAUTÉED FLOUNDER

■

4 SERVINGS

Before seafood's rise in popularity, breaded flounder was always an American favorite. But it was prepared with more oil than is now nutritionally desirable. Thanks to modern nonstick technology, this recipe, sparked by a lemony sauce, uses only 1 tablespoon of added fat.

Preparation tip: This recipe is also lovely with **PORGY** or **TROUT** fillets.

¼ **cup dried bread crumbs**
Salt to taste
Freshly ground black pepper to taste
  4 **FLOUNDER FILLETS (1¼ pounds total)**
  2 **teaspoons olive oil**
½ **cup dry white wine**
  1 **teaspoon minced garlic**
  2 **tablespoons fresh lemon juice**
  1 **tablespoon orange juice**
  1 **tablespoon chopped scallions**
  1 **teaspoon butter**
  2 **tablespoons chopped fresh chives**

Flounder

1. Place the bread crumbs in a shallow bowl, and season them with the salt and pepper. Dredge the fish in the seasoned crumbs, shaking off any excess.
2. Heat the olive oil in a nonstick skillet large enough to hold all the fillets in one layer. Place the fillets in the skillet, and sauté them for 2 minutes on each side or until they are browned.
3. Remove the fish to a platter, and cover it to keep it warm.
4. Add the wine, garlic, lemon juice, and orange juice to the pan, stirring the ingredients. Boil the mixture rapidly for 1 minute to thicken it.
5. Add the scallions, remove the skillet from the heat, and swirl in the butter. Pour the sauce over the fish, and serve the fish sprinkled with the chopped chives. ■

SAUTÉED SOFT-SHELL CRABS

■   8 FIRST-COURSE SERVINGS OR 4 MAIN-DISH SERVINGS

I feel fortunate that my close friends are not just wonderful, caring, interesting people, they are also great cooks. Especially Terry Quinn, who is now happily back in Brooklyn, after several years in Washington, D.C. He delighted me with a scrumptious meal of soft-shell blue crabs one evening in early June, soon after these marvelous creatures came into season. Among other gentle seasonings, Terry used fresh tarragon, relying on the subtle anise flavor of this herb to enhance the delicate sweetness of the crabs.

Preparation tips: Like Terry, I use the liquid released from ½ pound of sautéed mushrooms to start the crabs. However, if you will have no other use for the mushrooms, you can use ¼ cup of broth in its place. The slight kick from the hot paprika is wonderful, but sweet paprika can be used instead—perhaps mixed with a dash of cayenne. The crabs can be prepared about 1 hour in advance through step 3, then the recipe finished a few minutes before serving time. Or the fully cooked crabs can be kept warm for about 15 minutes in a warm oven.

Serving suggestions: As an appetizer, place 1 cooked crab on a small plate lined with a leafy vegetable such as red-leaf or Boston lettuce, arugula, or radicchio. Add the sautéed mushrooms to rice pilaf or to pasta mixed with sautéed vegetables.

    2 **teaspoons butter** *or* **margarine**
    ½ **pound mushrooms, sliced**
Liquid from sautéed mushrooms (see "Preparation tips")
    1 **teaspoon olive oil**
1½ **teaspoons minced garlic**
    1 **teaspoon balsamic vinegar**
    8 SOFT-SHELL CRABS, **cleaned (see page 81)**
Hot paprika to taste (see "Preparation tips")
    ¼ **cup chopped fresh tarragon**
    2 **tablespoons dry vermouth** *or* **dry white wine**
    4 **to 8 lemon wedges (optional)**

1. In a nonstick skillet large enough to hold all the crabs in a single layer, melt the butter or margarine, add the mushrooms, and sauté them over medium heat until they give off their liquid. Remove the mushrooms from the skillet with a slotted spoon or spatula, and place them in a

strainer over a bowl. Press the mushrooms gently with a spoon to extract all the liquid. Pour the liquid back into the skillet. Set the mushrooms aside for another use (see "Serving suggestions").

2. Add the olive oil, garlic, and vinegar to the skillet, stirring the ingredients well. Cook the ingredients over medium heat for about 30 seconds, then add the crabs, top side down, in one layer. Turn the heat to medium-high, and cook the crabs for 2 minutes. Turn the crabs over, and cook them 2 minutes longer.

3. Remove the skillet from the heat, and transfer the crabs to a work surface. Sprinkle the crabs on both sides with the paprika, and press the tarragon onto them. Return the crabs to the skillet, top side down.

4. Sprinkle the crabs with the vermouth or wine, and sauté the crabs over medium heat for about 3 minutes per side. To serve the crabs, place them top side up on individual plates, and put a lemon wedge on each plate (if desired). ∎

STIR-FRIED TUNA WITH BROCCOLI
■

4 SERVINGS

Norman Weinstein, teacher and master of Chinese cuisines, prepares the dish I have adapted here as a beef-and-broccoli stir-fry. Using tuna as a substitute for the beef works well. The tuna ends up looking like chicken but the flavor is its own.

Preparation tip: Although advanced preparation of ingredients and utensils is always important when you are cooking, it is essential in stir-frying because everything happens so fast. For this recipe, note that you will need several small bowls and large platters as well as a large colander, among other pieces of equipment. Fermented black beans are sold in Asian markets.

FISH
- 1 pound TUNA, about 1 inch thick
- 1 tablespoon soy sauce
- 1 tablespoon rice wine *or* dry sherry
- 1/2 teaspoon sugar
- 1 egg white

Cornstarch

Tuna

SAUCE
- 1 cup chicken broth, divided
- 2 tablespoons oyster sauce
- 2 teaspoons rice wine *or* dry sherry
- 1 tablespoon soy sauce
- 1 tablespoon sugar
- 2 tablespoons cornstarch

REMAINING INGREDIENTS
- 1 bunch broccoli
- 1 tablespoon fermented black beans, rinsed and drained
- 1 tablespoon minced garlic
- 1 teaspoon rice wine *or* dry sherry
- 3 teaspoons canola oil, divided
- 1/2 inch piece gingerroot, peeled and minced
- 3 scallions, cut into 2-inch lengths, including tender green tops
- 1/2 cup sliced bamboo shoots

1. To prepare the fish, cut the tuna into strips that are ¼ inch thick and 1 inch wide. In a shallow bowl, combine the soy sauce, wine or sherry, and sugar, stirring the ingredients until the sugar has dissolved. Stir in the egg white, mixing the ingredients well. Dip the fish into the mixture, coating the pieces well on all sides. Then lightly dust the fish slices with the cornstarch, tossing the fish slices gently to coat them with the cornstarch. Place the fish on a platter, cover the fish with plastic wrap, and refrigerate it for 30 minutes.

2. To prepare the sauce, in a small bowl, combine ¾ cup of the chicken broth with the oyster sauce, wine or sherry, soy sauce, and sugar, and stir the mixture until it is smooth and the sugar has dissolved. Set the sauce aside. Place the cornstarch in a small dish, and stir in the remaining ¼ cup of chicken broth. Set the cornstarch mixture aside.

3. To prepare the remaining ingredients, cut the broccoli into flowerets and the stems into thin diagonal slices. Immerse the flowerets and stems in salted, boiling water for 1 minute, then drain them in a colander, and rinse them under cold water to stop the cooking and preserve their color. Shake off the excess water, and set the broccoli aside.

4. In a small bowl, combine the black beans with the garlic and wine or sherry. Set the mixture aside.

5. To cook the stir-fry, toss the fish slices with 1 teaspoon of the canola oil. Heat a good-quality nonstick wok or very large nonstick skillet over medium-high heat. Add ½ teaspoon of the canola oil to the pan, spreading it with a spatula to thinly coat the bottom of the pan. Add half of the fish slices to the pan, and stir-fry them gently for 1 minute or until they are almost cooked through. Remove the cooked fish to a plate, and repeat the process with the remaining fish slices, adding them to the plate.

6. Add the remaining 1 teaspoon of the canola oil to the hot pan, add the gingerroot, and sauté it for 30 seconds, taking care not to burn it. Add the reserved black bean and garlic mixture and the scallions, and stir the ingredients well. Raise the heat to high, stir in the reserved broccoli and the bamboo shoots, and cook the vegetables, tossing them constantly, for 1 to 2 minutes or until the broccoli is tender-crisp. Remove the vegetables from the pan to a second plate, and set them aside.

7. Pour the reserved sauce into the pan, and bring it to a boil. Stir the reserved cornstarch mixture, then add it, stirring it slowly, to the pan. Cook the sauce, stirring it constantly, until it thickens.

8. Add the vegetables to the pan, and toss them to coat them with the sauce. Add the fish, and toss the ingredients gently to combine them well. Transfer the stir-fry to a large serving platter. ∎

STIR-FRIED SCALLOPS WITH BROCCOLI
■

8 SERVINGS

Parboiling the scallops before they are stir-fried gives them a custardy texture and enables you to prepare a stir-fried meal for 8 with only 1 tablespoon of oil.

Preparation tips: Although this is a handsome dish as is, slivers of red bell pepper, added in step 6 with the broccoli and mushrooms, enhance it even more. Be sure to allow 30 minutes for the scallops to marinate. Have all the ingredients ready before you begin to cook.

SEASONING MIX
- 12 very thin slices peeled gingerroot
- 2 scallions, cut into 1-inch pieces
- 2 teaspoons minced garlic

SAUCE
- 2 teaspoons cornstarch
- ½ cup cool chicken broth
- 2 tablespoons dry sherry
- 1½ teaspoons Asian sesame oil
- 1 teaspoon salt
- ½ teaspoon sugar
- ¼ teaspoon freshly ground white pepper

STIR-FRY
- 8 large dried Chinese mushrooms *or* shiitake mushrooms
- 2 pounds SEA SCALLOPS
- 2 scallions, cut into 1-inch pieces
- 2 quarter-sized slices gingerroot
- 2 tablespoons dry sherry
- 1½ teaspoons canola oil
- 1½ pounds broccoli flowerets, steamed for 3 minutes

1. To prepare the seasoning mix, combine all the seasoning ingredients in a small bowl. Cover the bowl with plastic wrap, and set the bowl aside.
2. To prepare the sauce, place the cornstarch in a small bowl, add the broth, stirring the ingredients until the cornstarch has dissolved. Add all the remaining sauce ingredients, mixing them well. Cover the bowl, and set it aside.
3. To prepare the stir-fry, place the mushrooms in a small saucepan, add water to cover, and bring the liquid to a boil. Turn off the heat, and let the mushrooms stand in the hot water for 5 to 15 minutes (depending upon the type of mushroom) or until they are softened. Drain the mushrooms, and slice the caps into slivers, discarding the tough stems. Set the mushrooms aside.
4. Slice the scallops crosswise in halves or thirds to make slices of equal thickness. Rinse and thoroughly drain the scallops, and place them in a large bowl.
5. Flatten the scallion pieces and gingerroot slices by placing them under the flat side of a chef's knife or cleaver blade, then pounding your fist on the blade. Place the sherry in a small bowl, and add the flattened scallions and gingerroot, squeezing them until they release their juices into the sherry. Discard the scallions and gingerroot. Add the flavored sherry to the scallops, tossing the scallops to coat them well. Cover the bowl with plastic wrap, and refrigerate the scallops for 30 minutes or longer.
6. Bring a quart of water to a boil in a large saucepan. Add the scallops, and cook them for 30 seconds. Drain them immediately in a colander.
7. In a large nonstick wok or skillet, heat the canola oil until it is hot. Add the reserved seasoning mix, and stir-fry it for 15 seconds, taking care not to burn the garlic. Stir the reserved sauce, and add it to the wok or skillet along with the steamed broccoli and reserved mushroom slivers. Add the scallops, bring the liquid to a boil, reduce the heat, and simmer the ingredients for 2 minutes or until the scallops are cooked through. ■

OYSTERS WITH BABY CORN AND PEA PODS

■

Most people are familiar with oysters only raw or in a stew or stuffing. But oysters can also be a treat in a stir-fry. In season—the fall and winter months primarily—seafood markets often carry shucked oysters, which are handy for preparing this dish. Like many other stir-fried dishes, this one requires only brief, last-minute preparation if the ingredients are readied in advance.

Preparation tips: Fermented black beans are sold in Asian markets. Note that the oysters should marinate for at least 30 minutes. Be sure to have all the ingredients ready before you start cooking.

SEASONING MIX

- 2 tablespoons fermented black beans, rinsed, drained, and chopped
- 2 tablespoons minced scallions
- 1 tablespoon minced garlic
- 1 tablespoon peeled, minced gingerroot

SAUCE

- 2 teaspoons cornstarch
- 1/4 cup water
- 2 tablespoons soy sauce
- 2 tablespoons minced scallion tops
- 1 tablespoon dry sherry
- 1 teaspoon sugar
- 1/2 teaspoon Asian sesame oil

STIR-FRY

- 2 quarter-sized slices gingerroot
- 1 tablespoon dry sherry
- 1 pint SHUCKED OYSTERS (see page 77)
- 1 tablespoon canola oil
- 1/2 pound sugar snap peas *or* snow peas, ends and strings removed (if using sugar snaps, parboil them for 2 minutes)
- 1 16-ounce can baby corn, drained

1. To prepare the seasoning mix, combine all the seasoning ingredients in a small bowl. Cover the bowl with plastic wrap, and set the bowl aside.
2. To prepare the sauce, place the cornstarch in a small bowl, and add the water, stirring the ingredients until the cornstarch has dissolved. Add all the remaining sauce ingredients, mixing them well. Cover the bowl, and set it aside.
3. To prepare the stir-fry, flatten the slices of gingerroot by placing them under the flat side of a chef's knife or cleaver blade, then pounding your fist on the blade. Place the gingerroot in a medium-sized bowl with the sherry. Squeeze the gingerroot to extract its juices into the sherry, and then discard the gingerroot.
4. Halve the oysters if they are very large. Add them to the seasoned sherry, tossing the oysters to coat them with the liquid. Cover the bowl with plastic wrap, and refrigerate the oysters for 30 minutes or longer.
5. Bring about 3 cups of water to a boil in a medium-sized saucepan. Add the oysters, cook them for about 45 seconds, then drain them.
6. Heat the oil in a nonstick wok or large skillet. Add the reserved seasoning mix, and stir-fry the ingredients for 15 seconds.
7. Stir the sauce, and add it to the wok or skillet along with the drained oysters. Stir-fry the oysters for 1 minute, then add the peas and corn. Stir-fry the mixture 1 minute longer or until the oysters are just cooked through and the vegetables are hot. ■

STIR-FRIED SQUID WITH SPRING VEGETABLES
∎

4 SERVINGS

My passion for asparagus always has me on the lookout for new ways to use this vegetable. A sign in a neighborhood Chinese restaurant for the special of the day, squid with asparagus, prompted me to create this low-fat stir-fry, which I have enjoyed both hot (with rice) and cold as a salad.

Preparation tip: Once the mushrooms have been soaked, this dish is quick to prepare. So start the rice, if you will be using it, before you start cooking. If you use whole squid that must be cleaned, buy 1¼ pounds of it, and see pages 78 and 79 for cleaning instructions.

> 8 **dried Chinese mushrooms**
> 1 **pound cleaned** SQUID
> 1 **tablespoon canola oil**
> 3 **quarter-sized slices gingerroot**
> 2 **large cloves garlic, slightly crushed**
> 2 **small whole dried chili peppers, seeded**
> 1 **cup dry white wine**
> Salt to taste
> Freshly ground black pepper to taste
> ½ **pound slender asparagus, sliced diagonally into 3-inch lengths**
> ½ **pound snow peas** *or* **sugar snap peas, ends and strings removed**
> 4 **scallions, including tender green tops, slivered diagonally into 2-inch lengths**
> Hot cooked rice (optional)

1. Place the mushrooms in a small saucepan, add water to cover, and bring the liquid to a boil. Turn off the heat, and let the mushrooms stand in the hot water for 15 minutes or until they are softened. Then drain the mushrooms, and slice the mushroom caps into strips, discarding the tough stems. Set the mushrooms aside.
2. Cut the squid bodies into ½-inch rings and the tentacles into bite-sized pieces. Rinse the squid in a colander, and set the squid aside to drain thoroughly.
3. Heat the canola oil in a nonstick (preferably) wok or deep skillet that has a lid. Add the gingerroot, garlic, and chili peppers to the oil, cooking them over medium heat until they brown. Using a slotted spoon, remove and discard the browned pieces, leaving the oil behind in the wok or skillet.
4. Add the squid to the flavored oil, and stir-fry it briefly until it just loses its raw look. Add the wine, salt, and ground pepper, bring the liquid to a boil, and cook the squid over medium heat for 3 minutes (do not over-

cook the squid or it will get tough). Remove the squid with a slotted spoon, and set it aside. Turn up the heat, and cook the remaining liquid for several minutes to reduce it by about one-third.

5. Add the asparagus and peas to the pan, cover the pan, and simmer the vegetables for about 3 minutes. Add the scallions, and cook the vegetables 1 minute longer, or until they are barely tender. Add the reserved mushrooms and the squid to pan, tossing the ingredients gently to combine them. Heat the mixture briefly, and serve it over the rice (if desired). ∎

SHRIMP AND MONKFISH IN LOBSTER SAUCE

8 TO 10 SERVINGS

As a child growing up in Brooklyn, New York, in the 1940s and 1950s, the dining treat I most enjoyed was the occasional Sunday family meal at a Chinese restaurant. In those days, Chinese food in the United States usually meant mild but flavorful Cantonese cooking (the influx of spicy dishes from Hunan and Sichuan provinces came much later). But we were more than happy with our wonton soup, chicken chow mein, and shrimp in lobster sauce. This recipe comes close to what I loved as a child, although it has much less fat. Lobster sauce, by the way, contains no lobster; rather, it is a sauce that is traditionally served over lobster.

Preparation tips: As with any stir-fry, it is essential to have all the ingredients ready, sauces mixed, and utensils on hand before you start cooking. If you plan on serving this dish to company, to simplify cooking chores, you can prepare the dish through step 3 an hour or so in advance, then reheat the sauce mixture and finish the cooking just before serving time.

Serving suggestion: Even more than most stir-fries, this one has a sauce that is excellent with rice. Be sure to start cooking the rice before you start the stir-fry. Chinese food is traditionally served with "sticky" rice—for 8 servings, start with 2 cups of rice and 3⅔ cups of cold water; for 10 servings, use 2½ cups of rice and 4½ cups of cold water. Cook the rice without salt or butter.

SAUCE
- 1 **cup chicken broth**
- 3 **tablespoons dry sherry**
- 2 **tablespoons soy sauce, preferably thin soy sauce, if available**
- ½ **teaspoon sugar**
- ¼ **teaspoon freshly ground white pepper**
- ⅔ **cup finely chopped scallions, including tender green tops**
- 1 **teaspoon Asian sesame oil (optional)**

REMAINING INGREDIENTS
- 1 **teaspoon canola oil**
- ⅓ **pound lean ground pork**
- 2 **tablespoons fermented black beans, rinsed, drained, and mashed**
- 1 **tablespoon minced garlic**
- 1½ **tablespoons cornstarch combined with 3 tablespoons water**
- 1½ **pounds MONKFISH, cut into 1-inch cubes**
- 1½ **pounds MEDIUM SHRIMP, peeled and deveined (if you wish)**
- 2 **egg whites *and* 1 whole egg, lightly beaten**
- **Hot cooked rice (see "Serving suggestion")**

1. To prepare the sauce, add all the sauce ingredients to a medium-sized bowl or 2-cup measuring cup, and stir the mixture well. Set the sauce aside.

2. Heat a well-seasoned or nonstick wok or very large skillet for about 30 seconds. Add the canola oil, and spread it around the cooking surface with a spatula. Add the pork, black beans, and garlic, and cook the ingredients over high heat, tossing them constantly, for 2 minutes or until the pork has lost its pink color.

3. Stir the reserved sauce, and add it to the wok or skillet, stirring the ingredients to combine them. Bring the mixture to a simmer, and cook it over medium-high heat for 1 minute.

4. Stir the cornstarch mixture to redissolve the cornstarch, and add the mixture slowly to the wok or skillet, stirring the ingredients constantly. Add the monkfish, and cook it for 1 minute, stirring it once or twice. Then add the shrimp, and cook the mixture, stirring it a few times, for 2 minutes or until the shrimp have all turned pink and opaque and the sauce has thickened somewhat.

5. Using a spiral motion, pour the beaten egg whites and egg over the contents of the wok or skillet, giving one stir after the entire egg mixture has been added. Immediately remove the wok or skillet from the heat, and serve the stir-fry over the rice. ∎

Monkfish

STEAMED BLACKFISH WITH LEEK SAUCE

■

4 SERVINGS

Blackfish, also known as tautog, is an Atlantic denizen that, in my kitchen, has repeatedly proved itself delicious. Its mild flavor makes it amenable to delicate sauces like the leek sauce I use here, which is really a thick vichyssoise with a bit of lemon for zip.

Preparation tips: See page 343 for tips on washing leeks. Leftover sauce will freeze well and can be used with any sweet, white-fleshed fish.

Serving suggestion: This is a very "light" dish that needs a substantial carbohydrate—spinach pasta with garlic and Parmesan, for instance—to give the meal some heft.

SAUCE

1½ **cups sliced, well-washed leeks, white and tender green parts only**
 ½ **cup peeled, sliced potato**
 ½ **cup (approximately) fish broth** *or* **chicken broth**
 1 **tablespoon fresh lemon juice**
 1 **teaspoon butter (optional)**
 2 **tablespoons snipped fresh dill** *or* **1 tablespoon dried dill**
 1 **teaspoon fresh chopped thyme** *or* ½ **teaspoon dried thyme leaves**
 ¼ **teaspoon freshly ground white pepper** *or* **black pepper**
Salt to taste

FISH

1¼ **pounds BLACKFISH FILLETS, cut into 4 portions**
Salt to taste
Freshly ground black pepper to taste
 8 **lemon wedges for garnish**

1. To prepare the sauce, place the leeks and potato in a small saucepan that has a lid. Add water to cover. Bring the water to a boil, cover the pan, reduce the heat, and simmer the vegetables for 15 minutes or until they are tender.
2. Drain the leeks and potatoes, and place them into the container of a food processor or blender along with the remaining sauce ingredients. Process the mixture until the sauce is smooth. Transfer the sauce to a covered saucepan or microwave-safe bowl, and set it aside until the fish is cooked.
3. Bring about 1 inch of water to a boil in the bottom of a pot that has a tight-fitting lid and has been fitted with a steamer rack.

4. Sprinkle the fish with the salt and pepper, and place the fish on a heat-proof plate that will fit on the steamer rack. Place the plate on the steamer rack, cover the pot, and steam the fish for 8 minutes or until the fish is just cooked through.

5. While the fish cooks, if necessary, reheat the sauce over low heat or in a microwave oven. When the fish is done, place the fish on individual plates, spoon some sauce over each serving, and garnish each plate with 2 of the lemon wedges. ■

Blackfish

STEAMED TILEFISH WITH BLACK BEAN SAUCE

4 TO 6 SERVINGS

My husband, who is not fond of "fishy" fish (as he calls them), adored this simple steamed fish, which has a pleasing texture and delicate flavor that takes nicely to the Chinese seasonings. Of three successful fish entrées that I served at a tasting dinner, this was the hands-down winner.

Preparation tips: This recipe would also work with RED SNAPPER, SEA BASS, STRIPED BASS, MULLET, or ANY FIRM-FLESHED WHITE FISH. I used my fish poacher with the insert turned upside down to steam the fish. Another possibility is to place the fish on a heatproof platter, and then put the platter in an oval or oblong roasting pan on an elevated cake rack or on the roasting-pan rack that has been placed on two or more empty, squat cans (6½-ounce tuna cans are perfect) that have had both ends removed. Alternatively, if the fish is too long for your cooking vessels, its head can be removed.

Serving suggestion: To my mind, nothing beats rice as the accompaniment to Chinese-style fish, but egg noodles would do.

FISH

1 WHOLE TILEFISH (about 2½ pounds), cleaned, head and tail left on, and gills removed
2 tablespoons soy sauce
2 tablespoons dry sherry
2 teaspoons Asian sesame oil
Freshly ground black pepper to taste (optional)
1 large carrot, cut into thin julienne strips about 2 inches long
3 large scallions, quartered lengthwise, then cut into 2-inch lengths

SAUCE

1 tablespoon cornstarch
2 tablespoons cold water
2 tablespoons fermented black beans, rinsed, dried, and chopped
1 tablespoon minced garlic
1 teaspoon peeled, minced gingerroot
¾ cup chicken broth
½ teaspoon sugar
½ teaspoon freshly ground white pepper
1 teaspoon canola oil

1. To prepare the fish, make three or four diagonal slashes about ½ inch deep on each side of the fish. Place the fish on a heatproof platter (or, if you are using a poacher, directly on the underside of the upturned poaching rack—see "Preparation tips").

2. In a small bowl combine the soy sauce, sherry, and sesame oil. Rub the mixture all over the fish—inside the cavity, on the sides, and into the slashes. Sprinkle the fish with the black pepper (if desired). Distribute the carrot and scallions over the top of the fish.

3. Place about 1½ inches of water in the poaching pan or in a cooking vessel that has a lid, has been fitted with a rack, and is large enough to hold the fish on the platter (see "Preparation tips"). Over high heat, bring the water to a boil, place the platter holding the fish on the rack in the pan, and cover the pan tightly (use heavy-duty foil if a tight-fitting lid is not available). Steam the fish for 15 minutes or until it is opaque at the thickest point.

4. While the fish steams, prepare the sauce. Place the cornstarch in a small bowl, and add the water, stirring the ingredients until the cornstarch has dissolved. Set the mixture aside. In a second bowl, combine the black beans with the garlic and gingerroot. In a third bowl, combine the broth, sugar, and white pepper, stirring the ingredients until the sugar has dissolved.

5. Briefly heat the canola oil in a small nonstick saucepan that has a lid. Add the black-bean mixture, and cook it over medium-high heat for about 10 seconds. Then quickly add the broth mixture, and heat the ingredients, stirring them often, until the mixture begins to simmer. Stir the reserved cornstarch mixture to redissolve the cornstarch, and slowly add it to the pan, stirring the ingredients constantly. Cook the sauce until it has thickened somewhat. Cover the pan to keep the sauce warm until the fish is done.

6. When the fish is cooked, push the julienned vegetables to one side. Divide the fish into portions, cutting along the slash lines down to, but not through, the bones. Using a metal spatula, lift the portions off the bones, and place them on individual plates. Top each portion with some of the julienned vegetables and the black-bean sauce. ∎

Tilefish

STEAMED "SCROD" ON SPINACH WITH CAPER SAUCE

4 SERVINGS

Buttermilk is an astonishing ingredient once you learn how to keep it from separating when it is heated. The trick is to bind it with a starch. Here, buttermilk takes the place of richer, fattier liquids to create a zesty sauce for one of the blander species of fish.

Preparation tip: If "scrod" (really cod) fillets are not available, try this with **TURBOT, BLACKFISH, HADDOCK,** or, if you can get them, **HALIBUT** fillets.

SAUCE
- ½ cup dry white wine
- ¼ cup broth (any kind *except beef*)
- 2 teaspoons cornstarch
- ½ cup buttermilk
- 1 teaspoon Dijon-style mustard
- 1 tablespoon white-wine Worcestershire sauce
- ¼ cup drained capers
- ¼ cup chopped fresh parsley

FISH
- 1¼ pounds "SCROD" (COD) FILLETS, cut into 4 portions
- 1 tablespoon fresh lemon juice
- Salt to taste
- Freshly ground black pepper to taste
- 1 pound fresh spinach, tough stems removed, carefully washed but not dried

TO PREPARE THE SAUCE

1. Combine the wine and broth in a small saucepan, bring the liquid to a rapid boil, and boil the liquid for 3 to 4 minutes or until it is reduced by half.

2. While the liquid boils, place the cornstarch in a small bowl, and gradually stir in the buttermilk. Set the buttermilk mixture aside.

3. When the liquid in the pan has been reduced by half, lower the heat, and, while the liquid simmers, stir in the mustard and Worcestershire sauce. Spoon 3 tablespoons of the hot liquid from the saucepan into the reserved buttermilk mixture, blending the ingredients thoroughly. Remove the saucepan from the heat, and add the buttermilk mixture slowly, continually stirring or whisking the ingredients. Return the pan to the heat, and bring the sauce to a boil. Cook the sauce, stirring it, for about 1 minute to thicken it.

4. Remove the pan from the heat, and add the capers and parsley. Cover the sauce to keep it warm, and set it aside.

TO PREPARE THE FISH

5. Sprinkle the fillets with the lemon juice, salt, and pepper, place the fish on a steamer rack over a pan of water, and bring the water to a full boil. Cover the pan, and steam the fish for 7 minutes or until it is cooked through.

6. While the fish is steaming, cook the wet spinach in a covered saucepan, stirring the spinach once or twice, for 3 minutes or until the spinach wilts. Drain the spinach in a colander, and place an equal serving of spinach on each of 4 dinner plates to create a bed for the fish.

7. Remove the fish from the steamer, and place 1 serving on top of each portion of spinach. Spoon some warm caper sauce over each serving of the fish, allowing the sauce to drizzle down onto the spinach. ∎

Cod

BOILED LOBSTER
■

Lobster lovers say there is nothing better than lobster that has been simply boiled in seawater. This may be true, but for those of us who are not close to the sea or who lack confidence in the purity of the seawater, just adding a generous amount of table salt to a kettle of tap water should do the trick. Lobster is very low in fat and not as high in cholesterol as was once thought. And it's so sweet by itself, it needs nothing more than a sprinkling of lemon juice or a low-fat vinaigrette or sauce to enhance its flavor. Boiled lobster is delicious served warm, at room temperature, or chilled.

Preparation tips: If you do not have a 10-quart (or larger) kettle, or if you are concerned about the length of time it takes for the lobsters to die, you can cook 2 lobsters at a time in a smaller kettle (6 or 8 quarts) using 3 to 4 quarts of water and 2 tablespoons of salt. Alternatively, the lobsters can be steamed: bring about 3 inches of water to a full boil in a large pot that has a tight-fitting lid, put the lobsters in head first, immediately cover the pot, and steam the lobsters for 12 to 14 minutes.

Serving suggestions: Be sure to have a nutcracker or two at the table for cracking the claws, or crack them before you serve the lobsters. Fresh corn on the cob is a classic partner for lobster, or try steamed potatoes sprinkled with chopped parsley and lemon juice. If you are serving more than 4 people and do not want to buy more than 4 lobsters, serve the same 4 lobsters, cut in half or into portions, supplemented with steamed mussels (see page 246).

> 6 **to 8 quarts water with 4 tablespoons salt**
> 4 LIVE LOBSTERS (1¼ **pounds each**)
> 4 **wedges of lemon**
> **Vinaigrette** *or* **sauce (optional—see pages 374 and 378)**

Lobster

1. Bring the salted water to a vigorous boil in a large kettle (10-quart size or larger—see "Preparation tips") that has a lid.
2. Plunge the lobsters, head first, into the boiling water. Cover the pot, bring the water back to a boil, and cook the lobsters for 12 minutes. Using tongs, remove the lobsters to a shallow bowl or pan.
3. When the lobsters are cool enough to handle, lay one of the lobsters on its back, preferably on a cutting board with a "ditch" that will catch the juices. Slit the undershell lengthwise from the head through the tail with a knife or kitchen scissors, and, if you wish, crack the claws with a nut-cracker. Then place the lobster top side up on a plate or serving platter. Repeat this step with the remaining lobsters.
4. Serve the lobsters with the wedges of lemon and (if desired) the vinaigrette or sauce on the side. ∎

POACHED WHOLE SNAPPER WITH TARRAGON VINAIGRETTE

■   4 SERVINGS

A poached whole fish is one of the simplest and most dramatic of seafood dishes. The principle is to submerge the fish in an aromatic broth and gently simmer it (the violence of boiling water would damage it), then bring the fish to the table whole, often with the edible portion of the fish skinned and embellished with a sauce or some vegetable decoration. This recipe calls for my most often-used vinaigrette spruced up with fresh tarragon and made lower in fat by replacing some of the oil with water.

Preparation tips: Although the recipe stipulates a fish poacher, if you do not have one, a roasting pan containing a rack is a good substitute. Wrap the fish in cheesecloth, making sure some of cloth at the head and tail hangs outside the pan as you simmer the fish, thus providing handles for lifting the fish out of the pan without breaking it. Also, if no tarragon is available, feel free to switch to any other herb commonly used with seafood—dill, for instance.

Serving suggestions: Since this dish is often viewed as a warm-weather one, it goes especially well with grilled vegetables such as zucchinis or mushrooms. If you are serving this to company, a satisfying first course might be the vichyssoise on page 217.

FISH

- 1 3-pound WHOLE RED SNAPPER, cleaned, head and tail left on, and gills removed
- 1½ cups sliced onion
- 1½ cups sliced celery
- ¾ cups sliced carrots
- 2 bay leaves
- 12 peppercorns
- 4 sprigs parsley
- 4 sprigs thyme
- ⅛ teaspoon cayenne
- 2 cloves garlic, peeled

DRESSING

- 2 tablespoons extra-virgin olive oil
- 2 tablespoons balsamic vinegar
- 2 tablespoons dry white wine
- 2 tablespoons water
- 2 tablespoons chopped shallots
- 1 tablespoon chopped fresh tarragon
- 1 tablespoon Dijon-style mustard

Salt to taste
Freshly ground black pepper to taste

1. To prepare the fish, rinse the fish in cold water, and place it on the rack of an 18-inch or 24-inch fish poacher. (If you do not have a poacher, see page 87 for alternatives.) So that you know exactly how much water will be required, set the rack in the poacher, and cover the fish with cold water

to a height that is about 1 inch above the fish. Remove the fish, pat it dry, and refrigerate it until it is needed. Set the rack aside.

2. Add all the ingredients for the fish *except the fish* to the water. Using 2 burners, bring the water to a boil, then reduce the heat, cover the pan, and simmer the vegetables for 25 minutes to form a court bouillon.

3. Place the fish on the poaching rack, and lower the rack into the court bouillon. Bring the liquid just to a simmer, cover the pan tightly, and simmer the fish for 15 minutes. (To maintain the gentlest simmer, it may be necessary to use only one of the burners.)

4. Turn off the heat, and allow the fish to rest in the court bouillon 15 minutes longer. Lift the rack with the fish out of the poacher, and place the rack on a solid work surface. With a paring knife, gently remove the skin from the top side of the fish. Transfer the fish to a serving platter, turning the fish over carefully so that the skinless side is down. Remove the skin on what is now the top side of the fish. Cover the fish lightly until it is ready to be served, but refrigerate it if it will not be served within 1 hour. The fish can be served at room temperature or chilled.

5. To prepare the dressing, place all the dressing ingredients in a bowl or small jar, and whisk or shake the ingredients until they are well blended.

6. To serve the fish, spoon some of the dressing over it, reserving the rest to be served on the side. Bring the platter to the table, and, using a spatula, slide 2 servings off the exposed side of the fish (as if you were filleting the fish—see page 74 for details). After serving one side, remove the skeleton by lifting it up from the tail, and cut the remaining fish into 2 portions. Pass around the dressing. ■

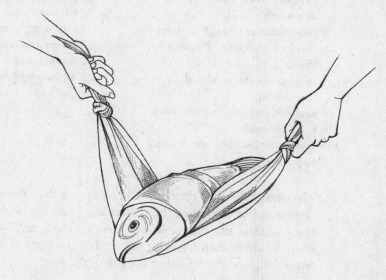

WINE-POACHED SALMON WITH MUSTARD-DILL SAUCE

■

Cold poached fish has long been a cook-ahead joy, and when the dish is made with salmon and accompanied by a simple sauce, the result is a meal fit for royalty. The garnishes are the only last-minute preparation needed.

Preparation tips: If you want to poach a whole, large salmon fillet, as I have done in this recipe, you may have to be creative in your cooking apparatus. I fashioned a large poacher out of a covered roasting pan (the kind used for big turkeys) by setting the fish on long bands of heavy-duty aluminum foil that I used to lift the cooked fillet from the pan in one piece. See page 87 for other poaching methods. To determine how much poaching liquid you will need, do a test run by placing the fish in the pan and adding water to cover by 1 inch; then remove the fish, and measure the amount of water remaining in the pan. Deduct 3 cups of water from this amount when you cook the fish since the 3 cups of wine will make up the difference.

Serving suggestion: The fish looks lovely served with garnishes of scored, thinly sliced cucumber and sliced tomatoes or halved cherry tomatoes.

FISH

1 LARGE SALMON FILLET (about 2½ pounds)

3 cups dry white wine *or* dry vermouth

6 cups water or enough to cover the fish by 1 inch (see "Preparation tips")

4 large garlic cloves, sliced lengthwise

4 shallots, cut into ¼-inch slices

1½ teaspoons salt

1½ teaspoons freshly ground white pepper

SAUCE

⅔ cup nonfat plain yogurt, *or* ⅓ cup nonfat plain yogurt and ⅓ cup nonfat sour cream

¼ cup sweet-hot mustard, *or* ¼ cup Dijon-style mustard and 4 teaspoons sugar

2 tablespoons white-wine vinegar

2 tablespoons snipped fresh dill

1. To prepare the fish, rinse the fish, and pat it dry. Remove the rack from a large poacher, and place the fish on the rack. Or, if you are using a roasting pan, rest the fish, skin side down, on three 12-inch-long doubled strips of aluminum foil arranged so that the ends of the strips extend up from the sides of the fillet to the top of the pan.

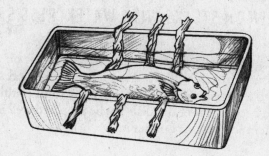

2. Place all the remaining ingredients for the fish in the poacher or pan, and bring them to a boil. Simmer the poaching liquid for 5 minutes, then lower the fish into the poacher or pan. Bring the liquid back to a boil, immediately reduce the heat to medium-low, cover the poacher or pan tightly (if necessary, seal the pan with aluminum foil), and gently simmer the fish for 8 to 10 minutes (depending upon the thickness of the fillet) or until the fish is opaque all the way through.

3. Remove the fish to a platter, allowing all the liquid to drain away, and, if foil strips were used, slide the foil out from under the fish. Allow the fish to cool briefly, cover it with plastic wrap, and refrigerate it until about 20 minutes before serving time (the fish is best served at room temperature).

4. To prepare the sauce, combine all the sauce ingredients in a small bowl. Cover the bowl, and chill the sauce until serving time.

5. To serve the fish, slice the fish into portions, placing each portion on an individual plate. (If the fillet was not skinned, remove the skin as you slice each portion.) Place a dollop of sauce on each plate (see "Serving suggestion"). ∎

POACHED SALMON STEAKS WITH WATERCRESS SAUCE

■
6 SERVINGS

Salmon is such a tasty, colorful fish that it needs almost no embellishment. Still, a low-fat sauce, particularly if it is made with fresh herbs, turns a simple poached fish into a gourmet treat. I am especially fond of this kind of recipe when I entertain because the entire dish can be prepared well in advance if it is served at room temperature, as I prefer it.

Preparation tips: While I use salmon steaks in this preparation, you may substitute 2 pounds of **SALMON FILLETS** or any other fish steak or thick fillet that can be poached such as **TILEFISH, COD,** or **HADDOCK.** Just be sure to adjust the cooking time according to the thickness of the fish. To prevent the cooked fish from falling apart when it is removed from the poaching liquid, the steaks or fillets could first be wrapped in cheesecloth. The sauces can be prepared 1 to 2 days ahead. If you plan to serve the fish cold, poach it at least 4 hours prior to serving it, and chill it after it cools.

Serving suggestions: The flavor is best if the fish is served close to room temperature. For an elegant service, place the fish on a large platter decorated with sliced tomatoes (or halved cherry tomatoes), cucumber slices, and small sprigs of watercress. In addition to the watercress sauce, the fish may be accompanied by the Mustard-Dill Sauce on page 376.

POACHING LIQUID
- 1 cup dry white wine
- ½ cup water
- 2 shallots, chopped
- 4 sprigs parsley
- 1 bay leaf
- ¼ teaspoon salt, or to taste
- 10 peppercorns
- ⅛ teaspoon red pepper flakes

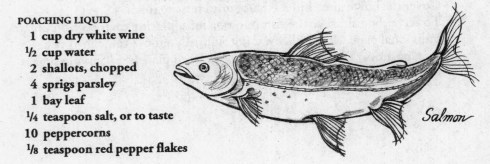

Salmon

FISH
- 6 small 1-inch-thick SALMON STEAKS (about 6 ounces each)
- ½ lemon, thinly sliced into 6 rounds

SAUCE

- ½ cup nonfat or low-fat plain yogurt
- ¼ cup finely chopped watercress leaves
- 2 teaspoons fresh lemon juice
- 1½ teaspoons coarse-grained mustard
- ⅛ teaspoon salt, or to taste
- ⅛ teaspoon freshly ground black pepper *or* white pepper

TO PREPARE THE FISH

1. In a skillet that has a lid and that is large enough to hold the fish in a single layer, combine all the ingredients for the poaching liquid, and bring them to a boil. Add the salmon, topping each steak with a slice of lemon. When the liquid returns to a boil, reduce the heat to medium-low, cover the skillet, and simmer the fish for 10 minutes (less if the fish is thinner than 1 inch).

2. With a large slotted spatula, remove the fish to a platter, and let the fish cool until it is warm. *Reserve the cooking liquid.* When the fish is cool enough to handle, remove the skin from the steaks, and discard the skin. Cover the fish with plastic wrap, and chill the fish until 20 minutes before serving time.

TO PREPARE THE SAUCE

3. In a small bowl, whisk together all the ingredients for the sauce. Cover the bowl, and chill the sauce until serving time.

4. Serve the fish accompanied by the sauce. ■

SMOKED SALMON WITH SWEET-AND-SOUR ONIONS

6 SERVINGS

Once I started using my stovetop smoker, it was hard to keep me away from it. With three fresh salmon fillets in hand and company coming, I created a recipe that would not only enhance the natural beauty and flavor of the fish, but would maximize the time I could spend with my guests. With the onions cooked, the parsley chopped, and the smoker set up in advance, all I had to do was turn on the stove to smoke the fish during our cocktail hour and microwave the onions for last-minute reheating.

Preparation tip: The fish can be smoked (step 3) while the onions cook.

2 teaspoons olive oil
2 very large onions, halved lengthwise and sliced crosswise (about 4 cups)
¼ cup red-wine vinegar
2 tablespoons maple syrup *or* honey *or* brown sugar
¼ teaspoon salt plus salt for the fillets, to taste
2 tablespoons applewood or other mild wood chips
3 SALMON FILLETS (about 2 pounds total), cut lengthwise into 6 portions
Freshly ground black pepper to taste
Vegetable-oil spray
2 tablespoons chopped fresh parsley for garnish

1. Briefly heat the olive oil in a large nonstick skillet. Add the onions, reduce the heat to medium-low, and cook the onions, stirring them every few minutes, for 20 minutes or until they are golden.
2. In a measuring cup or small bowl, combine the vinegar and maple syrup (or honey or brown sugar). Add the mixture to the onions, sprinkle the onions with the ¼ teaspoon of salt, and cook the ingredients stirring them often, until the liquid has evaporated. Keep the onions warm, or reheat them at serving time.
3. Place the wood chips in the smoker. Sprinkle the flesh side of the salmon fillets with the salt and pepper. Spray the grate of the smoker with the vegetable oil. Lay the fillets skin side down on the grate. Following the manufacturer's directions for your smoker, smoke the fish for 15 minutes or until it has cooked through.
4. Serve the fish topped with the warm glazed onions and the parsley. ■

SMOKED BLUEFISH WITH GREEN SAUCE

■

4 SERVINGS

When I tasted this smoked bluefish, it was scrumptious without any added seasoning or dressing. But if you are entertaining, you'll want to dress it up, and the green sauce does just that.

Preparation tips: The fish was smoked with alder chips (see page 111 for sources), which have a sweet flavor especially suited to fish. With my Camerons stovetop smoker, the smoking took about 14 minutes at medium heat. Follow the instructions accompanying your smoker. Or use **STORE-BOUGHT SMOKED FISH** of your choosing.

FISH
1¼ pounds BLUEFISH FILLETS, skin on, in 4 portions
Salt to taste
Freshly ground black pepper to taste
 8 lemon wedges for garnish

SAUCE
 ¼ cup low-fat cottage cheese
 ¼ cup nonfat or low-fat plain yogurt
 2 tablespoons fresh lemon juice
 2 tablespoons chopped fresh parsley
 2 tablespoons chopped chives
 1 teaspoon Dijon-style mustard

1. Sprinkle the fish lightly with the salt and pepper. Place the fish in the smoker, and smoke the fish skin side down according to the manufacturer's instructions. Remove the fish from the smoker, and place the fillets on individual plates.
2. While the fish smokes, place all the sauce ingredients in the container of a food processor or blender, and process them until they are smooth.
3. Serve the fillets warm or at room temperature, garnishing each serving with 2 of the lemon wedges and a dollop of sauce. ■

LOBSTER CAPELLINI WITH SMOKED SALMON

4 SERVINGS

The hardest part of this recipe was resisting the temptation to eat the salmon as it emerged from my stovetop smoker. My guests rhapsodized over this unusual dish, which features flavored pasta highlighted by bits of sun-dried tomatoes and fresh basil.

Preparation tips: The salmon can be smoked while the pasta water comes to a boil, and the sauce can be prepared (except for heating it and adding the pasta cooking liquid) while these two steps are in progress. Instead of lobster capellini, you can use plain or spinach capellini (see page 116 for a source for the lobster-flavored pasta). See pages 95 and 111 for information about home smokers.

MAIN INGREDIENTS
1 pound SALMON FILLETS, skin on
Salt to taste
Freshly ground black pepper to taste
Vegetable-oil spray
12 ounces lobster-flavored capellini
(see "Preparation tips")

SAUCE
1 ounce dry sun-dried tomatoes
(about ¼ cup)
2 teaspoons cornstarch
1 cup buttermilk, divided
½ cup chopped fresh basil leaves
1 tablespoon Dijon-style mustard
1 teaspoon white-wine
Worcestershire sauce
⅛ teaspoon cayenne
Salt to taste (optional)
Freshly ground black pepper to taste
½ cup (approximately) pasta
cooking liquid

1. Bring a large pot of salted and lightly oiled water to a boil. Cover the pot, and keep the water simmering while you prepare the salmon.
2. Rinse the salmon, pat it dry, and sprinkle the flesh side with the salt and pepper. Spray the smoker rack with the vegetable oil, and place the fish on it, skin side down. Smoke the fish according to the manufacturer's instructions (my smoker takes about 15 minutes after it is covered). When the fish is cooked, remove it from the smoker to a platter or cutting board. Using a fork, break the salmon into small chunks (bite-sized or a bit smaller), removing any bones and the skin as you proceed. Cover the salmon with foil to keep it warm.

3. While the salmon smokes, start the sauce. Soften the sun-dried tomatoes by letting them stand in boiling water to cover for about 5 minutes. Drain the tomatoes, pat them dry, and cut them into 1/3-inch dice.

4. Place the cornstarch in a small saucepan, preferably one with a nonstick surface, and add 1 tablespoon of the buttermilk, stirring the mixture to dissolve the cornstarch. Then stir in the remaining buttermilk. Add the sun-dried tomatoes, basil, mustard, Worcestershire sauce, cayenne, salt (if desired), and pepper. Set the pan over a very low heat, stirring the ingredients from time to time with a wooden or plastic slotted spoon or a fork.

5. Bring the pasta water back to a rolling boil, and add the capellini, stirring it well. Cook the pasta until it is al dente (the cooking is swift for this thin pasta, so start testing for doneness after 2 to 3 minutes). Drain the pasta, but be sure to *reserve about 1 cup of the cooking liquid.* Transfer the pasta to a heated bowl, and cover the pasta to keep it warm.

6. Stir about 1/2 cup of the pasta cooking liquid into the sauce mixture. Then add the sauce to the pasta, tossing the pasta to combine the ingredients well. If necessary, add some more of the reserved pasta cooking liquid to the pasta to produce a sauce of the desired consistency. Add the reserved salmon, toss the mixture gently, and serve the dish immediately. ∎

SMOKING IN A WOK

TUNA PASTA
■

Often, red sauces for pasta are prepared with one high-fat meat or another. You will find that good-quality canned solid white tuna packed in water is an excellent, low-fat alternative, adding the needed texture and protein and producing a sauce that is quick to prepare. The red pepper flakes are listed as optional with good reason: this is an ideal dish for children, appealing even to those who do not like fish; but hot pepper may not suit young taste buds.

1 tablespoon olive oil
1 cup chopped onion
1/4 cup chopped celery
1 teaspoon minced garlic
1 28-ounce can crushed tomatoes, *or* 1 28-ounce can plum tomatoes, drained and juice reserved, chopped into small pieces
1/2 cup water (omit if using juice from plum tomatoes)
13 ounces CANNED SOLID WHITE ALBACORE TUNA, packed in water
1 teaspoon dried oregano leaves
1/8 to 1/4 teaspoon red pepper flakes (optional)
Salt to taste
Freshly ground black pepper to taste
1 pound rotelle *or* other shaped pasta
1/4 cup chopped fresh parsley, preferably Italian (flat-leaf)
Freshly grated Parmesan

1. Heat the olive oil in a medium-sized saucepan that has a lid. Add the onion, celery, and garlic, and cook them gently, stirring them often, for several minutes until the onion wilts. Take care not to burn the garlic.
2. Add the crushed tomatoes and water or the chopped tomatoes with their liquid, and bring the ingredients to a simmer.
3. Drain the tuna, discarding the liquid. With a fork, break the tuna into small chunks, and add it to the tomato sauce along with the oregano, red pepper flakes (if desired), salt, and pepper. Cover the pan, and simmer the sauce for 10 minutes.
4. While the sauce simmers, bring a large pot of water to a boil. Add the pasta, and cook it al dente according to the package directions. Drain the pasta, and place it in a large bowl.
5. Add the sauce and the parsley to the pasta, and toss the ingredients to combine them well. Serve the pasta with the Parmesan on the side. ■

CREAMY SHRIMP AND FETTUCINE

■

4 SERVINGS

One method for flavoring pasta is to cook it in a seasoned broth. A modified version of that method is used in this recipe, the liquid being a classic combination of fish broth and wine. You'll find the sauce surprisingly creamy, despite its low fat content.

Preparation tips: There's no need to skin or seed the tomatoes here; just core and chop them. When tomatoes are in season, use fresh ones; out of season, canned tomatoes are preferable. Take care not to overheat the buttermilk or it will separate. See page 343 for instructions on washing leeks.

1 tablespoon olive oil
3 medium leeks, white and tender green parts only, thinly sliced, well washed, and drained
1 teaspoon minced garlic
1 cup dry white wine
¾ cup fish broth *or* clam juice
1 cup chopped fresh tomatoes (see "Preparation tips")
1 tablespoon chopped fresh tarragon *or* 1 teaspoon dried tarragon
Salt to taste
Freshly ground black pepper to taste
1 pound fettucine
1 pound MEDIUM SHRIMP (about 40), shelled and, if desired, deveined
2 tablespoons Pernod
1 cup buttermilk, warm but not hot
1 cup chopped parsley, preferably Italian (flat-leaf)

1. Heat the olive oil in a large, deep saucepan that has a lid, and add the leeks and garlic. Cook the vegetables, stirring them, for about 3 minutes. Add the wine, fish broth or clam juice, tomatoes, tarragon, salt, and pepper, cover the pan, and simmer the ingredients for 10 minutes.
2. While the sauce simmers, bring a large pot of water to a boil. Add the fettucine, and cook the pasta according to the package directions until it is almost al dente (it should still feel slightly hard in the center).
3. Drain the nearly cooked pasta, and add it to the simmering sauce. Add the shrimp to the sauce. Continue cooking the mixture, stirring it, for 3 to 4 minutes or until the liquid in the pan is nearly gone. Blend in the Pernod.
4. Remove the saucepan from the heat, and stir in the warm buttermilk until it is fully incorporated with the other ingredients. Before serving the dish, stir in the parsley. ■

SKIP'S SHRIMP AND SCALLOP CAPELLINI

■

4 SERVINGS

Skip Kennon is a talented composer-lyricist for the musical theater who also happens to have a way with food. After I introduced him to the flavored pastas produced by the Morisi family of Brooklyn (see page 116), he spent months devising ways to turn them into wonderful dishes that do little damage to the waistline. This, a particular favorite, is one that Skip often whips up for dinner guests.

Preparation tips: I added both the garlic and the peas to Skip's recipe, either or both of which can be omitted. Since this dish cooks quickly, have everything readied in advance. But don't start cooking until shortly before you are ready to eat.

Serving suggestion: All this dish needs to round it out is a crusty Italian bread and a green salad.

 ¾ **pound capellini (lobster-flavored, if available)**
 1 **cup clam juice**
 1 **tablespoon olive oil**
 2 **tablespoons minced onion**
 1 **tablespoon minced garlic (optional)**
 ⅛ **teaspoon cayenne, or to taste**
 ¾ **pound** MEDIUM SHRIMP, **peeled and, if desired, deveined**
 ½ **pound** BAY SCALLOPS **or halved** SEA SCALLOPS
 1 **cup frozen peas, thawed (optional)**
 ¼ **cup chopped parsley, preferably Italian (flat-leaf)**
Freshly ground black pepper (optional)
Freshly grated Parmesan or similar cheese (optional)

1. Bring a large kettle of salted and lightly oiled water to a rolling boil. Add the capellini, and cook it according to package directions until it is al dente. Take care not to overcook this thin pasta (it takes only a few minutes), and, as soon as it is done, drain it and keep it warm.
2. While the pasta cooks, in a small saucepan, bring the clam juice just to a boil, reduce the heat, and simmer the juice until it is reduced by about one-third. Remove the pan from the heat.
3. While the clam juice cooks, briefly heat the olive oil in a large nonstick skillet, add the onion, and sauté it over medium-low heat for 2 minutes. Add the garlic (if desired), and sauté the vegetables 30 seconds longer, taking care not to let them burn.

4. Stir the cayenne and the reduced clam juice into the onion mixture. Add the shrimp and scallops, and cook the ingredients over medium heat about 3 minutes. Add the peas (if desired), and cook the ingredients for 2 minutes or until the shrimp turn pink. Stir in the parsley.

5. Place a portion of pasta on each individual plate, and ladle the seafood mixture on top. Serve the pepper and grated cheese on the side (if desired). ■

SCALLOPS AND PASTA IN TARRAGON-TOMATO SAUCE

■
4 SERVINGS

For much of the year, fresh tomatoes are a dismal affair—so hard, tasteless, and waxy that canned ones are a great deal better. But when summer is in full swing and the tomatoes are abundant and off-the-vine ripe and delicious, there is nothing more satisfying than a light, fresh tomato sauce infused with just-picked herbs. And the sauce is easy to make. Here, I've combined the sauce with scallops and pasta. Scallops seem so rich—although they are in fact low in fat and calories—that a small amount goes a long way but still provides full flavor.

Preparation tips: Cook the pasta while you prepare the tomato sauce. If you use a pasta pot (a deep pot with a deep strainer basket), you can drain the pasta without dumping out the boiling water, allowing you to reheat the pasta in the hot water just before mixing it with the sauce.

1½ **pounds ripe tomatoes**
1 **pound** SEA SCALLOPS
Salt to taste, divided
Freshly ground black pepper to taste, divided
Vegetable-oil spray
¾ **pound fettucine** *or* **other pasta**
1 **tablespoon canola oil**
½ **cup finely chopped red onion**
1 **teaspoon minced garlic**
1 **tablespoon chopped fresh tarragon** *or* **2 teaspoons dried tarragon**
¼ **teaspoon red pepper flakes**
¼ **cup chopped fresh basil**
¼ **cup chopped fresh parsley**

1. Plunge the tomatoes into boiling water for 15 seconds. With a paring knife or vegetable peeler, remove the skin. Cut the tomatoes in half, remove the core, and chop the tomatoes coarsely.
2. Sprinkle the scallops with the salt and pepper. Spray a large nonstick skillet that has a lid with the vegetable oil, add the scallops, and sauté them over medium-high heat for 2 minutes or until they are evenly browned. Remove the scallops from the skillet, and set them aside. With paper toweling, wipe out any liquid that may have collected in the skillet.
3. Bring a large pot of salted, lightly oiled water to a rolling boil. Add the pasta, and cook it according to package directions until it is al dente. Drain it, and cover it to keep it warm.

4. While the pasta cooks, in the same skillet used for the scallops, heat the canola oil. Add the onion and garlic, cover the pan, and cook the vegetables until the onion is wilted. Add the tomatoes, tarragon, red pepper flakes, some salt, and some pepper, and simmer the sauce for 15 minutes. Add the reserved scallops, and continue simmering the mixture for 2 to 3 minutes or until the scallops are cooked through.

5. Place the pasta in a large bowl, and add the scallops and tomato sauce, tossing the ingredients to combine them well. Sprinkle the dish with the basil and parsley, and gently toss the ingredients again. ■

PASTA WITH SCALLOPS AND ARUGULA

■

Tangy greens—arugula, mustard greens, watercress—can turn an ordinary dish into an extraordinary one. If you happen to grow these in your garden or can buy them at a farmers' market, all the better.

Preparation tips: If arugula is unavailable or too expensive, you can substitute any tangy greens, such as mustard greens, or milder ones, like spinach or chard. As for the pasta, almost any shape that is not too dense or large will work. For color's sake, I prefer a tomato or spinach macaroni like rotini.

$^3/_4$ **pound (12 ounces) pasta (see "Preparation tips")**
3 **teaspoons olive oil, divided**
4 **teaspoons minced garlic, divided**
1 **pound arugula (see "Preparation tips"), well washed, tough stems removed, and leaves coarsely chopped**
$^1/_8$ **to $^1/_4$ teaspoon red pepper flakes, to taste**
Salt to taste, divided
Freshly ground black pepper to taste, divided
$1^1/_4$ **pounds BAY SCALLOPS**
$^1/_2$ **cup coarsely chopped parsley, preferably Italian (flat-leaf)**
$^1/_2$ **cup dry white wine**
$^1/_4$ **cup clam juice or fish broth or chicken broth**
Dash cayenne, or to taste

1. Bring a large pot of salted, lightly oiled water to a boil. Add the pasta, and cook it according to package directions until it is al dente. Drain it, transfer it to a large bowl, and keep it warm.
2. While the pasta cooks, briefly heat 2 teaspoons of the olive oil in a large nonstick skillet. Add 2 teaspoons of the garlic, stirring the garlic for about 20 seconds. Add the arugula and red pepper flakes, stirring the ingredients to combine them. Sauté the arugula until it has wilted. Sprinkle the arugula with the salt and pepper, transfer it to a bowl, and keep it warm.
3. Wipe out any liquid that may have collected in the skillet. Heat the remaining 1 teaspoon of oil. Add the remaining 2 teaspoons of garlic, and cook the garlic for about 10 seconds. Add the scallops, parsley, wine, clam juice or broth, cayenne, some salt, and some pepper. Bring the ingredients to a boil, reduce the heat to medium, and poach the scallops for 3 minutes or until they are just cooked through.
4. To the cooked pasta, add the reserved arugula and the scallops with their cooking liquid, tossing the ingredients to combine them well. ■

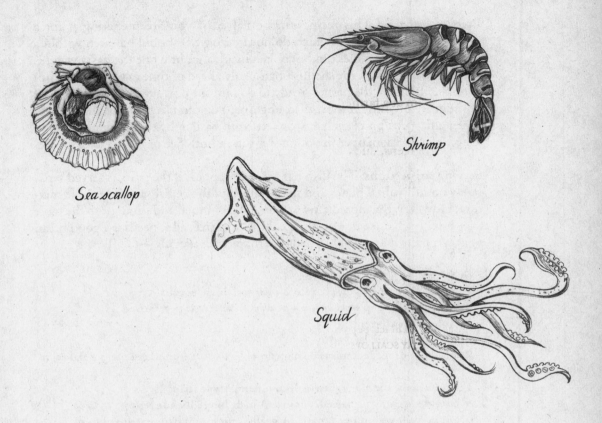

Sea scallop

Shrimp

Squid

SEAFOOD PASTA PRIMAVERA

■   8 SERVINGS

A glorious spring weekend featuring a company dinner prompted me to
think "primavera" and concoct this colorful dish that emphasizes three major
staples of my family's diet—pasta, shellfish, and vegetables. In keeping with
the balmy weather, I shied away from even a light cream sauce and instead let
the ingredients speak for themselves, sparked only by garlic, hot pepper, and
fresh herbs. There is no need, of course, to be limited to springtime vegetables.

Preparation tips: This recipe can be halved if you are preparing it for a smaller group. Leftovers (which do not freeze well) should be eaten within a few days. The vegetables can be cooked in advance or while the pasta water is coming to a boil. Get the shellfish pan-ready ahead of time as well, but do not cook the fish until the pasta is ready to go into the pot. For the pasta, I would not suggest anything heavier than linguine. You can use plain spaghetti, but I prefer a flavored pasta such as spaghetti with basil, lobster, squid ink, or even jalapeño or black pepper (if your tastes run to hot). See page 116 for a source.

Serving suggestions: The dish has more eye appeal if the pasta is served separately on individual plates and then topped with the fish-and-vegetable mixture. However, the ingredients can also be combined and brought to the table casserole style. Since this dish is a complete entrée, all it needs is a good bread to accompany it and a light salad—perhaps with arugula—to follow.

VEGETABLES
- ³⁄₄ **pound thin asparagus, cut into 2-inch to 3-inch lengths**
- ¹⁄₂ **pound sugar snap peas *or* snow peas, ends and strings removed**
- 1 **tablespoon olive oil**
- 2 **tablespoons minced garlic**
- 2 **tablespoons seeded, minced jalapeño *or* ¹⁄₄ to ¹⁄₂ teaspoon red pepper flakes, to taste**
- 1 **large onion, sliced lengthwise into julienne-type strips**
- ¹⁄₂ **pound zucchini, unpeeled, cut into 3-inch-long julienne strips**
- ¹⁄₂ **pound yellow summer squash, unpeeled, cut into julienne strips about 3 inches long**
- ¹⁄₂ **pound red bell pepper, cored, seeded, and cut into julienne strips about 2 inches long**

Salt to taste (optional)
Freshly ground black pepper to taste
- 2 **tablespoons chopped fresh basil *or* 2 teaspoons dried basil**
- 2 **tablespoons chopped fresh oregano *or* 1 teaspoon dried oregano leaves**

PASTA AND FISH
- 1 **pound spaghetti *or* linguine (see "Preparation tips")**
- 1 **tablespoon olive oil**
- 1 **tablespoon minced garlic**
- 1 **pound cleaned SQUID, bodies cut into rings, tentacles cut into bite-sized pieces**
- 1 **pound MEDIUM OR LARGE SHRIMP, peeled and deveined**
- 1 **pound SEA SCALLOPS, sliced crosswise into ¹⁄₄-inch-thick rounds**
- 1 **cup clam juice *or* fish broth *or* chicken broth, heated**
- ¹⁄₄ **cup chopped fresh parsley, preferably Italian (flat-leaf)**

TO PREPARE THE VEGETABLES

1. Steam the asparagus and sugar snap peas (but not snow peas, which need no advance cooking) for 3 minutes, or cook them in a microwave oven until they are barely tender-crisp. Set the vegetables aside.

2. In a very large skillet or wok, preferably one with a nonstick surface, briefly heat the olive oil over medium heat. Add the garlic, jalapeño or red pepper flakes, and onion, and cook the vegetables, stirring them often to keep the garlic from burning, for 2 minutes or until the onion wilts. Add the zucchini and yellow squash, and cook the vegetables for 1 to 2 minutes. Add the red bell pepper, and cook the vegetables, stirring them often, 1 minute longer. Add the reserved asparagus and peas. Season the vegetables with the salt (if desired) and ground pepper, and cook the vegetables, stirring them often, 1 minute longer. Add the basil and oregano, tossing the ingredients to combine them well. Set the vegetables aside, keeping them warm, until the fish is cooked and the pasta is nearly ready. If you wish to complete the dish in the same pan, transfer the vegetables to a bowl.

TO PREPARE THE PASTA AND FISH

3. Bring a large pot of salted, lightly oiled water to a rolling boil. Add the pasta, and cook it according to package directions until it is al dente. Drain the pasta, transfer it to a large serving bowl (see "Serving suggestions"), and keep it warm.

4. While the pasta cooks, briefly heat the olive oil in a very large skillet or wok, preferably one with a nonstick surface. Add the garlic, and, after 10 seconds, add the squid. Stir-fry the squid until it just turns milky white. Then add the shrimp, stir-frying the ingredients for 1 to 2 minutes or until the shrimp are about half pink. Add the scallop slices, and stir-fry the mixture 1 to 2 minutes longer or until the scallops turn milky.

5. Add the hot clam juice or broth, and, only if all the seafood has not cooked through, cook the fish mixture 1 minute longer.

TO ASSEMBLE THE DISH

6. Over medium heat, add the reserved cooked vegetables to the fish mixture, and toss the ingredients to combine them well. Cook the mixture just long enough to heat the vegetables through (cover the pan, if necessary). Remove the pan from the heat, and toss in the parsley.

7. Using individual plates, serve the fish-and-vegetable mixture on top of the pasta. Or toss the pasta with the fish-and-vegetable mixture until all the ingredients are combined, and serve the dish casserole style (see "Serving suggestions"). ■

WHITE CLAM SAUCE WITH PASTA

■
8 FIRST-COURSE SERVINGS OR 4 MAIN-DISH SERVINGS

To my mind, the greatest challenge in low-fat cooking is creating tasty, workable recipes that can rely on such naturally low-fat ingredients as skim milk and nonfat yogurt. Thus, it was particularly thrilling to discover that a delicious white sauce could be prepared without having to use fake this or that but, rather, real buttermilk. Despite its name, buttermilk is low in fat since it is the liquid that remains when fat is skimmed off fresh milk to make butter. There is one problem, though: when buttermilk (or yogurt, for that matter) is heated, it tends to separate. To prevent this, I first mix the buttermilk with a little cornstarch. Then this wonderfully tangy sauce holds together even when it is made in advance and reheated.

Preparation tips: See page 343 for guidance on washing leeks. Start the water for the pasta before steaming the clams, and start cooking the pasta after completing step 1.

> 4 dozen SMALL CLAMS (for example, littlenecks)
> 1 tablespoon olive oil
> ½ cup finely diced Canadian bacon (about 3 ounces)
> 1½ cups thinly sliced, well-washed leeks (see "Preparation tips")
> 1 teaspoon minced garlic
> 1 teaspoon fresh thyme leaves *or* ½ teaspoon dried thyme leaves
> ¾ cup strained clam liquor *or* bottled clam juice
> ¾ cup dry white wine
> 1 teaspoon white-wine Worcestershire sauce
> 1½ teaspoons cornstarch
> ¾ cup buttermilk
> 1 pound pasta, cooked al dente and kept warm
> ¼ cup finely chopped fresh parsley

1. Rinse the clams, place them in a very large kettle with a lid, cover the kettle, and place it over medium-high heat. Steam the clams, shaking the pot every 1 to 2 minutes, for about 7 minutes, by which time the clams should be fully opened. Remove the kettle from the heat, and let the clams cool. When they are cool enough to handle, remove the clam meat from the shells, but *save the clam liquor.* Discard the shells and any clams that failed to open. Strain the clam liquor through a very fine sieve or several thicknesses of cheesecloth. Set the clam liquor and the clams aside in separate containers.

2. In a large skillet, preferably one with a nonstick surface, heat the olive oil, add the Canadian bacon, and cook the bacon, stirring it often, over medium heat for about 2 minutes.

3. Add the leeks, garlic, and thyme, and sauté the ingredients for 2 minutes.

4. Add the ³/₄ cup of reserved clam liquor or clam juice, wine, and Worcestershire sauce. Bring the mixture to a boil, reduce the heat, and simmer the mixture for 2 minutes.

5. Place the cornstarch in a small bowl or measuring cup, and gradually stir in the buttermilk. Stir several tablespoons of the hot wine mixture into the buttermilk, then slowly pour the buttermilk mixture into the pan, stirring the ingredients constantly over medium-low heat. Add the reserved clams, and cook the mixture 1 minute longer.

6. Add the clam sauce to the cooked, drained pasta, and toss the pasta to combine it well with the sauce. Serve the pasta sprinkled with the parsley. ■

Clams

LINGUINE WITH CLAMS

■

4 TO 6 SERVINGS

For those who like their sauces uncreamed yet flavorful and interesting, I bring you a clam sauce par excellence that is made with only 1 tablespoon of oil but is heavy on the featured ingredient—clams, both canned and fresh. My tasters adored this dish, all the more so because it was wholesome as well as delicious. The teaspoon of raw garlic tossed in at the end is an especially nice touch suggested to me by Stevie Kim, a former New Yorker who now resides in Italy.

Preparation tips: Be sure to use top-quality canned clams such as Progresso brand or Gorton's. If your sun-dried tomatoes are packed in oil, drain them on paper towels, squeezing out the excess oil before you chop them. If you start with dry tomatoes, place them in a small bowl with boiling water for a few minutes to soften them. I cannot emphasize too strongly the importance of scrubbing the clam shells well, preferably with a brush and certainly under cold running water. Note that the ingredients call for *cooked* pasta, so start that first.

Serving suggestions: Although I specify linguine, the sauce could be served with other kinds of pasta, as long as the pasta is not too dense. Since this is an off-white dish with just a hint of red, I recommend a green vegetable as an accompaniment—for example, broccoli rabe or chard—to keep to the Italian theme.

  1 tablespoon olive oil
1½ cups thinly sliced onion
  5 teaspoons minced garlic, divided
  ¼ cup chopped sun-dried tomatoes (see "Preparation tips")
  ¾ teaspoon dried oregano leaves
  ¾ teaspoon dried basil
  ¼ teaspoon red pepper flakes
Freshly ground black pepper to taste
  ¼ cup dry white wine
  21 ounces CANNNED MINCED CLAMS, drained and ⅔ cup liquid reserved
  2 dozen LITTLENECK CLAMS, well scrubbed (see "Preparation tips")
  1 pound linguine, cooked al dente and kept warm
  ¼ cup chopped fresh parsley, preferably Italian (flat-leaf)

1. In a large, deep, nonstick (preferably) skillet or Dutch oven that has a tight-fitting lid, briefly heat the olive oil, add the onion, and sauté the vegetable for 3 minutes.
2. Add 4 teaspoons of the garlic and the sun-dried tomatoes, and sauté the vegetables for 2 minutes.
3. Add the oregano, basil, red pepper flakes, ground pepper, wine, and the reserved ⅔ cup of clam liquid, stirring the ingredients to combine them well. Bring the mixture to a boil, reduce the heat, and simmer the mixture for 5 minutes.
4. Add the drained canned clams, and return the mixture to a boil. Add the littleneck clams, cover the skillet or pan tightly, and cook the clam mixture over medium heat for about 5 minutes, or for about 2 minutes after the clams have opened, depending upon how well done you like your clams. Discard any clams that fail to open.
5. Place the cooked pasta in a large serving bowl. Add the clam mixture, and toss the ingredients to combine them. Before serving the dish, sprinkle the pasta with the remaining 1 teaspoon of garlic and the parsley, and lightly toss the ingredients again. ∎

ORZO WITH CLAMS
■

Every now and then, I like to offer a recipe for a meal that can be prepared in 20 minutes or less. Ironically, my orzo with clams closely resembles a clam risotto, which traditionally requires much tedious work. By using canned clams and orzo—a tiny, fast-cooking pasta—instead of rice, the result is much like risotto yet quickly and easily achieved. Cooking the orzo in stock rather than water produces an intense flavor.

Preparation tips: I recommend the Progresso brand or Gorton's canned clams, if they are available. Regardless of brand, the liquid in a can of clams contains salt, and to my taste the dish requires no more. However, I still list salt as an ingredient for those who might like a touch more. If you've got the time and inclination, you may make this dish using about 24 fresh LITTLE-NECK CLAMS, steaming them open, reserving and straining the liquor, and chopping the meat.

Serving suggestion: Since the dish is shapeless and lacks dramatic color, its appearance is greatly improved if it is served with a bright steamed vegetable like asparagus, broccoli, or carrots and garnished with a wedge of lemon to season the vegetables.

     3 **cups fish broth** *or* **clam juice**
     2 **cups water**
     1 **teaspoon canola oil**
     1 **pound orzo**
     2 **teaspoons olive oil**
     1/4 **cup chopped onion**
     1 **teaspoon minced garlic**
     2 **plum (Roma) tomatoes, seeded and cut into** 1/2-**inch cubes**
     1 **teaspoon seeded, minced jalapeño**
    21 **ounces (approximately)** CANNED MINCED CLAMS **and their liquid**
       (see "Preparation tips")
     2 **tablespoons grated Parmesan**
Freshly ground black pepper to taste
     1/2 **cup chopped fresh parsley**
Salt to taste (optional)

1. In a large saucepan, bring the broth or clam juice, water, and canola oil to a rolling boil. Add the orzo, stirring it to keep it from sticking. Boil the orzo rapidly for 4 minutes or until it is half-cooked and much of the liquid has been absorbed.

2. While the orzo boils, heat the olive oil in a deep, nonstick skillet large enough to hold the cooked orzo and its liquid. Add the onion and garlic, and sauté the vegetables, stirring them, for 1 minute, taking care not to burn the garlic. Add the tomatoes and jalapeño, and sauté the vegetables for 2 minutes. Add the clams and their liquid, and bring the ingredients to a boil.

3. Pour the orzo and all the remaining liquid from the saucepan into the skillet. Continue to cook the ingredients at a rapid boil, stirring them occasionally, for 4 to 5 minutes. The liquid should be almost completely absorbed, but the orzo should be very moist. Stir in the Parmesan, sprinkle the ingredients with the ground pepper, add the parsley, and toss the the ingredients until they are combined. Before serving the dish, add the salt (if desired). ∎

SQUID 'N' SPANISH RICE
■

Spanish rice is a homey dish that generally derives its protein from sausage or other red meat. In this version, which is prepared without the usual tomatoes, squid provides a seafood alternative that is far lower in fat and calories yet attractive and tasty. This stovetop casserole makes an excellent buffet dish.

    1 tablespoon olive oil *or* canola oil
    2 cups chopped onion
    2 cups chopped bell peppers (red *or* green, *or* both)
    1 tablespoon seeded, minced jalapeño (about 1 pepper)
1 1/2 tablespoons minced garlic (4 or 5 large cloves)
  1/4 teaspoon red pepper flakes
    1 tablespoon chopped fennel leaves *or* 1/2 teaspoon
      fennel seeds (optional)
1 1/2 teaspoons sugar
  1/2 teaspoon dried marjoram
  1/3 cup dry red wine
    2 pounds small cleaned SQUID
    3 cups (approximately) fish broth *or* chicken broth
2 1/2 cups uncooked long-grain white rice
  2/3 cup pimiento-stuffed green olives, sliced crosswise
      into 1/4-inch pieces
    2 cups frozen green peas, thawed

1. Briefly heat the olive oil or canola oil in a large nonstick saucepan or stovetop casserole that has a tight-fitting lid. Add the onion, bell peppers, and jalapeño, and sauté the vegetables, stirring them often, for 5 minutes.
2. Add the garlic, and sauté the vegetables 1 minute longer.
3. Add the red pepper flakes, fennel leaves or seeds (if desired), sugar, marjoram, and wine. Bring the mixture to a boil, reduce the heat, and simmer the mixture for 10 minutes.
4. While the mixture cooks, cut the squid bodies into 1/4-inch rings and the tentacles into bite-sized pieces. Add the squid to the saucepan or casserole, and simmer the ingredients for 40 minutes.
5. Place a colander over a large bowl, and transfer the squid mixture to the colander, catching the liquid in the bowl. Return the squid and vegetables to the pan or casserole, and transfer the liquid from the bowl to a 4-cup measure. Add enough fish broth or chicken broth to make 4 cups, and transfer the broth mixture back to the saucepan or casserole.

6. Add the rice, stirring it, bring the mixture to a boil, reduce the heat, cover the saucepan or casserole, and simmer the mixture for 20 minutes or until the rice is cooked and the liquid has been absorbed.

7. Stir in the olives and peas. Cover the saucepan or casserole, and let it stand for 1 minute or until the olives and peas are heated through. ■

JAMBALAYA

■

8 TO 10 SERVINGS

Jambalaya, one of the best Cajun-Creole contributions to American cuisine, is a highly seasoned combination of rice, meats, poultry, sausage, and/or seafood reminiscent of Spain's paella (see page 320). This tasty dish is ideal for a buffet as well as for a sit-down dinner for family or friends.

Preparation tips: In this recipe, in place of traditionally high-fat sausage, I use a smoked turkey sausage that is more than 90 percent fat-free. Or, for a hotter version, you may use hot andouille or smoked Italian sausage from North Country Smokehouse (see page 116). If you have no low-fat sausage available, slice the sausage, and slow-cook it first in a pan, in the oven, in the microwave oven, or in a pot of boiling water to reduce the fat content. Any firm-fleshed fish such as SHARK can be substituted for the monkfish, which I use because it holds together well. The chicken, fish, and shrimp can be prepared for cooking while the sauce cooks. Or the sauce can be prepared a day or more in advance through step 2, then reheated before the rice, broth, chicken, fish, and shrimp are added. Or you can cook the entire dish *except* the shrimp just before guests arrive, then arrange the uncooked shrimp on top of the casserole, and heat the jambalaya in a 350°F oven for about 5 minutes before serving the dish.

Serving suggestion: Round out the meal with a green vegetable such as collard greens, asparagus, or okra and/or a salad.

SAUCE

1 tablespoon olive oil

1/2 pound low-fat smoked sausage, thinly sliced (see "Preparation tips")

2 cups finely chopped onion

2 cups finely chopped green bell pepper

1 cup finely chopped celery

1 tablespoon minced garlic

2 cups coarsely chopped plum (Roma) tomatoes

1/2 cup tomato puree

2 bay leaves

1 teaspoon dried oregano leaves

1 teaspoon dried thyme leaves

1 teaspoon freshly ground white pepper

1/2 teaspoon salt, or to taste

1/2 to 1 teaspoon Tabasco sauce, to taste

1/4 to 1/2 teaspoon cayenne, to taste

MAIN INGREDIENTS

1 1/2 cups raw long-grain rice

3 cups fish broth (see page 179) *or* chicken broth *or* vegetable broth

1 pound boneless chicken breast, cut into 1-inch cubes

1 1/2 pounds MONKFISH, cut into 1-inch cubes

1 pound LARGE SHRIMP, peeled and deveined (if necessary)

1/4 cup finely chopped scallions, including some green tops

1. In a large, deep nonstick skillet or 5-quart Dutch oven that has a lid, heat the olive oil, add the sausage, and briefly cook the sausage to flavor the oil. Add the onion, green bell pepper, and celery, and cook the ingredients over medium-low heat, stirring them often, for about 10 minutes. Add the garlic, and cook the ingredients 5 minutes longer.

2. Stir in all the remaining sauce ingredients. Bring the mixture just to a boil, reduce the heat to medium-low, and cook the sauce for 10 minutes.

3. To the hot sauce, add the rice, and cook it, stirring it often, for 2 minutes. Add the broth, bring the liquid to a boil, reduce the heat to medium-low, cover the skillet or pot, and cook the rice mixture for 10 minutes. Remove and discard the bay leaves.

4. Stir the chicken into the half-cooked rice mixture, cover the skillet or pot, and cook the mixture for 5 minutes. Stir in the monkfish, distributing it well in the rice mixture, cover the skillet or pot, and cook the jambalaya for 5 minutes. Arrange the shrimp on the top of the jambalaya with their tails pointing toward the center. Cover the skillet or pot, and cook the jambalaya for 5 minutes or until the shrimp are pink and curled. If all the liquid has not been absorbed, take the covered skillet or pot off the heat, and let it stand a few minutes longer.

5. Sprinkle the jambalaya with the scallions before serving it, or top each serving with some of the scallions. ∎

GREEK-STYLE STUFFED SQUID

■

Squid arrive in the kitchen as perfect packages for stuffing. I found it hard to resist creating tasty fillings to go into their natural pouches. In this recipe and in the one that follows, I offer two rice-based stuffings, the first with a Greek cast and slightly sweetened by currants, and the second decidedly Italian with a little peppery kick. Since the same braising sauce is used with both, if you have the notion to do the two different stuffings at once, just double the sauce ingredients and the number of squid in this recipe.

Preparation tips: The size of the squid is important—the bodies should be at least 5 or 6 inches long but not more than 7. It is also important not to over-stuff the squid since they shrink when they cook and, if they are overstuffed, will burst open. And be sure your pan has a tight-fitting lid to prevent the liquid from cooking out. Toast the pine nuts in a skillet over low heat, stirring the nuts often. Note that the recipe calls for *cooked* rice.

SQUID AND STUFFING

8 cleaned SQUID (about 1¼ pounds), with bodies 5 to 6 inches long, tentacles chopped
2 teaspoons olive oil
½ cup finely chopped onion
1 teaspoon minced garlic
1 cup *cooked* rice, preferably brown rice prepared with a little salt
¼ cup toasted pine nuts
2 tablespoons currants, soaked in water for 10 minutes and drained
¼ cup finely chopped fresh parsley, preferably Italian (flat-leaf)
Salt to taste
Freshly ground black pepper to taste

BRAISING SAUCE

1 teaspoon olive oil
¼ cup finely chopped onion
1 teaspoon minced garlic
1 14-ounce can tomatoes, drained and juice reserved, diced
½ cup dry white wine
1½ teaspoons fresh lemon juice
¼ teaspoon salt, or to taste
⅛ teaspoon freshly ground black pepper

1. Make sure the squid bodies have been thoroughly gutted. Then rinse the squid, pat them dry, and set the bodies aside. Place the chopped tentacles in a dish, and set them aside.
2. To prepare the stuffing, briefly heat the olive oil in a medium-sized skillet, add the onion and garlic, and sauté the vegetables for 1 minute. Add the reserved chopped squid tentacles, and sauté the ingredients for 1 minute. Remove the skillet from the heat, and add all the remaining

stuffing ingredients *except the squid bodies,* stirring the ingredients to combine them thoroughly.

3. To stuff the squid, with your fingers or with a very narrow small spoon (like a demitasse spoon), place about 2½ tablespoons of the stuffing into each squid body, leaving some room in the cavity to allow for shrinkage when the squid cooks. When all the squid are stuffed, secure the opening of each by weaving a toothpick through it horizontally.

4. To prepare the braising sauce, use a skillet with a tight-fitting lid that is just large enough to hold all the squid in a single layer. Briefly heat the olive oil, add the onion and garlic, and sauté the vegetables for 1 to 2 minutes or until the onion is just soft. Add all the remaining braising-sauce ingredients, and bring the liquid to a simmer.

5. Add the stuffed squid to the sauce in a single layer. Bring the liquid back to a simmer, turn the heat to low, and cover the skillet tightly. Gently simmer the squid for 50 minutes to 1 hour (use the longer time for larger squid), checking after about 40 minutes to be sure the liquid has not evaporated and adding some wine or water if needed. Serve the squid hot with some of the sauce spooned over them. ■

Squid

ITALIAN-STYLE STUFFED SQUID

■

These stuffed squid are just as tantalizing as those in the preceding recipe, but here the flavorings are Italian, and the dish will remind you of stuffed pasta.

Preparation tips: The size of the squid is important—the bodies should be at least 5 or 6 inches long but not more than 7. It is also important not to over-stuff the squid since they shrink when they cook and, if they are overstuffed, will burst open. And be sure your pan has a tight-fitting lid to prevent the liquid from cooking out.

SQUID AND STUFFING

- 8 cleaned SQUID (about 1¼ pounds), with bodies 5 to 6 inches long, tentacles chopped
- 2 teaspoons olive oil
- ½ cup finely chopped onion
- 1 tablespoon minced garlic
- ¼ cup chopped mushrooms
- ¼ cup finely chopped green bell pepper
- ¾ cup *cooked* brown rice *or* white rice, prepared with a little salt
- ¼ cup grated Parmesan
- ¼ cup finely chopped fresh parsley, preferably Italian (flat-leaf)
- 1 tablespoon chopped fresh basil *or* 1 teaspoon dried basil
- 1 teaspoon chopped fresh oregano *or* ½ teaspoon dried oregano leaves
- ¼ teaspoon red pepper flakes

Salt to taste
Freshly ground black pepper to taste

BRAISING SAUCE

- 1 teaspoon olive oil
- ¼ cup finely chopped onion
- 1 teaspoon minced garlic
- 1 14-ounce can tomatoes, drained and juice reserved, diced
- ½ cup dry white wine
- 1½ teaspoons fresh lemon juice
- ¼ teaspoon salt, or to taste
- ⅛ teaspoon freshly ground black pepper

1. Make sure the squid bodies have been thoroughly gutted. Then rinse the squid, pat them dry, and set the bodies aside. Place the chopped tentacles in a dish, and set them aside.
2. To prepare the stuffing, briefly heat the olive oil in a medium-sized skillet, add the onion and garlic, and sauté the vegetables for 1 minute. Add the reserved chopped squid tentacles, and sauté the ingredients for 1

minute. Add the mushrooms and green bell pepper, and sauté the ingredients for 2 minutes or until the pepper has softened. Remove the skillet from the heat, and add all the remaining ingredients for the stuffing *except the squid bodies,* stirring the ingredients to combine them thoroughly.

3. To stuff the squid, with your fingers or with a very narrow small spoon (like a demitasse spoon), place about 2½ tablespoons of the stuffing into each squid body, leaving some room in the cavity to allow for shrinkage when the squid cooks. When all the squid are stuffed, secure the opening of each by weaving a toothpick through it horizontally.

4. To prepare the braising sauce, use a skillet with a tight-fitting lid that is just large enough to hold all the squid in a single layer. Briefly heat the olive oil, add the onion and garlic, and sauté the vegetables for 1 to 2 minutes or until the onion is just soft. Add all the remaining braising-sauce ingredients, and bring the liquid to a simmer.

5. Add the stuffed squid to the sauce in a single layer. Bring the liquid back to a simmer, turn the heat to low, and cover the skillet tightly. Gently simmer the squid for 50 minutes to 1 hour (use the longer time for larger squid), checking after about 40 minutes to be sure the liquid has not evaporated and adding some wine or water if needed. Serve the squid hot with some of the sauce spooned over them. ∎

CURRIED SHRIMP WITH CHICKPEAS

■

Curry powder, a mixture of seasonings, is readily available in markets large and small. In this recipe, however, I have prepared an Indian curry seasoned with my own spice mix.

Preparation tips: If you can get the spices listed, I urge you to try the recipe as written. Otherwise you can substitute 1 tablespoon or more of curry powder (including some hot curry powder, if you wish). As with stir-fries, in this recipe it is important to have all your ingredients pan-ready before you start cooking. Start the rice (if you are using it—see "Serving suggestions") when you start cooking the onions.

Serving suggestions: Rice or rice pilaf (perhaps with green peas added) is the perfect accompaniment. A green salad makes the meal.

SPICE MIX (SEE "PREPARATION TIPS")
  2 teaspoons ground cumin
  1 teaspoon ground turmeric
  1 teaspoon ground coriander
  1 teaspoon garam masala (see page 277)
  1 teaspoon paprika

MAIN INGREDIENTS
  1 tablespoon canola oil
  1 cup finely chopped onion
  2 teaspoons minced garlic
  1 tablespoon seeded, minced jalapeño (about 1 pepper) *or* hot chilis, or to taste
  1 pound plum (Roma) tomatoes *or* 1 28-ounce can drained plum tomatoes, diced
  4 tablespoons (¼ cup) chopped cilantro, divided
  1 tablespoon chopped fresh mint *or* 1 teaspoon dried mint
  1 19-ounce can chickpeas, rinsed and drained, *or* 2 cups cooked chickpeas
  1 pound MEDIUM SHRIMP, peeled and, if desired, deveined
  ½ teaspoon salt, or to taste
  ⅛ to ¼ teaspoon freshly ground black pepper, to taste

1. In a small bowl, combine all the ingredients for the spice mix. Set the mixture aside.
2. Briefly heat the canola oil in a large nonstick skillet or shallow 3-quart saucepan. Add the onion and garlic, and cook them, stirring them often, over medium-low heat for 5 minutes or until the onion begins to turn golden.
3. Add the reserved spice mixture and the jalapeño or chilis, and cook the ingredients over low heat, stirring them, for 1 to 2 minutes.
4. Add the tomatoes, 2 tablespoons of the cilantro, and the mint to the skillet or pan, and cook the mixture over medium-low heat, stirring it occasionally, for 5 to 10 minutes or until the tomatoes have nearly disintegrated.
5. Add the chickpeas, shrimp, salt, and pepper, turn the heat up to medium, and cook the mixture, stirring it several times, for 3 to 4 minutes or until all the shrimp have turned pink and have cooked through. Serve the dish piping hot with the remaining cilantro sprinkled over it. ∎

SEARED TUNA WITH LENTILS
■

Lentils make a spectacular base for salads—just as pasta, rice, or beans do. They give a salad belly-filling substance as well as superb nutrition. And they are a cinch to prepare. The red lentils I use in this recipe require only about 10 minutes of cooking. Here, a warm lentil salad becomes the bed for seared tuna, a complete meal of protein and carbohydrates that is beautiful to behold.

LENTILS
4½ cups homemade or canned
    chicken broth, divided
2 cups dried *red* lentils, washed
1 teaspoon olive oil
½ cup chopped onion
1 teaspoon minced garlic
¼ cup chopped celery
¼ cup chopped carrot
1 teaspoon chopped fresh thyme *or*
    ½ teaspoon dried thyme leaves
Salt to taste
Freshly ground black pepper to taste
1 tablespoon fresh lemon juice

FISH
1¼ pounds TUNA STEAKS about
    ¾-inch thick
Salt to taste
Freshly ground black pepper to taste
1 teaspoon hot chili powder
Vegetable-oil spray
1 tablespoon chopped cilantro *or*
    chopped fresh parsley

1. To prepare the lentils, bring 4 cups of the broth to a boil in a saucepan that has a lid. Add the lentils, lower the heat, cover the pan, and simmer the lentils for 8 minutes or until they are just tender.
2. While the lentils cook, heat the olive oil in another saucepan that has a lid and preferably a nonstick surface, and add the onion, garlic, celery, carrot, thyme, salt, and pepper. Cook the vegetables, stirring them often, until the onion begins to wilt. Add the remaining ½ cup of broth and the lemon juice to the vegetables, cover the pan, and simmer the vegetables for 5 minutes.
3. When the lentils are done, add them with any remaining liquid to the vegetables, and simmer the mixture for another 2 to 3 minutes. Set the lentil-vegetable mixture aside, cover it, and keep it warm.

4. To prepare the fish, sprinkle the tuna with the salt, pepper, and chili powder, and spray it with the vegetable oil. Heat a well-seasoned cast-iron skillet or a high-quality nonstick skillet (ungreased) for 3 minutes or until it is hot. Place the tuna in the hot skillet, and cook the tuna on one side for 2 minutes. Turn the tuna, and cook it on the other side 2 to 3 minutes longer, or until it is just cooked through.

5. Place a portion of lentils on each of 4 plates. Slice the tuna into 8 pieces, and place 2 pieces of the fish on top of each portion of lentils. Sprinkle each dish with the cilantro or parsley. ■

Tuna

MAKO SHARK CASSEROLE

■

Mako shark is caught up and down the Atlantic seaboard as well as in the Pacific. Although it was once regarded as a trash fish and discarded, it has become so popular in recent years that it is in danger of being overfished. Its texture and taste are superb, similar to swordfish but not as sweet or as flaky, and it is firm enough to hold its own in a soup or in a casserole like this one.

Preparation tips: If shark is not available and you have your heart set on this beautiful casserole, **SWORDFISH** will work well, as will **TUNA** or any other relatively firm fish. The shark's skin can be thick and rubbery and is usually removed before the fish is sold. If this is not the case, remove it yourself, using a sharp filleting or chef's knife. Insert the blade between the flesh and the skin, and, with a rhythmic sawing motion, cut close to the skin as you tug the skin away. In cooking this dish, an enameled cast-iron casserole is excellent because it distributes and holds the heat well and is good-looking enough to be taken directly from stove to table.

  1 tablespoon olive oil
  2 large leeks, white and tender green parts only, thinly sliced,
     well washed, and drained (see page 343)
  1 large red bell pepper, cored, seeded, and cut into 1-inch squares
  1 large baking potato, peeled and cut into $\frac{1}{2}$-inch cubes
  1 tablespoon minced garlic
  1 cup fish broth *or* clam broth *or* chicken broth
$\frac{1}{2}$ cup dry white wine
  1 tablespoon apple-cider vinegar
Salt to taste
Freshly ground black pepper to taste
 12 pearl onions, peeled
$1\frac{1}{4}$ pounds MAKO SHARK, skinned and cut in $1\frac{1}{2}$-inch cubes
  1 cup fresh or frozen and thawed green peas
$\frac{1}{2}$ cup chopped parsley, preferably Italian (flat-leaf)

Mako shark

1. Briefly heat the olive oil in a heavy stovetop casserole or heavy pot that has a tight-fitting lid. Add the leeks, red bell pepper, potato, and garlic. Over low heat, cook the vegetables, stirring them, for 3 minutes or until the leeks begin to soften.
2. Add the broth, wine, vinegar, salt, and ground pepper. Cover the casserole or pot, bring the ingredients to a simmer, lower the heat, and cook the mixture for 10 minutes. Add the pearl onions, cover the casserole or pot, and simmer the mixture for 5 minutes. Add the fish, and simmer the mixture 5 minutes longer.
3. Meanwhile, if you are using fresh peas, cook the peas in boiling water for about 3 minutes. Add the partly cooked or thawed peas to the casserole or pot, replace the cover, and simmer the ingredients 2 minutes longer. Before serving, taste the casserole, adjusting the seasonings, if necessary. Then sprinkle the casserole with the parsley. ■

SCALLOP AND BLACK BEAN TACOS

■

4 SERVINGS (8 TACOS)

Although they are traditionally made with seasoned meats, tacos can be delicious with a wide range of fillings, including fish. My tasters enjoyed this quick-to-prepare, good-looking combination, which can be used to fill both taco shells (crisp tortillas) and soft tortillas and either eaten as is or with toppings of your choice.

Preparation tips: Be sure to have the desired toppings prepared before you start cooking the filling. The filling can also be made in advance and gently reheated at serving time.

TACOS

1 pound SEA SCALLOPS, cut into
   ½-inch dice
Chili powder (hot and/or mild) to
   taste
Salt to taste
3 teaspoons canola oil, divided
1 tablespoon fresh lime juice
8 taco shells
½ cup finely chopped onion
½ cup finely diced red bell pepper
1 cup cooked corn kernels (fresh,
   frozen, or canned)
1 cup cooked black beans, drained
   and rinsed

POSSIBLE TOPPINGS
Shredded lettuce
Diced fresh tomatoes
Thinly sliced scallions
Chopped cilantro
Avocado, diced or cut into strips

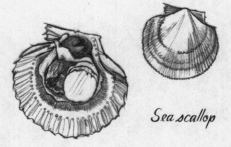

Sea scallop

1. Sprinkle the scallops generously with the chili powder and salt.
2. In a nonstick skillet, briefly heat 1 teaspoon of the canola oil over medium heat. Add the scallops, and sauté them, tossing them often, for 2 minutes or until they are just cooked through. Stir in the lime juice, transfer the scallops to a bowl, and keep them warm.
3. Follow package directions for heating the taco shells. Or heat the oven to 350°F, place the separated taco shells on a baking tray, and put the taco shells in the oven to warm.
4. While the taco shells heat, add the remaining 2 teaspoons of canola oil to the skillet. Heat the skillet, add the onion and red bell pepper, and sauté the vegetables for 2 minutes or until they are soft. Add the corn and beans, and cook the mixture just long enough to heat it through. Remove the skillet from the heat, and add the cooked scallops to the vegetable mixture, tossing the ingredients to combine them well.
5. Remove the taco shells from the oven, divide the scallop filling among the 8 taco shells, and serve the tacos, letting individual diners add the toppings of their choice. ∎

LEMONY MONKFISH WITH BULGUR

■

4 SERVINGS

Bulgur—parboiled, dried, cracked wheat—is a Middle Eastern staple that has been a family favorite since we were introduced to it by my college roommate, Linda Himot, who lived in Turkey for several years. The natural-food revolution made it readily available in health-food stores in whole-grain form, which has a wonderful, nutty flavor. While chicken is a more common companion, monkfish stands up well in this easy-to-prepare and quick-cooking bulgur-and-vegetable creation.

Preparation tip: Any firm-fleshed fish can be used in place of monkfish, including **SHARK, MARLIN, SWORDFISH, WOLFFISH,** and **OCEAN POUT.**

BULGUR
- 2 teaspoons olive oil
- 1 teaspoon butter *or* margarine
- 2 cups chopped onion
- 2 teaspoons minced garlic
- 1½ cups diced carrots
- 1½ cups uncooked bulgur, preferably whole-grain
- 3 cups boiling chicken broth
- 2 tablespoons grated lemon rind
- ¼ cup fresh lemon juice
- ¾ teaspoon cumin
- ½ teaspoon cardamom
- ½ teaspoon coriander
- ½ teaspoon salt, or to taste
- ½ teaspoon freshly ground black pepper

FISH
- 1 pound **MONKFISH**, cut into 1-inch cubes
- Salt to taste
- Freshly ground black pepper to taste
- ⅛ teaspoon cayenne, or to taste
- Vegetable-oil spray

Monkfish

1. In a large saucepan with a tight-fitting lid, briefly heat the olive oil and butter or margarine. Add the onion and garlic, and sauté the vegetables over medium-low heat until the onion is soft. Add the carrots and bulgur, and cook the ingredients, stirring them, for several minutes to toast the bulgur. Add all the remaining bulgur ingredients, and stir them to combine them well. When the liquid returns to a boil, reduce the heat to low, cover the pan, and cook the bulgur for 12 to 13 minutes (it probably will not have absorbed all the water).

2. While the bulgur cooks, sprinkle the monkfish with the salt, pepper, and cayenne. Spray the fish with the vegetable oil. Heat a nonstick skillet large enough to hold the fish in a single layer, add the fish, and sear the fish on all sides, cooking the fish for a total of 5 minutes.

3. Add the seared fish to the bulgur, tossing the ingredients gently to combine them. Cover the saucepan, and cook the bulgur-and-fish mixture for 2 minutes or until all the liquid has been absorbed. ■

LIGHT CRAB CAKES
■

Crab cakes are often extremely rich, made with lots of melted butter, whole eggs, or, perhaps, mayonnaise. Although this recipe takes a traditional approach, it keeps the fat to a minimum yet preserves the flavor and texture of the original.

Preparation tips: The lighter the crab cake, the fewer the fillers, and the more important it is to buy the highest-quality lump crabmeat you can find. Generally, a seafood shop will do better than a supermarket that lacks a good seafood counter. Be sure to take the 2-hour chilling step seriously; it is crucial in helping the patties hold together.

Serving suggestions: Serve the crab cakes with lemon wedges and reduced-fat mayonnaise into which you have blended the chopped herb of your choice, or try the Green Sauce on page 381 or the Fresh Corn Relish on page 498.

3 teaspoons butter *or* margarine, divided
2 tablespoons minced shallots
2 tablespoons minced red bell pepper
1 tablespoon tarragon vinegar *or* white-wine vinegar
1 pound LUMP CRABMEAT
3 tablespoons fresh lemon juice
2 egg whites, lightly beaten
1 tablespoon nonfat or reduced-fat mayonnaise
1/4 cup finely chopped fresh parsley
1/8 teaspoon Tabasco sauce
Salt to taste
Freshly ground black pepper to taste
1 cup dried bread crumbs
2 teaspoons olive oil *or* canola oil

1. In a small nonstick skillet, melt 1 teaspoon of the butter or margarine, add the shallots and red bell pepper, and sauté the vegetables, stirring them, until the shallots are wilted. Add the vinegar, raise the heat, and boil the vinegar rapidly until it has evaporated. Set the skillet aside to cool.

2. Place the crabmeat in a large bowl, sprinkle it with the lemon juice, and blend in the cooled shallot–red bell pepper mixture. Stir in the egg whites, mayonnaise, parsley, Tabasco sauce, salt, and ground pepper. Cover the bowl, and chill the mixture for 2 hours or longer.

3. With moistened hands, mold the crab mixture into 8 patties, and coat the patties on both sides with the bread crumbs. Discard the extra crumbs.

4. In a nonstick skillet or griddle large enough to hold all 8 crab cakes, heat the olive oil or canola oil with the remaining 2 teaspoons of butter or margarine, and cook the crab cakes over medium heat for 4 minutes. (If you can cook only 4 crab cakes at a time, use half the oil and 1 remaining teaspoon of butter or margarine for each batch.) With a spatula, turn each crab cake carefully, and cook the cakes on the other side 4 minutes longer. ∎

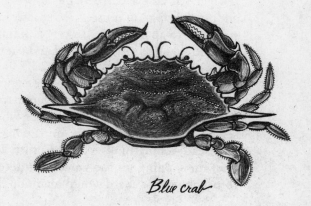

Blue crab

CIOPPINO

■

Californians, especially San Franciscans, like to take credit for inventing this spicy, tomato-based, Italian-style fish-and-shellfish stew (pronounced chuh-PEE-no). There is, however, a fish stew, *cioppin*, indigenous to Genoa, Italy, as well as a fish stew sans shellfish called *ciuppino*, enjoyed in Italy's Ligurian region. And one fish story has it that it was named for the Portuguese and Italian fishermen who would ask their neighbors to "chip in" seafood for the stew pot. Regardless of its provenance, it is delicious and versatile since it can be made with a wide variety of fish and shellfish, limited only by availability, taste, and budget. The stew is ideal for a large dinner party or buffet, although smaller gatherings should not be denied this treat.

Preparation tips: The sauce can be prepared in advance through step 2 and refrigerated or frozen. Be sure to bring it back to the boiling point before adding the clams or mussels. Alternatives include SCALLOPS (bay or halved sea scallops), CRAB LEGS, RED SNAPPER, HALIBUT, SEA BASS, or STRIPED BASS. The fish and shellfish can be cleaned and cut up while the sauce cooks.

Serving suggestions: I ladle the cioppino over capellini (the thinnest spaghetti). But any thin-stranded pasta, rice, mashed potatoes, egg noodles, or a macaroni that is not too dense would work as well. The stew may be served with or without an accompanying carbohydrate. However, do not forget bread—something small and crusty like a baguette (perhaps a sourdough one) for sopping up the sauce. Round out the meal with a green vegetable (broccoli rabe or chard would maintain the Italian theme) or a salad.

SAUCE

- 1 tablespoon olive oil
- 2 cups chopped onion
- ½ cup thinly sliced scallions, including some green tops
- 1 tablespoon minced garlic
- 1½ cups chopped green bell pepper
- ¾ cup chopped red bell pepper
- 1 cup diced celery
- 3 thin zucchinis (about ¾ pound), cut into ¼-inch slices
- ½ cup chopped fresh parsley, divided
- 1 28-ounce can plum (Roma) tomatoes, drained and juice reserved, chopped
- 1 16-ounce can tomato puree
- 1 6-ounce can tomato paste
- 2 cups dry red wine
- 2 teaspoons white-wine Worcestershire sauce

½ teaspoon Tabasco sauce
2 bay leaves
2 teaspoons dried basil, crumbled
1½ teaspoons sugar
1½ teaspoons dried thyme leaves, crumbled
1 teaspoon dried oregano leaves, crumbled
½ teaspoon red pepper flakes, or to taste
1½ teaspoons salt, or to taste
1 teaspoon freshly ground black pepper

FISH

18 SMALL CLAMS, well-scrubbed, or MUSSELS, debearded, in their shells
1 pound thick COD ("SCROD") FILLET, cut into 1-inch to 1½-inch cubes
¾ pound MONKFISH, cut into 1-inch cubes
½ pound SQUID, cut into ¼-inch rings or 1-inch pieces
1 pound MEDIUM TO LARGE SHRIMP, peeled and, if desired, deveined

1. To prepare the sauce, in a large (6-quart) nonstick pot that has a lid, briefly heat the olive oil. Add the onion, and sauté it for 3 minutes. Add the scallions and garlic, and sauté them for 1 to 2 minutes, taking care not to let the garlic burn. Add the green bell pepper, red bell pepper, celery, zucchinis, and ¼ cup of the parsley, and sauté the ingredients 2 minutes longer.

2. Add all the rest of the sauce ingredients, including the reserved juice from the tomatoes. Stir the ingredients to combine them well. Bring the mixture just to a boil over medium heat, reduce the heat to low, and simmer the sauce, uncovered, for 45 minutes, stirring it every 10 minutes or so. Remove and discard the bay leaves.

3. To prepare the fish, add the clams or mussels to the hot sauce, cover the pot, and cook the mixture over medium heat, checking after several minutes to see if the shellfish have begun to open. When the clams or mussels start to open, add the rest of the fish and shellfish, placing the shrimp on the top. Cover the pot, and simmer the stew for 5 to 7 minutes. Discard any unopened clams or mussels before serving the stew. Sprinkle the cioppino or individual servings with the remaining ¼ cup of chopped parsley. ∎

BOUILLABAISSE

■

I have loved this hearty stew for decades. But whenever I looked up a recipe for it, the long list of ingredients (and the many kinds of fish and shellfish called for) discouraged me from trying to make it myself. Then Piers Lewis, a good friend and efficient cook from St. Paul, Minnesota, served it at a supper party I attended. Knowing that he was not one to labor for hours in the kitchen or spring the entire week's food budget on one meal, I asked for his recipe. He explained that almost any combination of fish, including surimi (imitation crab), would work. His addition of rice makes this stew a complete meal if it is served with a salad. Here is my version.

Preparation tips: The bouillabaisse can be prepared in advance and gently reheated. But be careful not to overcook the fish. Alternatively, the soup can be prepared through step 2, reheated shortly before serving time, and then completed. Possible seafood substitutions are almost endless as long as the fish are boneless and not oily. If your soup kettle is not a nonstick one, you might want to do step 1 in a nonstick skillet, then transfer the sautéed vegetables to the larger pot.

1 tablespoon olive oil
1 cup chopped onion
1 cup chopped celery
1 teaspoon minced garlic
1 leek, diced and well washed, *or* 2 shallots, finely chopped
2 teaspoons fresh thyme leaves *or* 1 teaspoon dried thyme leaves
1 bay leaf
1 16-ounce can tomatoes, drained and juice reserved, chopped, *or* 2 cups crushed tomatoes
1 cup dry white wine
1 cup clam juice
1 cup water
1/4 cup chopped fennel bulb *or* 1/2 teaspoon crushed fennel seeds
2 tablespoons chopped fresh parsley
1/8 teaspoon saffron (optional)
Salt to taste (optional)
Freshly ground black pepper to taste
1 pound skinless FIRM FISH FILLETS (for example, red snapper, cod ("scrod"), catfish, walleye, orange roughy)
1 pound SCALLOPS, halved crosswise if large
1/2 pound SURIMI STICKS, halved lengthwise and sliced crosswise into 1-inch pieces

½ pound PEELED SHRIMP, halved crosswise if large, *or* other shellfish (such as clam or oyster meats)
1 tablespoon minced cilantro (optional)
2 to 3 cups *cooked* white rice (1 to 1½ cups dry rice)

1. In a 5-quart or 6-quart nonstick soup pot or Dutch oven (see "Preparation tips"), briefly heat the olive oil. Add the onion, celery, garlic, leek or shallots, thyme, and bay leaf, and sauté the ingredients over medium heat for about 5 minutes.
2. Add the tomatoes and their juice, wine, clam juice, water, fennel or fennel seeds, parsley, saffron (if desired), salt (if desired), and pepper. Bring the ingredients to a boil, reduce the heat to medium-low, and simmer the ingredients for 15 minutes.
3. Add all the fish and shellfish, and cook the stew over medium-low heat 15 minutes longer. Remove the bay leaf, and stir in the cilantro (if desired).
4. To serve the bouillabaisse, place ⅓ to ½ cup of the rice in each bowl, and ladle the stew over the rice. ∎

CAJUN CATFISH STEW

■

8 SERVINGS

Even though the consumption of catfish has spread from the Deep South throughout the nation, southern-style preparations remain among the best ways to show off the virtues of this sweet, firm-fleshed fish. Here is a colorful catfish recipe I devised that I serve over pasta.

Preparation tips: MONKFISH is an excellent alternative to catfish in this recipe. SWORDFISH would work well, too. Other vegetable possibilities include cut green beans and corn. Cajun spice mix is now sold in many supermarkets. But you can make your own by processing in the container of a blender or food processor 1/2 cup of sweet paprika, 2 tablespoons of cayenne, 2 tablespoons of freshly ground black pepper, 1 tablespoon of dried oregano leaves, 1 tablespoon of dried thyme leaves, 1 tablespoon of onion powder, 1 1/2 teaspoons of celery seeds, and 3/4 teaspoon of garlic powder (yield: 1 cup).

Serving suggestions: I love this stew over a black squid-ink pasta (calamari-flavored) such as a ricciolini. But it also works well with a plain pasta that is shaped to catch the sauce. Or you can skip the pasta and serve a hearty, crusty bread. Freshly grated Parmesan added just before serving the stew provides a nice finishing touch.

1 1/2 pounds THICK CATFISH FILLETS, cut into 1-inch pieces
    1 teaspoon (approximately) Cajun spice mix (see "Preparation tips"), divided
    1 tablespoon olive oil *or* canola oil
    2 cups diced onion (1/2-inch dice)
    1 tablespoon minced garlic
    2 cups diced celery (3 to 4 large ribs, cut into 1/2-inch dice)
    1 large green bell pepper, cored, seeded, and cut into 3/4-inch dice
    1 large red bell pepper, cored, seeded, and cut into 3/4-inch dice
  3/4 pound carrots, halved lengthwise, cut into 1/4-inch slices (about 2 cups)
1 1/2 pounds potatoes, peeled and cut into 1/2-inch dice (about 3 cups)
    3 small zucchinis (about 3/4 pound), halved lengthwise, then cut crosswise into
        1/2-inch slices
    2 cups fresh or frozen peas (optional)
    1 28-ounce can tomatoes, drained and juice reserved, cut into 3/4-inch pieces
  3/4 cup dry white wine
    1 teaspoon dried thyme leaves
  1/2 teaspoon red pepper flakes, or to taste
    1 teaspoon salt, or to taste (optional)
  1/2 teaspoon freshly ground white pepper, or to taste

1. Wash and dry the fish, and sprinkle it generously with the Cajun spice mix. Set the fish aside.
2. Briefly heat the olive oil or canola oil in a large saucepan (5 or 6 quarts) or Dutch oven that has a lid and, preferably, a nonstick surface. Add the onion and garlic, and sauté the vegetables for 3 minutes or until they are soft. Add the celery, green bell pepper, and red bell pepper, and sauté the vegetables 3 minutes longer.
3. Add the carrots, potatoes, zucchinis, fresh peas (if desired), tomatoes with their juice, wine, $\frac{1}{2}$ teaspoon of the Cajun spice mix, thyme, red pepper flakes, salt (if desired), and ground pepper, stirring the ingredients to combine them. Bring the ingredients to a boil over medium-high heat, reduce the heat, cover the pan, and simmer the mixture for 5 minutes.
4. Gently stir in the frozen peas (if desired) and the reserved catfish, making sure the fish is covered with liquid. Simmer the stew for 5 to 6 minutes or until the fish and vegetables are just done. ∎

FISH STEW WITH FRESH SALSA

■

4 TO 6 SERVINGS

This simple stew has a lot going for it. It is versatile—I've eaten it for breakfast, lunch, and dinner; it can be prepared without having to rely on a ready-made stock because it makes its own broth; it is adaptable (I've used several kinds of fish and various vegetables, according to availability); and it is highly nutritious and low in fat.

Preparation tips: Fish alternatives include COD, ROCKFISH, HALIBUT, or other thick white fish fillets or steaks. If thin zucchini are unavailable, slice larger ones lengthwise once or twice before making crosswise slices. The stew can be prepared completely in advance and reheated in the microwave oven or on top of the stove. The salsa can be made several days in advance. Or you can substitute a commercial salsa.

Serving suggestions: For a complete meal, serve the stew over cooked rice. Start cooking the rice when you start preparing the stew. Cook 1 cup of white or brown rice in 2 cups of water and ¼ teaspoon of salt. Place about ½ cup of rice in each serving bowl, and top the rice with the stew. The salsa can be passed around as a topping or mixed into the stew just before serving.

SALSA
- 2 cups peeled, chopped fresh tomatoes
- ⅓ cup finely chopped onion
- 2 tablespoons seeded, minced jalapeños (about 2 peppers)
- 1 teaspoon minced garlic
- 2 tablespoons minced cilantro
- 1 tablespoon red-wine vinegar
- 2 teaspoons olive oil *or* canola oil
- ¼ teaspoon salt
- Dash Tabasco sauce (optional)

FISH AND BROTH
- 3½ cups water
- 2 tablespoons fresh lemon juice
- 2 teaspoons white-wine Worcestershire sauce
- 1 bay leaf
- 2 sprigs parsley
- 1 whole clove garlic, peeled
- ⅛ teaspoon Tabasco sauce
- ½ teaspoon salt, or to taste
- ¼ teaspoon freshly ground black pepper
- 1 pound POLLOCK FILLETS, cut into 1-inch cubes

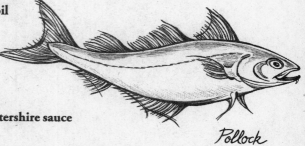

Pollock

STEW INGREDIENTS

1 tablespoon olive oil
1 cup finely chopped onion
1 cup diced green bell pepper
1 teaspoon minced garlic
2 cups thinly sliced carrots
1 cup thinly sliced celery
1 cup corn kernels
1 14-ounce can black beans, drained and rinsed, *or* 1²/₃ cups cooked black beans
½ pound zucchinis, preferably thin ones, thinly sliced (see "Preparation tips")
½ teaspoon salt, or to taste
½ teaspoon freshly ground black pepper, or to taste
2 tablespoons minced fresh parsley for garnish
1 tablespoon minced cilantro for garnish

TO PREPARE THE SALSA

1. In a nonreactive bowl, combine all the salsa ingredients. Cover and chill the salsa, but bring it to room temperature before serving it.

TO PREPARE THE FISH AND BROTH

2. In a large saucepan, combine all the ingredients for the fish and broth *except the fish.* Bring the ingredients to a boil, add the fish, return the ingredients to a boil, reduce the heat, and simmer the fish for 5 minutes.

3. Remove the pot from the heat. Pour the contents of the pot into a colander set over a large bowl, and reserve the broth. Discard the bay leaf, parsley sprigs, and garlic clove, and set the fish aside, keeping it warm.

TO PREPARE THE STEW

4. Wipe out the saucepan, and briefly heat the olive oil. Add the onion, green bell pepper, and garlic, and sauté the vegetables for 3 minutes over medium-low heat.

5. Add the reserved broth, carrots, celery, corn, and black beans. Bring the ingredients to a boil, reduce the heat, and simmer the mixture for 10 minutes.

6. Add the zucchinis, and simmer the mixture 3 minutes longer.

7. Add the reserved fish, and simmer the mixture for 2 minutes or until the vegetables are just tender and the fish is heated through. Season the stew with the salt and ground pepper, and garnish the stew with the parsley and cilantro.

8. Serve the stew with the salsa (see "Serving suggestions"). ■

MOROCCAN MONKFISH STEW
■

4 TO 6 SERVINGS

Moroccan seasonings and seafood have a natural affinity for one another, and monkfish is ideal for this nutritious, colorful, delicious dish.

Preparation tips: CATFISH is an excellent substitute for monkfish in this stew. If the stew is prepared in advance to be reheated at serving time, do not cook the stew longer than 5 minutes in step 4.

Serving suggestion: Try serving the stew over rice pilaf or, for a more traditional approach, couscous (simply add 3 cups of boiling broth to 1 1/2 cups of couscous, let the couscous stand for 5 minutes or until all the broth has been absorbed, then fluff the grain with a fork).

1/4 cup sliced almonds
1 tablespoon olive oil *or* canola oil
1 medium onion, halved lengthwise and thinly sliced crosswise
2 teaspoons minced garlic
2 cups chicken broth
2 teaspoons paprika
1 1/2 teaspoons ground coriander
1/2 teaspoon cayenne
1/4 teaspoon turmeric
1/2 teaspoon salt, or to taste
1/4 teaspoon freshly ground black pepper
2 medium carrots, thinly sliced on the diagonal (about 1 1/2 cups)
1 cup cooked chickpeas
1 medium zucchini, halved lengthwise and sliced crosswise (about 1 1/2 cups)
1 medium red bell pepper, cored, seeded, and cut into strips 1/3 inch × 1 1/2 inches
1 pound MONKFISH, sliced into strips 2 inches × 1 inch × 1/3 inch thick

1. In a skillet over low heat or on a baking sheet in an oven that has been heated to 350°F, toast the almonds until they begin to turn golden (about 8 minutes), tossing them several times to be sure that they do not burn. Set the almonds aside.
2. Briefly heat the olive oil or canola oil in a large nonstick skillet that has a lid, add the onion, and sauté it over medium heat for about 5 minutes. Add the garlic, and sauté the vegetables 1 minute longer.

3. Add the broth, paprika, coriander, cayenne, turmeric, salt, and ground pepper, stirring the ingredients to combine them. Add the carrots and chickpeas, bring the mixture to a boil, reduce the heat to medium-low, and simmer the ingredients for 5 minutes.

4. Add the zucchini, red bell pepper, and monkfish, and bring the mixture back to a boil. Reduce the heat to medium-low, cover the skillet, and simmer the stew for 8 minutes or until the fish is done and the vegetables are tender.

5. Serve the stew sprinkled with the reserved toasted almonds. ∎

CODFISH AND CLAM STEW
■

This simple stew is gently seasoned with saffron, which raises an "ordinary" fish like cod to an extraordinary level. Don't let the long ingredients list intimidate you; most of the items are seasonings.

Preparation tips: The entire dish can be prepared in advance and gently reheated at serving time or (preferably) prepared ahead through step 3, and the olives and fish added when the sauce is reheated for serving. The "hotness" of the stew can be controlled by adding to or eliminating the red pepper flakes or jalapeño, but the two really do add zip to the dish. Fresh tomatoes, especially in season, are preferable to the canned ones, which can be used in a pinch. If you can get fresh basil, use it both in the cooking of the stew and at the end; if only dried is available, use it just when cooking the sauce. Pitted black olives or cured olives can be substituted for the green olives, if you wish; halve the olives crosswise if only large ones are available. Add the clams to the stew if additional texture is desired.

Serving suggestions: I successfully served this stew over mashed potatoes. But it would also go well with rice, spaghetti, or egg noodles. A green vegetable or salad completes the meal.

 2 teaspoons olive oil *or* canola oil
 3 cups thinly sliced onion
 1 tablespoon minced garlic
 2 tablespoons seeded, minced jalapeño (about 2 peppers)
 1 cup dry white wine
 1/4 teaspoon crushed saffron
 4 tablespoons (1/4 cup) chopped fresh parsley, divided
 2 bay leaves
 1 tablespoon minced fresh basil *or* 1 teaspoon dried basil
 1/2 teaspoon dried oregano leaves
 1/8 teaspoon red pepper flakes
 2 cups chopped plum (Roma) tomatoes (about 6 fresh tomatoes)
 1 cup tomato puree
 1/2 teaspoon salt, or to taste
 1 teaspoon freshly ground black pepper
 1/2 cup small pimiento-stuffed green olives
 1 to 2 cups small SHUCKED CLAMS OR CHOPPED CLAMS, raw or canned (optional—see "Preparation tips")
1 1/2 pounds COD FILLETS, cut into 1-inch cubes
 2 tablespoons slivered fresh basil (optional—see "Preparation tips")

1. Briefly heat the olive oil or canola oil in a large, nonstick saucepan (5 to 6 quarts), and add the onion. Sauté the onion, stirring it often, over a medium-low heat for 5 minutes. Add the garlic and jalapeño, and sauté the vegetables 2 minutes longer, taking care not to let the garlic burn.

2. Add the wine and saffron, bring the ingredients to a simmer, and cook them gently for 5 minutes.

3. Add 2 tablespoons of the parsley, bay leaves, minced or dried basil, oregano, red pepper flakes, tomatoes, tomato puree, salt, and pepper. Bring the ingredients to the boiling point, and simmer the sauce over medium-low heat for 15 minutes.

4. Add the olives, clams (if desired), and cod. Simmer the stew for 7 to 10 minutes or until the clams and fish are just cooked through. Before serving the stew, remove the bay leaves, and stir in the remaining parsley and the slivered basil (if desired). ■

Cod

SPANISH-AMERICAN SHRIMP AND OKRA STEW
■

Many people avoid okra because they associate this highly nutritious vegetable with sliminess. But if okra is prepared whole and is not overcooked, none of its natural gums (which in fact are desirable cholesterol-lowering soluble fibers) touches the palate when the vegetable is consumed. On the other hand, those who enjoy a gumbolike texture should consider using larger okra and cutting them into bite-sized pieces.

Preparation tips: It is important to use small, tender okra if you are using them whole. Trim just the stem ends without cutting into the fleshy part. If you can get only large okra, they should be cut into pieces that are 1 1/2 inches to 2 inches long. Frozen okra can be substituted, but they should be added to the stew at the same time the shrimp and corn are added (in step 3) and cooked for 5 minutes at most.

Serving suggestions: This stew goes wonderfully with rice—white, brown, or mixed. If you prefer a pasta, use a small, tender macaroni like orzo.

    1 **tablespoon olive oil** *or* **canola oil**
    1 **cup sliced Spanish onion** *or* **white onion**
    2 **teaspoons minced garlic**
    1 **jalapeño or green chili, seeded and finely chopped, or to taste**
 1/4 **teaspoon red pepper flakes, or to taste**
    1 **14-ounce can plum (Roma) tomatoes, drained and juice reserved, cut into**
      1/2-inch slices
    2 **tablespoons fresh lime juice** *or* **fresh lemon juice**
    2 **tablespoons chopped fresh oregano** *or* **1 teaspoon dried oregano leaves**
 1/4 **teaspoon salt, or to taste**
 3/4 **pound small okra, ends trimmed (see "Preparation tips")**
 1/3 **cup small pimiento-stuffed green olives**
    1 **pound** MEDIUM SHRIMP, **peeled and, if desired, deveined**
    2 **cups fresh or frozen corn kernels**
Freshly ground black pepper to taste
 1/4 **cup chopped fresh parsley** *or* **2 tablespoons chopped cilantro**

1. Briefly heat the olive oil or canola oil in a 4-quart or 5-quart nonstick kettle or Dutch oven that has a lid, and add the onion, garlic, jalapeño or chili, and red pepper flakes. Sauté the ingredients, stirring them often, for 3 minutes or until they are just tender.
2. Add the tomatoes and their juice, lime or lemon juice, oregano, and salt. Bring the ingredients to a boil, reduce the heat to medium, and add the

okra and olives. Cover the pot, and simmer the ingredients for about 10 minutes (depending on the size of the okra—mine were about 2 inches long).

3. Add the shrimp, corn, and ground pepper. Cover the pot, and cook the stew over medium-low heat 5 minutes longer.

4. Serve the stew sprinkled with the parsley or cilantro. ■

SQUID AND CHARD STEW
■

4 TO 6 SERVINGS

This was a delicious surprise. Once again I was looking for novel ways to use my garden crop of chard. This quick-cooking Italian-style dish was the result.

Serving suggestion: This stew is lovely with rice, pasta (for example, a tomato or sweet-red-pepper linguine), or a simple, crusty Italian bread.

- 1 tablespoon olive oil
- 1 cup finely chopped onion
- 1 1/2 cups finely chopped fennel bulb (1 medium bulb)
- 1 tablespoon chopped fennel leaves ("feathers"—optional)
- 1 large stalk celery, chopped
- 1 tablespoon chopped celery leaves
- 1 tablespoon chopped fresh parsley
- 1 teaspoon minced garlic
- 1 pound chard, stems finely chopped and leaves coarsely chopped
- 2 pounds cleaned SQUID, bodies sliced in rings and tentacles cut into 1-inch lengths
- 2 cups fresh peeled and coarsely chopped tomatoes, *or* 1 14 1/2-ounce can tomatoes, drained and juice reserved, coarsely chopped
- 1 teaspoon salt, or to taste
- 3/4 teaspoon freshly ground black pepper

1. Briefly heat the olive oil in a large nonstick saucepan that has a lid. Add the onion, fennel bulb, fennel leaves (if desired), celery, celery leaves, parsley, and garlic. Sauté the vegetables, stirring them often, for 5 minutes.

2. Add the chard, cover the pot, and cook the vegetables over medium-low heat 5 minutes longer.

3. Add the squid, fresh tomatoes or canned tomatoes with their juice, salt, and pepper. Bring the mixture to a boil, reduce the heat, cover the pot, and simmer the stew for 5 minutes or until the squid is just done. (Do not overcook the squid, or it will become tough.) ■

TRIPLE-S SEAFOOD CHILI

∎

What makes chili chili are the seasonings, the consistency, and the beans. So why not replace the meat in chili con carne with seafood? Adding fish of three different textures turns chili into a healthful gourmet delight. I deliberately held back on the seasonings lest the seafood get lost, and I made sure to use seafood with enough texture to make its presence felt.

Preparation tip: If you choose to do some advance preparation, you can cook the chili through step 2. But to avoid overcooking the seafood, it is best to add it to the hot sauce shortly before serving time.

Serving suggestions: As with all chilis, this one goes best with rice. But it can also be served with mashed potatoes or orzo.

    1 tablespoon olive oil *or* canola oil
 1½ cups chopped onion
    2 tablespoons seeded, minced jalapeño (about 2 peppers)
    4 teaspoons minced garlic
    1 large red bell pepper, roasted, peeled, cored, seeded, and chopped, *or*
      ¾ cup chopped roasted peppers from a jar
    2 28-ounce cans tomatoes, drained and juice reserved, chopped
    2 tablespoons dry white wine
    2 tablespoons mild chili powder
   ½ teaspoon hot chili powder (optional)
 1½ teaspoons dried oregano leaves, crumbled
    1 teaspoon cumin
   ½ teaspoon dry mustard powder (do not substitute prepared mustard)
   ¼ teaspoon celery seeds
   ⅛ teaspoon cayenne, or to taste
   ½ teaspoon salt
   ½ teaspoon freshly ground black pepper
    1 16-ounce can black beans, drained and rinsed
    1 pound MAKO SHARK (or other shark), cut into 1-inch cubes
   ¾ pound SEA SCALLOPS, sliced in half crosswise
   ¾ pound cleaned SQUID, bodies cut into ¼-inch rings and
      tentacles cut into 1-inch pieces
   ½ cup chopped fresh parsley

1. Briefly heat the olive oil or canola oil in a large nonstick saucepan (5 to 6 quarts). Add the onion, and sauté it over medium-low heat for about 3 minutes. Add the jalapeño, garlic, and red bell pepper or roasted pepper, and sauté the vegetables, stirring them often, 3 minutes longer.

2. Add the tomatoes with their juice, wine, mild chili powder, hot chili powder (if desired), oregano, cumin, mustard powder, celery seeds, cayenne, salt, and ground pepper. Stir the ingredients to combine them well. Bring the mixture to the boiling point, reduce the heat, and simmer the mixture for 30 minutes.

3. Add the beans and shark, and cook the chili for 5 minutes. Then add the scallops and squid, and cook the chili for another 5 minutes or until the seafood is just cooked. Stir in the parsley before serving the chili. ∎

Mako shark

Squid

MUSSELS TO REMEMBER

■

8 FIRST-COURSE SERVINGS OR 4 MAIN-DISH SERVINGS

Mussels are nature's gift to weight-conscious, health-conscious gourmets: low in calories, fat, and cholesterol yet succulent and exquisite when steamed open and piled high in a shallow bowl or tossed, savory broth and all, with pasta and tangy wilted greens. I enjoy them piping hot, at room temperature, and chilled.

Preparation tips: Be sure to rinse the mussels well (no soaking necessary) and to debeard them carefully (see page 78) since they will be consumed as is when they emerge from the pot. If you will be serving them over pasta (and even if not), you might toss in about ½ pound of tender mustard greens or arugula during the last minute or so of steaming.

Serving suggestions: These are divine over pasta (see "Preparation tips"). French or Italian bread is also superb for sopping up the broth. If you use whole chilis, either remove them before serving the mussels or caution diners not to eat them. Be sure to give diners extra bowls in which to place the empty shells.

   1 **tablespoon olive oil**
  ³/4 **cup chopped onion**
   4 **teaspoons minced garlic**
   8 **whole dried chili peppers or ¼ to ½ teaspoon red pepper flakes**
  ½ **cup dry white wine**
   4 **pounds MUSSELS, cleaned and debearded**

1. In a large kettle (6 quarts or more) with a tight-fitting lid, briefly heat the olive oil. Add the onion, garlic, and chili peppers or red pepper flakes, and sauté the vegetables, stirring them often, over medium-low heat for 3 minutes or until the onion is soft.
2. Add the wine and mussels to the pot, and toss the ingredients to coat the mussels with the vegetable-wine mixture. Raise the heat to high, and, when the liquid reaches a boil, toss the ingredients once more, reduce the heat to medium-high, cover the pot, and steam the mussels for 5 minutes. Remove the pot from the heat, and let it stand, covered, 1 minute longer.
3. If the mussels are to be served with pasta, be sure to ladle some of the broth into the bowls along with the mussels. Discard any mussels that have not opened. ■

Great on the Grill

In America, grilling has long been a favorite way of cooking. Indeed, some of my friends—including a few who live in the frequently frozen land of Minnesota—grill outdoors year round. The grill is a perfect way to prepare many kinds of fish and shellfish, as you will see from the recipes that follow. I have several gas-powered grills (one each in Brooklyn, Woodstock, and Minnesota, the places where I do a significant amount of cooking) and have equipped them all with permanent ceramic bricks (in place of lava) to reduce flare-up. The bricks, available in most places where grills are sold, also produce an even cooking surface and are self-cleaning.

Warning: When using a commercial vegetable-oil spray to grease a grill grate, you must remove the hot grate from the grill before you spray it to guard against a flare-up that could burn you.

SKEWERED SWORDFISH

■

Skewers are ideal for grilling bits of food. But they perform other functions as well—for example, when vegetables and meats are joined, they absorb flavors from one another. There is also something entertaining about skewered food. I've seen children who dislike fish gobble it up after it came off a skewer. In fact, this swordfish dish was just such a success with several not-too-fond-of-fish children I know.

Preparation tip: The kind of skewers you use makes a difference in terms of convenience. While I prefer wooden skewers because they are gentler to the fish, they need to be soaked in water first to keep them from burning, and it helps further to put bits of foil on the ends of each skewer after the food has been placed on it. Metal skewers, on the other hand, are not only easier to deal with, but are indestructible. The most convenient kind comes with a frame that allows you to fit the skewers into notches and turn them in place easily.

Serving suggestion: These kebabs go beautifully with rice that has been cooked with chopped red and green bell peppers.

KEBABS
- 1 to 1¼ pounds SWORDFISH steak, about 1 inch thick
- 1 medium zucchini (about ½ pound)
- 1 medium red bell pepper (about ⅓ pound)
- 1 red onion (about ½ pound)
- 18 cherry tomatoes
- 6 skewers

Vegetable-oil spray *or* vegetable oil for brushing the grill grate

MARINADE
- 1 tablespoon olive oil
- 2 tablespoons Dijon-style mustard
- 2 tablespoons honey
- 1 tablespoon dry sherry
- 1 tablespoon fresh lemon juice

Salt to taste
Freshly ground black pepper to taste

1. Slice away the skin, if any, of the swordfish steak, and cut the fish into 18 cubes about 1 inch each.
2. Wash and dry the zucchini, and slice it into 18 rounds. Cut the pepper and onion into 18 pieces each.
3. Combine all the marinade ingredients in a large bowl. Add the fish and the vegetables, including the cherry tomatoes, and toss the ingredients to coat them thoroughly with the marinade. Cover the bowl, and chill it for 1 hour.
4. Start the grill.
5. Reserving the marinade, remove the fish and vegetables from the bowl, and string the individual ingredients alternately on the 6 skewers, using 3 pieces of each ingredient on each skewer.
6. When the grill is hot, remove the hot grill grate, spray or brush the grate with the vegetable oil, then replace the grate on the grill. Place the skewers on the hot grill, and cook the kebabs for 4 to 5 minutes, basting the kebabs twice with the marinade. Turn the skewers, and grill the kebabs for another 4 to 5 minutes, basting the kebabs twice. ■

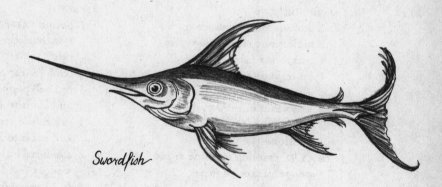

Swordfish

HAWAIIAN FISH KEBABS

∎

5 TO 6 SERVINGS

Kebabs are a joy to anyone who grills. They can be set up in advance on skewers, and they cook quickly over hot coals. With seafood kebabs, the result is tasty, moist fish that is just cooked through as well as tender-crisp vegetables. The Catfish Institute suggested this simple, delicious, colorful alternative to the traditional meat kebab. I made some changes in the marinade and added red bell pepper to the skewers.

Preparation tips: SWORDFISH is a fine (albeit more costly) alternative to the catfish used here. Fish kebabs work best on strong wooden skewers (metal ones can overcook the fish), but be sure to soak the skewers for 20 minutes or longer before preparing the kebabs. If you use metal skewers, try to use thin ones. If the fish fillets are thin, cut them into pieces 1 × 2 inches, and fold the long side in half when placing the fillets on the skewers. The kebabs can also be cooked in a broiler.

MARINADE
- 2 tablespoons soy sauce
- 2 tablespoons fresh lime juice
- 4 teaspoons Asian sesame oil
- 1 tablespoon peeled, grated gingerroot
- 2 teaspoons minced garlic
- 2 tablespoons finely chopped scallions
- ¼ to ½ teaspoon cayenne *or* red pepper flakes, to taste

KEBABS
- 1 pound CATFISH FILLETS, cut into 1-inch pieces (see "Preparation tips")
- ½ fresh pineapple, cut into chunks
- 1 red bell pepper, cored, seeded, and cut into 1-inch squares
- 1 green bell pepper, cored, seeded, and cut into 1-inch squares
- 1 small red onion, cut into 1-inch wedges
- 10 to 12 wooden skewers, soaked for 20 minutes, *or* thin metal skewers

Vegetable-oil spray *or* vegetable oil for brushing the grill grate

1. To a jar with a tight-fitting lid, add all the marinade ingredients, and shake them well.
2. Place the catfish in a shallow, nonreactive bowl or pan, and pour the marinade over the fish, tossing the fish to coat it thoroughly with the marinade. Cover the bowl or pan, and chill the fish for 30 minutes or longer.
3. Start the grill.

4. Reserving the marinade, remove the fish from the bowl or pan. String the pineapple, vegetables, and fish on the skewers, starting and ending with pieces of bell pepper. Brush the skewers on all sides with the remaining marinade.

5. When the grill is hot, remove the hot grill grate, spray or brush the grate with the vegetable oil, then replace the grate on the grill. Place the skewers on the hot grill, and cook the kebabs for 4 minutes on each side or until the fish is just cooked through. ■

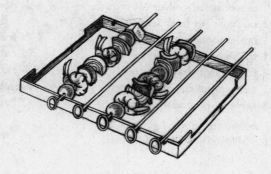

MONKFISH AND PINEAPPLE KEBABS

■

4 SERVINGS

This is a sweeter and simpler version of the Hawaiian Fish Kebabs on page 440. Although the flavorings are similar, the effect is quite different since the dish contains no vegetables.

Preparation tips: Monkfish sold in the stores frequently has a thin membrane covering some of the flesh; remove it with your fingers or a sharp knife, losing as little of the white flesh as possible. If you use wooden skewers, remember to soak them for 20 minutes or longer before preparing the kebabs.

Serving suggestion: Serve the kebabs over wild rice, garnishing each plate with sliced steamed bok choy or asparagus.

MARINADE

- 1/4 cup reduced-sodium soy sauce
- 2 tablespoons fresh lemon juice
- 1 tablespoon dry sherry
- 1 tablespoon Asian sesame oil
- 1/4 teaspoon Tabasco sauce
- 1 tablespoon chopped chives
- 1 tablespoon peeled, minced gingerroot
- 1 tablespoon minced garlic

KEBABS

- 1 1/4 pounds MONKFISH, cut into 1-inch cubes (32 pieces)
- 1/2 fresh pineapple, cut in 1-inch cubes (32 pieces)
- 8 skewers

Vegetable-oil spray *or* vegetable oil for brushing the grill grate

1. To a medium-sized bowl, add all the marinade ingredients, combining them well.
2. Add the fish and pineapple pieces to the marinade, tossing the ingredients to mix them well. Cover the bowl, and refrigerate it for 30 minutes or longer.
3. Start the grill.
4. Reserving the marinade, remove the fish and pineapple from the bowl. On each of the 8 skewers, alternate pieces of fish and pineapple until you have 4 of each ingredient on each skewer.
5. When the grill is hot, remove the hot grill grate, spray or brush the grate with the vegetable oil, then replace the grate on the grill. Place the skewers on the hot grill, and cook the kebabs, brushing them occasionally with the marinade, for 3 to 4 minutes on each side or until the fish is just cooked through. ■

GRILLED TUNA WITH ROSEMARY AND THYME

■

4 SERVINGS

Tuna is fabulous on the grill as long as it is not overcooked and, thus, dried out. However, you do not have to go to the extreme of some chefs who simply sear the fish on the outside, barely warming its interior. The sprigs of thyme in this recipe burn away as they come in contact with the heat, leaving behind a hint of their aromatic flavor.

Preparation tip: The grill must be hot for two reasons: you want attractive charred grill marks on the fish, and the initial high temperature will help to prevent sticking.

1¼ **pounds** TUNA STEAKS, **cut into 4 portions**
   2 **teaspoons olive oil**
   1 **tablespoon fresh lemon juice**
   1 **tablespoon chopped fresh rosemary** *or* 1 **teaspoon dried rosemary**
   8 **sprigs fresh thyme**
Salt to taste
Freshly ground black pepper to taste
Vegetable-oil spray *or* **vegetable oil for brushing the grill grate**

GARNISHES
Compound butter (optional—see the recipe on page 509)
   1 **tablespoon chopped fresh chives**
   4 **lemon wedges**

1. Start the grill.
2. Brush the fish on both sides with the olive oil. Sprinkle the flesh side with the lemon juice and rosemary. Press two sprigs of thyme onto each portion, then sprinkle the fish with the salt and pepper. Cover the fish with plastic wrap, and allow it to sit for 5 to 10 minutes.
3. When the grill is hot, remove the hot grill grate, spray or brush the grate with the vegetable oil, then replace the grate on the grill. Place the fish steaks on the hot grill, and cook them for about 3 minutes. Turn the steaks, and grill them for 4 minutes or until the fish is just cooked through.
4. Remove the fish from the grill, and place it on individual plates. Put a thin slice (about ¼ inch thick) of compound butter in the center of each piece of fish (if desired). Sprinkle the fish with the chives, and serve each portion with a wedge of lemon. ■

GRILLED SALMON FILLET WITH SESAME AND SCALLIONS

■
                                                                    4 SERVINGS

Although I regard salmon as among the most delicious of fish, generally in need of little adornment, a marinade and garnish now and then provide pleasing variety. Farm-raised Atlantic salmon, though generally considered less flavorful than the Pacific sockeye salmon, a summer favorite, has the virtues of being less expensive and available year round.

Serving suggestions: A green vegetable like snow peas, sugar snaps, or broccoli, or a green leafy vegetable like spinach or chard looks lovely on the plate with the salmon. In keeping with the Asian theme of the marinade, you might also serve plain boiled rice as the carbohydrate, perhaps topped with the remaining marinade that has been heated to a simmer and cooked for 1 minute on the stovetop or in a microwave oven.

FISH

1¼ pounds SALMON FILLET, skin on
Vegetable-oil spray *or* vegetable oil for
   brushing the grill grate
 1 tablespoon toasted sesame seeds
¼ cup thinly sliced scallion greens

MARINADE

 2 tablespoons fresh lime juice
 2 tablespoons dry white wine *or* dry
   sherry
 2 tablespoons soy sauce
 2 teaspoons Asian sesame oil
 1 tablespoon peeled, minced
   gingerroot
 2 teaspoons minced garlic
⅛ teaspoon red pepper flakes *or* ½
   teaspoon freshly ground black
   pepper
¼ cup finely chopped scallions,
   white parts only

1. Rinse and pat dry the salmon. Remove any bones with a tweezers, needle-nose pliers, or your fingertips. Place the salmon skin side down in a nonreactive pan or on a platter with a lip.
2. Combine all the marinade ingredients in a bowl or jar that has a tight-fitting lid, mix them well, and pour them over the salmon. Then turn the salmon skin side up, cover the pan or platter with plastic wrap, and place the fish in the refrigerator for 30 minutes to 2 hours.
3. Start the grill.
4. When the grill is hot, remove the grill grate, and spray or brush the grate with the vegetable oil, then replace the grate on the grill. (You can also use

a hamburger-style 2-sided grate to facilitate turning the fish.) When you are sure the grate is hot, place the fish on it, flesh side down.

5. Grill the fish for about 5 minutes, then turn it, and grill it about 5 minutes longer or for a total of 10 minutes to the inch measured at the fish's thickest part. When the fish is done, remove it to a serving platter flesh side up, and sprinkle the fish with the sesame seeds and scallion greens. ■

Salmon

GRILLED TROUT LE GRENADIN
■

6 SERVINGS

One of the most delightful fish dishes I ever ordered in a restaurant was grilled fillets of brook trout with spinach, mushrooms, and assorted nuts. This masterpiece was prepared by Chef Jacques Fougers at Le Grenadin Restaurant in mid-Manhattan. I enticed the chef to share the recipe, which I then prepared, with some modifications, for an elegant dinner party. This is a special event, deserving of a small serving of the "no-no" beurre blanc. So little of this buttery sauce is needed that the sin is hardly worth mentioning. But if you are a nutritional purist, it can be omitted.

Preparation tips: Although the dish has many steps, most can be done well in advance of dinner. You can prepare the spinach and scallions, toast the nuts, sauté the vegetables, and start the beurre blanc ahead of time. You have three options for cooking the fish. It can be grilled on a fish grate over charcoal or on a gas grill; it can be "grilled" on the stovetop in a shallow cast-iron skillet that has a built-in grating; it can be broiled. Although beurre blanc is traditionally prepared at the last minute, you can start the recipe before grilling the fish and then whisk in the butter as soon as the fish is done.

Serving suggestion: Complete the meal with a nonassertive carbohydrate like rice or mashed potatoes or a puree of parsnips or rutabaga and carrots.

MAIN INGREDIENTS
- 2/3 cup coarsely chopped pecans
- 1/3 cup sliced almonds
- 1/3 cup pine nuts
- 2 teaspoons olive oil, divided
- 3/4 pound mushrooms, sliced

Salt to taste, divided
Freshly ground black pepper to taste, divided
- 1 large red bell pepper, cored, seeded, and cut into 1 1/2-inch slivers
- 1 large green bell pepper, cored, seeded, and cut into 1 1/2-inch slivers
- 1 tablespoon minced garlic
- 1 pound raw spinach, tough stems removed, well-washed, and dried
- 6 BROOK TROUT or RAINBOW TROUT FILLETS (about 5 to 6 ounces each)

Vegetable-oil spray
- 1/3 cup sliced scallions for garnish

BEURRE BLANC
- 2 tablespoons minced shallots
- 1/4 cup dry white wine
- 2 tablespoons white-wine vinegar
- 2 teaspoons fresh lemon juice
- 1/8 teaspoon salt

Freshly ground white pepper to taste
- 3 tablespoons well-chilled butter, cut into small cubes

Trout

1. In a heavy skillet over medium-low heat, toast the pecans and almonds, tossing them often, for about 5 minutes. Add the pine nuts, and continue toasting the nuts for 2 to 3 minutes or until the pine nuts begin to turn golden brown. Take care not to let the nuts burn. Remove the nuts from the pan, and set them aside.

2. Start the beurre blanc by combining the shallots, wine, vinegar, and lemon juice in a small saucepan. Boil the ingredients until most of the liquid has evaporated, leaving behind about 2 tablespoons of liquid. Set the pan aside.

3. Heat the grill or broiler (see "Preparation tips").

4. Briefly heat 1 teaspoon of the olive oil in a large nonstick skillet, and add the mushrooms. Season the mushrooms with the salt and ground pepper, and sauté them for 2 minutes or until they are just wilted. Remove the mushrooms from the pan, and set them aside.

5. Wipe out the skillet, and heat the remaining 1 teaspoon of olive oil. Add the red bell pepper, green bell pepper, and garlic, and sprinkle the vegetables with the salt and ground pepper. Sauté the peppers for 3 minutes or until they are tender-crisp. Return the mushrooms to the skillet, and set the skillet aside. If you prefer, the vegetables can be transferred to a bowl for later heating in a microwave oven.

6. Place a mound of the uncooked spinach on each of 6 plates. Sprinkle the reserved nuts over the spinach, and set the plates aside.

7. Spray both sides of the trout fillets with the vegetable oil, then sprinkle both sides of the fillets with the salt and ground pepper. Place the fish on the hot grill or in the hot broiler. Grill the fish about 2 minutes on each side, or broil the fish for 4 minutes on one side. Remove the fish from the heat, but keep it warm.

8. Place the skillet with the mushrooms and peppers over low heat, or, if you have transferred the ingredients to a bowl, reheat them in the microwave oven.

9. Quickly reheat to boiling the saucepan in which you started the beurre blanc. Add the salt and ground pepper. Reduce the heat to low. Add the pieces of butter to the pan one at a time, whisking the ingredients constantly until the sauce is thick and smooth. When all the butter has been incorporated into the sauce, remove the pan from the heat.

10. Distribute the hot mushrooms and peppers over the spinach and nuts. Place one fillet on top of each mound of vegetables and nuts, and spoon some beurre blanc over each fillet. Garnish each serving with a scant tablespoon of the sliced scallions. ∎

GRILLED BLUEFISH WITH SUN-DRIED TOMATO VINAIGRETTE
■

The pungent tomatoes in the nippy sauce are an excellent counterpoint to this full-flavored fish.

Preparation tips: Sun-dried tomatoes sold dry are preferable to those packed in oil. (Since the latter are sometimes salty, if you use them, do not automatically add any salt to the dressing.) If you start with dry tomatoes, soften them by letting them steep for 5 minutes or so in boiling water; then drain and pat them dry before you chop them. Chopped pimientos, which are milder, can be substituted for the tomatoes. Fresh herbs are much preferred in this vinaigrette, which should be prepared at least 1 hour before serving time.

Serving suggestions: Boiled potatoes sprinkled with parsley and steamed asparagus are a nice complement and can share the vinaigrette with this dish.

VINAIGRETTE

- 2 tablespoons Dijon-style mustard
- 2 tablespoons fresh lime juice
- 2 tablespoons apple-cider vinegar
- 2 tablespoons dry white wine
- 2 tablespoons extra-virgin olive oil
- 2 tablespoons finely chopped shallots
- 1 tablespoon finely chopped fresh tarragon *or* 1 teaspoon dried tarragon
- 1 teaspoon minced garlic
- 2 tablespoons chopped sun-dried tomatoes (see "Preparation tips")
- 2 tablespoons chopped fresh basil *or* 1 teaspoon dried basil

Freshly ground black pepper to taste

FISH

Vegetable-oil spray *or* vegetable oil for brushing the grill grate
- 4 BLUEFISH FILLETS, skin on (about 5 to 6 ounces each)

Salt to taste (optional)
Freshly ground black pepper to taste

1. To prepare the vinaigrette, in a medium-sized bowl, whisk together the mustard, lime juice, vinegar, wine, and olive oil. Blend in the shallots, tarragon, garlic, sun-dried tomatoes, basil, and pepper. Cover the bowl, and let the mixture stand at room temperature for about 1 hour so that the flavor can develop.
2. Start the grill.

3. When the grill is hot, remove the hot grill grate, spray or brush it with the vegetable oil, then replace the grate on the grill. Spray or brush the fish on both sides with the vegetable oil. Sprinkle the fillets with the salt (if desired) and pepper.

4. Place the fish, flesh side down, on the hot grill, and cook the fish for about 4 minutes. Turn the fish, and grill it on the skin side 3 to 4 minutes longer or until the fish is just done.

5. Transfer the fish to individual serving plates, and spoon a little of the vinaigrette over each fillet. Serve the remaining vinaigrette on the side. ∎

Bluefish

GRILLED SESAME MACKEREL

■

4 SERVINGS

Because it is relatively oily, mackerel is what some people call a "fishy" fish. But in this recipe, the pronounced, typically Asian flavors cut right through that oiliness. And the sesame seeds provide a pleasant crunch.

Preparation tips: Use a tweezers or needle-nose pliers to remove the bones down the center of the fillets. Other full-flavored fillets such as POMPANO, SALMON, or BLUEFISH would work as well. Be sure to leave enough time for the fish to marinate. The only difficulty with this recipe is in trying to turn the relatively thin fillets on the grill without breaking them. A fish grate and a wide or long spatula and barbecue-length oven mitt will help with this.

FISH

2 tablespoons sesame seeds
4 MACKEREL FILLETS, skin on (about 4 to 5 ounces each), bones removed
Vegetable-oil spray *or* vegetable oil for brushing the grill grate

MARINADE

½ cup fresh lemon juice
½ cup reduced-sodium soy sauce
2 teaspoons Asian sesame oil
2 teaspoons peeled, finely chopped gingerroot
1 teaspoon minced garlic
Freshly ground pepper to taste

1. Place the sesame seeds in a small, hot skillet over medium-low heat, and toss them continuously until they are lightly toasted. Set the seeds aside.
2. Place the mackerel in a nonreactive pan or wide, shallow bowl.
3. In a small bowl or 2-cup measuring cup, combine all the marinade ingredients. Pour the marinade over the fish, cover the pan or bowl with plastic wrap, and place the fish in the refrigerator for 20 minutes.
4. Start the grill.
5. When the grill is hot, remove the grill grate, spray or brush it with the vegetable oil, then replace the grate on the grill.
6. Place the mackerel, *skin side up,* on the hot grill, and grill the fish for about 4 minutes. Carefully turn the fish, and sprinkle the fillets with the reserved sesame seeds. Pat the seeds gently with a spatula to be sure they adhere to the fish. Grill the fish for 2 to 3 minutes or until the fish is just cooked through. ■

SALMON TERIYAKI

■

Anyone who has ever eaten in a Japanese restaurant has no doubt seen the various teriyaki preparations. Although commercial teriyaki sauces are widely sold, it is easy to make your own: it is essentially a sweetened soy sauce that is used as a glaze.

Preparation tip: Be sure to take the basting instruction seriously. Baste frequently so that the fish will darken and absorb the sweetness of the glaze.

SAUCE
- 3 tablespoons soy sauce
- 3 tablespoons honey
- 2 tablespoons dry sherry
- 2 teaspoons peeled, finely chopped gingerroot
- 2 teaspoons olive oil

FISH
- Vegetable-oil spray *or* vegetable oil for brushing the grill grate
- 4 boneless SALMON FILLETS, skin on (about 6 ounces each)

1. In a small bowl, combine all the sauce ingredients.
2. Start the grill.
3. When the grill is hot, remove the grill grate, spray or brush it with the vegetable oil, then replace the grate on the grill.
4. Place the salmon on a platter, and pour enough sauce over the fish to coat the fish thoroughly, reserving the rest of the sauce for basting.
5. Place the fish, *flesh side down,* on the hot grill, and grill the fish for 3 to 4 minutes, basting it several times with the reserved sauce. Turn the fillets, and continue grilling them, basting them frequently, for 3 to 4 minutes or until they are just done. ■

GRILLED SALMON WITH FENNEL

■

The delicately flavored fennel sauce enhances rather than distracts from the richness of grilled salmon. I prepared huge quantities of the sauce one day after finding large fennel bulbs at bargain-basement prices.

Preparation tips: The sauce should be made before the salmon is put on the grill; it can be prepared hours or even a day ahead and reheated at serving time.

Serving suggestions: The greenish-white sauce and pink fish look fabulous and taste even better over a bed of nippy greens like arugula or watercress. Or serve a dark-green vegetable side dish like peas, broccoli, chard, or spinach. Since this recipe makes a lot of sauce, if you have any left over (and you will), try it mixed with rice or orzo as a side dish.

SAUCE

    1 tablespoon olive oil *or* canola oil
    1 cup finely chopped white onion *or* ½ cup finely chopped shallots
    1 large or 2 small fennel bulbs (save some of the feathery leaves), finely chopped (about 3 cups)
    2 teaspoons orange liqueur
  ½ teaspoon salt, or to taste
Freshly ground black pepper to taste
    2 tablespoons finely chopped fresh parsley
    1 to 2 tablespoons finely chopped fennel leaves ("feathers")

FISH

    4 SALMON STEAKS, ¾ inch to 1 inch thick (about 6 ounces each)
Salt to taste
Freshly ground black pepper to taste
Vegetable-oil spray

1. Heat the grill to medium-hot.
2. To prepare the sauce, briefly heat the olive oil or canola oil in a large skillet that has a lid, add the onion or shallots, and sauté the vegetable for 2 minutes or until it softens. Add the fennel bulbs, orange liqueur, salt, and pepper, and sauté the ingredients until the vegetables are soft. Turn off the heat, and cover the pan to keep the sauce warm. Or, if you are making the sauce in advance, set it aside to be reheated before serving. Stir in the parsley and fennel leaves just before serving time.

3. Sprinkle the salmon with the salt and pepper, and spray the fish with the vegetable oil (or remove and spray the fish grate, if you are using one, and then replace it). Place the steaks on the hot grill. Grill the fish for about 5 minutes on one side, turn the fish, and grill the fish for 4 to 5 minutes on the second side.

4. While the steaks grill, reheat the sauce, if necessary, and add the parsley and fennel leaves if you have not already done so. Place ample portions of the sauce on individual platters, and top the sauce with the salmon. ∎

GRILLED HALIBUT WITH GUACAMOLE

■

I had just arrived in Minnesota for my annual summer stay on the scenic St. Croix River and had stopped only to stock up at a local fish market before I had to fix a meal. With the few ingredients I had carried in a cooler from New York, I was able to prepare this lovely summer dish for supper. Although avocados are rich, the fat they contain is the heart-sparing monounsaturated kind, and no other fat is added to the guacamole.

Preparation tip: The guacamole can be prepared an hour or two ahead and kept covered and chilled. But it should be brought back to room temperature before it is served.

Serving suggestion: In keeping with the summery tone of this dish, you might serve it with corn on the cob, grilled zucchini or yellow squash, and sliced fresh tomatoes.

GUACAMOLE
- 1 **medium to large ripe avocado**
- ½ **cup seeded and finely diced plum (Roma) tomatoes**
- ¼ **cup finely chopped onion**
- 1 **tablespoon seeded, minced jalapeño (about 1 pepper)**
- 1 **teaspoon crushed or finely minced garlic**
- 4 **teaspoons fresh lime juice**
- 2 **dashes Tabasco sauce**
- ¼ **teaspoon salt, or to taste**

FISH
- 4 **SMALL HALIBUT STEAKS (about 6 ounces each)**
- **Vegetable-oil spray**
- 2 **teaspoons fresh lime juice**
- ½ **teaspoon (approximately) hot *and/or* mild chili powder**
- **Salt to taste, divided**
- **Freshly ground black pepper to taste, divided**

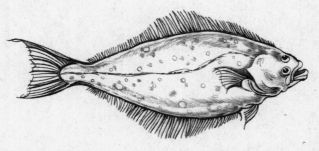

Halibut

1. Start the grill.
2. To prepare the guacamole, peel the avocado, remove the flesh from the pit, and place the flesh in a bowl. Mash it with a fork, leaving some small lumps. Add all the remaining ingredients for the guacamole, mixing the ingredients to combine them well. Cover the bowl with plastic wrap, and let it stand at room temperature (see "Preparation tip").
3. Rinse the fish, and pat it dry. Spray the steaks on both sides with the vegetable oil, then sprinkle the steaks on one side with the lime juice, chili powder, salt, and pepper. When the grill is ready, place the fish, seasoned side down, on a rack over the hot coals. Grill the steaks for 5 minutes, sprinkle them with additional salt and pepper, turn them, and grill them several minutes longer (a total of about 10 minutes for each inch of thickness).
4. Set the steaks chili-seasoned side up on individual plates. To serve the fish, drape one-fourth of the guacamole like a belt over each steak. ∎

GRILLED MARLIN WITH MANDARIN ORANGE SALSA

■
                                                                    4 SERVINGS

Marlin is a large ocean fish similar to, but usually less expensive than, sword-fish. Since, like swordfish, marlin can dry out when cooked, a pregrilling marinade helps to keep it moist. Add an interesting sauce like the one below and you have an elegant dish. One of the best supermarkets in the Midwest, Byerly's in the suburbs of Minneapolis, provided the basic recipe that I adapted.

Preparation tips: You can use SWORDFISH or TUNA steaks or any firm-tex-tured fish suitable for grilling or broiling in place of the marlin. The fish should marinate for 30 minutes or longer. As an alternative to grilling, the steaks can also be cooked in a hot broiler on a greased slotted broiler pan placed about 4 inches from the heat. In either case, the 10-minutes-to-the-inch cooking rule applies.

Serving suggestions: Rice is an excellent accompaniment, especially aromatic basmati rice cooked in broth.

SALSA
    1 cup coarsely chopped fresh or canned pineapple (save 1 tablespoon juice)
    1 11-ounce or 15-ounce can mandarin oranges, drained and coarsely chopped
    2 scallions, including green tops, thinly sliced
    1 jalapeño pepper, seeded and minced (1 tablespoon)
    1 tablespoon fresh lemon juice
    1/4 teaspoon salt, if desired
    1/8 teaspoon cayenne, or to taste

MARINADE
    2 tablespoons fresh lemon juice
    1 tablespoon pineapple juice
    1 tablespoon brown sugar
    1/2 teaspoon salt, if desired
    1/4 teaspoon freshly ground black pepper

FISH
1 1/4 to 1 1/2 pounds MARLIN STEAKS
Vegetable-oil spray *or* vegetable oil for brushing the grill grate

1. In a small glass or ceramic bowl, combine all the ingredients for the salsa. Cover the bowl, and refrigerate it until shortly before serving time.
2. In another small bowl, combine all the ingredients for the marinade. Place the fish in a nonreactive pan such as a glass baking dish, and pour the marinade over it. Turn the fish to coat it well with the marinade. Cover the dish, and chill the fish for 30 minutes or longer, turning it once or twice.
3. Heat the grill or broiler.
4. Remove the hot grill or broiler grate, spray it or brush it with the vegetable oil, then replace the grate. Remove the fish from the marinade, reserving the marinade. On the hot grill or in the hot broiler, grill or broil the fish for 4 to 5 minutes on one side. Brush the fish with the marinade, turn the fish, and grill or broil it for 4 to 5 minutes on the other side.
5. After turning the fish, heat the salsa for 2 minutes in a microwave oven; or transfer the salsa to a nonstick or stainless-steel saucepan, and briefly heat the salsa on the stove.
6. Serve the fish topped with the warm salsa. ■

GRILLED HALIBUT IN ROSEMARY MARINADE

■

The name *halibut* (*hali* = "holy"; *butte* = "flatfish") made its way here from medieval England, where "butt fish" were eaten only on holy days. The first time I made this dish I had only one halibut steak but had to provide six diners with tasting portions. They practically wept for more, it was so good.

Preparation tips: This is one case in which longer marination improves the fish. The steaks should marinate for at least 30 minutes or up to 2 hours before grilling them. They can also be broiled. The tangy marinade, if it is cooked down, can be used as a sauce. To make the sauce, remove the steaks from the marinade about 15 minutes before you plan to grill them, place the marinade in a nonreactive saucepan, and cook the marinade over medium-high heat until the liquid has been reduced by about two-thirds.

FISH
    2 HALIBUT STEAKS (about ¾ pound each)
Vegetable-oil spray

MARINADE
    ½ cup orange juice
    ½ cup fresh lemon juice *or* fresh lime juice
    ½ cup dry white wine
    3 tablespoons soy sauce
    2 tablespoons tequila or rum (optional)
    ¼ cup finely chopped red onion
    2 tablespoons chopped fresh rosemary leaves *or* 2 teaspoons dried rosemary, crushed
    2 tablespoons finely chopped fresh parsley
    1 tablespoon minced garlic
    ¼ teaspoon salt, or to taste
    ¼ teaspoon freshly ground white pepper *or* black pepper

1. Place the steaks in a nonreactive pan or shallow bowl such as a glass pie plate.
2. In a 2-cup measuring cup or medium-sized bowl, combine all the marinade ingredients, and pour the marinade over the fish steaks, lifting the fish to allow some of the marinade to get underneath. Cover the fish with plastic wrap, and refrigerate it for 30 minutes or up to 2 hours, turning the fish occasionally.
3. Heat the grill or broiler.
4. Remove the fish from the marinade, reserving the marinade if you plan to use it for a sauce (see "Preparation tips"). Spray the fish with the vegetable oil; or remove the grill or broiler grate, spray it with the vegetable oil, then replace the grate. On the hot grill or in the hot broiler, grill or broil the fish about 3 to 4 minutes on each side or until the fish is just opaque.
5. Cut the steaks in half before serving them. ∎

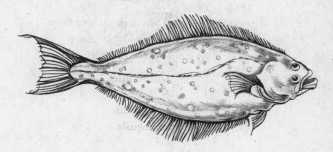

Halibut

GRILLED WHOLE TROUT
■

My first experience with grilling whole trout occurred when a Minnesota youngster named Henry caught more fish at a trout farm than his own family could eat. If there is a trout farm near you or if your local market has access to one, pick up some of the superfresh young trout and try grilling this lovely, often pink-fleshed fish. Fresh herbs are all that is needed to enhance the delicate flavor.

Serving suggestions: If you prefer to do the work for your diners, once the fish is cooked, the flesh can be gently lifted off the bones with a sharp spatula, starting from the backbone (top of the fish–see page 74 for details). Keep side dishes simple but colorful. For example, I served this with corn on the cob and green beans seasoned with sautéed garlic and onions. A lemon wedge is an appropriate accompaniment for each serving.

  4 **small WHOLE TROUT (1/2 to 3/4 pound each), cleaned**
Salt to taste
Freshly ground black pepper to taste
  4 **4-inch sprigs fresh rosemary**
  4 **4-inch sprigs fresh thyme**
  4 **cloves garlic, halved lengthwise**
Vegetable-oil spray

1. Start the grill.
2. Thoroughly wash the fish, and dry them well inside and out with paper towels. Sprinkle the fish inside and out with the salt, and sprinkle the outside of the fish with the pepper.
3. Place one sprig of rosemary and thyme and two garlic halves in the cavity of each fish. Spray the outside of the fish with the vegetable oil.
4. If available, spray two whole-fish grilling baskets with the vegetable oil, and place two fish in each basket. Or remove the hot grill grate, and spray it with the vegetable oil. Grill the fish over medium-hot coals for 3 to 4 minutes per side, covering the grill if it has a cover. Serve 1 fish per person (see "Serving suggestions"). ■

GRILLED WHOLE STRIPED BASS

■

4 SERVINGS

In recent years, admirers of the sweet white flesh of the striped bass have run into rough waters. The fish was not only dwindling in numbers, but proved prone to contamination by PCBs. In New York's Hudson River, a major spawning ground, the bass picked up this industrial carcinogen and stored it in its flesh by eating smaller contaminated fish and by passing contaminated water through its gills. But by the early 1990s, PCB contamination had declined considerably, and striped bass began to make a population come-back. At the same time, farm-raised hybrid striped bass began appearing in markets; these can be enjoyed safely and often.

Preparation tip: Whole striped bass is impressive-looking. If you can handle its size, leave the head and tail on. A whole-fish grilling basket will help immeasurably to keep the fish from breaking as you turn it. Remove the head only if the fish is too large for the grill or the grilling basket.

Serving suggestion: The charred grilled fish is so beautiful that diners deserve to see it before it is cut into serving portions. Bring it to the table whole, then fillet the cooked fish: take a large metal spatula, and carefully lift boneless servings from the central bone (see page 74 for details).

FISH
- 1 **3-pound STRIPED BASS** *or* 2 1½- to 2-pound striped bass, cleaned, head and tail left on and gills removed
- 5 sprigs thyme

Vegetable-oil spray

MARINADE
- 2 tablespoons dry white wine
- 1 tablespoon fresh lemon juice
- 1 tablespoon olive oil

Salt to taste

Freshly ground black pepper to taste

1. Place the fish on a large platter. With a sharp knife, make two or three ½-inch-deep slashes on each side of the fish. Place the thyme sprigs in the cavity of the fish.
2. In a small bowl, combine the marinade ingredients. Pour the marinade over the fish, and allow the fish to stand for about 20 minutes, turning it once or twice.
3. While the fish marinates, start the grill.
4. Remove the fish from the marinade, and spray both sides of the fish with the vegetable oil. Place the fish on the hot grill (in a fish basket, if it is available), and grill the fish for 20 minutes on each side. Transfer the fish to a serving platter (see "Serving suggestion"), and serve the fish hot or warm. ■

GRILLED WHOLE SALMON TROUT ORIENTALE

■

When I was a child, this is the fish my family knew as salmon. It is actually a big trout with pink flesh that is milder than salmon but still succulent. When it is raised on fish farms, its color is enhanced by carotene in its diet, which gives the fish a nutritional boost as well. The deception is not as extreme as it may seem since trout and salmon belong to the same family. When I prepared this dish, I had just started work on this book, and it seemed very ambitious because of the fish's size. But the recipe worked so well and the fish was so stunning to look at that my confidence soared.

Preparation tips: You can substitute any comparable whole, firm fish such as a STEELHEAD or large YELLOWTAIL SNAPPER. Since the most difficult part of the cooking is in turning the fish, a whole-fish grilling basket intended for this purpose is a wonderful aid. If you do not have a basket, two people, each with a long spatula, can together turn the fish without breaking it.

MARINADE

¼ cup fresh lime juice
2 tablespoons soy sauce
2 teaspoons olive oil
2 teaspoons Asian sesame oil
½ cup finely chopped fennel bulb
¼ cup finely chopped scallions
2 tablespoons minced garlic
1 teaspoon peeled, minced or grated gingerroot

FISH

1 4-pound SALMON TROUT, cleaned, head and tail left on and gills removed
¾ cup finely chopped fennel bulb
¼ cup chopped scallions, including green tops
Vegetable-oil spray

1. In a medium-sized bowl, blend together all the marinade ingredients.
2. Place the fish in a nonreactive pan, and pour the marinade over it. Marinate the fish in the refrigerator or in a cooler with ice packs for 1 hour, turning the fish once.
3. In a small bowl, combine the fennel and scallions. Place the fish on a large platter or cutting board, and fill the cavity of the fish with the fennel-scallion mixture. To keep the stuffing in place, close the cavity with skewers, or cover the stuffing with aluminum foil, pushing the edges of the foil directly into the cavity to secure the stuffing.
4. Start the grill.

5. When the grill is hot, remove the grill grate, spray it with the vegetable oil, then replace the grate on the grill. *Or* place the fish in a greased grilling basket. *Or* place a nonstick fine mesh grate over the grill.

6. Place the fish on the hot grill. Grill the fish over medium heat for 20 minutes. Flip the grilling basket, or, using two long-headed spatulas (see "Preparation tips"), turn the fish very carefully so that it does not break. If you have an adjustable grill, lower the heat, cover the grill, and cook the fish 20 minutes longer. If you have no choice about the heat, check the fish for doneness after about 12 to 15 minutes on the second side.

7. To serve the fish, place it on a cutting board or platter, and present the whole fish to fellow diners before serving filleted portions (see page 74) or using a sharp chef's knife to cut the fish crosswise into thick individual steaks. ■

GRILLED SQUID AND VEGETABLES
■

My friend Kris Kim was a frequent taster for the recipes in this book. Every so often, after tasting a dish, she would exclaim, "*This* is the best one you've done." She said it again for this dish, only this time she stated, "This is *really* the best one you've done!" And it is such a simple and colorful dish. I was inspired to try it after ordering grilled squid salad at an Italian restaurant. This is a leaner yet equally tasty version.

Preparation tips: You will need a mesh grilling grate and small squid for this dish. The squid bodies, which, like the tentacles portion, are cooked whole, should be no more than 3 inches long. Note that the squid should marinate about 1 hour. The entire dish can be made ahead and served at room temperature, or it can be prepared in minutes right before dining and served hot. But be sure to have all the ingredients ready before you start cooking.

Serving suggestion: This can be used as a salad, appetizer, or buffet offering. Don't plan on leftovers.

MARINADE/DRESSING
   3 tablespoons dry white wine
   4 teaspoons olive oil
   1 tablespoon balsamic vinegar
   1 tablespoon crushed garlic
Salt to taste (optional)
Freshly ground black pepper to taste

MAIN INGREDIENTS
   1 pound cleaned SMALL SQUID,
      including tentacles (see
      "Preparation tips")
   2 medium or 1½ large red bell
      peppers
   2 medium or 1½ large yellow bell
      peppers
   1 large sweet onion, peeled
Vegetable-oil spray
Salt to taste (optional)
Freshly ground black pepper to taste

1. In a 1-cup measuring cup, combine all the marinade/dressing ingredients.
2. Place the squid bodies and tentacles in a medium-sized bowl. Stir the marinade/dressing, and pour *one-third of it* over the squid, tossing the squid to coat them well with the ingredients. Cover the bowl, and place it in the refrigerate to marinate for about 1 hour, tossing the pieces occasionally.

3. While the squid marinates, core and seed the red bell pepper and yellow bell pepper, and cut them into 2 × 2-inch pieces. Cut off the ends of the onion, and cut the onion in half crosswise. Separate the layers of the onion, and cut them into 2 × 2-inch pieces. Spray the vegetables with the vegetable oil, and sprinkle them with the salt (if desired) and ground pepper.

4. When the squid is nearly done marinating, start the grill, and place a mesh grate on it. You will want it to be very hot before you start cooking.

5. When the grill is hot, remove the mesh grilling grate, spray it with the vegetable oil, then replace the grate. Place the vegetables on the grate, and grill them, turning the pieces several times, until they are barely tender and beginning to char at the edges. Transfer the vegetables to a serving platter, and, if you are serving the dish warm, cover them with foil to keep them warm.

6. Remove the mesh grilling grate, and again spray it with the vegetable oil, then replace the grate. With a slotted spoon, remove the squid from the marinade, discarding the marinade, and place the squid pieces on the grate. Grill the squid 2 minutes per side—they will become opaque when they are done. *Take care not to overcook the squid* since they will become tough. Add the cooked squid to the vegetables. Stir the reserved two-thirds of the marinade/dressing (*not* the liquid used to marinate the squid), and drizzle it over the squid-and-vegetable mixture. ■

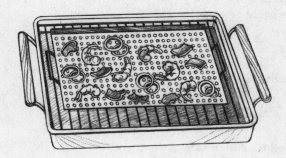

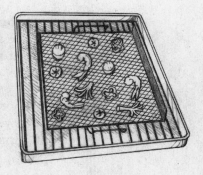

GRILLED SHRIMP WITH ROSEMARY AND CHIVES

■

4 SERVINGS

Since fresh rosemary has such a powerful, distinctive flavor, when you use it with any sort of seafood, you had better mean it. I meant it here—to give the shrimp a pronounced, herby flavor, redolent of summertime. Incidentally, rosemary plants will grow year round in well-drained flowerpots in a sunny window.

Preparation tip: I use a mesh grilling grate over the grill top to keep the shrimp from falling onto the coals. If none is available, then skewer the shrimp, and proceed with the recipe as given.

Serving suggestion: The shrimp are lovely surrounded by grilled vegetables such as zucchinis, bell peppers, and mushrooms.

MARINADE
- 1/4 **cup dry white wine**
- 2 **tablespoons fresh lemon juice**
- 1 **tablespoon olive oil**
- 1 **tablespoon chopped chives**
- 2 **teaspoons chopped fresh rosemary** *or* 1 **teaspoon dried rosemary**
- 1 **teaspoon chopped fresh thyme** *or* 1/2 **teaspoon dried thyme leaves**
- 1 **teaspoon Dijon-style mustard**
- 1 **teaspoon minced garlic**
- 1/4 **teaspoon Tabasco sauce**

Salt to taste
Freshly ground black pepper to taste

SHRIMP
1 1/2 **pounds** LARGE SHRIMP
Vegetable-oil spray *or* **vegetable oil for brushing the grill grate**

1. In a large bowl, combine all the marinade ingredients.
2. Peel and devein the shrimp, leaving the tails on. Place the shrimp in the marinade, cover the bowl, and refrigerate the shrimp for at least 1 hour.
3. Start the grill.
4. When the grill is hot, place the shrimp on a mesh grate that has been sprayed or brushed with the vegetable oil (or thread the shrimp on skewers), and grill the shrimp for about 3 minutes on each side. ■

GRILLED CURRIED SHRIMP

■

4 SERVINGS

There are advantages to marinating shrimp in yogurt. The yogurt is not only low in fat, but it gives the shrimp a pleasing brown color and leaves them delectably dry on the outside and moist on the inside. This recipe, with its Indian overtones, is sharp but not biting.

Preparation tips: The hotness of the curry can be adjusted to suit your own taste. I cooked the shrimp on a mesh grate that prevented them from falling onto the coals. If you have no grate, string the shrimp on skewers. The shrimp can also be "grilled" under the broiler about 6 inches from the heat source.

Serving suggestion: The shrimp are beautiful with a rice pilaf cooked with diced red bell pepper and tiny green peas.

MARINADE
- 1 **cup nonfat or low-fat plain yogurt**
- 3 **tablespoons fresh lime juice**
- 1 **tablespoon olive oil**
- 1/4 **cup chopped fresh mint** *or* 2 **teaspoons dried mint**
- 2 **teaspoons curry powder (can include some hot curry)**
- 1 **teaspoon minced garlic**

Salt to taste
Freshly ground black pepper to taste

SHRIMP
- 1 1/4 **pounds LARGE SHRIMP, peeled and, if desired, deveined**

Vegetable-oil spray
- 1 **tablespoon chopped cilantro for garnish (optional)**

1. In a large nonreactive bowl, combine all the marinade ingredients, blending them well.
2. Add the shrimp, and toss the shrimp to coat them with the marinade. Cover the bowl, and refrigerate the shrimp for 30 minutes to 1 hour.
3. While the shrimp marinate, heat the grill or broiler.
4. Remove the shrimp from the marinade, reserving the marinade. Place the shrimp on skewers, or on a mesh grate that has been sprayed with the vegetable oil, or on a broiler grate, if you are broiling the shrimp. Grill or broil the shrimp for about 2 1/2 minutes on each side, basting them once or twice with the reserved marinade. The shrimp should be cooked through but not dry. Sprinkle the shrimp with the cilantro (if desired), and serve the shrimp immediately. ■

SMOKY SOFT-SHELL CRABS

■

4 FIRST-COURSE SERVINGS OR 2 MAIN-DISH SERVINGS

My friend Terry Quinn is a genius when it comes to grilling and often devises unorthodox recipes that are taste sensations. This is one of them.

Preparation tips: Although the smoky flavor of the applewood chips is divine, if you do not have them or some other fragrant wood chip that would not overwhelm the crab's natural sweetness, just grill the crabs over hot coals or on a gas grill. The fishmonger will usually clean crabs for you, but if not, see page 81 for instructions.

1 **cup applewood chips (see "Preparation tips" and page 111 for source)**
1 **tablespoon butter** *or* **margarine**
2 **teaspoons minced garlic**
2 **tablespoons finely chopped fresh basil** *or* 2 **teaspoons dried basil**
1/8 **teaspoon cayenne**
1/2 **cup dry vermouth, divided**
4 **SOFT-SHELL CRABS, cleaned**
Vegetable-oil spray *or* **vegetable oil for brushing the grill grate**
Salt to taste
Freshly ground black pepper to taste
1/2 **lemon, cut into wedges**

1. Place the wood chips in a bowl, add water to cover by 1 inch, and set the wood chips aside to soak for at least 30 minutes.
2. Start a grill that has a cover.
3. Melt the butter or margarine in a large nonstick skillet. Add the garlic, basil, cayenne, and 1/4 cup of the vermouth. Add the crabs, and sauté them over a medium-high flame for 1 minute on each side. Transfer the crabs to a flat grilling basket or a mesh grate that has been sprayed or brushed with the vegetable oil. *Do not discard the contents of the skillet.*
4. Drain the applewood chips, and place them over the hot coals. Place the crabs upside down on the grill. Cover the grill, and hot-smoke the crabs for 4 to 5 minutes. Then turn the crabs over, and smoke them right side up 4 to 5 minutes longer. The legs and claws should become partially charred. Transfer the crabs to a serving platter, sprinkle them with the salt and pepper, and cover them to keep them warm.
5. While the crabs grill, reheat the skillet, and add the remaining 1/4 cup of vermouth, stirring the liquid over medium heat for about 30 seconds to reduce the alcohol. Spoon the contents of the skillet over the crabs, and serve the crabs with the lemon wedges. ■

Magic in the Microwave

When I told my friend Jo-Ann that I was working on a microwave section for this book, she couldn't believe it. Despite all the cookbooks and the newspaper and magazine articles devoted to microwaving, she—like many others I know—was persuaded that the microwave oven is not good for much of anything beyond reheating and defrosting. And I must admit that, although I had owned a microwave oven for years, I felt that way, too. Only under the pressure of creating a well-rounded seafood cookbook did I drag myself over to the microwave oven with a fish instead of a cup of lukewarm coffee in my hand. To my delight, I found microwaving to be a cool, clean, efficient way to cook fish. Although the process is similar in effect to steaming, there are subtle differences. When you microwave trout, for instance, the result is a pleasant firmness that is often lost in steaming. Now, I've got to get Jo-Ann to give it a whirl. And, if you are like her, join us. You'll be glad you did.

CAJUN-STYLE FILLETS

■

4 SERVINGS

This recipe is simplicity itself. If done with thin fillets such as flounder or ocean perch, no marinating time is necessary. Just pop the doused fish into the microwave oven, and cook it.

Preparation tips: I have made this dish with fillets of COD ("SCROD") and TRIGGERFISH, but almost any moderately firm, thin fillet would work well (for example, TURBOT or CATFISH). Cajun seasoning mix is now sold in most supermarkets in the spice section. Or you can prepare your own (see page 424).

Serving suggestion: The sauce that remains behind can be heated in the microwave oven for 1 minute and used over rice, orzo, or a baked potato, which may accompany the fish.

4 skinless THIN FILLETS, about 1¼ pounds
   total (see "Preparation tips")
2 tablespoons dry white wine
1 tablespoon fresh lime juice
1 tablespoon ketchup
2 teaspoons liquid from capers
1 teaspoon minced capers
1 teaspoon finely minced garlic
1 teaspoon cajun seasoning
   mix (see preparation tips)

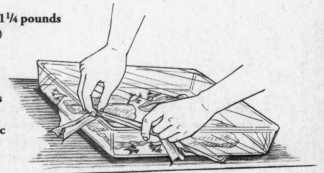

1. Rinse the fillets, and pat them dry. Place them in a single layer in a shallow, nonreactive, microwave-safe pan (a large glass or ceramic pie plate will do).

2. In a small bowl or measuring cup, combine all the remaining ingredients. Pour the mixture over the fillets, lifting the fish to coat it with the mixture on both sides. Pour off the extra liquid, reserving it if you wish (see "Serving suggestion"). Cover the fish with a microwave-safe lid or with plastic wrap turned up at one corner to allow the steam to vent.

3. Place the fish in the microwave oven, and cook the fish on high for about 4 minutes, giving the dish a quarter turn after 2 minutes if your microwave oven does not revolve. Check for doneness, and, if necessary, microwave the fillets 1 to 2 minutes longer or until the fillets are just cooked through. ■

COD CHINOISE

■

4 SERVINGS

This recipe is a working cook's dream. It requires no advance planning, takes only 5 minutes to set up and another 5 minutes to cook, and results in a delightful dish.

Preparation tips: If you are planning to serve the fish with rice, start the rice before you begin to prepare the fish. You can substitute for the cod any mild-flavored fillet that you might consider steaming, such as **HAKE, BLACKFISH, TILAPIA, ORANGE ROUGHY,** or **CATFISH.** However, in my experience, flounder is too delicate for microwave cooking.

Serving suggestions: As with most Chinese-style dishes, this one goes well with rice. A steamed green vegetable like broccoli, asparagus, or snow peas would add color and nutrients to this low-fat meal.

SAUCE
- 2 tablespoons orange juice
- 1 tablespoon reduced-sodium soy sauce
- 1 tablespoon hoisin sauce
- 1 teaspoon Asian sesame oil
- 2 teaspoons peeled, finely minced gingerroot
- 1 teaspoon finely minced garlic

FISH
- 1¼ pounds COD ("SCROD") FILLETS
- 2 tablespoons thinly sliced scallion greens

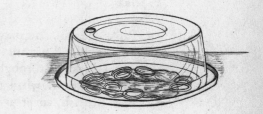

1. In a small bowl or jar that has a tight-fitting lid, combine all the sauce ingredients, whisking or shaking them to mix them well.
2. Place the fish in a shallow, microwave-safe baking dish. Turn under any thin ends of the fillets so that the fish is of equal thickness throughout. Pour the sauce over the fish, tipping the dish to distribute the sauce evenly over the fish. Sprinkle the scallions over the fish, and cover the dish with a microwave-safe lid or with plastic wrap turned up at one corner to allow the steam to vent.
3. Place the fish in the microwave oven, and cook the fish on high for 5 minutes, giving the dish a quarter turn after 2½ minutes if your microwave oven does not revolve. ■

TURBOT FOR TWO WITH LEMON-MUSTARD SAUCE

2 SERVINGS

Turbot, which is a thick flounder, is well suited to seasoning that gives it character yet does not mask its delicate flavor.

Preparation tips: If you wish to serve 4 diners, double all the ingredients. Alternatives to turbot include COD ("SCROD"), HAKE, TILAPIA, BLACKFISH, ORANGE ROUGHY, or any other white fish that has some texture.

Serving suggestion: The fillets also taste great cold, thus lending themselves to a salad-type service—for instance, by placing the fish on a bed of greens and surrounding it with halved cherry tomatoes and sliced baby zucchinis. Some of the liquid that collects in the baking dish when the fish cooks can then be used as a dressing.

FISH	SAUCE
¾ **pound** TURBOT FILLETS, **in 2 pieces**	1 **tablespoon lemon juice**
Salt to taste	2 **teaspoons Dijon-style mustard**
Freshly ground black pepper to taste	1 **teaspoon raspberry vinegar** *or* **white-wine vinegar**
Paprika	1 **teaspoon honey**

1. Rinse the fish, and pat it dry. Place the fish in a shallow, microwave-safe baking dish. Turn under any thin ends of the fillets so that the fish is of equal thickness throughout. Sprinkle the fish with the salt and pepper.
2. In a small bowl, whisk together all the sauce ingredients. Spoon the sauce over the fish, covering the entire surface of the fish with a thin layer of sauce.
3. Sprinkle the fish generously with the paprika, and cover the dish with a microwave-safe lid or with plastic wrap turned up at one corner to allow the steam to vent. Place the fish in the microwave oven, and cook the fish on high for 4 minutes or until the fish is just cooked through at its thickest part, giving the dish a quarter turn after 2 minutes if your microwave oven does not revolve. ■

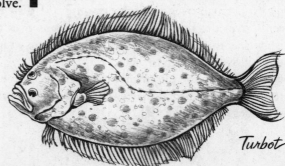

Turbot

BLACKFISH WITH GREEN HORSERADISH SAUCE

■

4 SERVINGS

Here, a room-temperature sauce is added when the fish is served, making this dish ideal for lunch or supper on a hot day.

Preparation tip: Any white fish with a reasonable amount of texture—COD ("SCROD") or ORANGE ROUGHY, for example—can be used in place of the blackfish.

SAUCE

- ¼ cup nonfat or low-fat plain yogurt
- 2 tablespoons finely chopped fresh parsley
- 1 tablespoon minced scallion greens
- 1½ teaspoons drained horseradish
- 1 teaspoon Dijon-style mustard
- 1 teaspoon fresh lemon juice
- ¼ teaspoon sugar
- ⅛ teaspoon salt
- ⅛ teaspoon freshly ground white pepper

FISH

- 1¼ pounds skinless BLACKFISH FILLETS
- 2 teaspoons fresh lemon juice

Salt to taste

Freshly ground black pepper to taste

Blackfish

1. In a small bowl, whisk together all the sauce ingredients. Let the sauce stand at room temperature while you prepare the fish.
2. Place the fish in a shallow, microwave-safe baking dish. Sprinkle the fish with the lemon juice, salt, and pepper.
3. Cover the dish with a microwave-safe lid or with plastic wrap turned up at one corner to allow the steam to vent. Place the fish in the microwave oven, and cook the fish on high for 5 minutes, giving the dish a quarter turn after 3 minutes if your microwave oven does not revolve. Check the fish for doneness, and, if necessary, return the fish to the microwave oven for additional 30-second cooking intervals.
4. Serve the fish topped with the sauce, or serve the sauce on the side. ■

TUNA WITH ORANGE JUICE AND FENNEL

■

4 SERVINGS

One of the most pleasant developments in modern nutrition is that as health-aware cooks use less oil, they increasingly turn to fruit juices for marinades and sauces. Here, orange juice, as a major component of an oil-free marinade and cooking liquid, lends just the right amount of tart sweetness to the ginger-flavored dish.

MARINADE
¼ cup orange juice
¼ cup dry white wine
1 teaspoon minced garlic
1 teaspoon peeled, minced gingerroot

MAIN INGREDIENTS
1¼ pounds TUNA STEAKS
1 cup thinly sliced onions
1 cup thinly sliced potatoes
1 cup thinly sliced fennel bulb
Salt to taste
Freshly ground black pepper to taste
2 tablespoons chopped fresh parsley

1. In a shallow bowl large enough to hold the tuna, combine all the marinade ingredients. Add the tuna, and marinate the fish in the refrigerator for 20 minutes, turning it once after 10 minutes.
2. Place the onions, potatoes, and fennel in a microwave-safe dish, and sprinkle the vegetables with the salt and pepper. Place the fish on top of the vegetables, and pour the marinade over the fish. Cover the dish with a microwave-safe lid or with plastic wrap turned up at one corner to allow the steam to vent.
3. Place the fish in the microwave oven, and cook the fish on high for 12 minutes or until it is cooked through and the vegetables are tender, giving the dish a quarter turn after 6 minutes if your microwave oven does not revolve. Arrange the fish over the vegetables on a platter, and sprinkle the fish with the parsley before serving it. ■

Tuna

MONKFISH WITH RED AND GREEN PEPPERS

■

4 SERVINGS

Monkfish, a firm but mild-flavored fish, is excellent in microwave recipes like this since it holds together so well. But the real stars of this dish are the vegetables; the colorful red and green peppers blend beautifully with the sliced onions and chopped tomato.

Preparation tip: Note that the gray membrane on the outside of the monkfish must be completely removed. This can be done with fingers and a paring knife. But be prepared to lose a bit of the white flesh.

    1 teaspoon olive oil
    2 teaspoons minced garlic
    1 cup sliced onion
1¼ pounds MONKFISH, membrane thoroughly removed, cut into 4 pieces
Salt to taste
Freshly ground black pepper to taste
 ¾ cup julienne strips green bell pepper
 ¾ cup julienne strips red bell pepper
    1 cup chopped fresh or canned tomatoes
 ⅛ teaspoon red pepper flakes
    1 tablespoon chopped cilantro *or* fresh parsley
 ¼ cup dry white wine
 ¼ cup chicken broth

1. Place the olive oil in a microwave-safe dish large enough to hold the fish in one layer. Add the garlic and onion, and microwave the vegetables on high for 1 minute.
2. Sprinkle the monkfish with the salt and ground pepper, and place it on top of the vegetables.
3. In a bowl, combine the green bell pepper, red bell pepper, tomatoes, red pepper flakes, and cilantro or parsley, and distribute the mixture over the fish. Pour the wine and broth over the vegetables and fish.
4. Cover the dish with a microwave-safe lid or with plastic wrap turned up at one corner to allow the steam to vent. Place the fish in the microwave oven, and cook the fish on high for 12 minutes or until the fish is cooked through, giving the dish a quarter turn after 6 minutes if your microwave oven does not revolve. Serve individual portions of the fish, surrounding each serving with the vegetables. ■

ORANGE ROUGHY WITH MUSHROOMS

■

A recipe developed by my friend Betty Marks, author of, among other books, the *Microwave Diabetes Cookbook,* was the inspiration for this easy, fast, no-fat-added dish. Orange roughy, a fish that is shipped here (usually frozen) from New Zealand, is mild and adaptable.

Preparation tip: Almost any thick, white fish fillet or steak can serve as an alternative to orange roughy, including COD ("SCROD"), BLACKFISH, HAKE, or POLLOCK.

Serving suggestion: Since this fish is light, a substantial carbohydrate like pasta or a baked potato (which can be cooked first in the microwave) would be a welcome accompaniment.

FISH
1¼ pounds ORANGE ROUGHY fillets
  2 tablespoons dry white wine
  ½ teaspoon dried dill
  ⅛ teaspoon paprika
Salt to taste
Freshly ground black pepper to taste

TOPPING
1½ cups thinly sliced mushrooms
  ¼ cup thinly sliced scallions,
      including some green tops
  2 tablespoons fresh lemon juice
Salt to taste
Freshly ground black pepper to taste
  1 tablespoon chopped fresh basil *or*
  1 teaspoon dried basil

1. Place the fish in a single layer in a microwave-safe baking dish. Turn under any thin ends of the fillets so that the fish is of equal thickness throughout. Pour the wine over the fish, and sprinkle the fish with the dill, paprika, salt, and pepper.
2. In a bowl, prepare the topping by combining the mushrooms, scallions, and lemon juice. Distribute this mixture over the fish. Sprinkle the topping with the salt, pepper, and basil.
3. Cover the dish with a microwave-safe lid or with plastic wrap turned up at one corner to allow the steam to vent. Place the fish in the microwave oven, and cook the fish on high about 6 to 7 minutes, giving the dish a quarter turn after 3 minutes if your microwave oven does not revolve. Then let the dish stand, covered, for 1 to 2 minutes before serving it. ■

SALMON WITH BROCCOLI AND MUSHROOMS

■

4 SERVINGS

Regardless of what George Bush and other antibroccoli people might say, I know broccoli is one of the healthiest, most beautiful, and delicious vegetables on earth. Here, it contributes to a dish that is as attractive as it is quick to prepare.

Preparation tip: Any moderately firm, flavorful fillet such as BLUEFISH, MACKEREL, or YELLOWTAIL should work well in this dish.

Serving suggestion: Mashed potatoes or couscous, millet, or bulgur would make a nice starchy accompaniment.

MAIN INGREDIENTS
1¼ **pounds** SALMON FILLET
Vegetable-oil spray
  2 **cups small broccoli flowerets**
  2 **cups sliced mushrooms**
  1 **tablespoon chopped fresh parsley**
  1 **tablespoon chopped fresh**
    tarragon *or* 1 **teaspoon dried**
    tarragon
  1 **teaspoon olive oil** *or* **canola oil**
Salt to taste
Freshly ground black pepper to taste

MARINADE
¼ **cup dry white wine**
¼ **cup chicken broth** *or* **fish broth**
1 **tablespoon fresh lemon juice**
1 **teaspoon minced garlic**

1. Place the fish skin side down in a shallow bowl. In a 1-cup measuring cup or small bowl, combine all the marinade ingredients, and pour this mixture over the fish. Let the fish marinate for 20 minutes.
2. Spray a microwave-safe baking dish with the vegetable oil. Place the fish skin side down in the dish, *reserving the marinade.*
3. Add all the remaining ingredients to the reserved marinade, and toss the ingredients to combine them well. Then pour the vegetable mixture over the salmon. Cover the dish with a microwave-safe lid or with plastic wrap turned up at one corner to allow the steam to vent.
4. Place the fish and vegetables in the microwave oven, and cook the fish on high for 10 minutes, giving the dish a quarter turn after 5 minutes if your microwave oven does not revolve. ■

LEMONY GROUPER WITH TOMATO-ROSEMARY SAUCE

■

4 SERVINGS

Grouper, which can easily dry out in a conventional oven, stays moist and maintains its texture in the microwave oven. This simple dish is elegant enough for entertaining.

Preparation tips: As long as it is kept covered and chilled, the fish can be set up through step 2 an hour or more ahead. Alternative fish include any fillet that is about ½ inch thick (or more), such as SEA BASS, ORANGE ROUGHY, SNAPPER, or COD ("SCROD").

    1 **large lemon, very thinly sliced crosswise**
    1 **GROUPER FILLET, about 1¼ pounds**
  ³/4 **cup diced plum (Roma) tomatoes**
    1 **teaspoon minced garlic**
 1½ **teaspoons fresh lemon juice**
  ½ **teaspoon white-wine Worcestershire sauce**
    2 **dashes Tabasco sauce**
  ¼ **teaspoon salt, or to taste**
  ⅛ **teaspoon freshly ground black pepper**
    2 **teaspoons coarsely chopped fresh rosemary leaves** *or* ³/4 **teaspoon dried rosemary, crumbled**

1. Line a microwave-safe baking dish with the lemon slices, arranging them in the shape of the fillet. Rinse the fish and pat it dry, and lay it on top of the lemon. If the fish has a thin tail, fold the tail under so that the fish is of equal thickness throughout.
2. To the container of a blender or food processor, add the tomatoes, garlic, lemon juice, Worcestershire sauce, Tabasco sauce, salt, and pepper. Puree the mixture. Then stir in the rosemary by hand. Pour the sauce over the fish. Cover the dish with a microwave-safe lid or with plastic wrap turned up at one corner to allow the steam to vent.
3. Place the fish in the microwave oven, and cook the fish on high for 5 minutes, giving the dish a quarter turn after 3 minutes if your microwave oven does not revolve. Check for doneness. If needed, microwave the fish for another minute or so. ■

Grouper

BLACKFISH OVER MIXED VEGETABLES

■

Blackfish, also known as tautog, is plentiful in my neighborhood in the summertime. During this season, the fisherman who comes to the local farmers' market finds these bottom feeders in his shellfish traps (they use their sharp teeth to eat crustaceans and mollusks) and sells them with the rest of his catch. The fish resembles a grouper and is firm yet mild in flavor.

Preparation tip: GROUPER or TILEFISH FILLETS could replace the blackfish.

FISH
1¼ pounds skinless BLACKFISH
    FILLETS, cut into 4 portions
Salt to taste
Freshly ground black pepper to taste
  1 tablespoon fresh lemon juice
  ¼ cup dry white wine
  4 fresh basil leaves
  4 lemon wedges for garnish

VEGETABLES
  2 teaspoons olive oil
  1 cup thinly sliced onion
  1 tablespoon minced garlic
  1 cup thinly sliced red bell pepper
  1 cup thinly sliced green bell pepper
  1 cup thinly sliced fennel bulb
  1 teaspoon fresh thyme leaves *or* ½
    teaspoon dried thyme leaves
Salt to taste
Freshly ground black pepper to taste

1. Sprinkle the fish with the salt and pepper, and place it in a microwave-safe baking pan with a rim that is ½ inch to 1 inch high. Pour the lemon juice and wine evenly over the fish. Place a basil leaf on the center of each piece of fish.

2. Cover the pan with a microwave-safe lid or with plastic wrap turned up at one corner to allow the steam to vent. Place the fish in the microwave oven, and cook the fish on high for 4 to 5 minutes or until the fish is just done, giving the pan a quarter turn after 2 minutes if your microwave oven does not revolve. Remove the pan from the microwave oven, and carefully pour off and *reserve the cooking liquid.* Cover the fish to keep it warm, and set it aside while the vegetables are being prepared.

3. Place the olive oil, onion, and garlic in a microwave-safe casserole dish, place the dish in the microwave oven, and cook the vegetables on high for 1 minute. Pour in the reserved cooking liquid from the fish, and stir in the remaining vegetable ingredients. Cover the casserole with a microwave-safe lid or with plastic wrap turned up at one corner to allow the steam to vent. Place the casserole in the microwave oven, and microwave the vegetables for 4 minutes or until they are cooked through but are still crunchy.

4. Place equal portions of the vegetables on each of 4 plates, and top each portion with a piece of fish. Garnish the plates with the lemon wedges. ■

SWORD(FISH) AND PLOWSHARE
■

4 SERVINGS

Rhubarb and tomatoes from my hand-plowed garden and the glimmer of peace that came with signing of the Israeli-Palestinian peace agreement inspired the biblically derived name for this recipe.

Preparation tips: Alternatives to swordfish include any steaklike fish such as **MARLIN, TUNA,** or even a thick piece of **SALMON.**

SAUCE

- 10 ounces fresh rhubarb, cut into ½-inch slices (about 2 cups)
- 4 small fresh plum (Roma) tomatoes, cut into ½-inch pieces
- ¼ cup red wine
- 1 tablespoon red-wine vinegar
- 1 tablespoon brown sugar
- ½ teaspoon salt
- ¼ teaspoon freshly ground black pepper

FISH

- 1¼ pounds SWORDFISH, cut at least 1 inch thick
- Vegetable-oil spray

1. Combine all the sauce ingredients in a microwave-safe bowl. Cover the bowl with a microwave-safe lid or with plastic wrap turned up at one corner to allow the steam to vent.
2. Place the bowl in the microwave oven, and cook the sauce for 5 minutes.
3. While the sauce cooks, rinse the fish, and pat it dry. Trim off any skin, and cut the steaks into pieces about 1 × 2 inches. Spray a shallow, microwave-safe pan with the vegetable oil, and place the fish in the pan in a single layer.
4. When the sauce is ready, pour it over the fish, covering it completely with the pieces of rhubarb and tomato. Cover the pan with a microwave-safe lid or with plastic wrap turned up at one corner to allow the steam to vent. Place the pan in the microwave oven, and cook the fish on high for 10 minutes, giving the pan a quarter turn after 5 minutes if your microwave oven does not revolve. ■

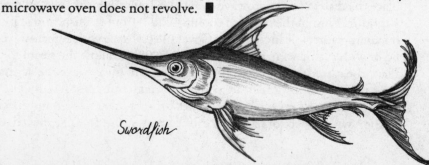

Swordfish

POACHED SHARK AND COUSCOUS

■   4 SERVINGS

This is another of those complete meals in a dish that the microwave oven seems especially good at producing. The vegetables and couscous are the main ingredients, with the fish used almost as a garnish.

Preparation tips: SWORDFISH, often more available than shark, is an excellent substitute. See page 343 for tips on washing leeks.

    1 cup finely chopped leeks, well washed, white and tender green parts only
 1/2 cup finely chopped carrot
 1/2 cup finely chopped celery
    1 cup dry white wine
 1/2 cup fish broth *or* chicken broth
1 1/4 pounds MAKO SHARK *or* other shark steak, skin removed, cut into 8 pieces
Salt to taste
Freshly ground black pepper to taste
1 1/2 cups couscous
    1 cup frozen green peas, thawed under warm running water
    2 tablespoons chopped fresh parsley
    4 lemon wedges as garnish

1. Place the leeks, carrot, celery, wine, and broth in a microwave-safe baking dish. Sprinkle the shark with the salt and pepper, and add it to the dish. Cover the dish with a microwave-safe lid or with plastic wrap turned up at one corner to allow the steam to vent. Place the dish in the microwave oven, and cook the fish on high for 12 minutes or until it is cooked through, giving the dish a quarter turn after 6 minutes if your microwave oven does not revolve.
2. With a slotted spoon, remove the fish to a platter, leaving behind the vegetables, and cover the fish with foil to keep it warm.
3. Stir the couscous, peas, and salt to taste (if desired) into the vegetables and their liquid in the baking dish, cover the mixture tightly, and allow it to sit for 5 minutes or until all the liquid has been absorbed.
4. Place an ample serving of couscous on each of 4 plates, distributing the couscous so that it covers most of the dish. Place two pieces of fish on top of each serving of couscous, sprinkle the fish and couscous with the parsley, and garnish each plate with a lemon wedge. ■

INDIAN-STYLE SEAFOOD WITH COUSCOUS
■

The flavorings here are piquant and almost quintessentially Indian, blending beautifully with the couscous. Couscous (or something like it, such as bulgur or millet) is essential for sopping up the sauce, filling out the meal, and giving the dish an exotic touch. As it is sold today, couscous is a busy cook's ideal fast food. Although this recipe can also be prepared on a stovetop in about the same amount of time, microwave cooking generates less heat, and the results are equally good.

Preparation tips: The instructions on packages of quick-cooking couscous nearly always call for the addition of 4 tablespoons of butter for 4 servings. I find that the butter (or margarine or oil) can be reduced to 2 teaspoons or less or omitted entirely and the couscous will remain moist, especially since it will be covered by the sauce from this seafood dish.

$1\frac{1}{2}$ **cups couscous**
  3 **cups boiling water**
Vegetable-oil spray
  2 **teaspoons cumin seeds**
  1 **teaspoon fennel seeds**
  1 **cup chopped onion**
$\frac{1}{4}$ **teaspoon cayenne, or to taste**
$1\frac{1}{2}$ **cups seeded and coarsely chopped (but not peeled) tomatoes**
  $\frac{1}{2}$ **pound MONKFISH, cut into 1-inch cubes**
  $\frac{1}{2}$ **pound BAY SCALLOPS**
Salt to taste
Freshly ground black pepper to taste
  1 **tablespoon fresh lemon juice**
  $\frac{1}{2}$ **teaspoon garam masala (see page 277)**
  1 **tablespoon chopped cilantro**

1. Combine the couscous with the water according to package directions, using no more than 2 teaspoons of butter, if any. *Or,* if you are using couscous purchased in bulk, place the couscous in a microwave-safe bowl, and pour the boiling water over it. Cover the bowl, and let it stand for 5 minutes or until all the water has been absorbed.

2. While the couscous absorbs the water, spray with the vegetable oil a microwave-safe baking pan that is at least 1 inch deep, and add the cumin seeds and fennel seeds. Place the uncovered pan in the microwave oven, and cook the seeds for 1 minute. Remove the pan from the microwave oven, and add the onion and cayenne. Place the uncovered pan in the microwave oven, and cook the onion for 2 minutes.

3. Remove the pan, blend in the tomatoes, replace the pan in the microwave oven, and cook the vegetables for 2½ minutes. Remove the pan, and add the monkfish, scallops, salt, and pepper. Cover the pan with a microwave-safe lid or with plastic wrap turned up at one corner to allow the steam to vent. Place the pan in the microwave oven, and cook the seafood on high for 4 to 5 minutes, giving the pan a quarter turn after 2 minutes if your microwave oven does not revolve. Test a scallop for doneness, and, if further cooking is needed, microwave the ingredients 1 minute longer.

4. When the seafood is cooked through, stir in the lemon juice, garam masala, and cilantro.

5. To serve the dish, warm the couscous, if necessary, in the microwave oven for 30 seconds. Divide the couscous among 4 individual plates, and spoon the seafood and sauce over the couscous. ■

WHOLE PORGY WITH TOMATO AND CUCUMBER

■

4 SERVINGS

Porgy, usually an inexpensive fish, has a handsome, round shape that makes it attractive when it is served whole. The fish's sweet flesh also lends itself well to microwaving and slides easily off the bone after it is cooked. Here, small porgies are served as individual portions, just as you might serve small trout.

Preparation tips: Since the fish can be served chilled, at room temperature, or warm, it can be cooked as far in advance as is convenient—up to 2 or 3 hours ahead. About ½ hour before serving time, simply toss the vegetables together; they require no cooking. **SMALL TROUT** are an excellent alternative to the porgies. Note that the salad ingredients should drain for at least 15 minutes.

FISH

> 4 **WHOLE PORGIES (about ¾ pound each), cleaned**
> 2 **tablespoons fresh lemon juice**

Salt to taste
Freshly ground black pepper to taste

> 8 **sprigs fresh mint**

DRESSING

> 1 **tablespoon olive oil, preferably extra-virgin**
> 1 **tablespoon fresh lemon juice**
> 2 **teaspoons minced shallots**
> 1 **teaspoon minced fresh mint**
> 1 **teaspoon minced fresh parsley**

Salt to taste
Freshly ground black pepper to taste

SALAD

> 1 **medium cucumber, peeled**
> 2 **large, ripe, fresh tomatoes, peeled, seeded, and cut into ¼-inch dice**

Salt to taste
Leafy greens (for example, romaine or Bibb lettuce)

1. To prepare the fish, sprinkle the porgies with the lemon juice, salt, and pepper, and place 2 sprigs of mint in the cavity of each fish. Cover the fish heads lightly with aluminum foil, and place the fish in a glass or other microwave-safe baking dish in one layer. Make sure the foil is contained within the dish. Cover the dish with a microwave-safe lid or with plastic wrap turned up at one corner to allow the steam to vent. Place the dish in

the microwave oven, and cook the fish on high for 7 to 8 minutes or until it is cooked through, giving the dish a quarter turn after 4 minutes if your microwave oven does not revolve.

2. Remove the fish from the oven, place them on a platter, and allow them to cool. When they are cool enough to handle, remove the foil, and, using your fingers and a paring knife (if needed), remove the skin from the bodies of the fish, leaving the heads and tails intact. If the porgies are to be served chilled, refrigerate them for 2 hours or more.

3. Combine all the dressing ingredients in a small bowl or a jar that has a tight-fitting lid, and whisk or shake the ingredients to blend them. Set the dressing aside.

4. To prepare the salad, cut the cucumber in half lengthwise, and, using a small spoon, scoop out the seeds. Again, cut the cucumber in half lengthwise, then into ¼-inch slices.

5. Place the cucumber in a strainer, add the tomatoes, sprinkle the vegetables with the salt, and allow the vegetables to drain for 15 to 30 minutes. Transfer the vegetables to a bowl.

6. Just before serving the fish, make a bedding of the greens on each of 4 plates. Toss the strained vegetables with the reserved dressing. Place one fish on each plate, and spoon the dressed tomatoes and cucumber over it. ■

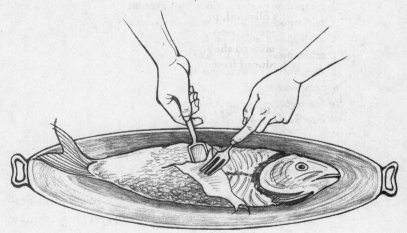

WHOLE MACKEREL CHINESE STYLE
■

4 SERVINGS

The Chinese often prepare whole, well-seasoned fish in a steamer (see, for example, Steamed Tilefish with Black Bean Sauce on page 368). Cooking in a microwave oven is a form of steaming, with the steam coming from the food as well as from any liquid in the pan. And, as with other steamed fish cooked Chinese style, in this recipe the flavorful skin is an integral part of the meal.

Preparation tips: The fish will look their best if they are cooked with their heads and tails intact. However, if you cannot fit whole fish into your microwave oven, I suggest cutting off the heads and, if at all possible, leaving the tails on since they make it easy to debone the fish after they are cooked.

Serving suggestion: As with all Chinese dishes, rice provides the perfect complement. But I have also enjoyed the mackerel with boiled potatoes and with fine noodles like capellini.

SAUCE
  2 teaspoons fermented black beans
  2 teaspoons minced garlic
  2 teaspoons peeled, minced gingerroot
  2 tablespoons reduced-sodium soy sauce
  1 tablespoon oyster sauce
  1 tablespoon rice vinegar
  1 teaspoon Asian sesame oil
  1/2 teaspoon sugar
  1/4 teaspoon red pepper flakes
  1/4 cup finely chopped scallions

FISH
  2 WHOLE MACKEREL (about 1 pound each), cleaned

1. To prepare the sauce, rinse the black beans, and drain them well. Place them in a small bowl, add the garlic and gingerroot, and mash the ingredients together with the back of a spoon (this step can also be done in a mortar with a pestle). Add all the remaining sauce ingredients *except the scallions,* and combine them thoroughly. Then stir in the scallions. Set the sauce aside while you prepare the fish.

2. Rinse the fish well inside and out, and pat them dry. Snip off the fins on the sides, top, and bottom of the fish. Cut off the heads of the fish only if the fish will not fit into your microwave oven. Cut three or four diagonal slits about ½ inch deep on each side of the fish. Loosely wrap the heads and tails in aluminum foil. Place the fish in a microwave-safe baking dish, making sure that the foil is contained within the dish.

3. Stir the reserved sauce, and spoon 1 tablespoon of the sauce into the cavity of each fish. Then spoon the rest of the sauce over both sides of the fish, forcing some sauce into each slit. Cover the dish with plastic wrap (use a double layer if you do not have plastic wrap designed for microwaving), turning up one corner of the wrap to allow the steam to vent.

4. Place the dish in the microwave oven, and cook the fish on high for 10 minutes, giving the dish a quarter turn after 5 minutes if your microwave oven does not revolve.

5. To serve the dish, present the fish whole. Then, working with 1 fish at a time and using a sharp knife, make a ¼-inch slice through the flesh at the top of the fish, and lift sections of fish off one side of the central bones. Place the sections of fish skin side up on a serving platter. With the bones of the fish now fully exposed, lift the tail, and pull the skeleton from the remaining side of the fish, which can then be placed on the platter in skin-side-up sections as well. Repeat this step with the second fish. Then spoon any sauce remaining in the baking dish over the fish. If desired, once the fish has been arranged on a serving platter, it can be reheated briefly in the microwave oven. ∎

Mackerel

WHOLE STRIPED BASS WITH DICED VEGETABLES

■

4 SERVINGS

Striped bass, even the small hybrids raised on fish farms, have such sweet flesh that they need little adornment. This recipe, which can be prepared in 20 minutes, gently dresses up the fish with subtly flavored vegetables.

Preparation tips: Any small, sweet-fleshed fish such as WHOLE PORGIES, could be used as a substitute for the bass. Or the recipe could be prepared with 1 large or 4 small FILLETS of, say, RED SNAPPER, SALMON, PERCH, or even BLUEFISH (if small fillets are used, the total cooking time may need to be reduced to about 8 to 10 minutes).

Serving suggestions: Although the recipe calls for 1 fish per diner, if you start with larger bass—1¼ pounds, for instance—1 fish will feed 2. In that case, you may choose to remove the fillet from each side of the cooked fish and serve it skin side up and topped with the vegetable mixture and parsley garnish. This dish goes well with steamed red new potatoes.

   4 small WHOLE STRIPED BASS (about ¾ pound each), cleaned and gills removed
 ½ cup finely diced carrots (⅛-inch pieces)
 ½ cup finely diced celery (⅛-inch pieces)
   2 tablespoons finely chopped celery leaves
 ¼ cup minced shallots
 ¼ cup dry white wine
 ¼ cup fish broth *or* chicken broth
   4 teaspoons fresh lemon juice
   1 teaspoon white-wine Worcestershire sauce
 ¼ teaspoon salt, or to taste
 ¼ teaspoon freshly ground black pepper, or to taste
   2 tablespoons chopped fresh parsley for garnish (optional)

1. Rinse the fish inside and out, and pat them dry. Loosely wrap the heads in aluminum foil. Place the fish in a microwave-safe baking dish, making sure that the foil is contained within the dish.

2. In a medium-sized bowl, combine all of the remaining ingredients *except the parsley*. Spoon some of the vegetable mixture into the cavity of each fish, and push some of the vegetables under the fish as well. Then pour the remaining vegetable mixture over the fish.

3. Cover the dish with a microwave-safe lid or with plastic wrap (use a double layer if you do not have plastic wrap designed for microwaving), turning up one corner of the wrap to allow the steam to vent. Place the dish in the microwave oven, and cook the fish on high for 12 minutes, giving the dish a quarter turn after 6 minutes if your microwave oven does not revolve.

4. Serve each diner a whole fish, spooning the vegetable mixture over it and (if desired) sprinkling it with the parsley. ■

Striped bass

FISH TACOS WITH CILANTRO PESTO

The unusual pesto that seasons this fish dish was devised by chef Norman Fierros of the La Pila restaurant in Phoenix, Arizona. It is a wonderful sauce that keeps for days and lends itself to many uses. *Simply Seafood* magazine suggests these possibilities: try it in place of mayonnaise or mustard on a sandwich; use it with any cooked fish—hot or cold—or on cooked vegetables; or dilute it with a bit of mild vinegar and use it as a salad dressing or a dip for raw vegetables.

Preparation tips: You will need a large bunch of cilantro to make this pesto. If you do not have enough or if you prefer a milder flavor, use some Italian (flatleaf) parsley leaves in place of some of the cilantro. Make the pesto while the fish marinates. Prepare the toppings just before you are ready to cook the fish. Alternatives to flounder include any small, thin, skinless fillets (for example, SOLE or OCEAN PERCH). If the fillets are large, cut them into pieces that are about 8 inches long and that weigh about 3 ounces each.

MAIN INGREDIENTS
- 8 small FLOUNDER FILLETS (about 3 ounces each or 1¼ to 1½ pounds total)
- 2 tablespoons fresh lime juice
- 2 tablespoons dry white wine
- 1 teaspoon crushed garlic
- 2 dashes cayenne, or to taste
- ¼ teaspoon salt
- ¼ teaspoon freshly ground white pepper
- 8 8-inch corn tortillas

PESTO
- ½ cup feta (about ¼ pound)
- 1 cup packed cilantro leaves (see "Preparation tips"), washed and dried
- 2 teaspoons seeded, minced jalapeño
- 1 tablespoon fresh lemon juice
- 1 tablespoon ice water
- 2 teaspoons minced garlic
- ¼ cup walnuts

TOPPINGS
- 2 cups shredded lettuce
- 2 cups chopped fresh plum (Roma) tomatoes
- 1 cup thinly sliced scallions, including green tops

1. Place the fish in a shallow, nonreactive bowl. In a small bowl, combine the remaining main ingredients *except the tortillas,* and pour the marinade over the fillets, lifting the fillets to be sure they are coated on all sides with the marinade. Cover the bowl, and refrigerate the fish for 20 minutes or longer.

2. To make the pesto, break the feta into chunks, place them in a small bowl, and add cold water to cover them by 1 inch. Let the feta soak for about 10 minutes, then drain it well.

3. Place the cilantro and jalapeño in the bowl of a food processor. Process them briefly to chop them. Then add all the remaining pesto ingredients, including the drained feta, and process the sauce until it forms a smooth paste.

4. To cook the fish, remove the fillets from the marinade, and place them in a shallow, microwave-safe pan or platter with a lip. Cover the pan or platter with a microwave-safe lid or with plastic wrap turned up at one corner to allow the steam to vent. Place the pan or platter in the microwave oven, and cook the fish on high for 4 minutes or until it is just cooked through.

5. Place the tortillas in a stack on a microwave-safe plate, and cover them with a very damp paper towel. Put the tortillas in the microwave oven, and heat them according to package directions or on high for 1 minute.

6. To serve the tacos, spread 1 tablespoon of the pesto on each of the warm tortillas. Place one cooked fillet in each tortilla, folding the tortilla to form an open half circle, then distribute the lettuce, tomatoes, and scallions over the fillets. ∎

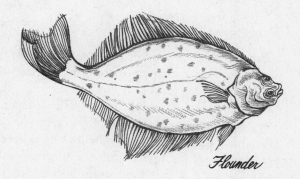

Flounder

WARM SWORDFISH SALAD
■
8 FIRST-COURSE SERVINGS OR 4 MAIN-DISH SERVINGS

As I have gradually expanded my repertoire of microwave-cooked fish, I have been increasingly impressed with the variety of dishes that this method can produce. The first time I tried cooking swordfish in the microwave oven I prepared a whole steak, then realized it would be even more inviting cut into chunks for a salad.

Preparation tips: Even though fish needs to spend no more than 30 minutes in a marinade, this salad is tastier if the swordfish spends the day in its flavorful bath. Bearing this in mind, you can place the fish in the marinade in the morning before going to work, and it will be ready to cook in the evening, when you return home.

SALAD

1¼ **pounds** SWORDFISH **steaks, cut about ¾ inch thick**

1 **8-ounce can sliced water chestnuts, drained**

1 **11-ounce can mandarin oranges, drained**

Leafy greens

MARINADE

¼ **cup orange juice**

2 **tablespoons reduced-sodium soy sauce**

2 **tablespoons ketchup**

2 **tablespoons chopped fresh parsley**

1 **tablespoon Asian sesame oil**

2 **teaspoons fresh lemon juice**

2 **teaspoons finely minced garlic**

½ **teaspoon dried oregano leaves**

¼ **teaspoon freshly ground black pepper**

1. Rinse the fish under cold water, and dry it well with paper towels. Trim away the skin and any brown parts, and cut the remaining flesh into ¾-inch cubes. Place the fish in a shallow, nonreactive pan or bowl, preferably one that will hold the fish in a single layer.
2. In a jar that has a tight-fitting lid or in a mixing bowl, combine all the marinade ingredients. Pour the marinade over the fish cubes, tossing the cubes to coat them well with the marinade. Cover the fish with plastic wrap, and refrigerate the fish for 30 minutes or longer (see "Preparation tips").

3. When you are ready to cook the fish, remove it from the marinade, *saving the marinade* in a container that can be used in the microwave oven, and place the fish in a microwave-safe pan—preferably on a rack—that will hold it in a single layer. Place the water chestnuts on top of the fish, and cover the pan with a microwave-safe lid or with plastic wrap turned up at one corner to allow the steam to vent.

4. Place the reserved marinade in the microwave oven, cook the marinade for 2 minutes, and set the marinade aside. Then place the fish in the microwave oven, and cook the fish on high for about 3 minutes. Add the orange sections to the pan, cover the pan as before, place the pan in the microwave oven, and cook the fish on high 1 to 2 minutes longer. Check for doneness, and, if necessary, cook the fish for an additional 30 to 60 seconds, *or* let the pan stand, covered, 2 minutes longer to complete the cooking.

5. While the fish cooks, arrange the leafy greens on individual plates. With a slotted spoon or spatula, remove the fish, water chestnuts, and oranges from the pan, and distribute them over the greens. Spoon some of the cooked marinade over the salad, and serve the salad warm or at room temperature. ■

SUMMERY TROUT AND CANTALOUPE SALAD

■

I prepared this dish one evening when it was 90 degrees in the shade. It is a perfect example of how the microwave oven allows you to cook fish well and fast without heating up the kitchen. Nothing else in the salad requires cooking. And the cantaloupe, as well as the dressing with its orange-juice base, impart a psychologically cooling touch like a refreshing tropical breeze.

Preparation tips: Since the dish looks best when the melon balls are uniform in size, use a melon baller. But if you do not own this piece of equipment and are careful, you can approximate the effect by thrusting a teaspoon into the melon and rotating the spoon. Since the fish cooks quickly, be sure all the other ingredients are ready before you put the trout in the microwave oven.

DRESSING
$1/4$ **cup orange juice**
2 **tablespoons balsamic vinegar**
1 **tablespoons canola oil**
1 **tablespoon Dijon-style mustard**
2 **tablespoons chopped shallots**
1 **teaspoon minced garlic**
$1/4$ **teaspoon salt, or to taste**
Freshly ground black pepper to taste

FISH
4 TROUT FILLETS (4 to 5 ounces each)
1 **tablespoon fresh lemon juice**
Salt to taste
Freshly ground black pepper to taste
4 **lemon wedges for garnish**

SALAD
4 **to 8 large leaves of romaine lettuce, thick ends removed**
1 **small red bell pepper, cored, seeded, and cut into julienne strips**
1 **small green bell pepper, cored, seeded, and cut into julienne strips**
4 **ounces mushrooms, quartered**
1 **cup ripe cantaloupe balls (about $1/2$ medium cantaloupe)**

1. To prepare the dressing, place all the dressing ingredients in a bowl or a small jar that has a tight-fitting lid, and whisk or shake the ingredients vigorously.

2. Place the trout fillets in a microwave-safe baking dish, sprinkle them with the lemon juice, salt, and pepper, and cover the dish with a microwave-safe lid or with plastic wrap turned up at one corner to allow the steam to vent. Place the dish in the microwave oven, and cook the fish on high for 4 minutes, giving the dish a quarter turn after 2 minutes if your microwave oven does not revolve.

3. Place 1 or 2 lettuce leaves on each of 4 plates to cover most of the surface. Place 1 trout fillet in the center of each plate, and distribute the remaining salad ingredients in an alternating fashion around the trout. Spoon the dressing over the salad and fish, and garnish each plate with a lemon wedge. ■

Trout

STUFFED WHOLE TROUT

■

This stuffing could be used with many different fish. But, like the trout, it is relatively delicate and the marriage perfect.

Serving suggestion: The fish looks best on a bed of lightly cooked or fresh greens, perhaps with steamed corn on the cob on the side.

   2 medium leeks
   2 tablespoons chopped fresh parsley
   1 teaspoon peeled, minced gingerroot
   1 teaspoon minced garlic
   4 small WHOLE TROUT (about ½ pound each), cleaned
   2 tablespoons fresh lemon juice
   2 tablespoons dry white wine
   1 tablespoon chopped chives
Salt to taste
Freshly ground black pepper to taste
   4 lemon wedges

1. Discard the tough, deep-green part of the leeks, wash the lighter green leaves, and set them aside. Carefully wash and finely chop the white and pale-green parts of the leeks.
2. In a small bowl, combine the chopped leeks with the parsley, gingerroot, and garlic.
3. Rinse the trout inside and out, pat them dry, then rub them inside and out with the lemon juice. Stuff each fish with one-fourth of the leek mixture. In a microwave-safe baking dish large enough to hold all 4 trout in one layer, place some of the reserved leek leaves.
4. Loosely wrap the head of each trout with aluminum foil, and place them in the baking dish, making sure that the foil is contained within the dish. Sprinkle the fish with the wine.
5. Cover the dish with a microwave-safe lid or with plastic wrap turned up at one corner to allow the steam to vent. Place the dish in the microwave oven, and cook the fish on high for 7 to 8 minutes, giving the dish a quarter turn after 4 minutes if your microwave oven does not revolve. Remove the dish from the oven, and, gently with a fork, test for doneness at the thickest part of one of the trout, cooking it for additional 30-second intervals if necessary.
6. To serve the trout, discard the foil and leek leaves. Let the trout cool slightly, and, using your fingers, peel the skin from the upper surface of each fish, leaving the head and tail intact. Serve 1 fish on each plate, sprinkled with the chives, salt, and pepper and garnished with a lemon wedge. ■

A Saucier's Apprentice: Salsas, Sauces, and Marinades

Sauces and saucelike accompaniments for dishes appear throughout this book as integral parts of individual recipes (see the index for a listing). The following, however, versatile enough to stand alone, were just too good to omit. The proper enhancements, as we all know, can turn an everyday meal into a notable one. The trick with all such accompaniments is not to overwhelm the main ingredient, but merely to complement it or bring it out. Too often, accompaniments come loaded with fat and calories. But I think that after you try a few of these, you will agree that this no longer has to be the case.

FRESH CORN RELISH

■

ABOUT 4 CUPS (8 SERVINGS)

Summer is spelled *c-o-r-n* to me. And as soon as the local crop appears, I start eating it every which way: on the cob and off, combined with other vegetables in soups and stews, salads and relishes. This colorful relish, which I serve with Hawaiian Fish Kebabs (see page 440), is one of the ways I use fresh corn. The relish is also a fine accompaniment to nearly any grilled or broiled fish.

Preparation tips: Although frozen or canned corn kernels are not nearly as good as fresh, they can be used in a pinch. The relish and the dressing can be prepared separately a day or two in advance and combined several hours before serving.

RELISH

2 cups *cooked* corn kernels, preferably fresh
1 cup finely diced green bell pepper
1 cup finely diced red bell pepper
½ cup finely diced celery
½ cup sliced scallions, including some green tops, *or* finely diced red onion
1 tablespoon seeded, minced jalapeño (about 1 pepper) or to taste

DRESSING

1 teaspoon grated lime zest
2 tablespoons fresh lime juice
2 tablespoons white-wine vinegar
1 to 2 tablespoons olive oil *or* canola oil, to taste
1 tablespoon minced cilantro, or to taste
1½ teaspoons cumin
½ teaspoon salt, or to taste
Freshly ground black pepper to taste

1. In a large bowl, combine all the relish ingredients.
2. In a small jar that has a tight-fitting lid, combine all the dressing ingredients, shaking the jar to mix the ingredients thoroughly. Pour the dressing over the relish, and toss the ingredients to combine them well. ■

CORN AND TOMATO RELISH

■

ABOUT 1½ CUPS

After an unrelenting winter, I decided to give summer a head start during April by making a typical warm-weather relish for some grilled salmon. Using corn I had cut from cooked cobs and frozen the summer before, I prepared this simple, fresh, and highly versatile relish.

1 cup *cooked* corn kernels
2 small plum (Roma) tomatoes, seeded and diced
¼ cup chopped green bell pepper
¼ cup chopped red onion
2 teaspoons seeded, minced jalapeño, or to taste
1 teaspoon minced garlic
2 tablespoons red-wine vinegar
1 tablespoon fresh lime juice
1 teaspoon olive oil
¼ teaspoon salt
⅛ teaspoon freshly ground black pepper
1 tablespoon chopped cilantro, or to taste

1. To a small bowl, add all the ingredients *except the cilantro*. Stir the ingredients to combine them thoroughly. Cover and chill the relish until shortly before serving time.

2. Just before serving time, stir in the cilantro. ■

MANGO RELISH

■

I got hooked on mangoes one June while I was working (and sweltering) in Central Desert, Baja, the beauty of the place matched only by a daily treat of perfectly ripened Mexican mangoes sprinkled with fresh lime juice. I have since used this luscious fruit to make all sorts of dishes, including this relish, which can accompany almost any grilled or broiled fish, especially a meaty steak like tuna or swordfish.

Preparation tips: The relish should be prepared at least 1 hour before serving time to allow the flavors to meld. Bring it to room temperature before serving it with grilled or broiled fish.

1 **large ripe mango, peeled, pitted, and diced**
1 **tablespoon honey (use only if mango is not sweet)**
¼ **cup sliced scallions, including some green tops**
½ **cup diced red bell pepper**
Grated zest and juice from ½ small lime
1 **teaspoon minced garlic**
½ **teaspoon peeled, minced gingerroot**
1 **tablespoon seeded, minced jalapeño (about 1 pepper), or to taste**
¼ **teaspoon salt**
1 **tablespoon chopped cilantro** *or* **2 tablespoons chopped fresh parsley**

Combine all the ingredients in a bowl. Cover the bowl, and chill the relish until about 1 hour before serving time. ■

PINEAPPLE AND RED PEPPER SALSA

■

ABOUT 1 CUP

This colorful salsa is a grand, not-at-all-hot accompaniment to a grilled or broiled fish steak such as tuna, swordfish, salmon, or mahi-mahi.

Preparation tip: The salsa can be made ahead through step 2, but the cilantro is best added just before serving time.

- ½ cup dry white wine
- ¼ cup rice vinegar
- 1 cup finely chopped fresh pineapple (about ¼ large pineapple)
- ¼ cup finely chopped red onion
- ¼ cup finely diced red bell pepper *or* roasted red pepper
- 2 tablespoons finely chopped cilantro

1. In a small, heavy, nonreactive or nonstick saucepan, combine the wine and vinegar, and bring them to a boil. Reduce the heat, and simmer the liquid until it has been reduced to about ¼ cup.
2. Stir in the pineapple, onion, and red bell pepper or roasted pepper. Cook the salsa over low heat for 5 minutes. Remove the pan from the heat, transfer the salsa to a bowl, and, when the salsa has cooled, cover and refrigerate it.
3. Just before serving time, stir in the cilantro. ■

KIWI SALSA

■

ABOUT 1 CUP

This is a minimally sweet salsa that goes well with grilled or broiled fish steaks such as salmon, swordfish, or tuna.

- 4 ripe kiwis, peeled and cut into ¼-inch dice
- 2 tablespoons finely chopped red onion
- ½ teaspoon grated orange rind
- 4 teaspoons orange juice
- 1 teaspoon olive oil
- ½ teaspoon salt
- ¼ teaspoon freshly ground black pepper

Combine all the ingredients in a small bowl shortly before serving time. Serve the salsa at room temperature. ■

ORANGE SALSA

■

ABOUT 1½ CUPS

As fruit-based condiments increase in popularity, the cook's imagination is allowed to run wild. I had a lot of fun with this one, a delicious accompaniment to almost any broiled or grilled fish but especially wonderful with a full-flavored fish like salmon.

Preparation tips: For maximum flavor, it is best not to add the capers and cilantro until 1 hour before serving time. As an alternative to these ingredients, try ½ cup of chopped fresh parsley instead of the cilantro and ¼ cup of rinsed, pitted, and coarsely chopped cured olives instead of the capers.

 2 navel oranges, peeled and separated into sections
 ⅓ cup finely chopped red onion
 2 teaspoons olive oil
1½ teaspoons minced garlic
 ¼ teaspoon cumin
 ¼ teaspoon salt
 ⅛ teaspoon cayenne
 2 tablespoons nonpareil (tiny) capers, rinsed, *or* 2 tablespoons
    rinsed and coarsely chopped large capers (see "Preparation tips")
 ¼ cup chopped cilantro (see "Preparation tips")

1. Slice the orange sections crosswise into pieces about ¼ inch thick, and place them in a small bowl.
2. Add the onion, olive oil, garlic, cumin, salt, and cayenne to the oranges, stirring the ingredients to combine them well. Cover the bowl, and refrigerate the salsa until shortly before serving time.
3. Before serving the salsa, stir in the capers and cilantro. ■

DIVINE CHINESE DIPPING SAUCE
■
ABOUT ½ CUP

The host of a party I attended gave me the recipe for this spicy sauce after I and fellow celebrants had sopped up every last drop of it.

Preparation tips: Be sure to mince the ingredients very finely. The sauce can be made days in advance and kept chilled. But it should be brought to room temperature before it is served.

Serving suggestions: The sauce is especially good with the Minced Fish Balls on page 158, Tuna Maki on page 162, Asian Seafood Roll on page 153, and California Rolls on page 160. I even like it with the Japanese-Style Gefilte Fish on page 156.

2 tablespoons chicken broth
2 tablespoons regular or reduced-sodium soy sauce
1 tablespoon rice vinegar
1 tablespoon chili sauce, preferably Chinese style
1 tablespoon Asian sesame oil
1 tablespoon minced scallion
2 teaspoons minced garlic
1 teaspoon peeled, minced gingerroot
1 teaspoon sugar
⅛ teaspoon red pepper flakes

1. Combine all the ingredients in a small nonreactive or nonstick saucepan. Bring the ingredients to a simmer, and cook the sauce for 2 minutes. Remove the pan from the heat, and let the sauce cool.
2. When the sauce has cooled, transfer it to a small serving bowl or glass jar, and refrigerate it. Bring the sauce back to room temperature before serving it. ■

RED-HOT SCALLION AND SESAME SAUCE

■

ABOUT ½ CUP

Some do, indeed, like it hot, and the heat of this Asian-style sauce can be adjusted simply by using more or less cayenne. The sauce was a favorite among a variety of accompaniments for a mixed grill of fish steaks.

Preparation tips: Sesame seeds can be toasted quickly in a skillet but must be watched and tossed every few seconds to keep them from burning. The sauce can be prepared in advance through step 2, but add the reserved scallions and crushed sesame seeds just before serving time.

Serving suggestions: Although I serve this with grilled fish, it would also be fabulous with the Minced Fish Balls on page 158 or the Japanese-Style Gefilte Fish on page 156 or hot or cold cooked shrimp.

> 2 teaspoons toasted sesame seeds, divided
> 4 tablespoons (¼ cup) finely chopped scallions, including light green tops, divided
> 2 tablespoons soy sauce
> 2 tablespoons water
> 2 teaspoons Asian sesame oil
> 1 teaspoon sugar
> 1 teaspoon minced garlic
> ⅛ to ¼ teaspoon cayenne, to taste

1. In a mortar with a pestle, crush 1 teaspoon of the toasted sesame seeds. Set the crushed seeds aside.
2. In a small bowl, combine the remaining teaspoon of sesame seeds with 3 tablespoons of the scallions and all the remaining ingredients *except the crushed sesame seeds.* Cover and refrigerate the bowl until shortly before serving time.
3. Before serving the sauce, add the remaining 1 tablespoon of scallions and the reserved crushed sesame seeds, and stir the sauce to combine the ingredients thoroughly. ■

TOMATO SAUCE WITH CAPERS

■

ABOUT ⅔ CUP

This is a versatile sauce that suits any mild-flavored fish from cod and flounder to snapper and skate. It can be used on top of both hot and cold fish that
has been baked, broiled, steamed, or grilled.

Preparation tip: The sauce can be prepared ahead as is, or you can make
larger quantities to be refrigerated for several days or frozen for weeks.

1 teaspoon olive oil
2 tablespoons finely chopped onion
2 tablespoons finely chopped capers
2 teaspoons minced garlic
½ pound plum (Roma) tomatoes, finely diced
¼ teaspoon dried basil *or* 1 teaspoon minced fresh basil
⅛ teaspoon dried thyme leaves
Freshly ground black pepper to taste

1. Briefly heat the olive oil over medium-low heat in a medium-sized skillet
   that has a cover and a nonstick surface. Add the onion, and sauté it for 2
   minutes. Add the capers and garlic, and sauté them, stirring the ingredients often, 1 minute longer.
2. Add the tomatoes, basil, thyme, and pepper. Cover the skillet, and simmer the mixture for about 5 minutes. If the sauce is to be used over cold
   fish, let it cool, then chill it before serving it. ■

TOMATILLO SAUCE

■

ABOUT 1 CUP

Tomatillos are, as you might guess, closely related to tomatoes. They are a popular ingredient in Mexican cooking. Here, they are made into a mild sauce with a southwestern flair that could be used to dress up a simple piece of cooked fish or shellfish. The sauce is best served warm or at room temperature; it becomes gel-like in the refrigerator.

Preparation tip: To roast the chilies, spear them one at a time, and hold them over a gas flame, until the skin chars on all sides. *Or* place them under the broiler, turning them often, until the skin chars all over. Then remove the blackened skin.

10 ounces tomatillos (about 4), papery skin removed and stem ends cut off
²/₃ cup chicken broth
¼ pound poblano or Anaheim chilies (about 2 peppers), roasted, cored, and seeded (see "Preparation tip")
¼ cup chopped onion
¼ cup packed cilantro leaves
¼ teaspoon salt, or to taste

1. Quarter the tomatillos, and place them and the broth in a small saucepan. Bring the broth to a boil, reduce the heat, and simmer the ingredients for 6 minutes or until the tomatillos are soft. With a slotted spoon, transfer the tomatillos to the container of a food processor or blender, *reserving the broth.*

2. Cut the chilies into eighths, and add them to the food-processor or blender container along with the onion and cilantro. Puree the ingredients, adding the reserved broth 1 tablespoon at a time as needed to produce a sauce with the consistency of heavy cream (about 2 tablespoons broth should do the trick). Blend in the salt.

3. Transfer the sauce to a bowl, cover it with plastic wrap, and chill it until you are ready to use it. Serve the sauce at room temperature or warmed, placing it on top of or under cooked fish or shellfish. If you wish to serve it warm, add it to the fish during the last minute or so of cooking time, or heat the sauce separately in the microwave oven. ■

MEXICAN MARINADE

■

ABOUT ½ CUP

This tequila-spiked marinade has incredible staying power in the refrigerator. A week of rain kept me from using it for a planned barbecue, then I forgot about it for a few more weeks, finally using it to season some blackfish fillets. It should also fare well on shrimp, catfish, tuna, or almost any fish that could benefit from moistening and flavoring before being grilled.

3 tablespoons tequila
2 tablespoons fresh lime juice
2 teaspoons olive oil
1½ tablespoons minced fresh basil
1½ tablespoons chopped fresh rosemary
1 teaspoon minced garlic
¼ teaspoon freshly ground white pepper
⅛ teaspoon salt

Place all the ingredients in a jar that has a tight-fitting lid or in a bowl, and shake or whisk the ingredients to combine them thoroughly. Keep the marinade chilled until you are ready to use it. ■

BASIL-PARSLEY MAYONNAISE

■

ABOUT 1 CUP

Even though I originally prepared this low-fat mayonnaise as a garnish for cold boiled lobster (see page 372), it would go equally well with many seafood dishes, including the crab cakes on page 418, or as a dip for cooked shrimp.

½ cup loosely packed basil leaves
½ cup loosely packed parsley leaves, preferably Italian (flat-leaf)
½ cup nonfat or reduced-fat mayonnaise, or a combination of the two
¼ cup nonfat or low-fat plain yogurt
2 tablespoons fresh lemon juice
½ teaspoon sugar

1. Combine all the ingredients in the container of a food processor or blender, and process the ingredients until the basil and parsley are very finely chopped and the ingredients are thoroughly mixed.
2. Transfer the mayonnaise to a serving dish, cover it with plastic wrap, and chill it until serving time. ■

CILANTRO CREAM

■

ABOUT ¾ CUP

This fat-free sauce makes a lovely topping for seafood tacos or for a vegetable-based or tomato-based seafood soup.

Preparation tips: If possible, prepare the sauce hours—or even a day—ahead to allow the flavors to meld. In place of the sour cream, you could start with ¾ cup yogurt and drain it through a yogurt strainer or several layers of cheese-cloth to thicken it.

¼ cup nonfat plain yogurt
¼ cup nonfat sour cream
1 tablespoon minced scallions
1 tablespoon fresh lemon juice
½ teaspoon seeded, minced jalapeño *or* green chili
¼ teaspoon sugar
¼ teaspoon freshly ground black pepper
⅛ teaspoon salt (optional)
⅓ cup finely chopped cilantro

1. In a small bowl, whisk together all the ingredients *except the cilantro.*
2. Stir in the cilantro, cover the bowl with plastic wrap, and chill the sauce until 20 to 30 minutes before serving time. Allow the sauce to come to room temperature before serving it. ■

COMPOUND BUTTER

■

8 TABLESPOONS

Compound butters infused with a variety of flavors have been a part of traditional French cooking for centuries. They do have a place in this low-fat book because so little is needed to add flavor, smoothness, and moisture to a dish, especially to grilled fish. The one offered here is a tried-and-true, simple classic, known in France as beurre maître d'hôtel. Like any butter, it can be kept frozen for months, poised to add that little touch of refinement at just the right moment.

8 **tablespoons (1 stick) sweet butter** *or* **butter-margarine mix, at room temperature**
2 **teaspoons fresh lemon juice**
1 **tablespoon chopped fresh parsley**
½ **teaspoon freshly ground pepper, preferably white**

1. In a small bowl, cream together the butter and lemon juice. Add the parsley and pepper, mixing the ingredients well.
2. On wax paper, form the mixture into a cylinder about the length of the original stick of butter. Wrap the wax paper around the butter, and roll the butter, using the same motion you would with a rolling pin, until it is smooth.
3. With the butter still sealed in the wax paper, chill it until it is hard.
4. If you wish to freeze it, first cut the chilled roll into slices ¼-inch thick, separate the slices with plastic wrap, and enclose the slices in a sealed plastic freezer bag.
5. To serve the butter, place a pat in the middle of a grilled, broiled, baked, poached, or steamed fish fillet. ■

Fish in Their Finite Variety:
A Seafood Glossary

The following glossary of edible fish is by no means all-inclusive. Rather, it lists important, useful, and interesting facts about the fish you are most likely to encounter in the market and on menus as well as in this book. All nutritional data are drawn from United States Department of Agriculture sources, primarily the agency's Agriculture Handbook Number 8–15. The data are for 3½-ounce (100 gram) portions, raw, except when indicated. The designation "n/a" under "Nutrients" means no data were available.

ANCHOVY—Family Engraulidae

Characteristics: Canned, they are salty, with pronounced flavor. Fresh, they are firm, mild-flavored, and flaky.

Preparation: Tiny and sleek, fresh anchovies can be grilled or broiled; canned, they are generally used as a seasoning in stews, salads, pasta dishes, dressings, and sauces. Because most canned anchovies are heavily salted and packed in oil, some cooks soak them in milk or white wine for 15 minutes before using them.

Origins: Anchovies flourish in most of the world's oceans.

Sidelight: The familiar dark-pink color of canned anchovies is a result of the curing process. Fresh, they are white-fleshed.

Peak season: Year round.

Nutrients:	RAW	CANNED
Calories/calories from fat	131/43.56	210/87.30
Protein (grams)	20.35	28.89
Fat (grams)	4.84	9.70
Saturated fat (grams)	1.28	2.20
Sodium (milligrams)	104	3.67
Cholesterol (milligrams)	n/a	n/a
Omega-3 (grams)	1.45	2.06

(*Note:* Data for canned anchovies were calculated after draining.)

BASS, SEA—*Centropristis striata*

Other names: Black sea bass, rock sea bass (actually another species of sea bass).

Confusions: It is neither striped bass nor blackfish.

Characteristics: It has mild, moderately firm white meat and is related to the grouper. It can grow to 8 pounds but is usually harvested at 1½ to 3 pounds.

Preparation: Any method. It is especially attractive cooked whole but can be cut into steaks or filleted.

Origins: Bottom fish from the northeast Atlantic coast.

Sidelight: Sea bass are born as females and become males between the ages of 2 and 5.

Peak season: January through August.

Nutrients:

Calories/calories from fat	97/18
Protein (grams)	18.43
Fat (grams)	2.00
Saturated fat (grams)	0.51
Sodium (milligrams)	68
Cholesterol (milligrams)	41
Omega-3 (grams)	0.60

BASS, STRIPED—*Morone saxatilis*

Other names: Striper, rockfish, rock.

Confusions: It is often confused with others in the bass group, most of which are less highly regarded. You had best purchase fillets with the striped skin on to be sure you are buying the real thing.

Characteristics: It is mild, moist, and slightly sweet with flaky, lean, but firm flesh and is regarded by many as the best eating fish of all. The wild fish is generally thought to be superior to the farmed hybrid variety, although the farmed striped bass, because it is readily available and really very good, is widely admired.

Preparation: Whole—poached or baked; fillets—broiled, grilled, poached, or microwaved.

Origins: The true striped bass resides in coastal waters until spawning time, when it heads for freshwater rivers. It is found along the Atlantic coast of the United States. Since pollution and overfishing have greatly diminished the availability of striped bass from the wild, almost all striped bass sold today are a farm-raised hybrid.

Sidelight: The striped bass's resilience and adaptability even in polluted waters (where it can encounter toxins that make it unsafe to eat) have helped it survive to see days of increasingly cleaner waters. Happily, the species is now reviving.

Peak season: Year round.

Nutrients:

Calories/calories from fat	97/20.97
Protein (grams)	17.73
Fat (grams)	2.33
Saturated fat (grams)	0.51
Sodium (milligrams)	69
Cholesterol (milligrams)	80
Omega-3 (grams)	0.75

BLACKFISH—*Tautoga onitis*

Other name: Tautog.

Confusion: It is not a black sea bass.

Characteristics: Mild to bland with a moderately firm texture, it is usually sold at about 3 pounds when whole but can be as large as 25 pounds.

Preparation: Poached, steamed, baked, or grilled. It is excellent in soups, stews, escabeche, and fish salads.

Origins: The Atlantic Ocean from Cape Cod to South Carolina.

Sidelight: Because it eats crustaceans and mollusks, it has prominent, human-looking teeth, complete with molars.

Nutrients:

Calories/calories from fat	164/85.23
Protein (grams)	18.48
Fat (grams)	9.47
Saturated fat (grams)	3.51
Sodium (milligrams)	65
Cholesterol (milligrams)	50
Omega-3 (grams)	0.57

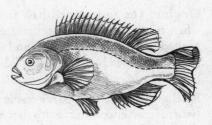

BLUEFISH—*Pomatomus saltatrix*

Other names: Snapper (the young bluefish), chopper.

Confusions: It is not related to fish in the snapper family.

Characteristics: It is rich, moderately oily, and strongly flavored with a bluish-gray cast and soft, flaky texture. Bluefish are sold fresh, whole and filleted. Frozen bluefish do not last well. Since much of the harvest is provided by sport fishermen, the quality of the fish must be carefully assessed before buying the fish. However, most store-bought bluefish is commercially caught.

Preparation: Baked, broiled, hot-smoked, or grilled. An acidic marinade is a foil for its oiliness. Smoked bluefish is an excellent main ingredient in a cold fish salad. It is usually regarded as inappropriate for poaching or chowders. A dark strip of meat on the fillet can have a strong, bitter flavor, especially when the fish is served hot—some people remove it before cooking.

Origins: Every spring, bluefish migrate toward shore and northward along the East Coast, and in October, as the days shorten in length, they swim south. The largest catches occur during these migrations in Chesapeake Bay and off New Jersey and Long Island. But bluefish are also found almost worldwide—in South Africa, Australia, and in the eastern Atlantic and the Mediterranean Sea.

Sidelight: They are cannibalistic fish, with ferocious feeding habits, a behavior that requires strong digestive enzymes that will attack and quickly spoil the bluefish itself if it is not gutted and iced soon after the catch.

Peak season: January through May, August through December.

Nutrients:

Calories/calories from fat	124/38.16
Protein (grams)	20.04
Fat (grams)	4.24
Saturated fat (grams)	0.92
Sodium (milligrams)	60
Cholesterol (milligrams)	59
Omega-3 (grams)	0.77

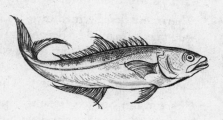

BONITO—*Sarda sarda* (Atlantic), *Sarda chiliensis* (Pacific), *Sarda orientalis* (striped)

Other names: Red baitfish, redbait, California bonito, Oriental bonito, belted bonito, pelamid, shortfinned tunny.

Confusion: It is not a bonito shark, which is a shortfin mako shark. It is, in fact, a tuna.

Characteristics: It has firm-textured, meaty flesh with very pronounced flavor. Its flesh is bright red when the fish is caught but turns an apricot color after the fish is bled. It is relatively small—weighing less than 10 pounds.

Sidelight: Bonito is an excellent substitute for tuna since it is one. But because it is considered less valuable than other tunas, the bonito is often treated as an outcast.

Nutrients:

Calories/calories from fat	108/8.55
Protein (grams)	23.38
Fat (grams)	0.95
Saturated fat (grams)	0.24
Sodium (milligrams)	37
Cholesterol (milligrams)	45
Omega-3 (grams)	0.22

CARP—*Cyprinus carpio*

Other names: European carp, German carp, mirror carp, grass carp, bighead carp, etc.

Confusions: Despite varying names and species, for culinary purposes, a carp is a carp. All are in the minnow family.

Characteristics: Farmed carp are mild and sweet-flavored; those caught in the wild may taste muddy, depending on the water quality. Common carp have dark flesh; grass and bighead carp are whiter. The flesh is moist, flaky, and soft with a high fat content. Whole carp are sold at weights of 2 to 5 pounds, although they can grow as large as 60 pounds. They are infamous for their Y-shaped flesh bones.

Preparation: Stuffed, steamed, poached, fried, baked, broiled, smoked. The carp's subtle flavor goes well with marinades and sauces. It is traditionally used to make gefilte fish.

Origins: Carp is a freshwater fish, indigenous to Eurasia, but is now common in freshwater lakes and ponds in many parts of the world.

Sidelight: Carp were one of the first candidates for farming: the Chinese had carp farms as early as 500 B.C. Because it reproduces so vigorously and destroys the habitats of other fish, the carp's introduction to the United States in 1876 was an ecological blunder.

Peak season: Year round.

Nutrients:

Calories/calories from fat	127/50.40
Protein (grams)	17.83
Fat (grams)	5.60
Saturated fat (grams)	1.08
Sodium (milligrams)	49
Cholesterol (milligrams)	66
Omega-3 (grams)	0.35

CATFISH, CHANNEL—*Ictalurus punctatus*

Other names: Channel cat, spotted cat, lake catfish.

Confusions: There are many catfish other than the channel catfish, which is the most widely eaten. A fish called ocean catfish, however, is not among them, although it is sometimes marketed as true catfish. It is actually an alternate name for the wolffish, a large, very firm-fleshed ocean fish that dines on shellfish.

Characteristics: Farmed catfish, forced to feed at the surface of the pond, generally have a sweet, mild flavor and soft, sometimes springy white flesh. Bottom-feeding, wild varieties may taste muddy, depending on the water quality. Catfish are adaptable enough to act as a substitute for many other fish such as flounder or cod. The farm production of catfish is regulated, as is the harvest of wild fish, by the Food and Drug Administration and the Departments of Agriculture and Commerce. Most catfish are produced in the Mississippi River Delta area—Mississippi, Alabama, and Arkansas—but California and Idaho also raise a significant amount.

Preparation: Baked, broiled, stewed, sautéed, poached, smoked, steamed.

Sidelight: Catfish—strange, whiskered animals to start with—took on a new sense of weirdness a few years back when a type called the walking catfish was inadvertently introduced to Florida from Thailand and immediately began showing off its particular talent: walking out of the water on its fins and crossing Floridian roads. The walking catfish is edible, but its skin is foul-smelling and its spines very sharp. Best to let it walk on.

Peak season: Year round.

Nutrients:

Calories/calories from fat	135/68.31
Protein (grams)	15.55
Fat (grams)	7.59
Saturated fat (grams)	1.77
Sodium (milligrams)	53
Cholesterol (milligrams)	47
Omega-3 (grams)	0.27

CAVIAR (Various)

Other names: American caviar, whitefish caviar, lumpfish caviar, salmon caviar.

Confusions: True caviar is sturgeon eggs, notably from Russia and Iran but also from the United States (all tins of caviar must indicate the country of origin). Fish roe prepared and marketed to resemble true caviar, such as whitefish or salmon roe, must indicate the fish from which it was taken.

Characteristics: True caviar—the extraordinarily expensive, salted eggs of the sturgeon—when properly processed, bursts in the mouth with intense flavor. The roe is removed from the sturgeon and washed on a screen that separates the eggs from their sac. After rinsing them, the eggs are drained and salted with about 5 ounces of salt for every 10 pounds of roe. The eggs must be stored in airtight containers and refrigerated. After 1 week, they reach their optimal flavor and should be eaten within 6 months. Refrigerated caviar tins should be turned from time to time so that the fat that coats the eggs does not rise to the top. The term *malossol* is Russian for "little salt." The caviar prepared with only 3 to 4 percent salt requires more careful storage and refrigeration than heavily salted types and is more expensive.

Variations:

Beluga	gray to black roe with the largest egg
Osetra	gray to gray-green medium roe with a nutty flavor
Sevruga	dark-gray small roe with fine flavor

Preparation: Good-quality caviar is best served as simply as possible, and used sparingly.

Sidelight: Sturgeon are such slow-maturing fish—some living to perhaps 100 years of age—that the beluga, for instance, does not begin to produce roe until it is 9 to 15 years old.

Peak season: Year round.

Nutrients (in 1 ounce):

Calories/calories from fat	71/45.09
Protein (grams)	6.89
Fat (grams)	5.01
Saturated fat (grams)	n/a
Sodium (milligrams)	420
Cholesterol (milligrams)	165
Omega-3 (grams)	n/a

CLAMS, HARD-SHELL—*Mercenaria mercenaria*

Other names: Quahogs, quahaugs, chowder clams, cherrystone clams, topneck clams, littleneck clams.

Confusion: The West Coast littleneck clam, which is rarely eaten raw, is a different species from the clam of the same name found on the East Coast.

Characteristics: Clams have a sweet, distinct flavor and are soft and juicy when cooked. If bootlegged shellfish are taken from contaminated waters, they can cause mild to serious stomach discomfort, perhaps even hepatitis, and should not be eaten, even if they are cooked. There are several sizes of hard-shell clams:

Littlenecks	1½ to 2⅓ inches across
Topnecks	2½ inches across
Cherrystones	2½ to 3½ inches across
Chowder clams	3½ inches or more across

Preparation: Small and medium clams can be served raw on the half shell, baked, sautéed, or steamed. Larger clams are less tender and are usually chopped to be used in soups, chowders, stuffings, and fritters.

Origins: The hard-shell clams known as quahogs are harvested along the North American Atlantic coast.

Sidelight: In some parts of the world, clams have been known to grow to 4 feet and more in length.

Peak season: Year round.

Nutrients:

Calories/calories from fat	74/8.73
Protein (grams)	12.77
Fat (grams)	0.97
Saturated fat (grams)	0.09
Sodium (milligrams)	56
Cholesterol (milligrams)	34
Omega-3 (grams)	0.14

COD, ATLANTIC—*Gadus morhua*

Other names: Rock cod, codling, scrod cod.

Confusions: Scrod, which is an unofficial name most often used for a small cod, is a term sometimes applied to other fish such as pollock. Also, cod is not lingcod, black cod, rock cod, or whitefish.

Characteristics: The Atlantic cod is a white-fleshed fish, mild-tasting, slightly sweet, with lean, tender meat that flakes easily. It is at its best when really fresh.

Preparation: It cooks very quickly, is best prepared with moist heat, and must not be overcooked. Steaming, braising, baking, sautéing, or poaching are the methods of choice.

Origins: The ocean waters off Canada, Norway, Denmark, Iceland, and from Virginia to the Arctic.

Sidelight: Historically, cod has been one of the most important of commercial fish and has long been subject to overfishing. Even in medieval times, salted and dried cod were in great demand for Lent.

Peak season: Year round.

Nutrients:

Calories/calories from fat	82/6.03
Protein (grams)	17.81
Fat (grams)	0.67
Saturated fat (grams)	0.13
Sodium (milligrams)	54
Cholesterol (milligrams)	43
Omega-3 (grams)	0.18

COD, PACIFIC—*Gadus macrocephalus*

Other names: Alaska codfish, gray cod, true cod, treska.

Characteristics: It is lean, tender, and mild-flavored, though not as sweet as the Atlantic variety nor as large.

Preparation: See **Cod, Atlantic.**

Origins: The waters off the West Coast from California to northern Alaska. Japan and Korea ship it frozen to the United States.

Peak season: Frozen, year round.

Nutrients:

Calories/calories from fat	82/5.67
Protein (grams)	17.90
Fat (grams)	0.63
Saturated fat (grams)	0.08
Sodium (milligrams)	71
Cholesterol (milligrams)	37
Omega-3 (grams)	0.22

CONCH—Family Strombidae

Other names: Lambi, scungilli.

Confusion: It is not a whelk, although conch and whelk are similar, and whelk is often listed on menus as scungilli.

Characteristics: Its sweet, springy flesh must be cooked long enough to eliminate toughness. The meat is often sold frozen and fully cooked.

Preparation: Chopped, it imparts excellent texture as well as flavor to soups, stews, chowders, and pasta sauces. Scungilli marinara, a southern Italian dish, is made with conch or whelk. Sometimes conch is eaten raw, sliced thin and with a sprinkle of lime juice.

Origins: The warm waters off the Florida Keys and in the Caribbean.

Sidelight: Conchs are herbivores but are so similar in appearance, taste, and texture to the carnivorous whelk that they can be prepared in the same way. Whelks are found along the East Coast from Rhode Island to the Gulf of Mexico. They break open the shells of mollusks with the turret of their own shell to extract the flesh with their tongue.

Nutrients:

Calories/calories from fat	137/3.60
Protein (grams)	23.84
Fat (grams)	0.40
Saturated fat (grams)	0.03
Sodium (milligrams)	206
Cholesterol (milligrams)	65
Omega-3 (grams)	0.01

CRAB, BLUE—*Callinectes sapidus*

Other name: Soft-shell blue crab (at growth stage only).

Characteristics: The blue crab has a sweet taste and flaky meat. In the brief period between the shedding of the old shell and the hardening of the new one, it is a soft-shell crab, and, at this stage, its whole body is eaten, including the shell, after the gills, mouth parts, and front spines are removed. Whole crabs should be bought live or cooked. Commercially packaged crabmeat, which has already been extracted from the shell, is sold cooked in either fresh or pasteurized form. There are several grades of crabmeat; lump is the best—big pieces with no bits of shell or cartilage.

Preparation: The hard-shelled variety is steamed or boiled and the meat extracted with a paring knife, mallet, and fingers. Its flesh is excellent in salads and in crab cakes. Soft-shelled, the crab is grilled, sautéed, and used in soups and stews.

Origins: Blue crab is found in the Atlantic from Cape Cod to Florida and in the Gulf of Mexico. It has also been introduced to the Mediterranean.

Sidelight: Because their shells are loaded with calcium, soft-shelled crabs, which are eaten shell and all, are an excellent source of the mineral. The crab's whole body is safe to eat because, during the period of shedding, the crab does not eat and purges itself.

Peak season: Mid-May to mid-September.

Nutrients:

Calories/calories from fat	87/9.72
Protein (grams)	18.06
Fat (grams)	1.08
Saturated fat (grams)	0.22
Sodium (milligrams)	293
Cholesterol (milligrams)	78
Omega-3 (grams)	0.32

CRAB, DUNGENESS—*Cancer magister*

Characteristics: Its meat is sweet, delicate, and flaky. Since the crab is large, the meat is relatively easy to extract. It is popular on the West Coast and is becoming increasingly known elsewhere. Dungeness crabs are sold alive, cooked whole, and as fresh (unpasteurized) canned meat. (This is unlike other large crabs—the king and snow crabs—which are available frozen year round.)

Preparation: It is most commonly steamed and eaten whole with butter or a sauce. Meat removed from the shell can also be used in soups, sautés, creamed dishes, and salads.

Origins: Off the West Coast, British Columbia, and Alaska.

Sidelight: A big crab, it can weigh as much as 3 pounds.

Peak season: December through February.

Nutrients:

Calories/calories from fat	86/8.73
Protein (grams)	17.41
Fat (grams)	0.97
Saturated fat (grams)	0.13
Sodium (milligrams)	295
Cholesterol (milligrams)	59
Omega-3 (grams)	0.31

CRAB, SOFT-SHELL

See **Crab, Blue.**

FLOUNDER (LEMON SOLE)—*Pleuronectes americanus*

Other names: Blackback or winter flounder when it is smaller than 3 pounds.

Confusions: It is often confused with dover sole, a fine European sole (although the name is used for a Pacific flounder as well).

Characteristics: This flatfish has mild, sweet-tasting, fragile white flesh that breaks into fine flakes when it is cooked. The designations "flounder" and "sole" are applied to the same species, usually depending on the size of the individual fish, the larger ones designated as sole.

Preparation: Simple preparations are best, such as sautéing, broiling, baking, or (for thicker fillets only) microwaving.

Origins: The waters off the Atlantic coast from Labrador to Georgia, and most common in the area from the Gulf of St. Lawrence to Chesapeake Bay.

Sidelight: Young flounder begin life swimming upright (like ordinary fish). But, as they mature, they rotate until they are on their sides on the bottom, and one eye migrates so that both end up on the top side of the head.

Peak season: Year round.

Nutrients:

Calories/calories from fat	91/10.71
Protein (grams)	18.84
Fat (grams)	1.19
Saturated fat (grams)	0.28
Sodium (milligrams)	81
Cholesterol (milligrams)	48
Omega-3 (grams)	0.20

FLOUNDER (ROCK SOLE)—*Pleuronectes bilineatus*

Other names: Rough-back, broadfin, and rock flounder.

Characteristics: Rock sole has a sweet flavor and is slightly meatier than other soles. It is caught off North America's West Coast from California to the Bering Sea and is also available on the Asian side of the Pacific Ocean. It usually weighs no more than 5 pounds.

Preparation: Because it is firmer than other flounders, rock sole is particularly adaptable to stuffing and rolling.

Peak season: Year round.

Nutrients:

Calories/calories from fat	91/10.71
Protein (grams)	18.84
Fat (grams)	1.19
Saturated fat (grams)	0.28
Sodium (milligrams)	81
Cholesterol (milligrams)	48
Omega-3 (grams)	0.20

FLOUNDER (YELLOWTAIL)—*Pleuronectes ferrugineus*

Other names: Yellowtail, rusty dab, sand dab.

Confusions: A snapper, an emperor, a rockfish, and a jack have "yellowtail" as all or part of their name.

Characteristics: It has a sweet, mild flavor and tender flesh with a small flake. Yellowtail flounder was the most popular flatfish in the United States a decade ago, but overfishing has created a severe decline in the supply.

Preparation: Methods that help preserve moisture such as poaching, steaming, sautéing, microwaving, and frying.

Origins: The Atlantic coast from Labrador to Virginia.

Peak season: June through August.

Nutrients:

Calories/calories from fat	91/10.71
Protein (grams)	18.84
Fat (grams)	1.19
Saturated fat (grams)	0.28
Sodium (milligrams)	81
Cholesterol (milligrams)	48
Omega-3 (grams)	0.20

GROUPER, BLACK—*Mycteroperca sp.*

Other names: Springer. Close relative of the gag, which is often sold as black grouper.

Confusions: Sometimes other related fish of lesser quality in the same family are mislabeled and passed off as grouper.

Characteristics: Black grouper has a mild, sweet flavor, more pronounced than red grouper, and lean, flaky white meat that retains its moisture well in cooking. It is a good substitute for the pricier red snapper.

Preparation: Broiled, baked, or grilled with the skin left on to preserve moistness. It holds up well in chowders and stews.

Origins: Tropical and subtropical waters. Mexico and other Latin American/Caribbean countries produce most of the U.S. supply.

Sidelight: Despite their name, groupers are loners but evidently get along well with people. Divers report cultivating relationships with individual groupers by revisiting them in their territory.

Peak season: January through April, year round in some areas.

Nutrients:

Calories/calories from fat	92/9.18
Protein (grams)	19.38
Fat (grams)	1.02
Saturated fat (grams)	0.23
Sodium (milligrams)	53
Cholesterol (milligrams)	37
Omega-3 (grams)	0.25

GROUPER, RED—*Epinephelus morio*

Other names: Cherna americana.

Characteristics: Red grouper has a mild to sweet flavor, milder than black grouper. It has a larger head than either black grouper or gag, and is reddish-brown in color. The mouth has a reddish lining. Red grouper is the most common grouper in the United States and is usually less expensive than black grouper or gag.

Preparation: *See* **Grouper, Black.**

Origins: Red grouper is primarily a warm-water, reef-dwelling fish, but it may be found all the way from Massachusetts to Brazil. It is most plentiful off Florida and in the Gulf of Mexico.

Peak season: Most of the year, from various countries.

Nutrients:

Calories/calories from fat	92/9.18
Protein (grams)	19.38
Fat (grams)	1.02
Saturated fat (grams)	0.23
Sodium (milligrams)	53
Cholesterol (milligrams)	37
Omega-3 (grams)	0.25

HALIBUT, ATLANTIC—*Hippoglossus hippoglossus*

Characteristics: It has very mild, sweet flesh, which is fine-grained, snow-white, and dense with firm flakes. It dries out easily if overcooked.

Origins: The North Atlantic from New Jersey to Greenland and on the northern European coast as far south as the English Channel. It generally lives in waters deeper than 200 feet.

Sidelight: The Atlantic halibut is a flounder, and the largest flatfish: the females grow to 700 pounds, although overfishing has made it rare to find one over 300 pounds.

Peak season: April through December.

Nutrients:

Calories/calories from fat	110/20.61
Protein (grams)	20.81
Fat (grams)	2.29
Saturated fat (grams)	0.32
Sodium (milligrams)	54
Cholesterol (milligrams)	32
Omega-3 (grams)	0.36

HALIBUT, PACIFIC—*Hippoglossus stenolepis*

Characteristics: It is similar to the Atlantic halibut.

Preparation: Because it is firm for a flatfish, halibut can be skewered for grilling and can be served baked, broiled, sautéed, or poached. It also does well in soups and chowders.

Origins: Pacific halibut is caught in the Gulf of Alaska for the most part, though it may be found as far south as California. Most often it is sold as steaks, although sometimes it is offered as huge fillets of perhaps 10 pounds called "fletches."

Peak season: March through August.

Nutrients:

Calories/calories from fat	110/20.61
Protein (grams)	20.81
Fat (grams)	2.29
Saturated fat (grams)	0.32
Sodium (milligrams)	54
Cholesterol (milligrams)	32
Omega-3 (grams)	0.36

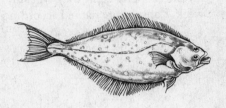

LEMON SOLE

See **Flounder (Lemon Sole).**

LOBSTER, AMERICAN—*Homarus americanus*

Other name: Northern lobster.

Confusions: It is frequently confused with the Spiny lobster or rock lobster, which does not have claws like the American lobster but is still delicious and is widely sold in the United States. The rock lobster is most often a warm-water crustacean, known sometimes as crawfish and, in France, as langouste.

Characteristics: The American lobster is mild and sweet-flavored; it has firm meat, the firmest meat being obtained from the tail. Lobsters should be alive when purchased, stored under refrigeration in an open container so that they do not suffocate, and covered with a damp dishtowel or seaweed to keep them moist. Properly kept, they will survive at least several hours and often up to one week. Lobsters are named according to size:

Chix	1 pound or less
Mediums	1 1/8 to 1 1/4 pounds
Selects	1 1/2 to 2 1/2 pounds
Jumbos	over 2 1/2 pounds
Culls	lobsters with 1 claw
Bullets (pistols)	lobsters with no claws
Shedders	newly molted, soft-shelled lobsters

Preparation: Steamed, baked, broiled, or boiled whole. (Some say that boiling the lobster detracts from its flavor.)

Origins: Lobsters are harvested in North Atlantic waters from Labrador to North Carolina. The largest harvests are in Canada, Massachusetts, and Maine.

Sidelight: Lobsters shed their shells on average once a year in the summer or fall, and the newly molted lobster has the sweetest meat although its texture is looser and more watery than hard-shelled lobsters.

Peak season: May through September.

Nutrients:

Calories/calories from fat	90/8.10
Protein (grams)	18.80
Fat (grams)	0.90
Saturated fat (grams)	n/a
Sodium (milligrams)	n/a
Cholesterol (milligrams)	95
Omega-3 (grams)	n/a

MACKEREL, ATLANTIC—*Scomber scombrus*

Other names: Boston mackerel, tinkers.

Characteristics: The oil-rich meat has an intense flavor and is soft, flaky, and moist. Gray when raw, it becomes creamy white after cooking. Mackerel belong to the migratory tuna family. They are small, usually weighing 1½ pounds or less. Immature mackerel, weighing less than 1 pound, are sold in the spring.

Preparation: The high oil content makes mackerel especially fine for grilling or smoking. It can also be baked, broiled, fried, braised in wine, and microwaved. The dark outer bands of stronger-tasting meat can be cut away before cooking, if desired.

Origins: The coastline of the northwestern Atlantic and eastern North Atlantic.

Sidelight: Although they are delicious, most mackerel, rather than being consumed by people, are still sold to pet-food manufacturers.

Peak season: March through December.

Nutrients:

Calories/calories from fat	205/125.01
Protein (grams)	18.60
Fat (grams)	13.89
Saturated fat (grams)	3.26
Sodium (milligrams)	90
Cholesterol (milligrams)	70
Omega-3 (grams)	2.30

MACKEREL, SPANISH—*Scomberomorus maculatus*

Characteristics: Spanish mackerel is larger, but has a weaker flavor and paler flesh than Atlantic mackerel. The meat is soft and gray or pink when raw, but it firms up when cooked. Spanish mackerel has a silvery body with spots ranging in color from yellow to deep orange. Like most mackerel, it is smooth and scaleless in appearance (the scales are actually very small).

Preparation: *See* Mackerel, Atlantic.

Origins: Spanish mackerel are caught in the waters from Chesapeake Bay to southern Florida and into the Gulf of Mexico. They are also found in far-flung areas of the Pacific and the Indian Ocean.

Sidelight: Not surprisingly, perhaps, given the capriciousness of fish names, Spanish mackerel are not caught off Spain, although the West African species might have been.

Nutrients:

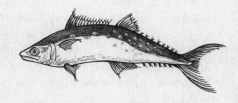

Calories/calories from fat	139/56.70
Protein (grams)	19.29
Fat (grams)	6.30
Saturated fat (grams)	1.83
Sodium (milligrams)	59
Cholesterol (milligrams)	76
Omega-3 (grams)	1.34

MAHI-MAHI—*Coryphaena hippurus*

Other names: Dolphin, dorado.

Confusion: It is a fish and, therefore, not even a close relative to the dolphin, which is a mammal.

Characteristics: It has a sweet, mildly pronounced flavor that can be made still milder by trimming away the darker portions of meat, if desired. The meat is very lean, white, and tender, and yields large, moist flakes after cooking.

Preparation: Baked, broiled, blackened, sautéed, grilled. It is also used in chowders and stews.

Origins: Mahi-mahi are harvested off Hawaii and Florida as well as elsewhere in the area of the Gulf Stream, and from Southern California to South America. They have been known to migrate far north—to Long Island—in warmer periods.

Sidelight: Until recently, this fish was virtually unknown in the United States outside of Hawaii and Florida. But now, with its less unsettling Hawaiian name, mahi-mahi is as trendy a fish in restaurants as one is likely to find.

Peak season: Almost year round.

Nutrients:

Calories/calories from fat	85/6.30
Protein (grams)	18.50
Fat (grams)	0.70
Saturated fat (grams)	0.19
Sodium (milligrams)	88
Cholesterol (milligrams)	73
Omega-3 (grams)	0.18

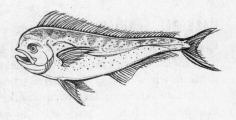

MAKO SHARK—*Isurus oxyrinchus*

Other names: Shortfin mako shark, bonito shark, mackerel shark, blue pointer, Atlantic mako shark, and Pacific mako shark.

Confusions: Mako shark is frequently confused with other sharks that can be good eating as well.

Characteristics: Its moist flesh has a pronounced meaty flavor. It is lean, firm, and dense, similar to swordfish. When it is cooked, it changes from bright orange or pink to ivory white. There is a dark-red bloodline in the steaks that may be removed. Mako shark can be distinguished from swordfish by its deep-blue, sandpapery skin (although other sharks have gray skin). It can taste of ammonia if it is improperly handled after capture: mako sharks carry urea in their bloodstream, and urea will turn to ammonia if the fish is not immediately bled and iced.

Preparation: Broiled, baked, grilled, poached, steamed, fried, stir-fried, blackened, and kebabs.

Origins: Harvested from subtropical or temperate waters in many parts the world.

Sidelight: Mako sharks usually weigh between 30 and 250 pounds when caught but have been known to reach weights of over half a ton.

Peak season: February through December.

Nutrients:

Calories/calories from fat	130/40.59
Protein (grams)	20.98
Fat (grams)	4.51
Saturated fat (grams)	0.92
Sodium (milligrams)	79
Cholesterol (milligrams)	51
Omega-3 (grams)	0.84

MARLIN—*Makaira sp.* and *Tetrapturus sp.*

Characteristics: Its meat is firm and flavorful and has less fat than swordfish (and, therefore, is more prone to drying out if overcooked). Marlin belongs to the same family as spearfish and sailfish—Istiophoridae.

Preparation: Grilled, smoked, baked, broiled. It is used in Japan for sashimi. The skin is very tough, so it is best to remove it before cooking.

Origins: There are four species of marlin that are common in tropical and temperate waters: blue marlin *(Makaira nigricans)* and white marlin *(Tetrapturus albidus)* are found in the Atlantic; striped marlin *(Makaira audax)* and black marlin *(Makaira indica)* are found in the Pacific.

Sidelight: Although marlin and swordfish seem to be kin since they taste alike and both have spearlike bills, they are in different families.

Nutrients:

Calories/calories from fat	121/36.09
Protein (grams)	19.80
Fat (grams)	4.01
Saturated fat (grams)	1.10
Sodium (milligrams)	90
Cholesterol (milligrams)	39
Omega-3 (grams)	0.60

MONKFISH—*Lophius americanus*

Other names: Anglerfish, lawyerfish, and lotte (in France).

Characteristics: It is sweet and is often said to be similar to lobster in taste. Its meat is dense and boneless (after the backbone is removed). It has long been popular in Europe but was, until recently, considered a trash fish in the United States. The membrane encasing the white flesh must be completely removed with a paring knife and fingers; be ruthless (even if you must lose some of the white flesh in the process) or the meat will be tough.

Preparation: Monkfish holds up well in soups and stews but may also be grilled, baked, poached, boiled, microwaved, and sautéed.

Origins: A wide range—from the Grand Banks to North Carolina.

Sidelight: The whole fish, which can grow to a size of 4½ feet and 45 pounds, is hideous-looking, with a huge, ugly head. But it is usually not brought to shore and so is rarely seen. Instead, fishermen remove the tail (from which two cylindrical fillets are cut) and throw the rest of the fish back into the sea.

Peak season: January through April, September through December.

Nutrients:

Calories/calories from fat	76/13.68
Protein (grams)	14.48
Fat (grams)	1.52
Saturated fat (grams)	n/a
Sodium (milligrams)	18
Cholesterol (milligrams)	25
Omega-3 (grams)	n/a

MULLET—Family Mugilidae

Other names: Lisa, Biloxi bacon, black mullet, jumping mullet, striped mullet, silver mullet.

Confusions: The fish known in Canada as mullet are really freshwater suckers. Also, kingfish are sometimes known as sea mullet or Virginia mullet but are not related to mullet. Red mullet, known in France as rouget, is from the family of goatfish, or Mullidae, and is also unrelated to the mullet.

Characteristics: Mullet has a medium oil content, moderately firm, juicy meat, and a rich, nutty flavor. It is best to cut away the dark strip of flesh along the side, thus eliminating a strong and possibly "muddy" flavor. This is especially advisable if the fish is to be frozen. The most popular species of mullet in the United States is the striped mullet.

Preparation: Grilled, smoked, poached.

Origins: Mullet are bottom feeders found in both salt water and fresh water all over the world and are particularly abundant in the Gulf of Mexico and in the Carolinas.

Sidelight: In Japan, mullet roe is salted, dried, and then sold at high prices as *karasumi.* In Italy, a similar preparation of the roe is known as *bottarga;* in Africa, *botargo;* in the Middle East, *batrakh.*

Peak season: Most of the year.

Nutrients:

Calories/calories from fat	117/34.11
Protein (grams)	19.35
Fat (grams)	3.79
Saturated fat (grams)	1.12
Sodium (milligrams)	65
Cholesterol (milligrams)	49
Omega-3 (grams)	0.32

MUSSELS—*Mytilus edulis*

Other name: Blue mussels.

Characteristics: Mussels have a distinctive, rich taste, and their meats are plump and tender. They range in color from white to orange.

Preparation: Steamed in water, wine, or an aromatic broth or microwaved au naturel. They can also be baked, sautéed, and cooked in sauces, and are excellent as hors d'oeuvres and in salads, soups, and pasta dishes.

Origins: Wild mussels are harvested year round from the East and West Coasts. Cultured mussels are grown in farms on ropes or posts or in "mussel parks."

Sidelight: Cultured mussels have up to three times more meat than wild mussels, but discerning diners say the wild ones have a more intense flavor.

Peak season: Year round.

Nutrients:

Calories/calories from fat	86/20.16
Protein (grams)	11.90
Fat (grams)	2.24
Saturated fat (grams)	0.42
Sodium (milligrams)	286
Cholesterol (milligrams)	28
Omega-3 (grams)	0.44

OCTOPUS—*Octopus vulgaris* (East Coast), *Octopus dofleini* (West Coast)

Characteristics: Octopus has mild-flavored, dense, chewy flesh. As it cooks, the flesh turns purplish on the outside, white on the inside.

Preparation: Octopus is often available already cooked. Fresh octopus, like squid, must either be cooked very briefly or boiled until the flesh is again tender—about 1 hour. Often, cooks are advised to tenderize the meat by pounding it. Octopus is usually cooked whole and then cut into smaller pieces according to the serving method. It is good marinated, grilled, or broiled and takes sauces very well. Cooked octopus is popular in Japan for sushi. The ink can be used as flavoring for sauces and pasta.

Origins: Octopus inhabit tropical and temperate oceans worldwide. Their diet consists almost entirely of other shellfish.

Sidelight: Like other cephalopods (squid, cuttle fish), the octopus uses two main methods for eluding predators. When it is threatened, it discharges the contents of its ink sac and flees, leaving a bulbous, octopus-shaped ink cloud hovering in its wake to fool the attacker. It is also able to change the color of its skin to blend into its surroundings.

Peak season: November and December (for fresh octopus from the East Coast).

Nutrients:

Calories/calories from fat	82/9.36
Protein (grams)	14.91
Fat (grams)	1.04
Saturated fat (grams)	0.23
Sodium (milligrams)	n/a
Cholesterol (milligrams)	48
Omega-3 (grams)	0.16

ORANGE ROUGHY—*Hoplostethus atlanticus*

Other name: Slimehead (a family name rarely used now that the fish has become popular).

Characteristics: Orange roughy are harvested at weights of about 5 pounds. Their meat is white and sweet, their flavor reminiscent of shellfish. Though low in fat, the fish remain moist when cooked and hold together well.

Preparation: Baked, poached, grilled, broiled, sautéed, microwaved, or steamed.

Origins: They are very deep ocean fish that are caught far out at sea, 200 miles or more off New Zealand and Australia, where the water reaches depths of 3,000 feet. They are also caught off the Spanish coast, north to Iceland. Orange roughy are shipped to North America frozen and occasionally as fresh fillets; however, markets usually thaw the frozen fillets before putting them on sale.

Sidelight: Orange roughy mature and reproduce very slowly. The average age of those caught in fishing nets is 30 to 50 years. Therefore, now that it has become a popular food fish, Australia and New Zealand monitor their stock of fish carefully.

Peak season: Frozen year round.

Nutrients:

Calories/calories from fat	69/6.30
Protein (grams)	14.70
Fat (grams)	0.70
Saturated fat (grams)	0.02
Sodium (milligrams)	63
Cholesterol (milligrams)	20
Omega-3 (grams)	n/a

OYSTER, ATLANTIC—*Crassostrea virginica*

Other names: Eastern oyster, American oyster.

Characteristics: Oysters have a distinctive, sometimes briny flavor. The meat is rather fatty for a shellfish and is smooth and moist. Because they are filter feeders, their flavor can be affected by the water in which they live. Often, oysters are named after the region in which they were grown, and connoisseurs can distinguish subtle differences in flavor caused by the different waters.

Preparation: Steamed, baked, roasted in the shell; or removed from the shell and sautéed or added to soups, stews, and stuffings. They are also eaten raw on the half shell.

Origins: Atlantic oysters are harvested in waters all along the East Coast, particularly the Gulf of Mexico, Chesapeake Bay, and Long Island Sound. During the last decade, weather, pollution, and disease diminished the supply. They are also farm-raised.

Sidelight: One of the most famous oyster dishes—baked oysters topped with vegetables and cream—originated in New Orleans and is called Oysters Rockefeller not because any member of that family had anything to do with it, but because of the richness of the dish.

Peak season: Year round.

Nutrients:

Calories/calories from fat	68/22.14
Protein (grams)	7.05
Fat (grams)	2.46
Saturated fat (grams)	0.77
Sodium (milligrams)	211
Cholesterol (milligrams)	53
Omega-3 (grams)	0.39

OYSTER, PACIFIC—*Crassostrea gigas*

Other name: Japanese oyster.

Characteristics: Pacific oysters are mild and sweet-tasting, with those from California having a slightly more pronounced flavor.

Preparation: *See* **Oyster, Atlantic.**

Origins: Almost all Pacific oysters are harvested from farms rather than the wild.

Sidelight: The Pacific oyster was brought to the United States from Japan early in the 1900s in an effort to revitalize the West Coast oyster industry. The only true, native West Coast oyster is the small Olympia, regarded as a delicacy.

Peak season: January through May, October through December.

Nutrients:

Calories/calories from fat	81/20.70
Protein (grams)	9.45
Fat (grams)	2.30
Saturated fat (grams)	0.51
Sodium (milligrams)	106
Cholesterol (milligrams)	n/a
Omega-3 (grams)	0.69

PIKE—Family Esocidae

Confusion: Walleyed pike is not a pike (*see* **Walleye**).

Characteristics: It has sweet, bland flesh with a flaky texture.

Preparation: Baked, roasted, broiled, grilled, fried. It is used to make the French poached dumplings called quenelles de brochette. It is also used for gefilte fish.

Origins: Pike inhabit rivers, streams, and lakes in the central and southern United States as well as elsewhere in the world. Pike are popular game fish and are also caught commercially.

Sidelight: Equipped with a large mouth, large teeth and jaws, and fierce feeding habits to go along with them, pike can decimate the fish populations within their territories.

Nutrients:

Calories/calories from fat:	88/6.21
Protein (grams)	19.26
Fat (grams)	0.69
Saturated fat (grams)	0.12
Sodium (milligrams)	39
Cholesterol (milligrams)	39
Omega-3 (grams)	0.11

POLLOCK—*Theragra chalcogramma*

Other names: Alaska pollock, walleye pollock, Pacific pollock.

Confusions: Pollock is sometimes sold as scrod, which more commonly refers to a young cod. The prevalent variety, Alaska pollock, is not like its Atlantic cousin, which is oilier and has darker flesh.

Characteristics: It is similar in flavor to cod (they are in the same family) but stronger; the meat is lean, white, moist, and moderately firm. Since it is a relatively small fish, weighing 1/2 to 2 pounds when caught, its fillets are smaller than a cod's.

Preparation: Baked, broiled, poached, steamed, sautéed. It is also commercially processed and textured to make surimi seafoods, a ready-to-eat seafood analogue.

Origins: Pollock is found throughout the North Pacific, with major stocks in the Gulf of Alaska and the Bering Sea. Pollock are either fully processed on boats or frozen immediately after they are caught and then brought to shore-based plants for processing.

Sidelight: Once a cheap alternative to cod, Alaska pollock has attained such popularity in Europe, Japan, and the United States that it is no longer such a bargain.

Peak season: Frozen, year round.

Nutrients:

Calories/calories from fat	81/7.20
Protein (grams)	17.18
Fat (grams)	0.8
Saturated fat (grams)	0.16
Sodium (milligrams)	99
Cholesterol (milligrams)	71
Omega-3 (grams)	0.37

PORGY—*Stenotomus chrysops*

Other name: Scup, sea bream, sheepshead.

Characteristics: Porgy is a sweet, flavorful fish.

Preparation: Grilled, poached, microwaved; it is also the ideal size for pan-frying. And you may roast, sauté, broil, and smoke it as well as use it in an escabeche and salads.

Origins: Porgies are found along the Atlantic coast from North Carolina to Florida and in the Gulf of Mexico. They grow to 2 to 3 pounds on average and are usually caught at about 1 pound. Porgy is the American name for sea breams that are found in many of the world's oceans.

Sidelight: Both names, *scup* and *porgy,* derive from a single Narraganset Indian word, *mishcuppauog. Pauog* refers to "fertilizer," for which the fish were used.

Peak season: Summer.

Nutrients:

Calories/calories from fat	105/24.57
Protein (grams)	18.88
Fat (grams)	2.73
Saturated fat (grams)	n/a
Sodium (milligrams)	42
Cholesterol (milligrams)	n/a
Omega-3 (grams)	n/a

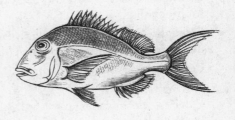

REDFISH—*Sciaenops ocellatus*

Other names: Channel bass, red drum, puppy drum, spottail bass, and red bass.

Confusion: Atlantic ocean perch is sometimes called redfish but is not the fish in the drum family that has become popular in recent years.

Characteristics: Its sweet and mild-tasting flesh has a soft, flaky texture.

Preparation: Baked, broiled, grilled, sautéed.

Origins: Redfish is found along the southeastern coast of the United States and in the Gulf of Mexico, but catching it is now prohibited in most of these areas because of overfishing, the result of the rise in popularity of a New Orleans dish called Blackened Redfish.

Sidelight: Redfish is a member of a noisy family of "drums and croakers," so called because they can make drumming or croaking sounds in the water that, according to one theory, may act as a kind of sonar, helping them navigate through murky estuaries.

Nutrients:

Calories/calories from fat	104/28.53
Protein (grams)	17.78
Fat (grams)	3.17
Saturated fat (grams)	1.09
Sodium (milligrams)	56
Cholesterol (milligrams)	61
Omega-3 (grams)	0.22

RED SNAPPER, AMERICAN—*Lutjanus campechanus*

Other name: Gulf red snapper.

Confusions: Any reddish snapper may show up with this name and command red snapper's usually higher price, although by federal decree there is only one true red snapper in a group of 105 snapper species. To make matters even more confusing, immature bluefish are called snappers.

Characteristics: The lean and moist flesh is semifirm and has a sweet, mild, distinctive flavor that makes it one of the best of the eating fish. Similar fish such as the vermilion snapper, the yellowtail snapper, and others are also excellent.

Preparation: Sautéed, grilled, baked, broiled, poached, steamed. Because it such a beautiful fish, it is especially impressive cooked whole.

Origins: The warm waters of the Atlantic, from North Carolina to Florida, and the Gulf of Mexico.

Sidelight: The name comes from the fish's tendency to snap its doglike teeth.

Peak season: Usually March through November, depending upon when harvest quotas are reached.

Nutrients:

Calories/calories from fat	100/12.06
Protein (grams)	20.51
Fat (grams)	1.34
Saturated fat (grams)	0.28
Sodium (milligrams)	64
Cholesterol (milligrams)	37
Omega-3 (grams)	0.31

SALMON, ATLANTIC—*Salmo salar*

Other names: Norwegian salmon.

Confusion: Sometimes Atlantic salmon is sold as Norwegian, regardless of its origins.

Characteristics: Its distinctive, mild flavor and oil-rich, moist flesh, combined with sufficient firmness to allow it to hold up under many cooking conditions, make this one of the most popular of all fish.

Preparation: Baked, broiled, poached, sautéed, grilled, smoked, microwaved.

Origins: Most commercial Atlantic salmon is produced in fish farms all over the world.

Sidelight: Although there is a debate over how much flavor has been sacrificed through widespread farming, a nice aquaculture bonus is that more smaller salmon—3 pounds or so—reach the market than before. They are perfect for cooking whole, serving 4.

Peak season: Year round.

Nutrients:

Calories/calories from fat	183/97.65
Protein (grams)	19.90
Fat (grams)	10.85
Saturated fat (grams)	2.18
Sodium (milligrams)	59
Cholesterol (milligrams)	59
Omega-3 (grams)	1.91

SALMON, CHINOOK—*Oncorhynchus tshawytscha*

Other name: king salmon.

Confusion: Any chinook under 6 pounds is likely to be the pink salmon, considered by many to be less desirable.

Characteristics: The chinook is oily, has an extraordinarily rich flavor and softer flesh than other salmons, and is among the most treasured of wild salmon. The color of the flesh ranges from rich salmon-red to almost white. There is a strain of chinook called white king that has very pale flesh.

Preparation: Baked, broiled, poached, sautéed, grilled, microwaved.

Origins: Caught from March to October in rivers in central California up to the Yukon River in Alaska and into Canada. It has been introduced to European waters as well. It is also farm-raised in British Columbia, Washington State, and New Zealand.

Sidelight: The chinook is the largest Pacific salmon, capable of growing to over 100 pounds.

Peak season: March through May, September through October (for wild).

Nutrients:

Calories/calories from fat	180/93.96
Protein (grams)	20.06
Fat (grams)	10.44
Saturated fat (grams)	2.51
Sodium (milligrams)	47
Cholesterol (milligrams)	66
Omega-3 (grams)	1.36

SALMON, CHUM—*Oncorhynchus keta*

Other names: Dog salmon, silverbright.

Characteristics: Chum has a relatively mild flavor, pale flesh with a firm texture. It is usually sold frozen and is relatively inexpensive.

Preparation: Baked, broiled, poached, sautéed, grilled, smoked, microwaved. Chum is also good in casseroles and in dishes where color is not a consideration.

Origins: Chums are always net-caught in the waters off Alaska and British Columbia and in Puget Sound. They are not farm-raised, although hatcheries raise their fry and release them into open water.

Peak season: August and September.

Nutrients:

Calories/calories from fat	120/33.93
Protein (grams)	20.14
Fat (grams)	3.77
Saturated fat (grams)	0.84
Sodium (milligrams)	50
Cholesterol (milligrams)	74
Omega-3 (grams)	0.63

SALMON, PINK—*Oncorhynchus gorbuscha*

Other name: Humpback.

Characteristics: Pink salmon are mild, but with a pronounced flavor. Their meat is pale and relatively low in oil for a salmon. Pinks are the smallest and most abundant of the Pacific salmon. They reach weights of 3 to 6 pounds during their 2-year lifespan. They can be sold fresh. But since they have a rapid spoilage rate and freeze less well than other salmon, most of the catch is sent to canneries.

Preparation: Baked, broiled, poached, sautéed, grilled, microwaved. When canned, this salmon is best when it is used in salads, fish cakes, mousses, and sauces.

Origins: They are harvested beginning in July in the waters off Alaska, British Columbia, Washington, and Oregon. The salmon population fluctuates, peaking every other year.

Peak season: August and September.

Nutrients:

Calories/calories from fat	116/31.05
Protein (grams)	19.94
Fat (grams)	3.45
Saturated fat (grams)	0.56
Sodium (milligrams)	67
Cholesterol (milligrams)	52
Omega-3 (grams)	1

SALMON TROUT—*Oncorhynchus mykiss*

Other name: Rainbow trout.

Confusion: Although salmon and trout are related and this fish has orangy flesh, the name is not an official designation. It is a trout and a close relative of the salmon.

Characteristics: Because the salmon trout is in fact a large trout that gets its salmon-colored flesh from its food, it makes for excellent eating when a big, handsome, relatively firm fish is desired.

Preparation: Poached, grilled, baked, broiled.

SCALLOPS, BAY—*Argopecten irradians*

Other names: Cape scallops, Cape Cod scallops, Nantucket or eastern bay scallops.

Confusion: Calico scallops, which are even smaller, are cheaper and are sometimes passed off as the more expensive bay scallops.

Characteristics: Bay scallops are mild and sweet and are considered the best-tasting scallop. The flesh is lean and firm but delicate. The color ranges from ivory to pink to light-apricot. The meat averages ½ to ¾ inch in thickness.

Preparation: Sautéed, poached, used in soups and stews (added near the end of cooking time). Because they are small, they cook very quickly and will get hard and dry if overcooked. Scallops lose their sweet flavor very quickly and so must be used fresh and handled with care.

Origins: Harvested from fall to spring in bays, harbors, and salt ponds on the Atlantic Coast from New England through North Carolina. They are most abundant from Cape Cod to Long Island. Bay scallops are usually collected with rakes or dredges onto small boats and then brought to shore for shucking. China, where scallops are cultivated, is now a leading supplier of bay scallops. Chinese scallops are usually sold as "previously frozen."

Sidelight: What we think of as the "scallop" is only part of the animal—the adductor muscle that closes the shell of this bivalve.

Peak season: October through December.

Nutrients:

Calories/calories from fat	88/6.84
Protein (grams)	16.78
Fat (grams)	0.76
Saturated fat (grams)	0.08
Sodium (milligrams)	161
Cholesterol (milligrams)	33
Omega-3 (grams)	0.20

SCALLOPS, CALICO—*Argopecten gibbus*

Confusion: They are not bay scallops, which are usually larger and more expensive.

Characteristics: Calicoes have sweet, nutty-flavored flesh, somewhat stronger in flavor than bay scallops, and are lean and firm. Calicoes are the smallest scallops, and their meat is also darker than bay or sea scallops.

Preparation: Calicoes cook very quickly and are best prepared sautéed, broiled, poached, baked, or added to chowders and stews almost at the end of the cooking time.

Origins: They are harvested in warm waters from North Carolina to Brazil, Florida being especially dominant.

Sidelight: Calicoes are dredged from deep waters and steamed open on shore. This steaming process, not used for other scallops, gives the meat an identifying feature—whitened outer edges—where the steam has partially cooked the scallop (for the savvy consumer, the whitened edges help distinguish calico from bay).

Peak season: May through December.

Nutrients:

Calories/calories from fat	88/6.84
Protein (grams)	16.78
Fat (grams)	0.76
Saturated fat (grams)	0.08
Sodium (milligrams)	161
Cholesterol (milligrams)	33
Omega-3 (grams)	0.20

SCALLOPS, SEA—*Placopecten magellanicus*

Confusions: It is neither a bay nor a calico scallop, both of which are much smaller.

Characteristics: It has a mild, briny taste and a lean, firm texture. It is the largest commercial scallop, with an adductor muscle 1 to 2 inches across.

Preparation: Sautéed, poached, grilled on skewers, broiled, baked, added to soups and stews.

Origins: Sea scallops are harvested all year in the Atlantic from Labrador to New Jersey. They are found in waters up to 900 feet deep, on firm sand or gravel bottoms, and are almost always shucked on board because they die quickly once out of the water. Scallops are farmed in Japan and British Columbia.

Sidelight: A similar scallop, the Pacific sea or weathervane scallop, is available locally in the Pacific Northwest.

Peak season: March through November.

Nutrients:

Calories/calories from fat	88/6.84
Protein (grams)	16.78
Fat (grams)	0.76
Saturated fat (grams)	0.08
Sodium (milligrams)	161
Cholesterol (milligrams)	33
Omega-3 (grams)	0.20

SCROD

See **Cod, Atlantic.**

Scrod is an old New England term used to designate the catch of the day, which would have been white fish such as cod, haddock, pollock, or hake. *Scrod* is understood nowadays to mean "small cod" but it is sometimes used for other codfish as well.

SHRIMP—Families Penaeidae and Pandalidae

Other names: Prawn (commercially used in the United States for very large shrimp).

Confusions: For consumers it can be difficult, if not impossible, to discern the specific variety of shrimp—there are many—or exactly where the shrimp came from.

Characteristics: Shrimp are sweet and firm or, if mishandled, mushy and tasteless. Good shrimp are spectacular unadorned by flavorings but will also stand up to assertive seasoning. Virtually all commercially available shrimp have had their heads removed and have been frozen in the shell (and often defrosted for sale). Although they are usually sold and priced by size—small, medium, large, or jumbo—these are not official descriptions, which leaves the consumer to decide, based on experience, how well size and price seem to match. The following will give you a rough idea of how many shrimp to expect when you buy 1 pound of unpeeled shrimp of a specific size:

Small	51–60
Medium	41–50
Large	31–40
Jumbo	21–25

The most important guide for freshness is a fresh smell and firm texture, with meat that completely fills the shell.

Preparation: Sautéed, broiled, grilled, steamed, boiled, smoked, microwaved.

Origins: Shrimp are caught wild and are farm-raised in many parts of the world, with Ecuador (home of the highly favored Ecuadorean or Mexican white shrimp) and Asia (the source of black tiger shrimp) sending much of their shrimp to the United States. Other popular shrimp are the Gulf pink, which comes from the Gulf of Mexico and West Africa, the Gulf white, and the Chinese white.

Sidelight: What is called the vein of a shrimp is really its intestinal tract and poses no known health risk. So whether or not you remove it is an aesthetic choice.

Peak season: Year round.

Nutrients:

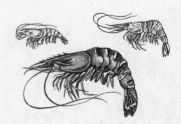

Calories/calories from fat	106/15.57
Protein (grams)	20.31
Fat (grams)	1.73
Saturated fat (grams)	0.33
Sodium (milligrams)	148
Cholesterol (milligrams)	152
Omega-3 (grams)	0.48

SKATE—Various Rajidae

Other name: ray.

Characteristics: Skate has a mild flavor, often likened to scallops. Only the pectoral fins ("wings") are eaten. They have a striated, fanlike configuration and corrugated texture. The skin is thick and inedible; it is generally removed before the skate is offered for sale. Like sharks, skates have skeletons made of cartilage, not bone, as well as urea in their blood, which will produce an ammonia smell if the skate is not bled just after being caught.

Preparation: Baked, sautéed, broiled, grilled, or added to soups.

Origins: Skates are bottom-dwelling fish found around the world in temperate, tropical, and cold waters. On the East Coast, clearnose, barn door, and little skates are the species caught commercially. On the West Coast, the species captured are the big skate, long-nosed skate, and California skate.

Sidelight: The slender, graceful wing of a skate can be hefty, with some West Coast skates propelled by wings weighing up to 5 pounds each.

Peak season: June through August.

Nutrients:

Calories/calories from fat	130/40.59
Protein (grams)	20.98
Fat (grams)	4.51
Saturated fat (grams)	0.92
Sodium (milligrams)	79
Cholesterol (milligrams)	51
Omega-3 (grams)	0.84

SOFT-SHELL CRAB
See **Crab, Blue.**

SQUID—*Illex illecebrosus, Loligo pealei*

Other name: Calamari.

Characteristics: It has lean, slightly sweet meat that is tender and firm. It is a close relative of the octopus and distant relative of bivalve mollusks. But with this shellfish, the shell is internal and is known as a quill or pen. The edible parts of the squid are the tentacles, the mantle (or tube), and the fins (or wings).

Preparation: Sautéed, stir-fried, baked, grilled, boiled, and used in salads, stews, and pasta sauces. It requires either brief or lengthy cooking. Cooking periods in between will make it tough.

Origins: The species considered most delicious is the Loligo or long-finned squid, which flourishes in waters off both the East Coast and West Coast. California squid are harvested from late November to March and from May through August, when they move inshore to spawn. East Coast squid are harvested from Massachusetts to North Carolina in varying quantities year round. Some squid come here from Asia already cleaned, with body and tentacled head separated, and frozen.

Sidelight: The freshness of whole squid can best be determined by how sweet it smells.

Peak season: January and February, June through December.

Nutrients:

Calories/calories from fat	92/12.60
Protein (grams)	15.58
Fat (grams)	1.38
Saturated fat (grams)	0.36
Sodium (milligrams)	44
Cholesterol (milligrams)	233
Omega-3 (grams)	0.49

SURIMI SEAFOOD

Other names: Seafood sticks and salad pieces, imitation crabmeat, and various brand names.

Characteristics: Surimi is a processed and textured fish paste usually made of Alaska pollock or, less often, New Zealand hoki. To the fish paste are added starch, coloring, flavoring, binders, and stabilizers so that an imitation of any of several kinds of seafood—lobster tail or claw, crab legs, or scallops—may be produced. Surimi may contain MSG (if sold in packages, the label must say so).

Peak season: Frozen, year round.

Nutrients:

Calories/calories from fat	99/8.10
Protein (grams)	15.18
Fat (grams)	0.90
Saturated fat (grams)	n/a
Sodium (milligrams)	143
Cholesterol (milligrams)	30
Omega-3 (grams)	n/a

SWORDFISH—*Xiphias gladius*

Characteristics: Swordfish is a moderately oily, flavorful fish with a firm, meat-like texture. Like tuna, swordfish can grow to be huge—more than half a ton.

Preparation: Grilled as steaks or kebabs, broiled, baked, pan-fried, smoked.

Origins: Swordfish are temperate- and tropical-dwelling fish, caught by longline and gill net off both the California and New England coasts in summer and fall, and in the Gulf of Mexico and off Florida's east coast in winter. Chile and Hawaii also supply large amounts of swordfish. It is imported frozen from Japan and Taiwan, and fresh from Greece, Taiwan, and Central and South America.

Sidelight: Swordfish, once shunned because of their tendency to accumulate mercury, are now monitored by the Food and Drug Administration for methylmercury content. Best advice: eat, enjoy—but not every day.

Peak season: March through November.

Nutrients:

Calories/calories from fat	121/36.90
Protein (grams)	19.80
Fat (grams)	4.01
Saturated fat (grams)	1.10
Sodium (milligrams)	90
Cholesterol (milligrams)	39
Omega-3 (grams)	0.60

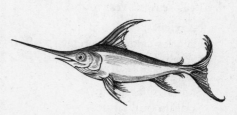

TILAPIA—Various Oreochromis species

Other names: St. Peter's fish (though not a legal market name).

Characteristics: It has mild, sweet flesh with tender flakes.

Preparation: Baked, broiled, sautéed, steamed, poached, or microwaved. Farm-raised tilapia are increasingly popular for sushi.

Origins: Native to Africa's fresh waters, but wild elsewhere, too, tilapia is now widely farmed in the southern and western United States. It is also supplied fresh from Costa Rica and Colombia.

Sidelight: As St. Peter's fish, the allusion to the saint is said to derive from this fish's role in the biblical story of fishes and loaves. However, the John Dory, a marine fish, is also known as Saint-Pierre (St. Peter's fish) and has been similarly credited.

Peak season: Year round.

Nutrients:

Calories/calories from fat	114/33.21
Protein (grams)	18.86
Fat (grams)	3.69
Saturated fat (grams)	0.78
Sodium (milligrams)	70
Cholesterol (milligrams)	68
Omega-3 (grams)	0.60

TILEFISH—Lopholatilus chamaeleonticeps

Characteristics: Tilefish is mild-tasting and firm. It resembles cod.

Preparation: Roasted, poached, baked, steamed, broiled, grilled, sautéed, hot-smoked, braised. It is also used in soups and stews, seviche, and escabeche.

Origins: From Cape Cod to the Gulf of Mexico and Brazil.

Sidelight: The tilefish, while it is alive, is brightly colored, though the color fades fast after death and is scarcely visible by the time the fish reaches the market. It prefers such deep water—over 300 feet is common—that commercial fishermen knew nothing about it until one was caught in 1879.

Peak season: Year round.

Nutrients:

Calories/calories from fat	96/20.79
Protein (grams)	17.50
Fat (grams)	2.31
Saturated fat (grams)	0.44
Sodium (milligrams)	53
Cholesterol (milligrams)	n/a
Omega-3 (grams)	0.43

TROUT, RAINBOW—*Oncorhynchus mykiss*

Other names: Salmon trout, when it is as large as 4 to 10 pounds; steelhead.

Characteristics: Rainbow trout has a mild, nutty flavor and tender, soft, flaky meat that holds together well during cooking (especially if the skin is left on).

Preparation: Baked, grilled, sautéed, poached, broiled, steamed, microwaved.

Origins: It is now farmed throughout the world and in almost all the states of the United States, with Idaho being the major producer, followed by North Carolina. Most rainbow trout are raised in long, rectangular raceways—shallow concrete outdoor ponds with flowing water.

Sidelight: The farming of trout, to stock recreational lakes, is many decades old, but the tremendous commercial development required advances in transportation and packaging that occurred in the 1960s. Many trout farms invite customers to catch their own.

Peak season: Year round.

Nutrients:

Calories/calories from fat	119/31.14
Protein (grams)	20.48
Fat (grams)	3.46
Saturated fat (grams)	0.72
Sodium (milligrams)	31
Cholesterol (milligrams)	59
Omega-3 (grams)	0.93

TUNA, BIGEYE—*Thunnus obesus*

Other name: Ahi in Hawaii (a name also applied to yellowfin tuna).

Characteristics: Richer in flavor than yellowfin tuna, the flesh has a meaty texture. It is a highly prized catch, with specimens ranging up to 400 pounds.

Preparation: Smoked, grilled, baked, broiled, stir-fried, or sautéed.

Origins: Found in tropical to temperate waters in the Pacific, Atlantic, and Indian Oceans, with most of the harvest coming from the Pacific.

Sidelight: The United States is only a minor producer of bigeye and exports much of its catch—which comes from the East Coast, New York to North Carolina—to Japan, the biggest producer and consumer of the fish and also the highest bidder for top-quality tuna.

Peak season: January through April, October through December.

Nutrients:

Calories/calories from fat	108/8.55
Protein (grams)	23.38
Fat (grams)	0.95
Saturated fat (grams)	0.24
Sodium (milligrams)	37
Cholesterol (milligrams)	45
Omega-3 (grams)	0.22

TUNA, SKIPJACK—*Katsuwonus pelamis*

Other names: Ocean bonito, lesser tuna.

Characteristics: It has a stronger flavor than other tunas. Its steaklike texture and taste make it an especially good fish to recommend to meat eaters. Often, the midline strip of darker meat is removed because the flavor can be too strong. Fresh skipjack has a short shelf life and will turn brown unless it is protected from air and kept very cold—under 40°F. A small tuna, skipjack grows only as large as 40 pounds and is usually harvested up to 20 pounds.

Preparation: It is best known as a canned product, but it can be prepared fresh in the same ways as other tunas.

Origins: Mostly found in the Pacific Ocean off southern California and Hawaii; also in the Gulf of Mexico. They may be found in the Atlantic during the summer as far north as New Jersey and Long Island.

Peak season: Year round.

Nutrients:

Calories/calories from fat	103/9.09
Protein (grams)	22
Fat (grams)	1.01
Saturated fat (grams)	0.33
Sodium (milligrams)	37
Cholesterol (milligrams)	47
Omega-3 (grams)	0.26

TUNA, YELLOWFIN—*Thunnus albacares*

Characteristics: Yellowfin tuna is similar to swordfish in flavor and milder than bigeye tuna. The meat has a firm texture and is bright red when raw, ivory when cooked.

Preparation: Most yellowfin is sold canned, as light-meat tuna, but it is excellent prepared fresh: grilled, smoked, baked, broiled, sautéed. It is also prized raw—for example, in sushi and sashimi.

Origins: Japan and the United States supply most of the yellowfin tuna. The major areas fished by the United States are off the western coast of Mexico, in the Gulf of Mexico, and in Hawaii; some are caught off the Atlantic coast.

Sidelight: In the eastern central Pacific, the nets commonly used to catch yellowfin inadvertently capture and kill dolphins as well. Consumer outrage over the dolphin killing led to a boycott that ended in 1990, when methods of harvest were modified and producers began marking some canned tuna as "dolphin safe." The best method for catching tuna is by hook and line since this does the least damage to the muscle tissue by minimizing the struggle.

Peak season: April through September.

Nutrients:

Calories/calories from fat	108/8.55
Protein (grams)	23.38
Fat (grams)	0.95
Saturated fat (grams)	0.24
Sodium (milligrams)	37
Cholesterol (milligrams)	45
Omega-3 (grams)	0.22

WALLEYE—*Stizostedion vitreum*

Other names: Walleyed pike, pickerel, yellow pike, yellow walleye, pike perch.

Confusion: Although walleye is most often called walleyed pike, it is not a pike, but is, rather, a member of the perch family.

Characteristics: It has fine, white flesh with a mild flavor and a flaky texture. It is a popular game fish. It grows as large as 20 pounds but is usually caught at a weight of about 3 pounds.

Preparation: Fried, marinated, roasted, steamed, baked, broiled, grilled.

Origins: It flourishes in many freshwater areas of the United States and Canada but is most important commercially in the Great Lakes region.

Sidelight: The fish gets its name from its reflective eyes, which are adapted to feeding at night.

Nutrients:

Calories/calories from fat	93/10.98
Protein (grams)	19.14
Fat (grams)	1.22
Saturated fat (grams)	0.25
Sodium (milligrams)	51
Cholesterol (milligrams)	86
Omega-3 (grams)	0.31

WHITEFISH—*Coregonus clupeaformis*

Other name: Lake whitefish.

Characteristics: A delicate, mild-flavored fish, with firm meat, it has a high oil content—the fat being an evolutionary development that protects it against the cold, fresh waters of the lakes it inhabits. Whitefish are related to salmon and trout but have pure white meat. They are usually harvested at a weight of about 3 pounds.

Preparation: Fried, poached, broiled, grilled, baked, smoked. It is a popular fish to use for gefilte fish.

Origins: Deep lakes—often iced over in winter—of the northern United States and Canada.

Sidelight: Lake fish, whitefish among them, have been a source of sport-fishing concern because of the possibility of contamination by PCBs and mercury. But the commercial harvest is monitored and should cause no problem if the fish are eaten in moderation. However, sport fishermen should heed state advisories about the consumption of these fish.

Peak season: Year round, although winter fishing is curtailed when lake ice weakens.

Nutrients:

Calories/calories from fat	134/52.74
Protein (grams)	19.09
Fat (grams)	5.86
Saturated fat (grams)	0.91
Sodium (milligrams)	51
Cholesterol (milligrams)	60
Omega-3 (grams)	1.26

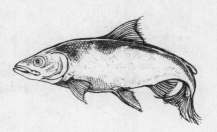

Index

About the Authors

JANE E. BRODY has been the Personal Health columnist of the *New York Times* since 1965. A native of New York City, she received her B.S. from Cornell University and her M.S. from the University of Wisconsin School of Journalism. Her previous books are the bestselling *Jane Brody's Nutrition Book*, *Jane Brody's Good Food Book*, *Jane Brody's Good Food Gourmet*, as well as *Jane Brody's New York Times Guide to Personal Health*, *Secrets of Good Health* (with Richard Engquist), and *You Can Fight Cancer and Win* (with Dr. Arthur I. Holleb).

A former editor of the *New York Times* Science Section, RICHARD FLASTE is a freelance writer and coauthor of *Pierre Franey's Cooking in America*, *Pierre Franey's Low-Fat Gourmet*, and *Pierre Franey's Kitchen*. He lives in Brooklyn, New York.